WORLD DAY OF PRAYER □ PASSOVER □ LAMMAS □ RATHA YATRA □ THANKSGIVING □ ASHURA □ YULE □ BAISAKHI □ LANTERN FESTIVAL

PURIM □

CHRISTMAS DAY □

MICHAELMAS □

EASTER □

Religious Holidays and Calendars

An Encyclopedic Handbook

2ND EDITION

Edited by
Karen Bellenir

RAMADAN □ LENT □ YOM KIPPUR □ MARDI GRAS

Omnigraphics, Inc.

Penobscot Building • Detroit, MI 48226

Editorial Staff, Second Edition

Karen Bellenir, *Editor*

Peter D. Dresser, *Managing Editor*

Omnigraphics, Inc.

Matthew Barbour, *Production Manager*

Laurie Lanzen Harris, *Vice President, Editorial Director*

Peter E. Ruffner, *Vice President, Administration*

James A. Sellgren, *Vice President, Operations and Finance*

Jane Steele, *Marketing Consultant*

* * *

Frederick G. Ruffner, Jr., *President, Publisher*

Library of Congress Cataloging-in-Publication Data

Religious holidays and calendars : an encyclopaedic handbook / edited
by Karen Bellenir. — 2nd ed.
    p. cm.
    Includes bibliographical references and indexes.
    ISBN 0-7808-0258-6 (alk. paper)
    1. Calendars—History.   2. Fasts and feasts.   I. Bellenir, Karen.
CE6.R45   1997
529' .3—dc21   97-24845
                                              CIP

Table of Contents

Part Three: Appendix, Bibliography, and Indexes

Introduction

Is today an ordinary day or a holy day? Throughout history and all around the globe people have asked that question. Holy day observances were—and still are—important for reasons as varied as the holidays themselves.

In the broadest sense, a calendar consists of the set of rules a society uses to determine which days are ordinary and which are holy. Religion and the calendar have been linked since antiquity. From the time of the ancient Egyptian, Babylonian, and Mesoamerican civilizations, members of the religious community determined how time was to be divided, established the beginning of a day, defined a week, described a month, and announced the new year.

Religious Holidays and Calendars: An Encyclopedic Handbook offers the researcher—whether student, scholar, or seeker—an overview of the time-keeping and holiday traditions of the world's religions. Although other reference works in the field focus on Christian and Jewish holidays or on the traditions of a single religion, no other existing source covers the unique relationship between religious calendars and religious holidays as does this *Handbook*. In addition to providing extensive information on familiar holidays of the world's majority faiths, this book also describes the primary holy days and festivals of minority religions as practiced in the United States or in the country of origin.

Features of the Second Edition

This revised and expanded second edition of *Religious Holidays and Calendars* features a new organizational strategy and a broader coverage of religious calendars and holidays. It begins with four essays on the historical development of lunar, lunisolar, and solar calendars, their sacred and secular uses, and calendar reform movements.

The holiday portion of this handbook has been reorganized to present the festivals, feasts, fasts, and holy days by religion according to the most appropriate calendar. This emphasis retains the significance of the entire holiday cycle.

An introductory essay for each major religion or religious group provides background information to assist the reader in understanding the importance of the holidays. An essay describing the specific issues related to the religion and its sacred calendar provides insight into the interrelationship between a religious group and its timekeeping systems and philosophies.

Holiday coverage has been expanded to include more than 450 individual entries of which more than 200 are new to this edition.

Scope

In some instances, the line between what is religious and what is not is less than clear. The notion that religion can be separated from secular society is primarily a Western concept that is often not paralleled in other cultures. So, in a sense, many celebrations including historic, social, political, promotional, and even sports-related, can be interpreted as being religious in nature. The holidays included in this book, however, are only those with a sacred component that celebrate, commemorate, or honor people, places, events, and concepts important to a specific religious community.

Organization of Religions

The religions included in this book are presented in a sequence chosen to reflect a logical pattern to the Western reader, presumably the most frequent user of this volume. Their order is not intended to imply any preference or supremacy.

The religion chapters begin in the Middle East, the birth place of many religions with which the Western reader will be most familiar. These are listed in order of the historical appearance of their founders: Abraham (Judaism), Zoroaster (Zoroastrianism), Jesus (Christianity), Muhammad (Islam), and Baha'u'llah (Baha'i). Several post-Christian movements of the last few centuries have been included in the Christian chapter. Although their inclusion may be seen by some as controversial, these groups often see themselves as heirs to the Christian tradition.

Moving eastward, the next group of religions are those with origins in the Indian subcontinent. Hinduism as the oldest is listed first, followed by Jainism, which is closely related to its Hindu heritage. Sikhism, combining elements from both Hinduism and Islam, is listed before Buddhism, which serves as a bridge to the religions of the Far East: Confucianism, Taoism, Chinese folk religions, and Shinto.

Continuing around the globe in an easterly direction, the next group of religions are those of the Native Americans. These are followed by faiths that link the American continents with Europe and Africa.

Names of Holidays and Spelling

Many of the holidays included in this book are known by more than one name. For example, the Pagan observance of Imbolc is also known as Imbolg, Oimelc, Oimelg, Brigid, Brigantia, and Gwyl Fair. Some of these alternates are variant spellings and others are different names used by various Pagan groups.

The holiday entries in this book list a primary name first followed by alternate names and variant spellings in parentheses. As much as possible spellings and forms for primary entries, calendar and month names, personal and place names, and concepts were standardized using the following guides: *The Encyclopedia of Religion*, Mircea Eliade, ed., Macmillan, 1987; *The Jewish Holidays: A Guide and Commentary*, Michael Strassfeld, Harper & Row, 1985; *Holidays, Festivals, and Celebrations of the World Dictionary* (second edition), Helene Henderson and Sue Ellen Thompson, eds., Omnigraphics, 1997. When such guidance was unavailable the forms and spellings listed reflect those that appeared most often in the sources consulted. Diacriticals unfamiliar to the non-specialist have been omitted. To ensure easy access to all the holiday entries irrespective of the form known by the reader, the alternate forms are included in the index.

Dates

Many methods of dating are described in this book. To avoid giving preference to any one religious system, the historical dates in this book are based on the Common Era system. The year numbers are the same as those used in Christian dating—which uses the designation B.C. (Before Christ) and A.D. (*Anno Domini*, a Latin term meaning "in the year of our Lord")—but the designations are B.C.E. (Before Common Era) and C.E. (Common Era).

Appendix, Bibliography, and Indexes

Appendix: Internet Resources for More Information

An annotated listing of web sites that includes addresses (URLs) and a general description of the information offered appears in an appendix. Selected sites deemed reliable were chosen to present a broad spectrum of calendar, holiday, and religious information. The listing is provided to serve as a starting point for people interested in further research; it is not an exhaustive list of all available sites. Inclusion is not an endorsement and omission is not a criticism.

Bibliography

The bibliography lists all of the sources used in compiling this *Handbook*. The topical arrangement will help researchers who are pursuing further study of religious holidays and calendars.

Indexes

Several indexes provide quick access to the information in this book. The **Alphabetical List of Holidays** presents all the primary and alternate holiday names along with variant spellings, religion, and page numbers. The **Chronological List of Holidays** offers a compilation of all the holidays in sequential order according to the months of the Gregorian calendar. Fixed holidays are shown on their actual dates; movable holidays are differentiated by the use of italic type and are shown according to their placement in 1997. The **Calendar Index** consists of two parts. The first part provides an alphabetical list of all the various calendars discussed in the text; the second part provides an alphabetical list of all the month names that appear on those calendars along with page ranges for holidays within them. The final index, the **Master Index** includes personal names, concepts, key terms, holidays, organizations, events, and other significant terms.

Acknowledgements

The production of this book would not have been possible without the support, encouragement, and assistance of many people. Aidan Kelly, Peter Dresser, and Linda M. Ross worked on the first edition of *Religious Holidays and Calendars* and established the foundation upon which this edition is built. Helene Henderson assisted in the chore of spelling standardization, located reference materials, provided inspiration, guided the way, and helped to make the process fun. Researcher Jenifer Swanson surfed the Internet to locate many valuable sites. The Rev. Jacque Zaleski, the Rev. David Jahn, and Dennis Kananen helped during the research phase by providing reference materials and insight;

special thanks also go to the reference librarians at William Tyndale College in Farmington Hills, Michigan. Helper Buffy Bellenir served by looking up answers to last minute questions, and indexer Theresa Murray created a masterful Master Index.

Lastly, and most importantly, thanks are due to Bruce Bellenir who visited libraries, bookstores, and sanctuaries; carried boxes, books, and calendars; installed computer programs and fixed hardware problems; proofread manuscripts; and, without complaint, ordered pizza, again.

PART ONE

The History of Calendars

CHAPTER 1

Basic Questions all Calendars Must Answer

Essential Role of Calendars

Societies have created calendars to order time in a systematic manner—a need which all human civilizations share. Like many other fundamental commodities in life, the calendar is so ordinary yet so important that one can hardly imagine a time when it did not exist. Its significance is so great that in many cultures the institution and maintenance of dating systems have been given sacred status and have fallen under the jurisdiction of religious authorities.

Calendars Attest to Human Ingenuity

As one begins to consider the state of the world before the evolution of the calendar, two questions invariably arise: How did people recognize their need for a calendar, and what did they do to construct one? Answers to these questions are intricately woven into the fabric of history and celebrate the wonder of human resourcefulness and creativity. Many different cultures have their own calendars, and the characteristics of these calendars are as diverse as the societies that developed them. All calendars, however, serve the common purpose of enabling people to work together to accomplish specific goals.

During the twentieth century, the Western civil calendar has become the international standard for business and diplomatic purposes, but many other calendars are also used by various religions, nations, and societies.

Origins of the Calendar

In the broadest sense, a calendar consists of the set of rules that a society uses to determine which days are ordinary and which are holy or holidays.

The Earliest Calendars Were Informal

Thousands of years ago, most people lived in small tribal societies which were based on hunting and gathering as a means of survival. The time-keeping methods of these groups would have been fairly uncomplicated because people could easily coordinate activities by word of mouth. Certainly they used days and perhaps even months as indications of time, but their needs probably did not demand anything more complex (such as a year, decade, or century). However, over the course of history, more and more people shifted from small hunting and gathering tribes to larger communities based on agriculture; this shift required that people become more interdependent with each other for survival. For example, farmers and city dwellers must come to the marketplace at the same time if they are going to do business. Therefore, the need for a tool to arrange these societal events became apparent.

Ancient Egyptians and Babylonians Systematize Their Calendars

The first people to formally address the need to integrate social activities were the ancient Babylonians and Egyptians. These two societies were similar in their agricultural base and demographics—large populations spread over significant expanses of land. The most common reason for the citizens of these empires to gather together would be the observance of religious festivals which would take place at regular intervals. Both societies recognized the necessity of a central time-reckoning system to facilitate the timely arrival of people to these festivals and placed the responsibility for the formation of this system into the hands of their respective religious communities.

To develop their calendars, both groups followed similar approaches. They divided time into three major divisions—what we now recognize as days, months, and years—and then went about calculating the exact duration of each category. The questions to be answered by the ancient Babylonians and Egyptians are the questions all subsequent calendar makers have had to address:

- How long is a day?
- How long is a month?
- How long is a year?

These values may seem obvious to a modern day observer, but it actually took centuries of ongoing observations, measurements, and calculations to set them.

How Long Is a Day?

The basic building block of all calendars is the day. The length of the day is set by the amount of time in which the earth completes one rotation on its axis.

During the fifth century B.C.E. (Before Common Era, which is equivalent to the term B.C.), the Babylonians divided this duration of time into twenty-four segments which we now know as hours. However, because accurate measurement of seconds and even minutes was not possible until the sixteenth century C.E. (Common Era, equivalent to A.D.), the length of those hours has not always been fixed.

Using the Sun to Measure the Day

Originally, the position of the sun was used to record the passing of time during the day. The problem with this was two-fold. First, because of the nature of the earth's revolution of the sun, the point at which the sun passes any given point from one day to the next varies slightly. Second, the devices used to mark the movement of the sun, such as sundials, were not precise and could not compensate for the change in the earth's position relative to the sun from season to season. For instance, according to a sundial, an hour in northern latitudes would have been twice as long in the summer as it would have been in the winter.

Early observers must have noted a pattern in the cycle of light and darkness. Even though the length of light and darkness varied, they were always balanced with each other. When light grew shorter, dark grew longer and vice versa. In any case, the custom of counting one period of light and one period of darkness as a unit for the purpose of time-keeping seemed natural.

A Starting Point Is Established

A question developed, however, about when to mark the beginning of this time-keeping unit. Two points seemed to make the most sense: sunrise or sunset. Hebrew culture chose to designate sunset as the beginning of a day. As a result, their sabbaths and holy days began at sunset on the evening before the daytime of the festival. This tradition carried over into Christian traditions and gave rise to the celebrations of "eves" such as Christmas Eve, New Year's Eve, and Halloween (All Hallow's Eve). Other groups chose sunrise as the beginning of the day.

Yet, because the balance of light and dark in the day was always shifting, societies still faced inconsistencies when using the sunrise or sunset to indicate the onset of the day. Because of the logistics of governing people over grand expanses of land, large empires were particularly troubled with widely varying starting points for the day. Theoretically, the day could begin several hours later in the western portion of an empire than it did in the eastern part. Therefore, societies began searching for a more constant point of origin for the day.

Astronomers in ancient Rome observed that no matter what time the sun rose or set, the time between the points at which the sun was directly overhead from day to day was always the same. The Romans established the point at which the sun was directly overhead as the beginning of the day. As history progressed, people realized that if there was a fixed time for midday, there would also be a fixed time exactly opposite that in the middle of the night—midnight. Once this was recognized, the advantages of naming midnight as the beginning of the day became clear. Rather than changing a date in the middle of the business day, the change could be made at night when most people were sleeping—or at least most business was not being conducted. Therefore, midnight became the most commonly accepted changing point for the day.

Classical Water-Clocks Increase Accuracy

Around 150 B.C.E., the water-clock or clepsydra came into use by the Greeks and Romans. These water-clocks measured time by allowing a steady flow of water to drip through a small opening into a collection chamber which was marked to indicate the passage of hours as the chamber filled. As the technical sophistication of clepsydras increased, a float attached to a rod was added to the collection chamber. As the water level rose, the rod moved, turning a gear with a pointer on one side. This pointer moved around a numbered dial which indicated the passage of hours.

During the middle-ages, an improvement in the design of the clock was made by replacing water with slowly descending weights to turn the gear. This change allowed the clocks to be mounted in the towers of churches which established a central time source for entire towns. However, even with all of these advances, the measurement of time was still not reliable.

Pendulums Swing Into Action

In 1581, Galileo's discovery that a pendulum moved at a constant rate of speed provided a basis for more accurate time-keeping. Building on this notion, the Dutch astronomer Christian Huygens invented a clock around 1657 in which a pendulum was kept moving by descending weights; the regular swinging of the pendulum moved the gears of the clock. Huygens's method proved to be quite precise, eventually allowing for the division of the hour into minutes and minutes into seconds.

How Long Is a Month?

The division of days into hours was very important, but a method of ordering a succession of days into larger units of time was necessary for long-term planning. The development of what we now call a month, which is based on the rotation of the moon around the earth, grew out of such an attempt to organize days together. When people began to observe the phases of the moon to define the month is not known, but evidence from ancient civilizations suggests that it was done very early in the history of mankind.

Watching the Phases of the Moon

Early observers noted patterns in the changing shape of the moon. Perhaps initially their observations began at the point when the moon appeared as a thin crescent in the western sky just after sunset. Then, a week later, the crescent would have grown to a half-circle which was rounded on the western side and flat on the eastern side. A few nights would pass and the moon would appear to have grown a hump on its previously flattened eastern side. (*Gibbous*, from a Latin word meaning "hump" is the name of this phase of the moon.) About a week later, a full disc would appear in the east almost exactly as the sun disappeared in the west. The full moon would last only one night; the next night the moon would rise in its gibbous phase, this time the western side would be slightly flatter than the eastern side. The western side would grow flatter each night until it became a half-circle again about one week after the full moon had appeared. The process would continue for another week until the crescent moon appeared in the east. Finally, one week later, no moon would appear. This phase became known as the new moon.

A month is the time that passes between one new moon and the next. The length of this period, called the *synodical month*, is about twenty-nine and one-half days.

The Priest Declares a New Month

When people were first beginning to use the phases of the moon as a basis for their month, the duty of watching for the new moon was very solemn and was administered by the religious leaders of the community. This tradition lasted long after astronomers had developed methods by which the appearance of the new moon could be predicted. In fact, it is from such an ancient Roman tradition that the word calendar comes. Each month, the high priest would watch for the new moon; when it occurred, he would *calare* (the Latin word for "declare") a new month. The first day of the month was called *calends* from which we derive our word calendar—a chart which records all of the *calends*.

What Is the Sidereal Month?

Ancient observers may have believed that the moon actually changed shapes, but astronomers soon discovered that this was not the case. While they were watching the skies, they certainly studied the moon's companions, the stars. As they did, they discovered that the moon changed its place nightly in relation to the other heavenly bodies. By observing the change in position night after night, they determined that it took about 27 days for the moon to come back to the first position in which it had been observed. This cycle was named the *sidereal month* and is slightly shorter than the synodical month.

Although the modern Western civil calendar is based on the synodical month, other calendars such as the Hindu calendar (which is based on the constellations of the zodiac), use the sidereal month. As time measurement became more precise, the length of the sidereal month was discovered to be 27 days, 7 hours, 43 minutes, and 11.5 seconds. The precision of this value became important as astronomers grappled with nature to divulge the secret of the length of the year.

How Long Is a Year?

Ascertaining the length of the year has been the most difficult issue faced by calendar makers. Although measuring the length of a complete cycle of seasons may not seem complicated, it actually creates significant problems for calendar systems.

In hunting and gathering societies, the need for time measurement beyond a month was not of extreme importance. Agrarian cultures, however, depend heavily on the ability to predict optimal planting and harvesting times—a process requiring an understanding of the cycles of weather. The inhabitants of ancient farming communities began to observe the weather in relation to the phases of the moon.

As the early astronomers watched, they observed a pattern of seasons. Each season contained several new moons or months. The seasons were marked by either warm or cold temperatures or a high or low level of precipitation that repeated after the passage of twelve months. These observations originally defined the year.

Babylonians and Egyptians Disagree

In the fifth century B.C.E., the Babylonians and Egyptians both arrived at a specific number of days in the year, but their conclusions were different. The Babylonians claimed that the year was 360 days long while the Egyptians more accurately estimated the year at 365 days. The discrepancy between the two lengths of the year has always been puzzling.

One possibility for the difference is that the Babylonians simply miscalculated the number; however, this is unlikely in light of their sophisticated astronomical and mathematical systems. Another explanation is that they rounded their figure from 365 days to 360 days to facilitate the interaction of the year with their base-twelve numerical system.

The problem with the Babylonian's five-day omission was that the months would not stay in line with the seasons of the year. Each year the beginning of each month would occur at least five days earlier in relation to the position of the sun. Eventually, the months would be completely dissociated with the seasons in which they originally occurred. To correct this problem, the Babylonians periodically added months to the calendar—a process termed *intercalation,* which can also be used to add "leap" days or weeks.

The Babylonians were not the only people to face the problem of keeping the months coordinated with the seasons. Even though the Egyptians calculated the length of the year more accurately, they too realized that their determination was not exactly perfect. In fact, the year cannot be divided into exact fractions that can be expressed in days.

The Solar System Affects the Length of the Year

Precise division of the year into days is impossible because the cycle of the seasons is determined by the earth's relationship to the sun *and* the moon. The movements of these heavenly bodies do not neatly coincide with the mathematical systems of any human civilization.

The quest to discover the secrets of how the universe fits together has motivated astronomers throughout history. In the second century C.E., Ptolemy, a Greek astronomer formulated the theory that the earth was the center of the universe and that the sun, stars, moon, and other planets revolve around it. In the fifteenth century C.E., the Polish astronomer Copernicus introduced the notion that the earth rotated on an axis and, along with the other heavenly bodies in the solar system, revolved around the sun. Shortly after the Copernican assertion, Galileo presented supporting evidence based on observations he made using a telescope. It is the solar cycle—the relationship among the earth, moon, and sun—that determines the cycle of the seasons.

The Gap Between the Lunar and Solar Cycles

Herein lies the difficulty of keeping the cycle of the months in line with the passing of the seasons: An 11.25-day difference exists between the 354-day lunar cycle on which the months are based and the 365.25-day solar cycle which determines the seasons. Three main ways of dealing with this discrepancy have been attempted. The first is to ignore the seasons and allow the lunar cycle to be the basis of the year as the Islamic calendar does. Another method is the lunisolar system like the Hebrew calendar which involves an elaborate system of calculations to add days or months to the lunar year until it coincides with the solar year. The third system is the pure solar calendar which originated with the Egyptians and allows the sun to determine not only the seasons, but the length of the months as well. In the following chapters, each of these systems will be explored.

CHAPTER 2

The History of Lunar and Lunisolar Calendars

The Chinese Calendar

The Chinese calendar, which has been used widely throughout the Asian world over the course of history, is based on the longest unbroken chain of time measurement in mankind's memory with its epoch believed to be 2953 B.C.E. Influences from the Hindu and Muslim have been introduced at various times, but none succeeded in changing the Chinese calendar. The traditional calendar has only diminished in its official use since the 1912 adoption of the Gregorian calendar for public use.

Part of the reason that the Chinese calendar has survived intact for nearly five millennium is that, until the middle of the twentieth century, the document was considered sacred. Any changes to the calendar were tightly controlled by imperial authorities, and the penalty for illegally tampering with the time keeping system was death. Therefore, although minor adjustments in the astronomical calculations have been made to the calendar, its essential structure today is the same as it was nearly five thousand years ago. Until the rise of Communism in China during the twentieth century, the official calendar was presented to the emperor, governors, and other dignitaries in an elaborate ceremony each year on the first day of the tenth month.

Three Celestial "Roads"

As most ancient time reckoning systems, the Chinese calendar is lunisolar. It is organized according to three paths or roads which map the movements of celestial bodies. The Red Road helps define the solar month and year by tracing the constellations in a line roughly corresponding with the equator. Each of the 28 constellations along the Red Road fall into one of 28 lunar mansions which vary in size from 1 to 34 degrees of the 360 degree circle in the sky around the earth. The earth's movement around the sun (or, according to a geocentric view of the universe, the sun's movement against the stars) is charted on the Yellow Road which also gives definition to the length of the solar year. The White Road follows the phases of the moon and is the basis for the lunar aspects of the Chinese calendar.

The Chinese Zodiac

The Chinese zodiac is not comparable to other systems. The "twelve branches" are derived from the twelve positions in the sky to which the seven stars of the Big Dipper point during the year. The Chinese use the zodiac in two different cycles to name their years. The first system matches the ten celestial signs with each animal of the zodiac (see Table 2.1). For example, the first zodiac sign is combined with the first celestial sign to form the year Kiah-tse. The second

TABLE 2.1. THE CHINESE ZODIAC AND CELESTIAL SIGNS		
Celestial Signs	**Zodiac Symbol**	**English Animal**
Kiah	Tse	Rat
Yih	Chau	Ox
Ping	Yin	Tiger
Ting	May	Hare
Wu	Shin	Dragon
Ki	Se	Snake
Kang	Wu	Horse
Sin	Wi	Sheep
Jin	Shin	Monkey
Kwei	Yu	Rooster
	Siuh	Dog
	Hai	Pig

year is Yih-chau, a combination of the second sign in each series. When all ten celestial signs have been paired, the eleventh zodiacal sign is matched with the first celestial sign. Thus the cycle continues through sixty years.

The Chinese use this system not only for counting years, but also for counting days. When it is used to enumerate days, it is known as the kah-chih system. The pattern of repeating the ten celestial signs probably led to the development of the hsun—the Chinese ten-day equivalent of the week.

The second cycle for naming the years is used less frequently and never in conjunction with the other. Like the first system, it is a sixty year cycle, but instead of using celestial signs as counterparts to the zodiac, it uses the elements of the earth: wood, fire, earth, metal, and water (see Table 2.2).

Subdivisions within the Chinese Year

The Chinese year is divided into twenty-four parts. The Chinese New Year takes place on the new moon nearest to the point which is defined in the West as the fifteenth degree of Aquarius—roughly February 4 or 5 according to the Western civil calendar.

Each of the twelve months in the Chinese year is twenty-nine or thirty days long and is divided into two parts defined as the period of time covering 15 degrees of the sky—about two weeks. The Chinese calendar, like all lunisolar systems, requires periodic adjustment to keep the lunar and solar cycles integrated.

Intercalation in the Chinese calendar takes place each time a month contains the beginning and end of only one of the 15 degree divisions.

Beginning with the New Year the names for the 24 divisions are:

1. Spring Begins	13. Autumn Begins
2. Rain Water	14. Limit of Heat
3. Excited Insects	15. White Dew
4. Vernal Equinox	16. Autumnal Equinox
5. Clear and Bright	17. Cold Dew
6. Grain Rains	18. Hoar Frost Descends
7. Summer Begins	19. Winter Begins
8. Grain Fills	20. Little Snow
9. Grain in Ear	21. Heavy Snow
10. Summer Solstice	22. Winter Solstice
11. Slight Heat	23. Little Cold
12. Great Heat	24. Great Cold

The Calendars of India

Throughout its history, India has used a plethora of calendars and dating systems of which there have been two basic types: a civil calendar which changed with each new regime (the current civil holidays are listed in Table 2.3), and a religious calendar maintained by the Hindus. Although each geographical region had its own Hindu calendar, most of the calendars shared some elements that they gleaned from a common heritage. When India became a unified and independent nation in the mid-twentieth century, the differences among regional calendars included over thirty methods for determining the beginning of the era, the year, and the month. These variations in the Hindu calendar were the culmination of nearly 5,000 years of history.

TABLE 2.2. PARTIAL CYCLE OF THE CHINESE ZODIAC AND ELEMENTS OF THE EARTH

Zodiac Symbol	English Animal	Element
Tzu	Rat	Wood
Chou	Ox	Wood
Yin	Tiger	Fire
Mao	Hare	Fire
Shin	Dragon	Earth
Ssu	Snake	Earth
Wu	Horse	Metal
We	Sheep	Metal
Shin	Monkey	Water
Yu	Rooster	Water
Hsu	Dog	Wood
Hai	Pig	Wood
Tzu	Rat	Fire
Chou	Ox	Fire
Yin	Tiger	Earth
Mao	Hare	Earth

TABLE 2.3. HOLIDAYS ON THE INDIAN CIVIL CALENDAR

Western Date	Holiday
March 22	New Year's Day
April 13	Vaisakhi (Old New Year's Day)
August 15	Independence Day
October 2	Mahatma Gandhi's birthday
January 14	Pongal or Makar-Sankranti: three-day festival of sidereal entrance of the Sun into Capricorn
January 26	Republic Day

India's Original Calendar

Before 1000 B.C.E., India's first time reckoning system emerged. It was based on astronomical observations and consisted of a solar year of 360 days comprising 12 lunar months. The discrepency between the length of the solar and lunar years was corrected by intercalating a month every 60 months.

In 1200 C.E, the Muslims brought to India the use of their calendar for administrative purposes, and the British introduced the Gregorian calendar in 1757. Despite these occurrences, however, each separate state maintained a calendar which its citizens used in their daily interactions. Throughout India's colonial days, the entrenchment of these local calendars created havoc for the central government because any given date would have up to six different interpretations throughout the country. The difficulties continued as an indigenous government took control in 1947.

For a more detailed discussion of the Hindu calendars, see the calendar section in Chapter 10.

Western Traditions

The earliest Western system for constructing calendars was developed by Babylonian, Sumerian, and Assyrian astronomers living in the Mesopotamian valley hundreds of years before the birth of Christ. These calendars were based on the phases of the moon and were closely related to the religious life of the cultures that developed them. The influence of the Mesopotamian civilizations on the global art of calendar making was far reaching because many of the techniques they developed were adopted by future societies.

The Babylonian Calendar

Of the various cultures that thrived in the Mesopotamian valley, the Babylonians seem to have had the most significant influence on calendar making. Many details of the evolution of the Babylonian calendar have been lost over the centuries, but it is known that the calendar was lunar in nature, had a system of intercalation, had months divided into seven-day units, and had days with twenty-four hours.

Intercalation Reconciles Nature's Incongruous Cycles

Because these early calendar makers were pioneers in the field, they were among the first to be confronted with the discrepancy between the lunar and solar cycles—a problem that had the potential to render any calendar system ineffective. To reconcile the two natural courses, the Babylonians worked out a schedule whereby an extra month was periodically intercalated. The process of intercalation, termed *iti dirig*, seems to have been rather arbitrary at first, but by 380 B.C.E. a formal system had developed. The plan consisted of a 19-year (235 month) system in which an extra month was added in the third, sixth, eighth, eleventh, seventeenth, and nineteenth years. Many other cultures, including the Greeks, developed similar intercalation schemes which may have been based on the Babylonian model.

The Babylonians Introduce the Seven-Day Week

Although the origin of the week has been a subject of much research and debate among scholars since the time of Plutarch (46-119 C.E.), most agree that the Babylonians are the primary source for the week in the Western civil calendar. Many researchers also conclude that the Babylonians devised the week as a part of their religious practices. They have observed that years, months, and days are all based on natural cycles, but the week is not. This observation has led to some questions: Why does the week have seven days? Why are the days named after celestial bodies? Why are the days not arranged according to the order of the planets in the solar system? Many proposed solutions to these quandaries have surfaced over the course of time.

The Babylonian View of the Universe

A different view of the universe may account for the structure of the week. Lawrence Wright articulates a theory on the origin of the week in his *Clockwork Man*, which may help a modern audience understand the ancient mind-set. Using available historical and archeological information, Wright has attempted to reconstruct the Babylonian view of the universe.

Wright proposes that the seven-day week was not based on any naturally occurring pattern, but was the result of other influences within Babylonian society. He suggests that the week may have been based on 168 hours rather than seven days.

Moreover, he suggests that the order of days may be explained by the Babylonian belief in the earth as the center of the astronomical cycles they observed. Thus, if one lines the sun, moon, and planets up according to the Babylonian estimation of their distance from the earth (Saturn, Jupiter, Mars, Sun, Venus, Mercury, Moon) rather than their order in the solar system, an interesting pattern arises. If each hour of the day is assigned a planet, by the time all of the hours have been assigned, and each planet has been given the first hour of one day, a seven-day sequence has been completed. For example, beginning with the first day, assign the first hour to the farthest planet from the earth, Saturn. That day would be known as Saturn's day or Saturday. Assign each hour of the day to another planet so that the second hour would be assigned to Jupiter, the third to Mars, and so on, repeating the sequence of planets until each hour of the day has been assigned to a planet. A twenty-four hour period requires that each planet be assigned three times and three planets four times. The first hour of the second day is named for the next planet in the sequence, or the Sun (hence, Sunday). Although the Babylonians had different planet and day names, they occurred in the same pattern as the current Western calendar observes.

Another Theory Based on an Astrological System

Another explanation for the order of the week may be that the Babylonians attached special significance to the days of the week and hours of the day. This suggests that the divisions may have been important to Babylonian religious practices.

Archeological evidence reveals that the Babylonian religion involved worship of the "visible gods," the seven lights in the sky that the Babylonians believed wandered against the background provided by the fixed stars—a type of astrological system similar to the Greek zodiac. Each day of the Babylonian month was sacred to one of these seven gods. Thus a seven-day pattern of gods' days would have emerged. This pattern would have offered a convenient division of the month.

Although in English the names of the week bear the influence of the Anglo-Saxons, the days in Latin and the Romance languages correspond to the ancient Babylonian "visible gods."

The Sabbath May Have Its Beginning in Babylon

The Sabbath is a common occurrence in many cultures. Historians suggest that the Babylonians may have been the first to develop this idea. In fact, the modern word "sabbath" can be traced to the Babylonian "shabattu" which means seventh. The Babylonians considered the days numbered 7, 14, 19, 21, and 28 "evil days" since the god of the underworld was the deity governing those days. Some scholars have proposed that the seven- day week was translated into other cultures by the ancient Hebrews, who adopted the concept when they were subject to Babylonian rule. From there, over a period of thousands of years, the Hebrews were diffused into nearly every culture on earth, taking their traditions with them.

Details of the Babylonian Calendar

Details of the Babylonian calendar are few, but some are known. It appears that the major festival of Babylonian society was the New Year celebration which took place in the spring of the year during the Babylonian month of Nisanu. On the first day of the festival, a ritual marriage was performed between the king and the high priestess, who symbolized the sovereignty of the land. On this day, the Babylonian creation myth (called *Enuma elish* from its opening words, "When on high") was read aloud. On the fifth day, Rites of Atonement were observed. During the Rites the king, as a representative of the people, endured a ritual of abasement to atone for the sins of the people against the gods. On the seventh day, the Festival of the Sun, or spring equinox, took place.

The Greek Calendar

The Greeks also possessed an ancient calendar system. The classical Greeks had calendar systems that varied among the city-states. The political powers of each city-state retained the right to intercalate months and days to reconcile the lunar and solar cycles. These intercalations were arbitrary and seem to have been more closely associated with political whimsy rather than natural cycles. The most influential calendar system was the Athenian.

The Athenian calendar consisted of twelve lunar months that alternated between 29 and 30 days in length, plus an intercalary month of 30 days. This extra month, Poseideion Deuteros or second Poseideion, was inserted into the calendar after the sixth month Poseideion. Also, an extra day could be added to the last month, Scirophorion, to keep the months in phase with the moon.

When the Athenians became rulers of the Delian League in the sixth century B.C.E., they realized the need to have an official calendar that could be used by all the League's members. Hence in 582 B.C.E. they regulated the intercalation of months by using an eight-year, or octennial, cycle in which a month was added to the third, fifth, and eighth years.

The Athenians Divide Months into Three "Decades"

The Athenian calendar began in midsummer and comprised twelve months:

1. Hecatombaion	7. Gamelion
2. Metageitnion	8. Anthesterion
3. Boedromion	9. Elaphebolion
4. Pyanopsion	10. Mounychion
5. Maimactrerion	11. Thargelion
6. Poseideion	12. Scirophorion

These months were divided into three "decades" of ten days each. The first ten days were called the "waxing moon"; the middle ten days were called "full moon"; and the last nine or ten days were called the "waning moon." Dates were assigned according to these decades, and days within the last decade were numbered from the end of the decade. For example, the first day of the month was called the "first day of the waxing moon" of whatever month. The eleventh day would be "the first day of the full moon." The twentieth day was called "the tenth day of the full moon," but the twenty-first day was called "the tenth day of the waning moon" (or the ninth day, if the month had only 29 days).

An Eight-Year Cycle Reconciles the Lunar and Solar Patterns

The Grecian concept of an eight-year cycle was devised by Cleostratus of Tenedos (c. 500 B.C.E.) and advanced by Eudoxus of Cnidus (390 to c. 340 B.C.E.). Called the octaëteris, the Greek cycle was based on a solar year of 365 days; thus, the eight-year cycle was composed of 2,920 days. The octennial cycle closely matched the length of 99 lunations (a total of 2920.5 days), which made it a promising link between lunar and solar calendars.

The actual length of a solar year is 365.24 days, and eight solar years have a length of 2921.93 days. Therefore, the calendar based on the octaëteris accumulated an error of 1.5 days every eight years. After about a century of use, the discrepancy had accrued to nearly 30 days. When the Greek scholars realized the problems with their calendar, some of them began to search for a more effective system to reconcile the lunar and solar calendars.

The Metonic Cycle Is Developed

The most significant of all the early attempts to relate the lunar calendar to the tropical year was the Metonic cycle. First devised about 430 B.C.E. by the Athenian astronomers Meton and Euctemon, the system is based on a nineteen-year cycle which intercalates months in seven of the nineteen years.

To determine the length for the tropical year, Meton and Euctemon made a series of observations of the solstices—the point at which the sun's noonday shadow cast by a vertical pillar, or gnomon, reaches its annual maximum or minimum. Assuming the value of the synodic lunar month to be 29.5 days, the two astronomers computed the difference between 12 lunations and the tropical year at 11 days. To accommodate the lunar cycle and create a rule that would be accurate on a long-term basis, Meton and Euctemon constructed a nineteen-year cycle. It consisted of twelve years of twelve lunar months each and seven years each of thirteen months for a total of 235 lunar months. The cycle contains 110 "hollow" months (of 29 days) and 125 "full" months (of 30 days), which comes to a total of 6,940 days. The difference between this lunar calendar and a solar calendar of 365 days amounted to only five days in nineteen years and, in addition, gave an average length for the tropical year of 365.25 days.

In practice, Meton's cycle is even more precise than he realized. The five-day difference that arose over the course of the cycle was based on a slightly inaccurate day count. Astronomers who came after Meton have discovered the actual length of 235 lunar months to be 6939.69 days and the number of days in nineteen solar years to be 6939.602. Thus, the actual difference between the two cycles accrues to less than one day in nineteen years—a discrepancy easily corrected by occasionally adding days to or subtracting them from the year.

There are two primary accomplishments of the Metonic cycle: it established a lunar calendar with a rule for intercalating months to keep it in step with the tropical year; and it gave a more accurate average value for the tropical year. Although none of the Greek calendars appear to have adopted the system, the Persians did around 380 B.C.E. The Metonic system then passed into the Hebrew liturgical calendar which is still based on the cycle, as are the formulas used by the Christian churches to calculate the date of Easter.

Callippus Enhances Meton's System

The Metonic cycle was improved by Callippus of Cyzicus (c. 370-300 B.C.E.). He developed the Callippic cycle which is a variation on the Metonic cycle. Consisting of four nineteen-year cycles, the Callippic system takes into account that 365.25 days is a more precise value for the tropical year than 365 days. The Callippic period encompasses 940 lunar months, but its distribution of hollow and full months differs from Meton's 440 hollow and 500 full months. Callippus adopted 441 hollow and 499 full months, reducing the length of four Metonic cycles by one day. The total number of days in the Callippic cycle, therefore, is 27,759. When this total is divided by 76 (the number of years in the cycle), the result is 365.25 days exactly. Thus, the Callippic cycle fits 940 lunar months precisely to 76 tropical years of 365.25 days.

Hipparchus' Discovery of the Precession of the Equinoxes

Hipparchus, who flourished in Rhodes about 150 B.C.E., was probably the greatest observational astronomer of antiquity. He discovered that the equinoxes—where the ecliptic (the sun's apparent path) crosses the celestial equator (the celestial equivalent of the terrestrial equator)—were not fixed in space but moved slowly in a westerly direction. The movement, now known as the precession of the equinoxes, is small, no more than two degrees of arc in 150 years. Yet, it was important to the development of the calendar because the tropical year is measured with reference to the equinoxes. The precession reduced the value of the year that was accepted by Callippus.

Hipparchus calculated the tropical year to have a length of 365.242 days, which was very close to the present 365.242199 days. He also computed the precise length of a lunation, using a "great year" of four Callippic cycles. He arrived at the value of 29.53058 days for a lunation, which, again, is comparable with the present-day figure, 29.53059 days. Hipparchus' adjustments made the Metonic cycle the most accurate long-range time keeping system available to scientists until well into the modern age.

Use of the Metonic Cycle for Liturgical and Astronomical Calendars

Meton's innovative cycle fell victim to the political winds of the day and was not recognized by the political establishment of Greece during his lifetime. Fortunately, Greek religious leaders and classical astronomers did use Meton's cycle to calculate their calendars. The cycle has been passed down through the course of history as subsequent calendar makers, including the Julian and Gregorian reformers, have adapted its basic formula to fit their systems.

Religious Holidays and the Greek Liturgical Calendar

The celebration of religious holidays in the Athenian months followed some consistent patterns. For example, the first and seventh day of each month was sacred to Apollo, and the first and fifteenth days were sacred to Selene. Festivals of other gods fell into consistent patterns as well. Dionysus tended to be celebrated on days 11 to 13; sacrifices to Zeus on day 14; the cycle of games on days 11-15. Therefore, by knowing the Greek pattern of religious celebration, scholars can accurately surmise the specific dates on which the festival of a deity was observed. By following these patterns, scholars have been able to reconstruct the Athenian calendar with a high degree of accuracy (see Table 2.4).

Days in the Greek calendar began at sunset just as in the Hebrew calendar. Since the Renaissance, the religious practices of the Greeks have been studied with interest, and have been revived by various Neoclassic and Neo-pagan groups.

The Eleusinian Mysteries

The most important Athenian festival was that of the Eleusinian Mysteries, which has intrigued scholars for centuries. Because the contents of the Mysteries were an Athenian state secret, the details of the festival are not known. The Mysteries fell into two periods. The earlier, in Anthesterion, was called the Lesser Mysteries, and probably involved a ritual or drama about the life, death, and resurrection of Dionysus. The later, in Boedromion, was called the Greater Mysteries, and was definitely centered on the myth of the Rape of Persephone, as told in the Greek poem called the Homeric *Hymn To Demeter*.

Some have surmised that initiation into the Lesser Mysteries was a prerequisite to participation in the Greater Mysteries. This may not be accurate, however, especially as the Romans began to influence the Greeks. Many Romans and other inhabitants of the Roman empire came to Athens in Boedromion to be initiated at the Greater Mysteries.

Preparation for the mysteries began formally on Boedromion 15. The Hierokeryx (sacred herald) would stand on the Painted Porch in Athens and, in the presence of the Hierophant ("high priest" of Eleusis), announce the assembly for the Mysteries. After several days of sacrifices and preparations, the Procession of the Mysteries would leave Athens on the morning of Boedromion 19, reaching Eleusis after sunset, which was then Boedromion 20 because the Athenian day began at sunset. Based on the known rituals, the celebration of the Mysteries probably lasted three nights. The festivities included a torchlit search for Kore and an initiation of the candidates who were sworn to secrecy as the key of the Hierophant was laid upon their lips. The agenda may have also included a ritual drama about the reunion of Demeter and Kore; evidence indicates that a ritual or mime of the Rape of Kore took place during the Thesmophoria. Finally, there was probably a ritual in the Telesterion. It is possible that the entire festival lasted nine days or longer based on the tradition of a nine-day fast which was clearly a part of the observation of this event. Therefore, the ending date of the festival can certainly be placed on or after Boedromion 23, nine days after the Proclamation of the Mysteries on Boedromion 15.

British Traditions

Time-Reckoning Begins with Stonehenge

The first evidence of a time reckoning system in Britain is the monument of Stonehenge. Historians suppose that the construction was originally used to mark solstices and equinoxes, and was built over a fifteen hundred year period beginning around 3000 B.C.E. Little is known about the builders of Stonehenge.

TABLE 2.4. ATHENIAN LUNISOLAR CALENDAR

Hekatombaion, "sacrifice of a hundred," 30 days.

1 . . . .Consecrated to the deities Selene and Apollo. This day always coincides with the appearance of the first visible crescent moon after the summer solstice.

4 . . . .Consecrated to the deities Aphrodite and Hermes, and the hero Herakles.

6 . . . .Consecrated to the deity Artemis.

7 . . . .Consecrated to Apollo. The Hekatombaia festival held, honoring Apollo. Hyakinthia begins.

8 . . . .Consecrated to the god Poseidon and to the Hero of Athens, Theseus.

9 . . . .Hyakinthia ends.

11-15 . .Nemean Games held in years two and four of each four-year cycle.

12 . . . .Consecrated to the Titan deity Kronos, the father of Zeus.

15 . . . .Consecrated to the moon goddess Selene.

16 . . . ."Federation Day." Consecrated to the goddess Aphrodite Pandemos, Peitho, and to the Horae, or season, Eirene, the personification of Peace.

21-28 . .Panathenaea, the "All-Greek Festival of Athena."

30 . . . .Consecrated to the fertility goddess Hekate.

Metageitnion, 29 days

1 . . . .Consecrated to Selene and Apollo.

4 . . . .Consecrated to Aphrodite, Hermes and Herakles.

6 . . . .The deities Artemis and Kronos honored with the sacrifice of a scapegoat.

6-14 . . .Pythian games held at Delphi in year three of each four-year cycle.

7 . . . .Consecrated to Apollo; Metageitnia held in honor of Apollo. The people of Salamis sacrificed a pig to each of the deities Apollo Patroos, Leto, Artemis, and Athena Agelaa.

7-15 . . .Karneia, a festival honoring Apollo Karneus; festivities included feasts, footraces, and musical contests.

8 . . . .Consecrated to the god Poseidon and to Theseus (Athenian Hero).

10 . . . .Athletic contests held at Olympus in honor of the goddess Hera in year one of each four-year cycle.

11-15 . .Olympic Games, held in year one of each four-year cycle.

15 . . . .Consecrated to the goddess Selene.

29 . . . .Consecrated to the goddess Hekate.

Boedromion, "month of helpers," 30 days.

1 . . . .Consecrated to the deities Selene and Apollo.

4 . . . .Consecrated to the deities Aphrodite and Hermes, and to the hero Herakles.

5 . . . .Genesia = Nekusia = Nemesia, the clans' feast of the dead.

6 . . . .Consecrated to the goddess Artemis.

6-7 . . .Boedromia held, honoring the deities Artemis and Apollo.

7 . . . .Consecrated to the god Apollo.

8 . . . .Consecrated to the god Poseidon and to the Hero of Athens, Theseus.

13 . . . .Commencement of preparations for celebration of the Eleusinian Mysteries.

15 . . . .Consecrated to the goddess Selene. The advent of the Mysteries announced from the Painted Porch.

16 . . . .Synoekia, the sacrifice of two oxen to the god Zeus (in the form Zeus Phratrios) and the goddess Athena (in the form Athena Phratria), "of the clans."

19-23 . .The Great Mysteries of Eleusis.

30 . . . .Consecrated to the goddess Hekate.

TABLE 2.4. ATHENIAN LUNISOLAR CALENDAR, continued

Pyanopsion, "month of boiling beans," 29 days.

1 . . . .Consecrated to the deities Selene and Apollo.
4 . . . .Consecrated to the deities Aphrodite and Hermes, and to the Hero Herakles.
6 . . . .Consecrated to Artemis. Proerosia held at Eleusis, a pig sacrificed to Theseus.
7 . . . .Consecrated to Apollo. Pyanopsia festival held with the expulsion of a scapegoat.
7-9 . . . .The Stepterion, Herois, and Charilla festivals held in honor of Apollo, once every eight years, at Delphi. A boy, representing Apollo, was placed in a hut called the palace of Python. The hut was set afire, and the boy removed from it and ritualistically "sent into exile." Then all the celebrants were purified at Tempe, and returned to Delphi in procession along the Pythian Way.
8 . . . .The Oschophoria, a celebration honoring the god Poseidon, held with footraces, feasting on beans, and carrying of grapes. Also, the Great Festival of Theseus.
9-13 . . .The Thesmophoria, "bringing of treasures," honoring Demeter and Kore; celebrated by women.
9 . . . .Sthenia held, honoring Demeter and Kore.
10 . . . .Anodos, "ascent," procession to the Thesmophorion, a temple of Demeter.
11 . . . .Nesteia, "fasting," observed.
12 . . . .The women built bowers, squatted on the ground, and ate roast pork.
13 . . . .Kalligeneia, "bearer of beautiful children," in which the rotting remains of the pigs sacrificed at the previous Skira were brought up and mixed with the seed corn to improve the crop.
11-13 . .Apaturia or Koureotis, festival observed by adolescent boys.
13 . . . .Apaturia, day three—children, young men who had just reached the age of maturity, and newly married women were enrolled in the phratries (clans) of Athens, with appropriate sacrifices.
14 . . . .Anarhusis, marked by the sacrifice of oxen to the god Zeus Phratrios and the goddess Athena.
15 . . . .Consecrated to the goddess Selene. The festival of Hera held at Olympia every four years.
16 . . . .Birthday of Homer, death of Demosthenes.
28 . . . .Chalkeia and Hephaestia: torch race for the goddess Athena and the god Hephaestus.
29 . . . .Consecrated to the goddess Hekate.

Maimakterion, sacred to the god Zeus Maimaktes, "stormy," 30 days.

1 . . . .Consecrated to the goddess Selene and the god Apollo.
4 . . . .Consecrated to the goddess Aphrodite, the god Hermes, and the hero Herakles.
6 . . . .Consecrated to the goddess Artemis.
7 . . . .Consecrated to Apollo.
8 . . . .Consecrated to the god Poseidon and the Hero of Athens, Theseus.
14 . . . .Maimakteria held, marked by the sacrifice of sheep to Zeus Maimaktes.
15 . . . .Consecrated to Selene.
30 . . . .Consecrated to the goddess Hekate.

Posideon, sacred to the god Poseidon, 29 days.

1 . . . .Consecrated to the goddess Selene and the god Apollo.
4 . . . .Consecrated to the goddess Aphrodite, the god Hermes, and the hero Herakles.
6 . . . .Consecrated to the goddess Artemis.
7 . . . .Consecrated to Apollo.
8 . . . .The festival of Poseidea held, honoring the god Poseidon and the Hero of Athens, Theseus.
11-13 . .The Rural Festival of Dionysus.
12 . . . .The Haloa, honoring the "Green Demeter" (fertility goddess) and an agricultural Poseidon/Dionysus figure.
15 . . . .Consecrated to the goddess Selene.
29 . . . .Consecrated to the goddess Hekate.

TABLE 2.4. ATHENIAN LUNISOLAR CALENDAR, continued

Posideon Deuteros, "second month sacred to Poseidon," 30 days.

(This was the intercalary month in the Athenian system.)

1 . . . .Consecrated to the goddess Selene and the god Apollo.
4 . . . .Consecrated to the goddess Aphrodite, the god Hermes, and the hero Herakles.
6 . . . .Consecrated to the goddess Artemis.
7 . . . .Consecrated to Apollo.
8 . . . .Consecrated to the god Poseidon and the Hero of Athens, Theseus.
15 . . . .Consecrated to Selene.
30 . . . .Consecrated to the goddess Hekate.

Gamelion, sacred to the goddess Hera Gamelia, "of marriage," 30 days.

1 . . . .Consecrated to the goddess Selene and the god Apollo.
4 . . . .Consecrated to the goddess Aphrodite, the god Hermes, and the hero Herakles.
6 . . . .Consecrated to the goddess Artemis.
7 . . . .Consecrated to Apollo.
8 . . . .Consecrated to the god Poseidon, and the Hero of Athens, Theseus.
10 . . . .Lenaion held on the island Mykonos, marked by sacrifices to the goddess Demeter and Kore.
12-14 . .The festival of Lenaia held, honoring the god Dionysus.
14 . . . .The Gamelia held, honoring the goddess Hera.
15 . . . .Consecrated to Selene.
30 . . . .Consecrated to the goddess Hekate.

Anthesterion, sacred to the god Poseidon, 29 days.

1 . . . .Consecrated to the goddess Selene and the god Apollo.
4 . . . .Consecrated to the goddess Aphrodite, the god Hermes, and the hero Herakles.
6 . . . .Consecrated to the goddess Artemis.
7 . . . .Consecrated to Apollo. Celebration of Apollo's birthday, at Delphi, and commemoration of his return to Delphi following a three-month absence in winter.
8 . . . .Consecrated to the god Poseidon and to the Hero of Athens, Theseus.
11 . . . .The Anthesteria, "feast of flowers," a three-day festival of the god Dionysus and the dead which began with the Pithoigia, "opening of wine jars."
12 . . . .Anthesteria, day two, and Choes, "cups" or "jugs." Celebration included the blessing of new wine before the god Dionysus, the use of libations (a sacrifice performed by pouring a liquid onto the ground), and drinking contests. A ship-shaped wagon containing a statue of Dionysus was drawn in procession from the seashore to the Boukolion, the temple of Dionysus as Bull God, where the Basilinna (the wife of the Archon Basileus, or King Archon) underwent a ritual marriage to Dionysus. Dionysus' santuary in Limnae was opened.
13 . . . .Anthesteria, day three, and Chytroi, "pots." Pots of cooked fruit sacrificed to chthonian Hermes and the spirits of the dead.
15 . . . .Consecrated to the goddess Selene.
20-23 . .Lesser Mysteries of Eleusis.
23 . . . .The Diasia held, marked by a burnt offering of pigs made to Zeus Meilichios.
29 . . . .Consecrated to Hekate.

Elaphebolion, "month of shooting stags," sacred to the goddess Artemis, 30 days.

1 . . . .Consecrated to the goddess Selene and the god Apollo.
4 . . . .Consecrated to the goddess Aphrodite, the god Hermes, and the hero Herakles.
6 . . . .The festival of Elaphebolia held, honoring the goddess Artemis.
7 . . . .Consecrated to Apollo.
8 . . . .Consecrated to the god Poseidon and the Hero of Athens, Theseus.

TABLE 2.4. ATHENIAN LUNISOLAR CALENDAR, continued

Elaphebolion, continued

9-13 . . .The "Greater"—or "City Festival"—of Dionysus, when the dramatic contests were held.
14 . . . .The Pandia held, honoring Zeus.
15 . . . .Consecrated to Selene.
30 . . . .Consecrated to the goddess Hekate.

Mounichion, sacred to the goddess Artemis, 29 days.

1 . . . .Consecrated to Selene and Apollo.
4 . . . .Consecrated to Aphrodite, Hermes, and Herakles. The people of Salamis performed sacrifices to Herakles, Kourotrophos ("nourisher of youths"), Alkmene, and Maia.
6 . . . . .Consecrated to Artemis. The Brauronia held at Brauron, and the Tauropolia at Halai, for Artemis.
7 . . . .Consecrated to Apollo.
8 . . . .Consecrated to Poseidon and Theseus.
11-15 . .Isthmian Games in years two and four of each four-year cycle.
15 . . . .Consecrated to Selene.
16 . . . .The Munychia held, honoring Artemis as Moon Goddess.
29 . . . .Consecrated to Hekate.

Thargelion, sacred to Apollo, 30 days.

1 . . . .Consecrated to Selene and Apollo.
4 . . . .Consecrated to Aphrodite, Hermes, and Herakles.
6 . . . .Birthday of Artemis.
7 . . . . .The Thargelia, birthday of Apollo, celebrated with the carrying of the eiresione; condemned criminals were dedicated as pharmakoi, "scapegoats," hung with figs, and driven out of Athens.
8 . . . .Consecrated to Poseidon and Theseus.
11-13 . .The Agrionia, a festival honoring the god Dionysus, associated with the myth of the daughters of Minyas, or of Proetus, in Boeotia, Rhodes, Sparta, Kos, and Byzantium.
15 . . . .Consecrated to Selene.
24 . . . .The Kallynteria held, sweeping out Athena's temple. Torch race for Bendis, the moon goddess of Thrace.
25 . . . .The Plynteria held, washing Athena's robe and statue in the sea.
30 . . . .Consecrated to Hekate.

Skirophorion, sacred to the goddess Athena, 29 or 30 days.

1 . . . .Consecrated to Selene and Apollo.
4 . . . .Consecrated to Aphrodite, Hermes, and Herakles.
6 . . . .Consecrated to Artemis.
7 . . . .Consecrated to Apollo.
8 . . . .Consecrated to Poseidon and Theseus.
12 . . . .The Skirophoria or Skira held. Pigs sacrificed to Demeter by being thrown down into rocky chasms, where the scavenger birds could not get at them.
13 . . . .The Arrhephoria, "carrying secret objects," honoring Athena and Aphrodite. Two young girls of noble birth were given unidentified, wrapped objects which they then carried at night, through a secret tunnel, from the Acropolis to the Sanctuary of Aphrodite in the Gardens.
14 . . . .The festival of Diipolia, or Buphonia, held, and an ox sacrificed to Zeus.
15 . . . .Consecrated to Selene.
29/30 . .Consecrated to the goddess Hekate. Diisoteria held, honoring Zeus and Athena.

Please note when using this and other calendars in this volume that ancient sources are often incomplete or misleading so dates contained herein are approximate.

Druid Priests and New Religious Traditions in Britain

Originally hailing from northern Europe, the Celtic tribes migrated to Britain in the sixth century B.C.E., bringing with them their religious holidays and customs. The Druids, who were priests of the Celtic tribes, governed the rites observed in the celebration of festivals on the first day of February, May, August, and November. These holidays were based on the weather patterns in northern Europe, rather than the solar cycle that the earlier Britons formed their religion around. These two sets of holidays became a point of division between the Celts and Britons and have remained such throughout the history of the island until the present.

Traditionally, the days observed by the Britons were called quarter days and fell on the solstices and equinoxes (around March 22, June 22, September 22, and December 22); they also marked the date on which quarterly rent was due. The Celts' holidays became known as cross-quarter days and celebrated the changes in season. Almost all of these days have several different names, reflecting their long and complex history.

The Celtic Worldview

The Celts' worldview divides everything into equal and opposite halves. Aylwin and Brinsley Rees point out in their *Celtic Heritage* that the Celtic worldview saw everything that exists as divided into two joined but opposing halves and that the seam between the two halves represents danger or evil.

This helps explain some of the festivals and holidays of the Celtic people. For example, their year began on Nov. 1 with a festival, Samhain, marking the end of good weather. The Celts believed that ghosts and fairies could slip into this world from the netherworld on the eve of this festival because it was the meeting place between the good half and bad half of the year.

Similarly, the Celts believed twilight and dawn were perilous times because fairies were most likely to steal into this realm and carry people off at these times. The two halves of the year were divided by Candlemas and Lammas; the night and the day were divided in half by midnight and noon.

The practice of beginning a celebration on the evening before a holiday, such as All Hallows Eve, is derived from the structure of the Celtic calendar. Like most other ancient societies, the Celts began their days at sunset. Therefore, like the Hebrews and others, their observation of festivals and holidays began at sunset.

Religious Conflict Influences the Calendar

In the second century C.E., Diocletian's persecution of Christians caused many believers to flee from the Roman Empire. Some of these people settled in Ireland and there established Christian communities and monasteries among the Celts.

Over the next four centuries, the Irish Church developed apart from the Roman Church which dominated the rest of the British Isles. In the sixth century, Irish missionaries began proselytizing in England and came into conflict with the previously established Roman Church. The two branches of Christianity competed with one another for official recognition and converts during the next hundred years, often engaging in heated debate over doctrinal issues. In 664 C.E., the Council of Whitby was called by Oswy, King of Northumbria, to settle some of the differences—most significantly, the method of determining the date of Easter.

The conflict over the date of Easter centered on the method used to calculate the phases of the moon. By the seventh century, the Roman Church had adopted the 532-year Victorian cycle to regulate the calendar. The Celts, on the other hand, still used the eight-year cycle developed in Rome before Diocletian's persecutions; the Celts also used the Eastern method for determining the night of the full moon. Therefore, the two methods arrived at significantly different dates for the celebration of the most sacred of Christian holidays. Eventually, the Roman Church prevailed and was declared to be the official Church in England.

The Christian Era Is Developed

In 532 C.E. Dionysius Exiguus, Abbot of Rome, calculated that Christ had been born about 753 years after the foundation of Rome (753 A.U.C.—Anno Urbis Conditæ— which means in the year from the building of the city), and made that year the beginning of a new chronology. This date was determined by taking the average of the dates of 747 A.U.C. (according to events in the Gospel of Matthew) and 759 A.U.C. (as indicated by events recorded in the Gospel of Luke) as the date of Jesus's birth. Although the accuracy of this date is no longer accepted, the Western civil calendar as well as several other systems still use the Christian era for dating because of the complications involved in changing to any other method.

Saxon Influence Changes the Calendar

During the Roman domination of the southern British Isles, the Roman calendar was adopted. The influence of the Roman system faded, however, under subsequent barbarian rule. The most significant of the barbarian groups to affect the calendar was the Saxons. They brought a lunisolar system of time reckoning with them when they came to power in England in the seventh century C.E.

The calendar was composed of twelve lunar months with a thirteenth month intercalated once every three years (see Table 2.5). The day began at sunset and was subdivided into segments beginning at noon and midnight. Yule, or the winter solstice, was the major festival of the year, and scholars have surmised that the summer solstice, Litha, was also an occasion of grand celebration.

Some variables affecting the months are uncertain and have been tentatively reconstructed as follows: The placement of the fall, or autumnal, equinox determined the order of the months, and fall equinox occurred during a month called Holymonth. If the fall equinox occurred in the month after Weedmonth, the order of months went Weedmonth, Holymonth, Winterfull. In years in which the equinox would not occur in the month after Weedmonth, the month order was Weedmonth, Harvestmonth, Holymonth, and Winterfull. The designation of the month containing the fall equinox was clearly pagan in origin because there were no significant Christian festivals observed near the fall equinox during the seventh century.

TABLE 2.5.
THE SAXON CALENDAR

Name of month	Alternative name	Western civil month
Afteryule	Wolfmonth	January
Sproutkale	Solmonth	February
Hlydamonth		March
Eostremonth		April
Threemilks		May
Forelitha	Shearmonth	June
(Threelitha)	(Intercalated month)	
Afterlitha	Meadmonth	July
Weedmonth		August
Harvestmonth	Holymonth	September
Winterfull	Holymonth	October
Bloodmonth		November
Foreyule		December

The two months called Hlydamonth and Eostremonth were named after the goddesses Hlyda and Eostre. Although details about the Goddess Eostre are few, historians suggest that it is from her name that English-speaking people derive the name "Easter" for the Feast of the Resurrection, which other languages call "Pasch," or something similar derived from the Hebrew word for Passover. The notion of the Easter Rabbit is also derived from Eostre, for the rabbit was one of her sacred animals. Furthermore, this rabbit lays Easter eggs because in some of the Mystery religions of the Roman period, an egg dyed scarlet was the symbol of the reincarnation and immortality promised to the initiate. The mixture of Christian and pagan traditions is clearly the result of Pope Gregory's policy of temperance and toleration which was articulated in a letter to Augustine of Canterbury early in the seventh century C.E.

Bede Popularizes the Use of the Christian Era in Dating

Information about both the Celtic and Saxon calendars as well as the Church controversies is found in Bede's *Ecclesiastical History of the English People*. The work was extremely popular among those who could read in the eighth and ninth centuries, and used the dating system of Dionysius Exiguus (B.C./A.D.) for the first time. It is because of Bede's work that this method of dating was spread throughout the Christian world.

Under Dionysius's system, March 25 was New Year's Day. The English adopted this for the ecclesiastical year in the twelfth century and the legal and civil year in the fourteenth century. The only exception was if March 25 fell during Holy Week—especially on Good Friday. If this occurred, New Year's Day was moved to April 1. This move may be behind the origin of April Fool's Day.

Quarter and Cross-Quarter Days Become an Outlet for Protest

An interesting pattern related to the observance of quarter and cross-quarter days (see Table 2.6) became evident in England during the early middle ages. Quarter days, marked by the solstices and equinoxes, divided the year into four segments. The four cross-quarter days fell at the mid-points of the quarters. The major Christian festivals were tied to the quarter days— Christmas to the winter solstice, Easter and the Annunciation to the spring equinox, St. John's Eve and Whitsuntide to the summer solstice, Michaelmas to the fall equinox. Therefore, pagan protestors of the Christian establishment embraced the cross-quarter days as occasions for rebellion and celebration of traditions associated with their own belief systems. This may be the reason May

Eve and Halloween are associated with witches; but, in fact, both the quarter days and the cross-quarter days are equally pagan in origin.

Pagan and Christian Traditions Melded Together

Through the course of time, the pagan agricultural and weather festivals have become so meshed with Christian movable feasts that depend on Easter that it is difficult to distinguish the pagan traditions from those of the Christians.

Of the cross-quarter holidays, Halloween is the only one still observed in the United States; the British have switched the festivities to Guy Fawkes' Day. May Day has become laden with political connotations which have removed any religious meaning from the day. Candlemas is still a minor church festival, but is otherwise remembered only as Groundhog Day.

Lammas is completely forgotten in America, although it is still the reason for the British bank holiday on the first Monday in August, and is kept as a harvest festival in rural Ireland.

TABLE 2.6. CROSS-QUARTER HOLIDAYS

Date	Christian Name	Gaelic Name
February 2	Candlemas	Oimbelg
May 1	May Day	Beltane
August 2	Lammas	Lughnasadh
November 1	Halloween	Samhain

CHAPTER 3

The History of Solar Calendars

The previous chapter discussed lunar and lunisolar calendars. Addressed here is the third system of reckoning time, the solar calendar, which disregards the phases of the moon and stays in step with the seasons. Most Western nations use this system as did the citizens of ancient Egypt and Rome. In addition, the Mesoamerican Mayan and Aztec civilizations used a complex calendar that included a solar component.

The Mayan and Aztec Calendars

Olmec Origins

The calendars developed by the Mayans and Aztecs shared many characterists that may have derived from an earlier calendar developed by their predecessors, the Olmec people. The Olmec civilization flourished in middle America between 1300 B.C.E. and 400 B.C.E. Their calendar system was based on astronomical observances and contained different cycles that interacted to monitor the timing of both ritual and social events. Because the Olmec people did not develop a written language, little is known about the precise workings of their calendar.

Mayan Calendar

Mayan civilization rose up after Olmec society had declined. The Classical Mayan era is typically dated between 200 and 900 C.E. The Mayan people lived in the areas of Central America presently occupied by parts of Mexico, Guatemala, Belize, and Honduras.

The Mayan calendar system employed a complex correlation of two cycles. One cycle, called the haab (which means "cycle of rains"), had a solar basis and was used for agricultural purposes. In some areas the new year began in the summer, but at various times during the Mayan era and in different parts of the Mayan domain, other times were recognized as the beginning. The length of the year, however, was constant.

Similar to the modern solar year, it consisted of 365 days. The year was subdivided into smaller components, but unlike many other early calendars, these subdivisions were not based on lunations. The 365-day year was made up of eighteen named months, each of which had 20 named days, plus a five-day period, called Uayeb, at the end of the cycle.

In addition to the components of the solar year the Mayans also recognized smaller periods of time (analogous to weeks) that consisted of 13 numbered days. There were 28 such periods in the course of a solar year. The counting of months and weeks was done independently, but every 260 days (20 times 13) the cycle of months and weeks would begin anew.

This 260-day cycle formed the basis of the Mayan ritual calendar, often referred to as the tzolkin. Other names include Count of Days, Divinatory Calendar, Sacred Calendar, Sacred Almanac, and Earth Calendar. Scholars have puzzled over the origin and significance of the number 260. Some speculate it was important because it marked the approximate time between the planet Venus's emergence as evening star and its emergence as morning star; others consider it a factor that could be used in calculating many astronomical events; some note that it corresponds with the length of human gestation; and others see an association with planting and harvesting cycles.

The name day on which the tzolkin cycle began was called the Year Bearer. It was used to describe characteristics of the coming year. Because of the mathematics of the interlocking haab and tzolkin cycles, only four of the name days served as Year Bearers.

The ritual tzolkin cycle operated in conjunction with the solar haab cycle to form a complex and far reaching time-keeping system built on progressions of repetitive cycles. One of the most basic of these cycles is called the Calendar Round.

The Calendar Round covers a time period equal to 52 solar years or 73 ritual years. The time is significant because in every Calendar Round all the possible combinations of haab and tzolkin cycles will have been experienced and they will re-synchronize at the same starting point. This is because 52 solar years covers a time period of 18,980 days, and 73 ritual years also covers a time period of 18,980 days.

Although the Calendar Round covered a number of years, it was not long enough to cover the full extent of time envisioned by its users. Consequently, Mayans also developed a system known as the Long Count. The Long Count measured time from a mythical beginning of the current age until a distant point in the future when it was believed that the age would come to a close. The beginning of the age, according to Mayan calculations and transposed to the current Gregorian calendar, occurred in 3114 or 3113 B.C.E., and it will end in 2011 or 2012 C.E. (The year discrepancy seems to be related to a question regarding compensation for a presumed year 0 between the years 1 B.C.E. and 1 C.E.)

Mayans used a system of pictorial inscriptions (called glyphs) along with dots and bars to record Long Count dates. The Long Count method of recording dates worked on the basis of recording the time that had elapsed from the theoretical beginning point. It tracked

cycles of time by marking periods known as days, unials, tuns, katuns, and baktuns. These time cycles are expressed using a five-decimal numeric notation with the shorter periods to the right and longer periods to the left. For example, a date such as 11.3.2.9.6 would mean that 11 baktuns, 3 katuns, 2 tuns, 9 unial, and 6 days had passed since the beginning. When a cycle of shorter periods equaled the next larger period, the number re-set to zero and the number for the next period increased by one. The complete cycle within the Mayan Long Count calendar covered a time period of 13 baktuns.

The Aztec Calendar

Between the 14th and 16th centuries, Aztec civilization predominated in the area currently occupied by central and southern Mexico. There is no evidence that the Aztecs employed a Long Count calendar system, but the agricultural and ritual calendars they followed had many similarities with the Mayan Calendar Round.

The Aztecs recognized a solar year that was divided into eighteen months of twenty named days. At the end of the year, a 5-day period of bad-luck days brought the total number of days in the year to 365. The ritual calendar, which also served as a tool for divination, consisted of twenty months of thirteen days, for a total of 260 days. The passing of each of these months was marked by a festival, but the completion of a 52-year cycle, when the solar and ritual calendars would re-mesh at their starting points, was a momentous occasion.

One of the chief concerns addressed in Aztec religion was the ability of the cosmos to continue. At the end of every 52-year cycle people feared that the world would be destroyed. To commemorate the end of a cycle and help usher in a new one, the New Fire Ceremony (also called Binding of the Years) was held. Old fires were extinguished before dusk and people waited for a cosmic sign indicating that the sun would be reborn. To strengthen the power of the sun on its course, human sacrifices were offered. The passing of the constellation Pleiades through the zenith at midnight was the awaited sign. When it occurred, it signified

TABLE 3.1. MAYAN MONTH AND DAY NAMES

18 Month Names	20 Day Names
Pop	Imix
Uo	Ik
Zip	Akbal
Zotz	Kan
Zec	Chicchan
Xul	Cimi
Yaxkin	Manik
Mol	Lamat
Chen	Muluc
Yax	Oc
Zac	Chuen
Ceh	Eb
Mac	Ben
Kankin	Ix
Muan	Men
Pax	Cib
Kayab	Caban
Cumku	Ezznab
	Cauac
	Ahau

5-Day Period

Uayeb

TABLE 3.2. NUMBER OF DAYS IN LONG COUNT PERIODS

Period	Consists of	Number of Days
unial	20 days	20 days
tun	18 unials	360 days
katun	20 tuns	7,200 days
baktun	20 katuns	144,000 days
complete cycle	13 baktuns	1,872,000 days

the promise of another 52-year period, and the fires would be relit.

The Aztec Calendar Stone (or Sun Stone) was discovered in the late 18th century during excavations in Mexico City and is currently housed in Mexico's Museum of Archaeology and History. It conveys both mythological and astronomical information. Thought to have been carved during the late 15th century, the stone is dedicated to the sun, the primary Aztec deity. The Calendar Stone is circular with a diameter of 3.7 meters (just under 12 feet). It weighs 25 tons. The carvings on its face include depictions related to the creation and re- creation of the universe and the twenty named days of the Aztec months.

The Egyptian Calendar

The Egyptians Developed Multiple Calendar Systems

The earliest Egyptian calendar was regulated by the cyclical (helical) rising of the star Sirius or Sothis, which coincided with the annual flooding of the Nile. This calendar was only twelve minutes shorter than the true solar year—a much more accurate system than most of its contemporaries.

In time, the inherent discrepancies between the lunar and solar cycles caused problems for the Egyptians. Although details of the difficulties are not known and while the lunar calendar was preserved for agricultural use, a second calendar was developed for civic purposes. In this civil calendar, the year was composed of twelve 30-day months and five days added to the end of the year for a total of 365 days. Its days, unlike those of other ancient calendars, began at sunrise.

TABLE 3.3. NAMED DAYS OF THE AZTEC MONTH	
1. Crocodile	11. Monkey
2. Wind	12. Grass
3. House	13. Reed
4. Lizard	14. Jaguar
5. Snake	15. Eagle
6. Death	16. Vulture
7. Deer	17. Movement
8. Rabbit	18. Knife
9. Water	19. Rain
10. Dog	20. Flower

There was no intercalation to compensate for the one-quarter day difference between this year and the true solar year of 365.25 days; consequently, the Egyptian civil year gained one day on the true solar year every four years. Therefore, over the course of 1,460 solar years, or 1,461 Egyptian years, the months of the Egyptian calendar would move completely through the seasons. This 1,461 year period is known as the Sothic Cycle.

Egyptian Legend Explains the Calendar

Egyptian religious myths sought to explain the origin of the civil calendar. The legends of the Osiris-Isis cycle indicate that the Egyptian calendar originally incorporated a year of 360 days. To this calendar of twelve 30-day months, the god Thoth added five days—the birthdays of the gods Osiris, Isis, Horus, Nephthys, and Set. When this civil calendar was introduced, its first day—the first of the month Thoth—coincided with the helical rising of Sirius.

Three Seasons

The importance of the Nile River to the survival of civilization near its delta was reflected in the Egyptian calendar. The months of the year were divided into three seasons of four months each, and these seasons were based on the flood stages of the Nile. The season of Inundation occurred when the river flooded its banks; Going Forth was the time of planting crops after the river had receded; and Deficiency was when the river was at its lowest point, but ironically, it was harvest time for the crops. Individual months within the seasons were indicated only by numbers: the third month of Inundation, the second month of Deficiency, and so on.

A Second Lunar Calendar

Over the course of time, the Egyptians realized that the discrepancies between their two calendar systems caused problems as they tried to set the dates of holidays. They were accustomed to using the original lunar calendar, but this became confusing when the new civil calendar came into use. The best solution, they decided, was to create a third calendar—another lunar one— for use in planning religious activities. This calendar, however, was related to the civil year and not, as the agricultural one was, to the helical rising of Sirius. It was kept in sequence with the civil year by the addition of an intercalary month each time the beginning of the lunar year preceded the beginning of the civil year. Eventually, a twenty-five year intercalation schedule was adopted.

Augustus Caesar Stabilized Egyptian Sothic Calendar

The Egyptian Sothic-cycle calendar remained in use and unchanged until Roman times. After Alexander the Great conquered Egypt in the fourth century B.C.E., his successor Ptolemy III declared a change to the calendar which added a day every four years beginning in 238 B.C.E. Egyptian priests, however, unwilling to give control of their sacred practices over to a foreign ruler, ignored the decree. Finally, in 30 B.C.E., Augustus Caesar enforced Ptolemy's order, stabilizing the calendar so that the first day of Thoth always fell on August 29.

The Roman Calendar and Julian Reform

Legendary Beginnings

According to writers during the Augustan period, the first Roman calendar was developed either by King Romulus, to whom the founding of Rome is attributed, or by King Numa, the supposed founder of the Roman religious system. Although there is no concrete evidence to support either of these theories, their existence attests to the importance the Romans assigned to their calendar. To have given it the honor of being developed by the leading figures in their history reflects the great need the Romans saw for the ordering of time.

Civil Unrest over Access to the Calendar

The first Roman calendar for which there is historical evidence dates to 450 B.C.E.. It was a list of "named days" (holidays on which the legal system shut down) that was published by the Decemvirate. Access to this information was limited to the aristocracy of priests and magistrates which meant that the average citizen did not officially know when he could attend to his legal matters. This caused such tension that in 304 B.C.E., Flavius was forced by plebeian outcry to post a calendar in the Roman forum that designated the legal days for conducting business. This calendar has become known as the pre-Julian calendar.

One interesting result of the popularization of the calendar in this manner was that many Romans began using the calendar as a decoration in their homes. Ornate renditions of Roman calendars (both pre-Julian and Julian versions) appear on the walls of Roman ruins which date as recently as the fourth century C.E. These pieces of artwork provide a great deal of the information about the Roman time reckoning system.

The Pre-Julian Calendar

The year, according to the pre-Julian calendar, was 355 days long, and roughly corresponded to a lunar year. It was divided into ten months which varied in length. Four months had 31 days: Martius, Maius, Quinctilis, and October. Seven months had 29 days: Januarius, Aprilis, Junis, Sextilis, September, November and December. One month, Februarius, had 28 days.

Each month was divided into three sections by special days: the Kalends was the first day of the month; the Nones was the fifth day of a short month or the seventh day of a long month; the Ides was the thirteenth day of a short month or the fifteenth day of a long one. All of the other days were designated in relation to one of these special days. For example, Martius (March) 10 would be called the sixth day before the Ides. (The Romans counted inclusively. While March 15 was the Ides, it was also counted as the first day of the set before the Ides. Thus, March 14 would be the second day before the Ides, and so on.) Apart from these dividing days, there were forty-five named days in the Roman calendar, most of which were significant for religious reasons.

Roman Beliefs

The Romans seemed to be a highly superstitious people. One of the Roman superstitions, a mistrust of even numbers, affected the calendar in several ways. First, it may have been the reason for the alternation of the length of month between 29 and 31 days rather than using twelve 30-day months. Also, the one month that did have an even number of days, February, was considered unlucky. The second way in which the Roman aversion to even numbers affected the calendar was that festivals that were noted as three-day festivals would actually take place over five days because the Romans did not count the even days in between.

The Roman System of Intercalation

To keep the months and years of the calendar in line with the seasons and solar year, an extra month was intercalated every other year. The Roman method of intercalation was quite unusual compared with other methods. They reduced the month of February to 23 or 24 days and intercalated a 27-day month after the shortened February. Holidays that were normally observed on the 24th and 27th of February were moved to the 23rd and 26th days of the intercalated month.

The problem with the Roman system of intercalation was that, over a four year period, a three to four day discrepancy built up between the calendar and the solar year. Instead of adjusting the length of the intercalary month, the Romans chose to omit it all together every time the man-made calendar accrued at least twenty-seven days more than the solar cycle.

The unusual nature of the intercalary schedule has long been a question among scholars. One highly plausible reason for the placement of the intercalation is that two holidays that fell at the end of February, the Regifugium and the Equirria, were significantly related to holidays in March and needed to fall in close proximity to them.

Celebrations of the Kalends, Nones, and Ides

According to the Roman writer Varro, who was a contemporary of Julius Caesar, the Kalends, Nones, and Ides were each celebrated in specific ways. On the Kalends, the pontifex maximus stood in the Curia Calabra on the Capitoline Hill and announced when the Nones would fall (thus indicating whether a month was long or short). The Nones was the day on which the festivals for the month were announced (all festivals took place between the Nones and the Kalends of the next month). The customs surrounding the Ides are less clear; it was apparently a day of ritual sacrifice (which adds to the poignancy of Julius Caesar's assassination on that date in 44 B.C.E.).

The origin of the customs surrounding the Kalends, Nones, and Ides dates to the time before the public had access to the calendar. According to Macrobius, a fifth century C.E. historian, the customs were developed while a lunar calendar was in place. A pontifex minor was assigned the task of watching for the crescent of the moon to be visible at night. When this occurred, he would inform the pontifex maximus (the most powerful religious leader of Rome) who would declare the Kalends the next day. The ceremony of declaration involved several sacrifices and a declaration of the day of the Nones. Word of when the Nones would occur was spread throughout the countryside and people traveled to Capitoline Hill for the announcement of which festivals would be celebrated during that month. The Nones occurred when the moon was at the first quarter. The sacrifice on the Ides coincided with the full moon.

These ceremonies, which served as a type of calendar for the people, would have become superfluous by the first century B.C.E. when the calendar was published openly. However, the traditions were maintained as part of the religious structure of Rome over which the pontifex maximus presided. There was also a strong political reason for the pontifex maximus to retain the official power of declaring months. Apparently even after the publication of the calendar, the pontifex maximus, as the most powerful religious leader, had a high degree of influence on its structure. This became significant because the pontifex

maximus was an elected official and could manipulate the calendar to hasten or stall elections according to his popularity (or lack thereof). By the time Julius Caesar came to power, the Republican calendar was more than three months out of line because of political tampering. Julius Caesar was able to reform the Roman calendar, not because he had become the supreme military and political leader, but because he had been elected pontifex maximus in 63 B.C.E. when he was a relatively young man.

Julian Reforms to the Republican Calendar Impact History

During his campaigns in Egypt, Caesar realized that the Egyptian solar calendar was simpler and more efficient than the traditional Roman calendar. When he returned to Rome, he charged an Alexandrian astronomer, Sosigenes, with the task of reforming the Roman system.

In 46 B.C.E., this plan was put into action: First, to reconcile the Roman year with the tropical year, 46 B.C.E. became, by decree, 445 days long. This was accomplished by lengthening most of the months, and adding two extra months. Caesar declared that this year was the "last year of confusion," but his constituents preferred to call it simply the "year of confusion."

Second, 45 B.C.E. marked the first year of the new system. The date for the beginning of the New Year was moved from March 25 to January 1. January had 31 days and in regular years February had 29 days. Beginning with March, the rest of the months alternated regularly between 31 and 30 days. Every four years a second February 24 was added between the regular February 24 and February 25 as the leap day. Julius Caesar thus produced the sequence familiar to the Western civil calendar of three common years of 365 days, and a leap year of 366 days. More importantly, he produced a calendar that required no intercalations, and that was therefore immune to political tampering. To commemorate this achievement, he had the month of Quinctilis renamed Julius.

Augustus Added Changes

Several years after the assassination of Julius Caesar, a misunderstanding of his leap-year rule emerged. Because of the Roman habit of counting inclusively, they began to count the fourth year of each leap-year cycle as the first year of the next one. This meant that they were adding the extra day every three years. Augustus Caesar corrected this problem between 8 B.C.E. and 8 C.E. by declaring that the leap years would be left out during this time. The Western civil calendar traces its cycle of leap-year dates to this occurrence.

Augustus also made other changes to the calendar which seem to have resulted more from pride than practicality. The month Sextilis was renamed Augustus to honor his own reform of the calendar, and he took a day from February and added it to his own month. Then, to avoid having three 31-day months in a row, he switched the lengths of September, October, November, and December. Although the switch disrupted the pattern established by Julius, it produced the sequence the Western civil calendar still maintains.

Augustus also revived many of the old Roman religious festivals. These events, however, had little meaning to the majority of Roman citizens who had not practiced them for generations. A great deal is known about how these festivals were celebrated from Ovid's *Fasti*, which gives an account of the monthly practices of the Roman people. Unfortunately, only a portion of the manuscript exists.

The Gregorian Reform of the Julian Calendar

The changes Julius instituted were a vast improvement over any previous system, but they had one significant fault. The Julian calendar was based on a year of 365.25 days long, but the true solar year is 365.2422 days long. This error of 11 minutes 14 seconds per year amounted to three days every 400 years. In 45 B.C.E., when Julius Caesar established his calendar, the spring equinox fell on March 25. By 325 C.E., when the Council of Nicaea met to fix the Easter rule, the spring equinox was falling about March 21. This discrepancy had a greater impact on the dates of the Christian Movable Feasts than on agricultural or civil events.

Although the problem was noticed and considered by Church councils for 1200 years, the first action on the matter was not taken until 1545 when the Council of Trent authorized Pope Paul III to investigate the problem and find a solution. After nearly forty years of investigation, a proposal was submitted by Jesuit astronomer Christopher Clavius to Pope Gregory XIII. In 1582, the Pope issued a papal bull (a type of official edict) instituting an adjustment based on Clavius's plan.

The Gregorian reform instituted several significant changes: First, it subtracted ten days from the month of October 1582. By making the day following the feast of St. Francis (October 5), October 15, the date of the spring equinox was brought back to March 21.

Second, to bring the year closer to the true tropical year, a value of 365.2422 days was accepted. This value, which differed by 0.0078 days per year from the Julian calendar reckoning, amounted to 3.12 days every 400 years. It was therefore decided that three out of every four centennial years should be common years, and one a leap year. This resulted in the rule that a centennial year is a leap year only if it is divisible by 400. Therefore, 1700, 1800, and 1900 do not count as leap years, but the year 2000 does.

Third, the Gregorian reform set January 1 as the new year which in Britain was different from the old system where December 25 was commonly recognized as the new year. The Gregorian calendar, therefore, gained the title "New Style" as opposed to the Julian "Old Style."

Gregorian Reform and Determining the Date of Easter

Prior to the Gregorian reforms, a medieval system known as golden numbers was used to determine dates for full moons and provide a date for the Christian celebration of Easter. At the time of the Gregorian reforms, however, the golden numbers system was rejected because it was astronomically inaccurate. The actual full moon could appear up to two days before or after the golden numbers indicated. (For a more complete discussion of golden numbers see the calendar section in Chapter 7—Christianity and Post-Christian Movements). Once again, the Church looked to Clavius and Lilius, whose calculations lay behind the Gregorian reform, for a more accurate system to calculate the date of Easter. Lilius used a method, termed the *epact*, that was already being used informally under the Julian calendar. The epact, which is derived from the Greek word meaning "to intercalate," is a system of numbers used to determine the age of the stage of the moon on the first day of the year.

The informal epact system was not completely accurate though, because it was based on the Metonic cycle, like the golden number system. This cycle occupied a period of 6,939.75 days, whereas to be accurate for the Moon, it should have lasted for 6,939.9 days. Although the difference is small, it amounts to one day in about 307 years; after this period, the New Moon would occur one day earlier than the epact table indicated.

Lunar and Solar Corrections Are Made

When the Gregorian calendar was adopted, the discrepancies in the epact system were taken into account. A correction (known as the lunar correction) was introduced which adjusted the age of the Moon, making it one day later on specific centennial years in a 2,500-year cycle. Seven of these adjustments were made, one every 300 years and an eighth time after a subsequent 400 years.

To keep the system of epacts in step with the other changes instituted by the Gregorian reforms, Clavius proposed another correction—a solar correction. The Gregorian calendar omitted most centennial leap years to accommodate the more accurate length of the year. Clavius's plan maintained that in ordinary centennial years, the number of the epact should be reduced by one. These two corrections kept the lunar and solar cycles in harmony with one another in relation to the date of Easter.

The epact system facilitated long-range planning more effectively than the previous system of golden numbers. It simplified the method of determining the dates of new and full moons throughout the year. Also, since the dates of full and new moons could be determined into infinity, the date of Easter could also be calculated to the same extent.

Religious Differences Slow the Spread of the Gregorian Calendar

Adoption of the Gregorian reforms seems to have been greatly based on religious similarities and differences. Roman Catholic countries carried out the reform promptly, but the Orthodox Christian countries did not. The disagreement is not over the facts of astronomy, but over community identity: the Eastern Orthodox Church seems to prefer to celebrate Easter on a date different from that chosen by Roman Catholics, in order to emphasize its independence from Rome.

There was also resistance to the changes in Protestant countries since the calendar revision was proposed in the wake of the Reformation.

France, Italy, Luxembourg, Portugal, and Spain adopted the New Style calendar in 1582, and most of the German Roman Catholic states, as well as Belgium and part of the Netherlands, adopted it by 1584. In Switzerland, the change took place over 229 years, between 1583 and 1812. In 1587, Hungary was the last country to adopt the New Style before a break of more than one hundred years after which Protestant nations began to accept the system. The first of these to adopt the New Style were Denmark and the Dutch and German Protestant states in 1699-1700. The Germans, however, maintained their tradition of determining Easter through the use of the Tabulae Rudolphinae (Rudolphine Tables), astronomical tables based on the 16th-century observations of Tycho Brahe. They adopted the Gregorian calendar rules for Easter in 1776.

From the mid-eighteenth century on, a steady stream of countries embraced the New Style. In 1752, Britain and the colonies adopted the New Style, with Sweden following in 1753. In 1740, however, the Swedes had taken on the German Protestant astronomical methods for calculating Easter; they did not accept the Gregorian calendar rules for this practice until 1844. When Alaska became part of the United States in 1867, it adopted the New Style. Japan converted in 1873, Egypt in 1875. Between 1912 and 1917, there was a flurry of activity which resulted in its acceptance by Albania, Bulgaria, China, Estonia, Latvia, Lithuania, Romania, Turkey, and the former Yugoslavia. Russia embraced the New Style in 1918, immediately after the Revolution. Greece was the last major country to accept the calendar, doing so in 1923.

Confusion in Britain

When the switch to the New Style was made in Britain, the discrepancy between the Old and New Styles had accrued to 11 days. The difference was corrected in 1752 by a declaration that the day following September 2 of that year would be September 14. The legislators were faced with an unexpected response as many British citizens took to the streets demanding, "give us back our 11 days." The protest was not easily quelled even though the declaration had been passed with careful consideration given to make sure no one would suffer financial or other penalties.

Many British people continued to celebrate their holidays Old Style well into the nineteenth century—a practice revealing the deep emotional resistance to calendar reform. Even today, in western Ireland, the Celtic harvest festival of Lughnasad is celebrated more or less Old Style on the Sunday nearest August 13. George Washington, who was born on February 11, continued to celebrate his birthday Old Style after the calendar reform by moving it to February 22.

CHAPTER 4

Calendar Reform Since the Mid-Eighteenth Century

Since the mid-eighteenth century, many proposals for calendar reform have been made. The objective of these reforms has been to develop a straightforward, universal, secular calendar. Three of these proposals have received significant attention in the Western world: the French Republican Calendar, the International Fixed Calendar, and the World Calendar.

The French Republican Calendar

Shortly before the French Revolution, calls for the secularization of the calendar began to be heard in France. The first rumblings for reform came in 1785 and 1788. The storming of the Bastille in July 1789 intensified the demands, and support swelled for the notion of a new calendar which would start from "the first year of liberty."

In 1793 the National Convention took notice of the demands and appointed Charles-Gilbert Romme, president of the committee of public instruction, to develop a new system. He delegated the technical matters to two eminent mathematicians, Joseph-Louis Lagrange and Gaspard Monge, and gave Fabre d'Eglantine the responsibility of renaming the months. Their proposal was submitted to the convention in September 1793. The delegates immediately ratified the new calendar which became the official system on October 5, 1793.

The new calendar, known as the French Republican Calendar, was retroactive to September 22, 1792, the day the Republic was proclaimed. (September 22 also happened to coincide with the autumnal equinox in 1792.) September 22 was declared the New Year of the Republican calendar which had, in total, 365 days. The months were divided into twelve 30-day periods with the five extra days added to the end of the year (September 17 through 22 in the Gregorian calendar).

The extra days were to be used for festivals and vacations in celebration and honor of virtue, genius, labor, opinion, and rewards. In a leap year the additional day was to be added to this period and was celebrated as the festival of the Revolution. Leap years continued to be inserted every four years, but the first leap year was inserted one year early so the Republican and Gregorian cycles would not coincide. Each four-year period was known as a Franciade.

The seven-day week was replaced with a ten day period called a *décade*. Each month, therefore, contained three *décades*, the tenth day of which was a rest day. The day was reorganized into portions divisible by ten, but this was too great a change for the whole society to adopt and was abandoned because of popular disapproval.

Fabre d'Eglantine renamed the months according to the meteorological characteristics of the periods. Table 4.1 lists the names and approximate Gregorian calendar dates.

The appeal of the French Republican Calendar was limited, for obvious reasons, to France. By September 1805, because of the difficulties of harmonizing the French system with the international standard, the Republican calendar had fallen into almost complete disuse. On January 1, 1806, the Gregorian calendar replaced the French Republican system as the official calendar of France. The failure of the French Republican Calendar tended to discourage any further attempts at calendar reform for a long time.

Twentieth-Century Reform Proposals

In the 1930s, the former Soviet Union made a brief attempt at calendar reform. By shortening the week to five days and giving workers a random day off within the week, the factories could operate continually which would, in theory, increase production. This experiment failed, however, because the social structure could not bear the stress of the change.

The two other prominent twentieth-century proposals for calendar reform have been the International Fixed Calendar and the World Calendar. Both of these calendars recognize that astronomically the current Western civil calendar is sufficient; however, they offer slightly modified designs which would make its arrangement more convenient.

The International Fixed Calendar

The International Fixed Calendar is divided into thirteen 28-day months, with one day added to the end of the year. All of the present month names remain the same with the thirteenth month named Sol and added between June and July. The extra day follows December 28, and is not included in any month or in any week. Leap day is treated in the same way and intercalated every four years after June 28. In this calendar, every month contains exactly four weeks, beginning on a Sunday and ending on a Saturday. (The Tree Calendar currently used by some Pagans follows a similar pattern.) The main criticism of the International Fixed Calendar is that it does not divide into four equal quarters and is therefore inconvenient for business purposes.

World Calendar

To answer the major criticism of the International Fixed Calendar, the World Calendar was devised. Its four quarters are composed of 91 days each, with an additional day at the end of the year. Each quarter is divided into three months: the first month has 31 days and the second and third have 30 days each. The extra day and leap day are treated in the same manner as in the International Fixed Calendar, following December 30 and June 30, respectively.

Critics of this system argue that it is no better than the current Gregorian system because each month extends over part of five weeks, and each month within a given quarter begins on a different day. However, each of the four quarters is identical to the others, so a three month calendar could represent the entire year.

Both of these systems seem to be more convenient than the Gregorian calendar because of their streamlined detail. However, the problem with introducing reforms to the world community lies in the fact that the calendar has traditionally carried and continues to carry deep religious significance to all people. Thus, the success of any calendar reform will depend on its adaptability to the many different religious expressions of the modern world.

TABLE 4.1.
FRENCH REPUBLICAN CALENDAR

French Month	English Translation	Approximate Gregorian Dates
Vendémiaire	Vintage	September 22–October 21
Brumaire	Mist	October 22–November 20
Frimaire	Frost	November 21–December 20
Nivôse	Snow	December 21–January 19
Pluviôse	Rain	January 20–February 18
Ventôse	Wind	February 19–March 20
Germinal	Seed-time	March 21–April 19
Floréal	Blossom	April 20–May 19
Prairial	Meadow	May 20–June 18
Messidor	Harvest	June 19–July 18
Thermidor	Heat	July 19–August 17
Fructidor	Fruits	August 18–September 16

PART TWO

Calendars and Holidays for Religious Groups

CHAPTER 5

Judaism

Overview

What Is Judaism?

Judaism is one of the oldest, continuously observed religions in the world. Its history extends back beyond the advent of the written word. Its people trace their roots to a common ancestor, Abraham, and then back even farther to the very moment of creation.

Throughout history Jewish beliefs and practices have changed and varying expressions of faith within the Jewish community have arisen, but its core belief—the belief that separates Jewish faith from the faiths of other religions—has remained unchanged. This belief is characterized by faith in a specific creator God and by an individual and community attempt to live a life of holiness.

According to Jewish belief, the law given to the Jewish people by God contained everything they needed to live a holy life, including the ability to be reinterpreted in new historical situations. Judaism, therefore, is the expression of the Jewish people, attempting to live holy (set apart) lives in accordance with the instructions given by God.

The Relationship between God and the Jewish People

The Jewish people believe in one God, the creator of the world. The *Shema*, an expression of Jewish belief, states: "Hear, O Israel, the Lord is our God, the Lord is One."

The Jewish people believe they have a unique, distinct relationship with this God, but not an exclusive one. Other people can have the same type of relationship if they accept the teachings, practice the rituals, and adhere to certain ethical requirements. Communication with God is accomplished through prayer and meditation. The Jews await the coming of a Messiah who will usher in God's kingdom.

Authorities and Sacred Writings

Although obedience to the Law is central to Judaism, there is no one central authority. Sources of divine authority are God, the *Torah*, interpretations of the *Torah* by respected teachers, and tradition. Religious observances and the study of Jewish Law are conducted under the supervision of a teacher called a Rabbi.

The Torah

The Hebrew Bible contains 24 books—a collection of writings that were compiled over a time period of about 1,000 years. They provide revelation from God to the Jewish people. It is the main source for all other teachings. The first five books are attributed to Moses, who received the Law from God. These five books are called the *Pentateuch* and the scrolls upon which they are written are called the *Torah*. The word *Torah* is also sometimes used to refer to the entire body of Jewish scared writings and tradition.

The *Torah* and its interpretations provide explanations of how to live a life that will bring the follower near to God. Its edicts are binding. All aspects of life are governed by the *Torah*; rules not specifically stated in the writing are inferred and interpreted by sages.

The Mishnah and Talmud

The *Mishnah* is a collection of rabbinic teachings covering a wide range of human endeavor including: agriculture, giving, holy day observances, rituals, family law, civil and criminal law, and moral teachings. The writings were compiled during the first and second centuries C.E. The *Mishnah*, in its final form, was adopted around the year 200 C.E.

The *Mishnah* is the first part of the *Talmud*. The *Talmud* contains further reflections on the *Mishnah*. Although there are two Talmuds, the *Jerusalem Talmud* and the *Babylonian Talmud*, the *Babylonian Talmud* is the one with the greater status. It was prepared during the fourth and fifth centuries C.E.

History of Judaism

In the Beginning

Jewish history begins at the beginning: with the creation of the world by a sovereign Creator God, and the Jewish people claim an unbroken heritage from that time through the succeeding ages. According to their beliefs, the unfolding of history is not merely a chain of episodes, but the playing out of a relationship between the Creator and his Creation.

The relationship between God and Creation became fractured when people, using the free will they had been given, disobeyed God's instructions. This disobedience opened the way for death and pain to enter the human experience. The eventual salvation and reunification between the world and God will come when people once again realize that they must accept the teachings about the God of the Jews.

A Chosen People

According to Jewish thought, God's way was originally open to all the people of the earth. Only after they had rejected him, did he turn to a specific group— the Jews. God entered into a covenant with the Jews for the purpose of demonstrating himself to the world. For this reason, the Jews are known as a "chosen people." They were chosen by God to be an example to the world. If the Jewish nation disobeyed God they would be punished; if the nation repented and obeyed God, they would be rewarded with grace and hope. The first people identified specifically with the faith that is now known as Judaism were Abraham, Isaac and Jacob. These ancients are called the Patriarchs.

Abraham, known to the Jews as the father of their faith, entered the land of Canaan, later called Palestine, sometime around 1800 B.C.E. According to the Biblical account, Abraham left Mesopotamia, the land of his father, in response to God's call. God promised Abraham that he would become the father of a special, chosen nation. Circumcision was established as a sign of the covenant between the people and God.

Moses

Later, Abraham's descendants, called the Hebrew people, moved to Egypt during a time of famine. Although originally welcomed into the land, they subsequently became slaves. This period in Jewish history—when they were "strangers" in a foreign land— gave rise to the custom of practicing hospitality. It also set the stage for one of the central themes in Jewish thought—deliverance.

Escape from Egypt was accomplished under the leadership of Moses. The Exodus, or leaving, occurred around 1250 B.C.E. Following the Hebrew people's departure, Moses received the Law from God in an encounter on Mount Sinai. This receiving of the law by Moses is the most significant event in Jewish history because it represents the receiving of divine revelation and the re-establishment of the covenant between God and his chosen people.

Although the *Ten Commandments* are perhaps the best known part of the Jewish Law, the total Law consisted of much more than these edicts. It included 613 commandments (248 things to do and 365 things to not do). In their totality and as they are interpreted, the Jews believe that the laws express God's will. They believe they have a duty to God and a duty to their fellow humans to obey them. Obedience results in peace. Disobedience brings strife and exile.

After receiving the Law, the Jewish people began settling in the land of Canaan. They initially developed a tribal governing structure which evolved as their population grew, culminating in nationhood under a monarch.

Rise and Fall of the Kingdom

The first King was Saul. He was succeeded by David (1013 to 973 B.C.E.), who was in turn succeeded by his son, Solomon. Under Solomon's leadership, the First Temple in Jerusalem was constructed.

The Temple became the central focal point of the Jewish religious experience. It was a place for the communal expression of faith, for ritual sacrifices, and for the presentation of offerings. The Temple was a destination for pilgrims and the seat of religious authority.

Following Solomon's reign, however, the people strayed from their obedience to God with tragic consequences. In 722–721 B.C.E., the ten northern tribes were conquered by the Assyrians and sent into exile.

Ancient Manuscripts Led to Reforms

According to the Biblical account in *II Kings 22*, apparently even the most rudimentary knowledge of the rituals surrounding the festivals had been lost until, during renovations of the Temple in Jerusalem, the High Priest, Hilkiah, discovered what he claimed were ancient manuscripts of the Law of Moses. These documents reportedly detailed the ceremonies necessary for observing the ancient Hebrew holidays. Hilkiah presented the discovery to King Josiah who required that all Hebrews observe its provisions. Participation in the religious feasts and festivals of Israel was mandated by King Josiah around 621 B.C.E.

Sweeping changes were made to the religious practices of the Hebrews as a result of the reforms. These included the establishment of Passover as a national festival and the designation of Jerusalem as the only acceptable site for observing the three Hebrew pilgrimage feasts: Passover, Pentecost, and Sukkot. Also, attendance of these feasts was made mandatory for all able-bodied men in Israel; they were required to bring their tithes, or religious taxes, to the Temple on these occasions.

Babylonian Conquest

Religious reforms did not last and the Judeans (the southern Tribe descended from Judah, from whom the name "Judaism" is derived) were then conquered by Nebuchadnezzar, the King of Babylon. The Babylonians destroyed the Temple in 587–86 B.C.E., took the ruling class of Israelites captive, and deported them to Babylon where they lived in exile for fifty years.

The Jewish people, in exile and without their Temple, began to focus on seeking God's favor by returning their obedience to him. Other faith expressions, such as communal prayer and the study and interpretation of the *Torah*, began to rise in prominence. Some researchers have suggested that many elements of modern Judaism, such as monotheism, were formalized at this time.

Return from Exile

The restoration of Jerusalem, the temple, and the Jewish community began when the Jewish people returned to their homeland in 539 B.C.E. They were permitted to return from exile after Cyrus, King of Persia, conquered the Babylonians. The temple was rebuilt in 515 B.C.E., and under the leadership of the priest Ezra, temple rituals were re-established.

According to some historians, the time spent in exile had a significant impact on Jewish theology. Persian influences, especially those of Zoroastrianism, blended with traditional Jewish thought helping to shape ideas about good and evil and developing the role of angels.

Greeks Rise in Influence

Jewish self-rule was short-lived. The Greeks rose to power in 331 B.C.E. Judaism was outlawed and the Temple was captured.

The Temple's importance to the Jewish nation cannot be overstated. It provided access to God. The priests in the temple performed the functions necessary for the atonement of sin and for reconciliation with God. Pilgrims came to the temple to celebrate mandated festivals. Without the Temple, it was impossible to perform many of the sacred requirements of the faith.

The Temple was recaptured in a military victory led by Judah Maccabee. It was miraculously purified and re-dedicated in 165 B.C.E., an historical event remembered annually during the celebration of Hanukkah.

Greek influences, however, made a lasting impact on the practice of Judaism. The Greek focus on education led to increased interest in studying the *Torah* and resulted in a blending of traditional law with sophisticated intellectual discourse.

This trend led to the development of a group called the Pharisees, who held a dual focus on study and piety. Pharisees were a new type of leader—not priests nor traditional holy men—but teachers who rose to positions of eminence through the study of the *Torah*, Jewish oral traditions, and interpretations of the *Torah*. Their authority increased during the first century C.E.

The Second Temple Falls

The Romans were the next rulers in Jerusalem. Under their dominion, in 70 C.E., the second Temple was destroyed. One wall remained standing. Termed the Wailing Wall, it remains—two thousand years later—a place where pilgrims converge and serves as a symbol of Jewish exile and hope.

During previous times in Hebrew history when the Jews had been deprived of their Temple and its central role in communal rites, alternate methods of practicing the faith had emerged. Following 70 C.E., Jewish practices once again refocused on different avenues of religious expression. Houses of Prayer (beit tefillah) and Houses of Study (beit midrash) emerged. A House of Prayer was a location where prayer services were conducted three times a day: morning, afternoon, and evening, coinciding with the times when sacrifices had been offered at the Temple. Houses of Study developed when masters rose up and students gathered around them. The act of studying the *Torah* became an act of worship.

During the latter years of the first century C.E., Rabbinic Judaism became more firmly established and rabbinical academies gained in popular acceptance. An effort to gather together the oral interpretations and teachings from rabbinic houses of study was made. The result was the production of the *Mishnah*, which was first canonized as biblical literature in 90 C.E. The *Mishnah* was later also studied, interpreted, and elaborated upon.

During the fifth and sixth centuries C.E., rabbinic commentaries were consolidated to produce the Palestinian and Babylonian *Talmuds*. The *Babylonian Talmud*, which emerged as the preeminent *Talmud*, was edited in the fifth century but contained writings dating back to the third century B.C.E. The traditional text of the Jewish Bible was established during the eighth and ninth centuries C.E..

Persecutions

Beginning in the fifth century C.E. the changing political situation in Israel and in Babylonian areas led to persecutions of Jews. Jewish people once again faced exile from their traditional homeland. Two centers of Jewish life emerged: The Ashkenazi Jews settled in central and eastern Europe; and the Sephardi Jews settled in Spain and the Near East. The two groups developed different traditions and languages. The Yiddish language, a mixture of Hebrew and German along with other Slavic characteristics, emerged among Ashkenazi populations. Ladino, with Hebrew, Spanish and Provencal characteristics, developed among Shephardi groups. Despite their differences, however, both groups remained as autonomous, distinctively Jewish communities.

The Jews were often a minority group within their larger culture, and they held firmly to their unique identity. Because they were easily identified and different from the majority classes, they were also frequently subject to periodic uprisings against them. These resulted in oppression, persecutions and executions. As political sentiments shifted, Jews were expelled from places such as England, France, Spain, and Portugal. Throughout centuries of oppression, the Jews held to their hope of being reestablished in their homeland, and the coming of the Messiah who would rule over the land in perfect peace.

A Common Identity

During the time of the exile, the Jewish calendar helped the dispersed Jewish communities celebrate their common heritage. The calendar, along with shared rituals and sacred objects, served to unite Jewish communities and provided a means for Jews to assimilate into new Jewish communities when forced to move from one place to another. The first Jewish community in the New World was founded in 1654 at New Amsterdam, New York.

During the 18th century, new social patterns brought about by the European Enlightenment affected Judaism in two ways: Non-Jewish populations influenced by liberal thinking became more tolerant, helping bring an end to oppression and persecution; and, modern thought and reform brought new ideas and new expressions into the Jewish community, transforming old theological ideas. Modern reforms led to the development of sects of Judaism resisting traditional Orthodoxy.

Returning to the Promised Land

Throughout their history, the Jewish people have been subject to exiles from their homeland. They lived in Egypt, Persia, Babylonia, and around the globe. A Jewish nationalistic movement, called Zionism, emerged during the late 19th and early 20th centuries. Its goals were to re-establish Hebrew as the Jewish language and to resettle the Jewish people in Israel.

Zionistic sentiments were heightened by renewed persecutions in Europe at the hands of the German Nazis. During the war years, an estimated six million Jews were killed. Jews began returning to Palestine in large numbers. The state of Israel was founded in 1948.

Judaism Today

A Dispersed People

Jewish people live not only in Israel, but all over the world. According to statistics for the early 1990s there were more than 18 million people of Jewish descent worldwide. The two largest Jewish communities were in North America (6.8 million) and the Asian continent, including the Middle East (6.3 million). Other areas with more than a million Jewish inhabitants included the countries of the former Soviet Union, Europe, and South America. Smaller Jewish communities also existed in Africa and the Pacific Island nations.

The Synagogue

Jews worship the same God honored by their forefathers. Services are held in homes and in synagogues (the word synagogue means assembly). A synagogue can be created where ten or more Jewish men live close enough to meet together for worship and study. The synagogue typically serves as the center of the Jewish community. It is a place for worship, a place for learning, and a location for social functions. The leader in a synagogue is called a rabbi. Rabbis are not priests; they are teachers or lawyers. Chazzan are people who read from the scriptures and recite prayers. Cochen are priests who are descendants from the ancient temple priests.

Archetecturally, a synagogue is a square or rectangular building. It contains the Arc which is situated so that it faces Jerusalem. The Arc contains the scrolls of the Law (the *Torah*). A reading-desk called the bema is where the Law is read and where prayers are said.

Sects within Judaism

Orthodox

Orthodox Judaism is characterized by an affirmation of the traditional Jewish faith, strict adherence to customs such as keeping the Sabbath, participating in ceremonies and rituals, and the observance of dietary regulations.

Reform or Progressive

Reform Judaism began in Germany during the European Age of Enlightenment (18th century). As some groups of Jews sought to reconcile their traditional beliefs with modern thought and learning, they abandoned many ancient ceremonial traditions. Reform Judaism stresses modern biblical criticism and emphasizes ethical teachings more than ritualistic observance. Rabbi Isaac Wise was a leader who brought the reforms to the United States. One of the first issues addressed on this continent was the use of English in the synagogue. Reform Jews also place a diminished emphasis on nationalistic themes.

Conservative

Conservative Judaism sought to build a middle ground between Orthodox and Reform. Conservative Jewish congregations seek to retain many ancient traditions but without the accompanying demand for strict observance. Conservative synagogues typically use both English and Hebrew and men and women sit together; however, the tradition of wearing a head covering is maintained.

Hasidism

Hasidism is a mystical sect of Judaism that teaches enthusiastic prayer as a means of communion with God. It includes an emphasis on personal experience rather than abstract study and contains components such as miracles and shamanism.

Hasidism, with roots in the Middle Ages, was revived during the 18th century in Europe under Rabbi Israel Baal Shem. The movement was organized into schools headed by a local leader called a Rebbe. Leadership passed from the Rebbe to his heir, either a son or a follower.

As a result of the persecution of Jews during World War II many Hasidic Jews emigrated to the United States. Many are located in Brooklyn, New York.

Zionism

Zionism refers to the nationalistic movement to return the Jewish people to the land of Israel. It was begun in Europe during the late 19th century and reached its pinnacle during the years surrounding World War II. Zionistic efforts culminated in the establishment of the state of Israel in 1948. Zionistic efforts continue, typically through fund raising campaigns to support the growth of Israel. Although many Jewish people are Zionistic to some degree, there are also anti-Zionistic groups.

Reconstructionist

The Reconstructionist movement began early in the twentieth century in an effort to "reconstruct" Judaism with the community rather than the synagogue as its center. Its organizers sought to recognize the diversity within Judaism and unite all factions into a unified religious society.

The Jewish Calendar

A Lunar Calendar

The Jewish calendar is based on a lunar model. This means that the phases of the moon determine when a month begins and ends. Many of the major holidays occur on the full moon—which is the fifteenth day of the Jewish month.

History of the Hebrew Calendar

Structural details of the ancient Hebrew calendar are fragmentary. The first written evidence of a Hebrew calendar is the Gezer Calendar, a stone carving which lists the tasks associated with the agricultural duties for each of a series of 12 yereah (the Hebrew word for lunation or month). Historians believe this early calendar was derived from the Canaanite cycle sometime before the establishment of the Jewish monarchy around 1050 B.C.E. References in the Old Testament to the Hebrews using Canaanite month names help to support this theory. The months that are recorded in the Hebrew scriptures (Aviv, Ziv, Etanim, and Bul) correspond to the modern Jewish months of Nisan, Iyyar, Tishri, and Heshvan.

While many technical aspects of the Hebrew calendar remain a mystery, it is known that the lunar and solar cycles were reconciled in some manner because the Passover month always occurred in a specific season. This would be impossible unless the calendar also took the solar cycle into account.

Differences between Judean and Samaritan Calendars

Conflict arose over religious reforms in the seventh century B.C.E. under King Josiah. The mandates required all able-bodied men to attend three pilgrimage feasts at the Temple in Jerusalem and there present their offerings. These decrees angered many Hebrews who lived outside the region of Judea because they had been practicing their religious ceremonies in local houses of worship for hundreds of years. The distance and inconvenience of traveling to Jerusalem caused many of these people to break away from the reform movement and worship at their traditional sites.

The splinter group, located in northern Israel, became known as the Samaritans. As a result of the break in religious practices and the ensuing conflicts that arose, the Samaritans and Israelites developed slightly different practices regarding their calendars. The custom of the Samaritans was to figure the start of the month according to the absence of a moon while the Israelites defined the "new moon" as the evening on which the crescent of the waxing moon is first visible locally. A difference of one to three days is possible between these two systems. Both groups sought to impose their method over the other; each sect felt if they embraced the other method, they would break the law and offend God. This conflict was a source of division among Jews for centuries, but the Israelite method was the one which prevailed.

Exile in Babylon Influences the Hebrew Calendar

The Babylonians conquered Jerusalem around 586 B.C.E. The Babylonian influence on the Hebrew calendar is clearly evidenced by many similar elements within both systems. Scholars surmise that the Hebrews adopted many elements of the Babylonian calendar because the Babylonian system was clearly established by the sixth century B.C.E., and there is no evidence to suggest that the Hebrew system was explicitly defined at that time.

Structurally the influence of the Babylonians on the Hebrew calendar was manifested in the adoption of the Babylonian month names, the establishment of Nisanu 1 as the point from which regnal years of the king were reckoned, and the incorporation of the seven-day week. As a result of these structural changes, the Hebrew calendar became a distinct entity with well-defined rules for calculating the passage of time.

Aside from technical elements, the Babylonian and Hebrew systems have other similarities. For example, both groups employ the wedding motif in various celebrations. One of the most important Hebrew celebrations, Passover, falls at the same time as the Babylonian new year, and both occasions incorporated some similar ceremonial rites. The Hebrews adopted some Babylonian rites into their own new year which occurs in the fall. Sir James Frazer argues in his *Golden Bough* that the account of Esther and Mordecai, the story at the center of the Purim celebration, is drawn from the Babylonian legend of Ishtar and Marduk.

In any case, the Babylonian-inspired calendar was used by the Hebrews until 70 C.E. except for the period during which Alexander the Great and the Ptolemies imposed the use of the Macedonian system (322–200 B.C.E.).

Complications Resulting from the Diaspora

The Babylonian and Israelite calendars both based the beginning of the month on the sighting of the new moon. In Hebrew society, the High Priest appointed watchmen to look for the new moon. When it appeared, the watchmen would report back to the High Priest who would proclaim the beginning of a new month. The Priests took great care to confirm the accurate proclamation of a new month because Hebrew religious practices prohibit the celebration of certain holidays on particular days of the week and require a specific number of days between festivals. Rosh Hashanah (New Year), for example, cannot fall on a Sunday, Wednesday, or Friday, but must fall 163 days after Passover.

The system of observing the new moon became impractical after the destruction of the Temple in 70 C.E. and the subsequent Diaspora of the Jews (the scattering of the community into distant geographic areas). The central system for proclaiming a new month could not adequately meet the needs of a dispersed population. As an attempt to solve this problem, a messenger system was instituted whereby a series of "runners" would travel from town to town bringing official word of the new month once it had been declared in Jerusalem.

In order to circumvent the difficulties involved in notifying outlying communities of the precise sighting of a new moon, a tradition arose in which some holidays were observed for two days. This practice ensured that the holiday was celebrated on its specified day. The tradition of celebrating holidays for two days is still observed by some Jewish groups.

An Equation Determines the New Month

By 200 C.E., Hebrew priests had developed an equation to replace the sighting method of determining the beginning of months. This formula was known only by a select group of priests in Jerusalem who continued to be the official voice to proclaim the new month. At the same time, many Hebrew communities were taking the matter into their own hands by appointing their own watchmen rather than waiting for the official word. This situation caused great strife and division among the Hebrews because, once again, the start of the new month varied from region to region. This division became especially crucial on the point of the celebration of Passover.

In 358 C.E., the High Priest Hillel II recognized the potentially destructive nature of the problem and, to maintain the unity of the Hebrew people, he made the secret equation public. Hillel's decision has been hailed as one which helped preserve the Hebrew faith through ensuing periods of dire crisis. Even though individual enclaves of Jews were often completely isolated from one another, they were able to maintain a sense of unity and identity partly because of their common religious calendar and observances.

From the time of Hillel II until the present, the Hebrew calendar has evolved into one of the most intricate systems of time reckoning in existence. The calendar includes such elements as varying year lengths, varying month lengths, and leap years—all of which are designed to meet the requirements of Judaic law regarding the celebration of feasts, festivals, and holidays.

TABLE 5.1. THE HEBREW LUNISOLAR CALENDAR

Name of Month	Number of Days
Nisan; liturgical new year	30
Iyyar	29
Sivan	30
Tammuz	29
Av	30 (29 if both Heshvan and Kislev are full)
Elul	29
Tishri; civil new year	30
Heshvan	29 or 30
Kislev	29 or 30
Tevet	29
Shevat	30
Adar	29 (30 when We-Adar is added)
We-Adar	29 (added in leap years)

NOTES:

Nisan is traditionally designated as the first month because it is when Moses led the Israelites out of Egypt.

In order to accommodate laws that forbid food preparation on the Sabbath, even in conjunction with required feasts and fasts, the first day of the seventh month, Tishri, cannot fall on a Sunday, Wednesday or Friday.

The month of Heshvan is also sometimes called Marheshvan.

The "leap month" We-Adar may also be called Adar Sheni meaning "second Adar."

Leap months are added in the third, sixth, eighth, eleventh, fourteenth, seventeenth, and nineteenth years of every 19-year cycle of years.

Thus, beginning with the equation made public by Hillel II, the Hebrew calendar became schematic and independent of the true New Moon. In fact, if the dates of the Hebrew calendar are compared with the dates for astronomical full and new moons, they will often differ by several days. The "new moon" is defined as the evening on which the crescent of the waxing moon is first visible locally, not as the astronomical new moon, which will always be one to three days earlier. The "full moon" is defined as the fourteenth evening after the "new moon" (first crescent), not as the astronomical full moon, which may occur up to three days earlier.

Days, Weeks, Months, and Years

The structure of the modern Jewish calendar is lunisolar with the months based on the moon and the years on the sun. The day is 24 hours long but each hour is divided into 1,080 parts each of which are approximately 3.3 seconds long. The day officially begins at 6:00 p.m., but for religious purposes, sunset is considered the beginning of a new day.

The 12 months of the Hebrew calendar alternate between 29 and 30 days. Two months, Heshvan and Kislev, have variable lengths. Months containing 30 days are known as "full" and the 29-day months are called "defective." The calendar includes an intercalary month, We-Adar, which is 30 days in length.

To meet the requirements of the Jewish religious law and reconcile the lunar cycle with the solar cycle, the Hebrew calendar has years ranging in length from 353 to 385 days. First, to bring the 19-year lunar cycle into harmony with the 28-year solar cycle, the intercalary month, We-Adar, is added in years 3, 6, 8, 11, 14, 17, and 19 of the lunar cycle. Second, to ensure that their religious regulations are fulfilled, the months of Heshvan and Kislev vacillate between 29 and 30 days. Years in which both months are full are called "complete" years (shelema). If it is a regular year, it will contain 355 days; a complete leap year (in which We-Adar is added) will contain 385 days. A "normal" (sedura) year is one in which Heshvan is full and Kislev is defective and will contain either 354 or 384 days. "Defective" (hasera) years, totaling 353 or 383 days, occur when both Heshvan and Kislev contain only 29 days.

There are similarities between the Hebrew calendar and the Greek Metonic cycle. The Hebrew calendar picks up a common thread with the Greek Metonic cycle for reconciling the solar and lunar cycles. Although We-Adar is intercalated in seven out of every 19 years like the Metonic cycle, the specific years to which the month is added is different from the most prominent of the Greek methods, the Athenian calendar. The reason for the difference in the patterns is that We-Adar is added whenever it is needed to push the 15th ("full moon") of Nisan after the spring, or vernal, equinox because the Passover cannot be held before the equinox.

Naming Years

The basis for naming years in the Hebrew calendar is a code indicating the characteristics of the year. The character of a year (qevi`a, literally "fixing") indicates the important technical details of the coming year. It is signified by three Hebrew letters: the first and third give the days of the weeks on which the New Year occurs and Passover begins, the second is the initial of the Hebrew word for defective, normal, or complete. There are 14 types of qevi`a, seven in common and seven in leap years. According to Hebrew scholars, the era used to number the years of the Jewish calendar (designated anno mundi or A.M.) had its epoch in the year of Creation which they believe was 3761 B.C.E.

—— " ——

To Maimonides the call of the Shofar seemed to say...

Awake, ye sleepers, and ponder your deeds; remember your Creator and go back to Him in penitence. Be not of those who miss reality in their hunt after shadows, and waste their years in seeking after vain things which cannot profit or deliver. Look well to your souls and consider your acts; forsake each of you his evil ways and thoughts, and return to God, so that He may have mercy upon you.

—— " ——

TABLE 5.2. THE JEWISH HOLIDAY CYCLE	
Dates	**Holidays**
Nisan	
10	Preparation for Passover
14	Fast of the First Born
15–21	Passover (Pesach)
22	Maimona
16–Sivan 5	Sefira (Counting of the Omer)
27	Yom ha-Shoah
Iyyar	
4	Yom ha-Zikkaron
5	Yom ha-Atzma'ut
18	Lag b-Omer (33rd Day of the Omer)
26	Yom Yerushalayim
Sivan	
6	Shavout
Tammuz	
17	Sevententh of Tammuz
17–Av 9	Three Weeks
Av	
9	Tisha be-Av
Elul	
1	New Year for the Herds
Tishri	
1–2	Rosh Hashanah
1–10	Teshuva
3	Fast of Gedaliah
10	Yom Kippur
15–21	Sukkot
21	Hoshana Rabbah
22	Shemini Atzeret
23	Simhat Torah
Kislev	
25–Tevet 2	Hanukkah
Tevet	
10	Asarah be-Tevet
Shevat	
15	Tu Bishvat
Adar (or **We Adar** in Leap Years)	
13	Ta'anit Esther
14	Purim
Variable	
	Sabbath of Rabbi Isaac Mayer Wise

Jewish Holidays

Weekly Observances

Sabbath
Friday/Saturday

The word sabbath means rest.

According to Jewish tradition, when God created the world, he rested on the seventh day. The Jewish Sabbath commemorates this rest. It is observed as a day of respite from work and is often accompanied with special rituals and meals.

The Sabbath begins at sunset on Friday evening and ends on Saturday evening. Although Sabbath observances vary greatly among members of the different sects of Judaism, synagogues typically offer both evening and morning services. Evening Sabbath services are typically attended by men while the morning services are more likely to be family oriented. Traditional evening synagogue services are called Kabbalat Shabbat (Welcoming the Sabbath) and Oneg Shabbat (Joy of the Sabbath). The services may include a Kiddush ceremony in which a cup of wine is symbolically raised to sanctify (set apart) the sacred day.

In the Jewish home, the sabbath celebration begins just before sunset when the woman lights the sabbath candles and recites prayers for God's blessing on her and her family. Although tradition assigns this duty of lighting the candles to the woman of the house, candles must be lit by men when no women are present. Candles are lit before sunset because Jewish law forbids the kindling of fire on the Sabbath. Some observant families extend the prohibition against kindling fire to include the turning on of electric lights or the operation of electric appliances during the Sabbath. Orthodox Jewish families light the Sabbath candles 18 minutes prior to sunset. Jewish calendars and newspapers publish exact times for every day of the year. Although there is no maximum number of candles, there must be a minimum of two. In Sephardic Jewish communities, candles are frequently lit in honor of deceased family members.

The Sabbath dinner is an evening meal eaten in the home with all family members present. Families may also invite others to partake of the Sabbath dinner with them in honor of the Jewish tradition of hospitality. The meal is accompanied by many symbolic items including a clean table cloth, two loaves of bread, and a cup of wine. As the meal begins, the man of the house chants praises and recites verses from the Hebrew Bible. He blesses the cup of wine and the bread and then serves his family. The evening may also include the singing of traditional songs and the collection of money to be given to the poor.

Saturday morning synagogue services typically begin with blessings, hymns and psalms and the barchu (call to worship). The Shema, a traditional formulaic prayer, is recited and the *Torah* is read. In some U.S. Jewish synagogues the *Torah* is read entirely in Hebrew, in others Hebrew and English are mixed, and in still others the reading is entirely in English. A commentary or discussion may follow the reading.

Saturday lunch is typically simple and often includes the second portion of bread from the previous evening's meal. The afternoon of rest is adhered to with varying strictness among the different sects of Jews.

The Sabbath ends at sunset, which is officially declared when three stars are visible. If it is cloudy, the Sabbath ends when it is no longer possible to tell the difference between a blue thread and a white thread held at arm's length. The ceremony marking the end of the Sabbath is called Havdalah (or Habdalah) which means "Separation," and it signifies the separation between the Sabbath and the rest of the week. Havdalah may be observed in the synagogue or home. In the synagogue, the ceremony often includes benedictions recited over wine and spices and the handling of a burning taper. In the home, it may include blessings and the kindling of fire through the ritual lighting of a special multi-wicked candle.

Annually

Nisan (March/April)

Preparation for Passover
Nisan 10

The first holiday in the Jewish year is Passover or Pesach (Nisan 15). The tenth day of Nisan marks the official beginning of preparations for the Passover.

Nisan, is the first month of the Jewish calendar. Months are counted beginning in the spring despite the fact that the Jewish New Year begins in Tishri, the seventh month. This peculiarity is thought to have occurred due to the adoption of the Babylonian calendar system during the time of the exiles.

Fast of the First-born
Nisan 14

The Fast of the First-born is the only Jewish fast which is observed for reasons other than atonement for sin or petition. Practiced symbolically by firstborn males on the day before Passover, the fast appears to serve as a reminder of how the firstborn sons of the ancient Hebrews were miraculously spared while the Egyptians lost their firstborn sons to the Angel of Death. The obligation to fast may be avoided by participating in a síyyum—the study of a particular passage of the *Talmud*.

Passover (Pesach)
Nisan 15-21 (or 22)

Passover, or Pesach, is the Hebrew celebration of spring and of their deliverance from slavery in Egypt. It is also known as the Feast of Unleavened Bread.

According to the account in the book of *Exodus*, when Pharaoh refused to let Moses lead the Hebrews from Egypt to the Promised Land, God sent ten plagues on the Egyptians, including locusts, fire, and hailstones. Pharaoh, however, refused to yield. The tenth plague was the visitation of the Angel of Death who was sent to kill the first-born sons of the Egyptians (see FAST OF THE FIRST-BORN, Nisan 14). Hebrew families were instructed to sacrifice a lamb and place its blood on the doorposts of their homes as a signal to the Angel to "pass over" their sons. When the Egyptians discovered what had happened, they ordered the Israelites to leave the country immediately.

The observance of Passover was one of three pilgrimage festivals established by the Deuteronomic reform in 621 B.C.E. (the other two are Shavuot and Sukkot). Before the reform, the festivals of the Passover and the Unleavened Bread had been celebrated by families in their homes. The Deuteronomic laws, however, required that the lamb for the Passover meal be sacrificed only at the temple in Jerusalem. This provision mandated that all Hebrew people had to come to Jerusalem for these festivals.

In Hebrew the three pilgrimage feasts are called the "shalosh regalim" or "three (foot) pilgrimages" because all adult males over the age of thirteen traditionally made a pilgrimage to Jerusalem for the celebration of those festivals. After the destruction of the Temple in Jerusalem in 70 C.E., the law requiring a central celebration of the festivals became impossible to fulfill. The holidays continued to be celebrated locally, however, with traditional merrymaking.

The rabbis restored the Passover to its former status as a family festival celebrated at home. Uncertainties of the ancient calendar, however, led to the custom of celebrating the Passover for eight days outside of Jerusalem during the period of the Second Temple. Orthodox and Conservative Jews living outside of Israel have retained this custom. In contrast, Reform Jews have reverted to the original seven-day dating.

With the reestablishment of Israel as a nation, the pilgrimage aspect of the festivals has experienced a revival. The tenor of the pilgrimages has changed, however, and for many the journey is one of sorrow in which they join with thousands of others at the Wailing Wall to mourn the destruction of the Temple.

The heart of the Passover celebration, however, remains a family-oriented traditional liturgy known as the Seder, which indicates the order of services. The Seder is among the most universally observed elements of Judaism, even among those who do not practice most traditional Hebrew concepts. The Seder includes a customary meal which consists of symbolic foods such as a "pascal lamb," bitter herbs, and wine. Matzo, a flat, unleavened bread, represents the hurry in which the Israelites left Egypt—they did not have time to let their bread rise.

The Seder dinner is traditionally conducted on Passover eve with the entire family. It is both a meal and a worship ceremony. The *Haggadah* is a worship book used during the Seder. The word Haggadah means "retelling" and it recounts in question and answer form the story of the Jewish emancipation from slavery in Egypt.

The symbolic foods present at the Seder meal are: a roasted shank bone (symbolizing the passover lamb); a roasted egg (representing the festival sacrifice); bitter herbs (typically horseradish, to recall the bitterness of slavery); haroset (an apple-nut mixture that symbolizes making bricks without straw); parsley dipped into salt water (symbolizing renewal); matzo bread (representing the unleavened bread prepared when the Jews left Egypt in a hurry); and, four cups of wine (representing the fourfold promise of redemption). The cup of Elijah, placed in the middle of the table symbolizes hospitality. A pillow or cushion on the leader's chair represents freedom.

The matzo bread plays a role in a traditional Passover game. During the meal one piece of the three matzos is broken in half, and one half is set aside until the end of the meal. This half is called the Afikomen. The children take the Afikomen, hide it, and do not give it back until the leader gives a gift or promises to give a gift.

Although Passover is celebrated primarily in the home, it is also observed in minor ways in the synagogue. During Passover services, additional psalms may be read. Also, in some congregations, Passover marks the time when a traditional prayer for rain recited during the fall and winter months is replaced with a prayer for dew.

Maimona (Maimuna)
Day after Passover (Nisan 22)

Jews in North Africa commemorate the philosopher and rabbi, Moses Maimonides, on the evening of the last day of Passover and the day that follows. Since the news of Maimonides's death in 1204 reached many Jews during

Passover, they were not able to mourn his passing, as custom would normally dictate, by eating bread and an egg. So they postponed it until the following day.

Sefirah (Counting of the Omer)
Nisan 16-Sivan 5

Sefirah is the season between Passover and Shavuot. It is a minor Jewish festival lasting 50 days. In the traditional synagogue liturgy, a custom of announcing the "counting of the omer" is observed by counting the number of days. An omer is a sheaf of wheat, and the festival has its origins in practice of bringing offerings to the Temple (see SHAVUOT).

Although the season is not observed by many modern Jews, Sefirah was held in greater esteem during the Middle Ages. It was kept as a period of abstinence and repentance during which the Jewish people remembered historical massacres of their ancestors, particularly those that occurred in 134–35 C.E. under the reign of the Roman Emperor Hadrian and during the Crusades between 1095 and 1270 C.E. By tradition, weddings and other celebrations were not held during Sefirah.

Yom ha-Shoah
Nisan 27

This solemn occasion is observed by Jews as the "Day of the Holocaust." It commemorates the mass killing of six million Jews by the Nazis during World War II. People of many faiths also mourn on this day in remembrance of Jewish victims along with the other six million people who were exterminated in Nazi death camps during the same period.

Observance of Yom ha-Shoah focuses on the fact that this catastrophe shocked and impoverished all mankind. It is dedicated to the hope that human beings will never forget the horror of the Holocaust and that they will assure that it never happens again.

In Israel on Yom ha-Shoah all public entertainment is closed and a three-minute siren blast is sounded. In the United States, observances often include civic ceremonies and the teaching of history. Synagogue services may include special readings from Lamentations or Psalms. Typically such services are solemn with a quiet, dark atmosphere. Memorial candles are frequently lit as part of the service.

Iyyar

Yom ha-Zikkaron (Remembrance Day)
Iyyar 4

Yom ha-Zikkaron is primarily observed by Jews living in the state of Israel. It is a day set aside to honor the memory of those who died fighting for Israel's independence and continued existence.

Yom ha-Atzma'ut (Day of Independence)
Iyyar 5

Yom ha-Atzma'ut, the day on which Israel became a sovereign nation (May 15, 1948), is celebrated primarily in secular fashion with public gatherings, parades, singing of traditional music, and dancing. Frequently collections are also taken to support the state of Israel.

Lag ba-Omer (33rd Day of the Omer)
Iyyar 18

On the thirty-third day of Sefirah, restrictions relating to abstinence and repentance were relaxed for one day. Some authorities believe that this exception was created to accommodate rejoicing over the stopping of a plague among the Jews in the second century C.E. It is also possible that this celebration combines Hebrew traditions with an ancient pagan festival day, featuring customs much like those of May Day.

Yom Yerushalayim (Jerusalem Day)
Iyyar 26

Yom Yerushalayim commemorates the capture of Jerusalem during the Six Day War in 1967. The Six Day War was an important part of the struggle between Israel and the nation's Arab neighbors.

Sivan

Shavuot (Shabuoth; Pentecost; Feast of Weeks)
Sivan 6

Shavuot, or the Feast of Weeks, occurs fifty days after Passover and is the second of the three pilgrimage festivals (the other two are Passover and Sukkot.) This festival, which is also called Pentecost from the Greek word for "fiftieth," marks the end of the barley harvest and the beginning of the wheat harvest.

Historically, all adult Hebrew males were required to bring their first omer (or sheaf) of barley to the Temple in Jerusalem on this day as an offering of thanksgiving for the harvest.

When Moses led the nation of Israel out of slavery in Egypt, Shavuot gained a new name: the Festival of the Giving of the Law. It is on this day that Jews celebrate Moses' descent from Mt. Sinai with the Ten Commandments given to him by God. In the homes of Orthodox and Conservative Jews, Shavuot is celebrated for two days, but Reform Jews celebrate only one day.

During Shavuot it is customary to read from the book of *Ruth* in the synagogue. Other customs include decorating with plants and flowers. Shavuot is also traditionally a time when young people who have come of age are accepted into the synagogue as full members.

Tammuz

Fast of the Seventeenth of Tammuz (Shivah Asar be-Tammuz)
Tammuz 17

The seventeenth day of Tammuz is one of four traditional days of fasting in the Jewish calendar (the other three are: the FAST OF GEDALIAH—Tishri 3, the ASARAH BE-TEVET—Tevet 10, and TISHA BE-AV—Av 9). The purpose of the fast is to mourn over Jerusalem.

The fast is observed by conservative Jews as a 24-hour fast beginning at daybreak. Some Jews extend the fast into a three-week season of mourning by imposing other restrictions on themselves such as abstaining from pleasure or from the eating of meat until after the fast of Tisha be-Av.

Three Weeks
Tammuz 17–Av 9

The three-week period between the Fast of the Seventeenth of Tammuz and the Ninth of Av is a time of mourning for the Jewish people because it is associated with the destruction of the Temple in Jerusalem. As the days draw closer to the ninth of Av, the signs of mourning increase in severity. Although there are differences between Ashkenazi (Jews with Northern and Eastern European ancestry) and Sephardic (Jews from the Iberian peninsula) customs, the restrictions include not shaving or cutting one's hair, not wearing new clothes, and not eating fruit for the first time in season. Beginning with the first day of Av, the Ashkenazi custom is not to eat any meat nor drink any wine until after Tisha be-Av, while Sephardim refrain from meat and wine beginning with the Sunday preceding the Ninth of Av. On Tisha be-Av itself, it is not permitted to eat or drink, to wear leather shoes, to anoint with oil, to wash (except where required), or to engage in sexual relations.

Av

Tisha be-Av
Av 9

There are four traditional days of fasting in the Jewish calendar; all are associated with the destructions of Jerusalem (see also FAST OF GEDALIAH—Tishri 3, ASARAH BE-TEVET— Tevet 10, and SEVENTEENTH OF TAMMUZ—Tammuz 17).

The ninth day of the month Av marks the date on which both the First and the Second Temples were destroyed, in 586 B.C.E. and 70 C.E. It also commemorates the fall of Judea to the Romans after the Bar Kochba rebellion in 135 C.E. and marks the Jewish expulsion from Spain in 1492.

Traditionally the three week period prior to the Tisha be-Av is a time when weddings and celebrations are not held. In the synagogue, services are somber and the *Torah* may be draped in black. Readings are customarily taken from the book of *Lamentations*.

The fast of Tisha be-Av is observed by conservative Jews with fasting and mourning from evening to evening. When Tisha be-Av falls on the day after the Sabbath, the Havdalah ceremony concluding the Sabbath observance is modified to include only one blessing over light. Other traditional Sabbath blessings are omitted or said at the conclusion of the fast of Tisha be-Av.

Although the fast is observed by some groups of Jews, it is less popular among others. One reason suggested to explain the lessening of interest in this commemoration is that grief over the destruction of the Temple is waning among modern Jews in favor of grief over the Holocaust. Others suggest that because Tisha be-Av focused on grief in exile, the day should be re-focused toward hope that the Messiah will come now that the nation of Israel has been established. According to legendary belief, the Messiah will be born on Tisha be-Av.

Elul

New Year for the Herds
Elul 1

This minor observance has its roots in the Jewish people's agricultural heritage.

The month of Elul is observed as a time of preparation; preparing for the High Holy Days beginning with Rosh Hashanah on Tishri 1. The season is observed with prayers called Selichoth (asking for forgiveness of sin) and with the blowing of a Shofar (Ram's horn).

Tishri

Rosh Hashanah
Tishri 1–2

Although Tishri is the seventh month in the Jewish calendar, Tishri 1 marks the beginning of the Jewish New Year. The first of ten High Holy Days, Rosh

Hashanah starts a period of introspection, abstinence, prayer, and penitence which culminates with the observance of Yom Kippur, or the Day of Atonement.

During the liturgy on Rosh Hashanah, the story of Abraham is read in the synagogue and the ram's horn or shofar is sounded to commemorate Abraham's willingness to obey God's command that he sacrifice his son Isaac. God honored Abraham's obedience by providing a ram for the sacrifice instead. The shofar also serves to symbolize the individual's need to experience spiritual awakening and renewal.

Special food is prepared for the New Year celebration, including round loaves of challah bread to symbolize the continuity of life and apples dipped in honey representing sweetness and health. Another tradition associated with Rosh Hashanah is the buying of new clothes, symbolizing new beginnings.

Fast of Gedaliah (Tsom Gedalyah; Tzom Gedaliahu)
Tishri 3 (the first day following Rosh Hashanah)

In 586 B.C.E., the Babylonian King Nebuchadnezzar destroyed Jerusalem and its first Temple. He enslaved most of the city's Hebrew inhabitants, but allowed a number of farmers and their families to remain in Jerusalem under the supervision of a Hebrew governor named Gedaliah ben Ahikam. Eventually those people who had fled to the hills during Nebuchadnezzar's attack returned to Jerusalem, and joined the farmers who had been left behind.

Distrustful of Gedaliah, some members of the community accused him of traitorous collaboration and assassinated him, along with the small garrison of soldiers Nebuchadnezzar had left stationed in Jerusalem. Subsequently, many of the farmers fled with their families to Egypt; those who remained behind were either killed or taken to Babylon.

These events triggered Judah's final collapse. The Jewish Fast of Gedaliah commemorates the tragic consequences of Gedaliah's assassination. Currently, this fast is observed by conservative Jews, as part of the synagogue liturgy.

Teshuva
The ten days between Rosh Hashanah and Yom Kippur

The Hebrew word for this time period, "teshuva," means turning. It is a season set apart as a time for reflection, introspection and repentance. Custom dictates that people apologize to one another for wrongs they have committed. The Sabbath that falls during Teshuva is called Shabbat Shuvah.

Yom Kippur (Day of Atonement)
Tishri 10

Yom Kippur, the Jewish "Day of Atonement" is the holiest day of the Jewish year. Also known as Yom Tov (Day of Goodness), it is observed by strict fasting and ceremonial repentance.

The meal eaten prior to the beginning of the fast does not include the traditional blessings. Special candles may be lit in memory of close family members who have died.

The synagogue services on the eve of Yom Kippur are traditionally called the Kol Nidre services. The term Kol Nidre refers to a specific prayer which begins with the Hebrew words for "all vows." In the prayer, the people renounce all thoughtless vows they may have made during the preceding year and forgive all debts owed to them and all wrongs done to them. According to Jewish belief, only then will God forgive them for their violations of his laws. In the Middle Ages, it was understood that the Kol Nidre prayer was a renunciation of any vows a Jew had been forced to make under threats of violence or death. This prayer, therefore, allowed Jews to renounce forced conversions to Christianity and to continue to be accepted as Jews by the Jewish community. The tone of the Kol Nidre service is somber, penitential, and confessional.

The fast of Yom Kippur is observed with varying degrees of strictness among American Jews. Some may abstain from all food and water until after sunset; others may observe modified fasts. Children, pregnant and nursing mothers, and people in ill-health do not fast. Some families cover their table with a white cloth until the day is over.

Other traditions associated with Yom Kippur include wearing prayer shawls or other distinctive dress, attending all-day prayer services, and sharing a break-the-fast meal with family and friends. One special garment worn by men is a white robe called a kittel. The kittel is typically received by men on their wedding day, and it is worn on Yom Kippur, during the Passover meal, and at the time of death it is worn as a shroud.

Sukkot (Feast of Tabernacles)
Tishri 15–21

Sukkot (also known as Sukkoth, Succoth, Sukkah, and Suka) was one of three pilgrimage feasts established by the Deuteronomic reform in 621 B.C.E. It is also called the Feast of Tabernacles, Booths, or the Ingathering. Like the other pilgrimages, Sukkot was a celebration of the harvest. In later times it came to be a commemoration of the wandering of the Israelites in the wilderness where they lived in tent-like booths.

One traditional way Jewish families observed Sukkot was to build small booths or tabernacles and live in them during the week-long festival. A booth is called a sukkah. Some families begin the preparation for Sukkot by driving the first nail of their sukkah as soon as Yom Kippur ends and before the fast is broken. Some Orthodox congregations build a sukkah in the synagogue. Reform Jews may construct centerpieces for their tables that represent the huts used by their ancestors during the years of nomadic wandering.

The booths are built of materials that are not intended to be permanent. This impermanence symbolizes the shortness of human life and man's dependence on God. According to rabbinic laws, the roof must be constructed in a way that permits rain to penetrate and so that those inside can see the starlight. These things serve to remind the people that God is over all. During the festival, the booths are decorated with produce. All Jews are invited to visit a sukkah and have a meal in it.

Synagogue services are typically held on the first or first and second days of Sukkot. During the ceremony it is traditional to wave a bouquet of tree leaves. Four special trees are used: palm, willow, citron, and myrtle. The twigs are tied together and waved in six directions (the four compass points and up and down) at special times during the service as an act of rejoicing. This action symbolizes the belief that God is everywhere. By tradition, the Sukkot service also includes prayers for rain.

Hoshana Rabbah
Tishri 21

The seventh day of Sukkot, Hoshana Rabbah, has a special significance. As an extension of the Day of Atonement, it is the last possible day for people to seek and attain forgiveness for the sins of the previous year. On this day, the ceremony in the synagogue differs from that of the other six days of the Sukkot festival. The service reflects a blending of the harvest celebration with the religious significance of the day. Mankind's dependence on rain is emphasized through symbolic rituals, and a solemn liturgy for repentance from the sins of the previous year is conducted.

Shemini Atzeret (Feast of the Assembly or Solemn Assembly)
Tishri 22

Shemini Atzeret, the eighth day of assembly, comes at the end of Sukkot. It is celebrated in some synagogues with a special service during which the scroll of Ecclesiastes is read. Occasionally Shemini Atzeret and

Simhat Torah celebrations are combined and called Atzeret HaTorah (Assembly of the *Torah*).

Simhat Torah (Feast of Rejoicing over the Law)
Tishri 23

The ninth day of the Sukkot festival cycle, Simhat Torah, has been celebrated since the Middle Ages. It was established as a day to celebrate the reading of the Law.

Simhat Torah celebrations may include synagogue services in which the *Torah* scrolls are removed from the ark and carried in a procession marked by wedding imagery, candles, and flags. Readings include the last portion of *Deuteronomy* and the first portion of *Genesis*. Celebrants consider it a special privilege to read one of the passages. The person who reads the last section is called Chasan Torah, or Bridegroom of the Law; the person who reads the first section of *Genesis* is termed, Chasan Bereshith or Bridegroom of Genesis. Special blessings on the children in the congregation may also be part of the service.

Kislev

Hanukkah (Chanukah; Festival of Lights; Feast of Dedication; Feast of the Asmoneans)
Kislev 25 to Tibet 2

Hanukkah is the Jewish Festival of Lights, celebrated for eight days, starting on the twenty-fifth day of Kislev. It commemorates the Maccabean recapture and rededication of the temple in Jerusalem in 165 B.C.E.

The story comes from the First and Second Books of the Maccabees. Antiochus, king of Syria, had forbidden Jews to practice their religion, and the temple was desecrated. Faithful Jews fled to the mountains. Under the leadership of Judah Maccabee they retook the town and temple. After military victory was achieved, they wanted to rededicate and purify the temple. The rededication ceremony required light for eight days, but only enough oil remained to kindle the necessary light for one day. The miracle of Hanukkah is that oil burned for the required eight days.

The celebration of Hanukkah is not commanded in Hebrew scriptures, as is the observance of many other Jewish holidays. It is, however, observed in synagogues with special readings and praise songs. Central themes of the service are liberty and freedom.

The best-known custom associated with Hanukkah is the lighting of the eight-candle menorah. The shamash is a special candle in the middle of the menorah that is used to light the others. One new candle is lit each night from right to left so that the light grows throughout the festival (although some groups of Jews practice the opposite—diminishing the number of candles throughout the Hanukkah observance). The eight candles represent: faith, freedom, courage, love, charity, integrity, knowledge, and peace. As the candles are lit, family members praise God and say a prayer. The menorah is traditionally placed in a window so that passersby can see it.

Other Hanukkah traditions include eating latkes (potato pancakes), parties, games, and dances. In one popular game, the dredl game, children spin a dredl (a top-like toy) in a contest to win coins or candies.

Many Jewish families in the United States have adopted the practice of gift-giving during Hanukkah. It is supposed that this is a practice borrowed from the Christian celebration of Christmas. Some families also decorate Hanukkah bushes and celebrate the holiday on December 25. Other families celebrate Hanukkah on its traditional dates and may present gifts to family members on each of the eight days of Hanukkah.

Tevet

Asarah be-Tevet (Tenth of Tevet)
Tevet 10

One of four traditional days of fasting is observed on the Asarah be-Tevet (the other three are the FAST OF GEDALIAH— Tishri 3, the SEVENTEENTH OF TAMMUZ—Tammuz 17, and TISHA BE-AV—Av 9). The fast on the tenth day of the month Tevet remembers the beginning of the siege of Jerusalem by the Army of Nebuchadnezzar. Currently this fast is observed only by conservative Jews as part of the synagogue liturgy.

Shevat

Tu Bishvat (Bi-Shevat; Hamishah Asar Bishvat; the New Year for Trees)
Fifteenth day of Shevat

The New Year for Trees is a minor Hebrew festival which is somewhat analogous to Arbor Day in the United States. The earliest reference to this holiday appeared late in the Second Temple period, at which time it was the final date for levying the tithe on the produce of fruit trees.

The practice of honoring trees is important because according to tradition, in ancient Palestine fathers planted trees when children were born; cedar for boys and cypress for girls. A child's tree grew during his or her childhood and was then cut down to make posts for the wedding canopy.

The observance of Tu Bishvat was revived in the 1940s with the return of Jewish colonists to Israel, the former Palestine. A massive reforestation program was undertaken by the settlers to reclaim barren land. It became customary to plant a tree for each newborn child—a cedar for a boy and a cypress or pine for a girl.

Today, Israeli children celebrate Tu Bishvat by planting trees and participating in traditional outdoor games. In other countries, the festival features the consumption of fruits from trees that grow in the Jewish homeland, such as oranges, figs, dates, pomegranates, and especially almonds—the first tree to bloom in Israel's spring.

Adar/We Adar

Ta'anit Esther (Fast of Esther)
Adar 13 (or We-Adar 13 in leap years)

This fast is observed in commemoration of Queen Esther's fast during the plot to slaughter the Persian Jews during the reign of Ahasuerus (Xerxes I) (see PURIM).

Purim (Feast of Lots)
Adar 14 (or We-Adar 14 in leap years)

Purim is a joyful occasion to celebrate the deliverance of the Hebrews from an evil plot to exterminate them, which was put forward by an advisor to the Persian King, Ahasuerus (Xerxes I). Haman, who hated the Jews but had a particular bile toward a man named Mordecai, selected the execution day by means of purim, or casting lots. Unbeknownst to King Ahasuerus or Haman, Ahasuerus's wife Queen Esther was Jewish, and Mordecai was her cousin. Esther prayed and fasted, and then she appealed to her husband to stop Haman's plans. Ahasuerus responded to his wife's plea and had Haman executed instead.

The *Book of Esther* is read in the synagogue on Purim, and it is a tradition to give the children noisemakers with which they try to drown out the name of Haman whenever it is read. During Purim celebrations, *Esther* is not read from the typical holy scrolls but from a special parchment scroll called the *Megillah*. Other customs associated with Purim include carnivals, parties, costumes, dances and a special three-cornered pastry called hamantash.

From this holiday, other Purim have followed. Many Jewish communities observe their own festivals commemorating their deliverance from harrowing circumstances. For example, the Padua Purim celebrated on Sivan 11 honors the Jews' deliverance from a terrible fire in 1795. The Hitler Purim observed in Casablanca on Kislev 2 remembers the escape of the city from German domination in World War II.

Sabbath of Rabbi Isaac Mayer Wise
Last Sabbath in the month of March

Each year, on a date that varies in the Jewish calendar, adherents to Reformed Judaism honor both the birth and death of Rabbi Isaac Mayer Wise (1819–1900). In 1873, Rabbi Wise organized a few scattered liberal congregations into what has become the Union of American Hebrew Congregations. In 1875, he founded the Hebrew Union Seminary, and in 1879 he founded the Central Conference of American Rabbis.

———— " ————

The Jewish people believe in one God, the creator of the world. The *Shema*, and expression of Jewish belief, states:

"Hear, O Israel, the Lord is our God, the Lord is One."

———— " ————

TABLE 5.3. ALPHABETICAL LIST OF JEWISH HOLIDAYS

Holiday	Date(s)
Asarah be-Tevet	Tevet 10
Bi-Shevat	
see Tu Bishvat	
Booths see Sukkot	
Counting of the Omer	
see Sefirah	
Day of Attonement	
see Yom Kippur	
Day of Goodness	
see Yom Kippur	
Day of Independence	
see Yom HaZtzuma'ut	
Fast of Esther	
see Ta'anit Esther	
Fast of Gedaliah	Tishri 3
Fast of the First-born	Nisan 14
Feast of Dedication	
see Hanukkah	
Feast of Lots see Purim	
Feast of Rejoicing	
over the Law	
see Simhat Torah	
Feast of Tabernacles	
see Sukkot	
Feast of the Asmoneans	
see Hanukkah	
Feast of the Assembly	
see Shemini Atzeret	
Feast of Weeks	
see Shavout	
Festival of Lights	
see Hanukkah	
Hamishah Asar Bishvat	
see Tu Bishvat	
Hanukkah	Kislev 25–Tebet 2 (or 3)
Hoshana Rabbah	Tishri 21
Jerusalem Day	
see Yom Yerushalaym	
Lag b'Omer	Iyyar 18
Maimona	Nisan 22
New Year for the Herds	Elul 1
New Year for Trees	
see Tu Bishvat	
Passover	Nisan 15–21
Pentecost see Shavout	

Holiday	Date(s)
Pesach see Passover	
Preparation for Passover	Nisan 10
Purim	Adar 14 (We-Adar 14*)
Rabbi Isaac Mayer Wise	
see Sabbath of	
Rabbi Isaac Mayer Wise	
Rosh Hashanah	Tishri 1–2
Sabbath	Friday/Saturday
Sabbath of	
Rabbi Isaac Mayer Wise	Last Sabbath in March
Sefirah	Nisan 16–Sivan 5
Seventeenth of Tammuz	Tammuz 17
Shavout	Sivan 6
Shemini Atzeret	Tishri 22
Simhat Torah	Tishri 23
Solemn Assembly	
see Shemini Atzeret	
Sukkot	Tishri 15–21
Ta'anit Esther	Adar 13 (We-Adar 13*)
Tabernacles see Sukkot	
Tenth of Tebet	
see Asarah be-Tevet	
Teshuva	Tishri 1-10
Thirty-third (33rd) Day	
of the Omer	
see Lag ba-Omer	
Three Weeks	Tammuz 17–Av 9
Tisha Be-Av	Av 9
Tsom Gedalyah	
see Fast of Gedaliah	
Tu Bishvat	Shevat 15
Tzom Gedaliahu	
see Fast of Gedaliah	
Wise, Rabbi Isaac Mayer	
see Sabbath of Rabbi	
Isaac Mayer Wise	
Yom ha-Shoah	Nisan 27
Yom ha-Zikkaron	Iyyar 4
Yom ha-Atzma'ut	Iyyar 5
Yom Kippur	Tishri 10
Yom Tov see Yom Kippur	
Yom Yerushalayim	Iyyar 16
*in Leap Years	

CHAPTER 6

Zoroastrianism

Overview of Zoroastrianism

What Is Zoroastrianism?

Zoroastrianism is a monotheistic religion founded by a prophet named Zoroaster. It is based on a belief in one god, the "Wise Lord" called Ahura Mazda (or alternately Ohrmazd). Some people, preferring to emphasize the name of the god, refer to the religion as Mazdaism, and because the Parsis are the largest surviving group of Zoroastrians, the faith is also sometimes called Parsiism.

Zoroastrians believe that the world, underworld, and heaven were created and are controlled by Ahura Mazda. They anticipate the coming of a series of three Saoshyants (saviors) at the end of history. The last Saoshyant will usher in a timeless age marked by the perfect rule of Ahura Mazda. Zoroastrians believe all people will eventually be judged and purified.

Opposing Ahura Mazda is Angra Mainyu, the Lord of Darkness and Lies. He is sometimes thought of as an evil twin to Ahura Mazda and sometimes considered a lesser spiritual being. In the cosmic struggle between the two opposing forces, however, Zoroastrians hold confidence that Ahura Mazda will eventually prevail.

Ahura Mazda and Angra Mainyu both have spiritual helpers. Ahura Mazda's helpers, called the Amahraspand (or alternately the Amesha Spentas; the names mean "Beneficent Immortals"), serve in a role somewhat similar to that of archangels. They are spiritual beings that represent Ahura Mazda's attributes and human virtues. In addition, each one presides over an aspect of creation.

Angra Mainyu's spiritual helpers, called the daevas (also spelled daivas), consist of the false gods identified by Zoroaster. The battle between good and evil that forms the framework for human history in Zoroastrian understanding can either be understood as a struggle that takes place within the human mind or as a struggle that takes place in the physical world.

According to Zoroastrian literature, earthly history exists within a 12,000 year period which is subdivided into four sections of three thousand years each. The first period begins with creation. It includes the life of the first man and ends when evil attacks the world. The second period marks the beginning of the comingling on earth of good and evil; the third period begins when evil makes its primary attack against the world; and the final period begins when the true religion is revealed to the prophet; it culminates when the three saviors are made known, one in each millennium of the final three-thousand year period.

Fire serves as the most important symbol in Zoroastrianism. Although Zoroastrians do not worship fire, fire is a central icon and the focal point of many acts of worship.

The Relationship between God and the Zoroastrian People

Zoroastrians believe that Ahura Mazda created people with bodies and souls and that he gave them the freedom to choose between good and evil. Obedience to Ahura Mazda involves working against evil and treating others justly. The three cardinal virtues are: good thoughts, good words, and good deeds.

Zoroastrianism teaches that people each live one life, a concept that differs sharply from the reincarnation beliefs of their neighbors in India. During a person's life, the outcome of his or her moral struggle will determine his or her destiny. Judgment occurs upon death. Righteous people pass over the Chinwad (also spelled Chinvat) Bridge, enter into the "best existence," and receive a place with Ahura Mazda; evil people fall off the bridge into the "worst existence" where they will endure suffering. Both good and evil people, however, will be resurrected and purified at the end of time.

The Zoroastrian faith is propagated by marriage and childbirth. Traditional Zoroastrians eschew intermarriage with people of different faiths and do not practice a policy of attempting to convert people to their faith. Zoroastrians believe that all religions are equal; therefore, converting from one faith to another is folly.

Sacred Writings

Avesta

Zoroastrian holy writings are called the *Avesta*. The name comes from the name of the language in which they are written—Avestan. Avestan, the ancient Persian language, is related to Sanskrit. Like the scriptures of many religions, the *Avesta* is made up of assorted texts and recorded oral traditions that were centuries old when they were compiled. In addition, because many of the original texts were lost or destroyed during Greek, Muslim, and Mongol invasions, some of the documents were recreated from the memories of priests. The canon of 21 volumes (called nasks) as it exists today was established between the fourth and sixth centuries C.E.

Three of the most important parts of the *Avesta* are the *Yasna*, the *Yashts*, and the *Vendidad*. The *Yasna* (which means "Act of Worship") has a set of five hymns ascribed to Zoroaster as its central core. These are called the *Gathas*. The *Yashts* (which means "Hymns of Praise") consists of hymns to spiritual beings; they are used in sacrificial ceremonies. The *Vendidad* (which means "Law against Demons") contains myths and laws to assist people in their struggle against evil powers.

Commentaries

The Pahlavi texts are another important source of Zoroastrian writings. They were produced during the Persian Sasanian dynasty (226 C.E. to 651 C.E.) and compiled during the ninth century C.E. The Pahlavi texts include commentaries, translations, glossaries and explanations of doctrines. Individual books include: The *Zand* (Interpretation) and the *Bundahishn* (Book of Primordial Creation). Other books cover topics such as wisdom, apologetics, cosmology and eschatology.

History

The founder of the Zoroastrian religion was the prophet Zoroaster, as he is commonly called in Western countries. Zoroaster is the Greek form of the Persian name Zarathustra; the Parsi form of his name is Zarthosht.

Historical details of Zoroaster's life are few. According to tradition, he lived in Persia (a region that is now occupied by Iran and Afghanistan) during the sixth or seventh century B.C.E. Some scholars, however, place the date earlier, between 1500 to 1000 B.C.E., and some accounts place him much earlier between 8000 and 9000 B.C.E.

According to Zoroastrian teaching, the religion proclaimed by Zoroaster was not new, but a revival of an old religion that had been forgotten. It proclaimed that the world was created by the god Ahura Mazda and that the first man Gayomard (or Gayo Maretan) lived in an era unblemished by evil. Death, disease, hunger, and other types of corruption were caused by the hostile actions of Angra Mainyu, a spiritual being who killed Gayomard. From Gayomard's body, the first human couple sprang into existence. Mankind lived for a while during a Golden Age in a homeland that was lost due to climate changes that forced its inhabitants, the Aryans, to migrate. After the migration and under the influence of Angra Mainyu, people turned away from Ahura Mazda and focused their attention on false gods. Zoroaster's message was intended to reestablish the ancient religion.

TABLE 6.1.
THE SEVEN AMAHRASPAND

Vohuman (variants: Vohu Mano or Vohu Manah)
attribute or virtue: Good Mind; Good Thought
presides over: animals

Ardwahist (variants: Asha or Asha Vahishta)
attribute or virtue: Righteousness; Best Truth
presides over: fire and energy

Shahrewar (variants: Kshathra or Khshathra Vairya)
attribute or virtue: Sovereignty; Desirable Dominion
presides over: metals and minerals

Spandarmad (variants: Armaiti or Spenta Armaiti)
attribute or virtue: Beneficent Devotion
presides over: earth and land

Hordad (variants: Hauvatat or Haurvatat)
attribute or virtue: Welfare; Wholeness
presides over: the waters

Amurdad (variants: Ameretat or Amerdad)
attribute or virtue: Immortality
presides over: plants

Spenamino (variant: Spenta Mainyu)
attribute or virtue: Creative Energy
presides over: mankind

Zoroaster began his religious work at approximately age 30 when he was admitted into Ahura Mazda's presence for the purpose of receiving instruction. Over a several-year period, he also received visions from Ahura Mazda's spiritual helpers. Zoroaster admonished people to accept Ahura Mazda as the One True God and to renounce other gods and spirits, especially Angra Mainyu, who was the Lord of Evil. In addition, Zoroaster advocated a settled, agrarian life over nomadic existence, and he opposed the practice of offering blood sacrifices.

At first Zoroaster did not win many converts. After an 11-year period of unsuccess, he moved northward and came under the protection of a regional king, Kay Vishtasp (also known as Hystaspes). With the king's support and military power, Zoroaster's message began to spread.

Zoroastrianism flourished and waned in concert with the success of the Persian Empire. Its two peaks occurred during the Achaemenid dynasty (559 B.C.E. to 330 B.C.E.) and the Sasanian dynasty (226 C.E. to 651 C.E.).

During the early Achaemenid period, Cyrus (also called King Kurush), expanded the Persian Kingdom. In 539 B.C.E. he conquered Babylon. Jews who had previously been held captive by the Babylonians, were permitted to return to their homeland in Jerusalem under Cyrus's decree. Some scholars theorize that the contact between the Jews and the Zoroastrians at this time introduced many Zoroastrian concepts into Judaism and subsequently into Christianity and Islam. Among the doctrines with a basis in Zoroastrianism are: the notion of a struggle between spiritual forces of good and evil; the expectant waiting for a savior to be born of a virgin; the ultimate victory of good; the resurrection of the dead; and the final destruction and re-making of the world.

By the time of Darius I (c. 522–486 B.C.E.), Zoroaster's teachings and influence had extended throughout the entire Persian empire, and Ahura Mazda was proclaimed to be the god of the Persians. Darius I (also known as Darius Hystaspis) was succeeded by Xerxes who ruled during the mid-fifth century B.C.E. and was later followed by Artaxerxes II (c. 402–359 B.C.E.). Militarily, the tide turned and the Persian Empire began to decline until it fell to the Greeks under Alexander the Great in 331 B.C.E.

Zoroastrianism experienced a revival during the Persian Sasanian dynasty (226–651 C.E.). During the formative years of the new Persian era, the high priest Kerder was influential in reviving Zoroastrianism and promoting it. The faith was made the official religion of the empire. The resurgence of the faith lasted until the middle of the seventh century when Persian lands fell to Muslim rule. Although Zoroastrians were initially tolerated, the combined pressures of political and economic factors led many Zoroastrians to either convert to Islam or flee. Many of those who left their traditional homeland moved to India and settled in the area around the modern city of Bombay. Those who remained behind lived in small communities in the area now occupied by present-day Iran.

Zoroastrianism Today

Today the two main population centers of Zoroastrianism continue to be in the vacinity of northwestern India and in Iran. Smaller communities, however, exist all over the world including North America (Canada and the United States), England and other parts of Europe, Australia, and Sri Lanka. The total number of Zoroastrians is uncertain, but many estimates indicate that there are between 100,000 and 130,000 followers of the faith worldwide.

Worship

There are three types of Zoroastrian fire temple: An Atash Behram contains the highest grade of consecrated fire. There are eight of these in India. They were built between the 11th and 19th centuries. The oldest Atash Behram contains a fire that has been burning continuously for more than 1,000 years. An Atash Adaran is a temple containing a middle grade of consecrated fire. It may be built where ten or more Zoroastrian families live and come together for worship. The lowest grade of consecrated fire is contained in a temple called an Atash Dadgah. It may be set up in a private home and used for family worship.

Zoroastrian rituals include actions, words, and objects that are intended to symbolically represent spiritual realities. The five main Zoroastrian prayers are called Ahuna Vairya, Airyema, Ishyo, Ashem Vohu, and Yenhe Hatam. These are recited in the ancient Avestan language.

Important rites in the lives of Zoroastrian people include initiation rites, marriage rituals, confession and penance, purification rites, and death rights. In addition to personal observances, the Zoroastrian year includes a number of regular holidays. These include a set of six seasonal festivals, called gahambars, that are celebrated to honor the six created things: sky, water, earth, plants, animals, and man.

Several different types of rituals serve different purposes and can be performed in different settings. The Yasna is a high liturgy that can be performed only in a fire temple by priests who have been ritually prepared. The name for the ceremony is taken from the name of the sacred book from which the text for the service is recited. The ceremony consists of twelve parts and serves as a symbolic sacrifice of haoma, a plant believed to be endowed with spiritual properties. In the ritual, the plant is pounded and its juice is extracted. The resulting liquid is given to participants to drink. The act symbolizes the anticipation of drinking special ambrosia which will be prepared by the Saoshyant when he comes.

Another type of Zoroastrian ritual is the Jashan. A Jashan ceremony can be performed in a fire temple, meeting-house, hall, or private home. Typically it is conducted by two priests, but it can be done by laypeople. The Jashan requires the use of complex symbolic elements and specific prayers or manthras. A manthra is a formulaic passage from the Sacred writings that is recited in the Avestan language because of the spiritual power associated with it.

The seven Amahraspand (or Amesha Spentas) are represented in the ceremony:

- Vohuman, who presides over animals, is represented by milk.

- Ardwahist, who presides over fire and energy, is represented by the ceremonial fire.

- Shahrewar, who presides over metals and minerals, is represented by the consecrated implements used to tend the fire.

- Spandarmad, who presides over earth and land, is represented by the place in which the ceremony is held.

- Hordad, who presides over the waters, is represented by a container of water.

- Amurdad, who presides over plants, is represented by fruit and flowers.

- Spenamino, who presides over mankind, is represented by the people conducting the ceremony.

During the Jashan ceremony portions of the sacred writings are recited. The specific portion will vary depending on the occasion. Many of the prayers in the ceremonies are also altered according to the time of day the ceremony is held.

At specific points during the prescribed prayers, the priests conducting the ceremony perform a ritual of placing and exchanging flowers. The ceremony also includes prayers of praise for the particular spiritual being who is receiving honor. A Jashan ceremony concludes with a benediction and the sharing of certain foods, such as the fruits and nuts used around the area of the ceremony.

Sects

Although there are no "denominations" in Zoroastrianism, there are differences in how the faith is expressed. These differences fall along a wide spectrum of belief between conservative and liberal interpretations. Some of the doctrines under dispute include: the practice of disposing of dead bodies by Dakhma-nashini (corpse destruction by flesh eating birds); segregating women during their menstrual cycles; prohibiting non-Zoroastrians from entering Fire Temples; wearing the Sudreah/Kushti (a sacred garment given to an individual at their initiation into the Zoroastrian faith); and reciting prayers in the original language (vs. reciting them in translation). Zoroastrian sects also differ on which version of the Zoroastrian calendar they follow.

Fire: Fire serves as the most important symbol in Zoroastrianism. Although Zoroastrians do not worship fire, fire is a central icon and the focal point of many acts of worship. There are three types of Zoroastrian fire temple: Atash Behram, Atash Adaran, and Atash Dadgah.

The Zoroastrian Calendars

The first Zoroastrian calendar was a lunisolar calendar based on the Babylonian calendar. It was adopted during the Achaemenid dynasty (559 B.C.E. to 330 B.C.E.). The calendar consisted of 12 months, each comprising 30 days. A 13th month was intercalated every six years to keep the calendar aligned with the solar year. Each of the 12 months was dedicated to a spiritual being and each day in the cycle of 30 days was likewise dedicated to a spiritual being. Days on which the month name and day name coincided were held in special honor.

During the Sasanian period (226 C.E. to 651 C.E.), the calendar was revised. Instead of adding a 13th month every six years, five days were added to the end of the year, making for a total of 365 days. Each of the last five days were dedicated to a specified group of Gathas (prophetic utterances of Zoroaster). Because a year of 365 days did not coincide exactly with the solar year of 365.24 days, a plan to intercalate a 13th month every 120 years was adopted. The year the last Sasanian King ascended to the throne, 631 C.E., serves as the epoch of the calendar (for example, 1997 C.E. is the Zoroastrian year 1366).

During the tenth century C.E., some Zoroastrians in Islamic Iran fled to India and some remained in Iran. The two communities lost contact with each other. In subsequent years the practice of intercalating a 13th month every 120 years was inconsistently applied and differently followed in the separate communities; however, both groups ultimately abandoned the practice. Without the intercalation, the days for specific observances progressed through the seasons, moving back 30 days every 120 years.

During the early eighteenth century, contact between the Parsi community in India and the Iranian Zoroastrians was reestablished and a discrepancy between their calendars was discovered: the Parsi calendar was one month behind the Iranian calendar. Some people, under the assumption that the Iranian calendar was more accurate, adopted it and called it the Qadimi (ancient ones) calendar. Others, holding firm to their own tradition, called their calendar the Shahanshahi (royalist) calendar.

TABLE 6.2. ZOROASTRIAN HOLIDAY CYCLE

Dates	Holidays	Dates	Holidays
Frawardin		**Aban**	
1	Nawruz (NoRuz; Nu Roz; Jamshed Navaroz, Patati)	10	Aban Parab
6	Hordad Sal (Khordad Sal)	**Adar**	
19	Feast of Frawardignan	9	Adar Parab
Ardwahist		**Dae**	
3	Feast of Ardwahist	1	Feast of Dae
11–15	Maidyozarem (Maidhyoizaremaya; Mid-Spring Feast	8	Feast of Dae
Hordad		11	Zarthastno Diso (Zardosht no Diso)
6	Feast of Hordad	15	Feast of Dae
Tir		16–20	Maidyarem (Maidhyairya; Mid-Year or Winter Feast)
11–15	Maidyoshahem (Maidhyoishema; Mid-Summer Feast)	23	Feast of Dae
13	Tiragan	**Vohuman**	
Amurdad		2	Feast of Vohuman
7	Feast of Amurdad	**Spendarmad**	
Shahrewar		5	Feast of Spendarmad
4	Feast of Shahrewar	26–30	Muktad (Hamaspathmaidym (Coming of the Whole Group of Farohars; Farvardegan Days; Festival of all Souls; Parsi Remembrance of the Departed)
26–30	Paitishahem (Patishahya; Feast of Bringing in the Harvest)	**Gatha Days**	
Mihr		1–5	Five intercalary days extend the celebration of Muktad to 10 days. The Gatha Days are: Ahunawad; Ushtawad; Spentomad; Wohukhshathra; and Wahistotoisht
1	Feast of Mithra (Mithrakana)		
16	Mihragan		
26–30	Ayathrem (Ayathrima; Bringing Home the Herds)		

TABLE 6.3. THE ZOROASTRIAN CALENDARS

Number of Month	Month Names*	Alternate Spelling*	Approximate English Meaning
1st	Frawardin	Fravardin	Humanity
2nd	Ardwahisht	Ardibehest	Truth and Righteousness
3rd	Hordad	Khordad	Perfection
4th	Tir	Tir	Sirius (Dog Star)
5th	Amurdad	Amardad	Immortality
6th	Shahrewar	Shehrevar	Benevolent Dominion
7th	Mihr	Meher	Fair-dealing
8th	Aban	Avan	Water (Purity)
9th	Adar	Adar	Fire
10th	Dae	Dae	Creator
11th	Vohuman	Bahman	Good Mind
12th	Spendarmad	Aspandarmad	Holy Devotion

Days of the Month:	Day Names*	Alternate Spelling*	Approximate English Meaning

(the first section focuses on the devine attributes of Ahura Mazda)

1st	Ohrmazd	Hormazd	Wisdom
2nd	Vohuman	Bahman	Good Mind
3rd	Ardwahist	Ardibehest	Truth and Righteousness
4th	Shahrewar	Shehrevar	Benevolent Dominion
5th	Spandarmad	Asfandarmad	Holy Devotion
6th	Hordad	Khordad	Perfection
7th	Amurdad	Amardad	Immortality

(the second section focuses on qualities of light)

8th	Dae-pa-Adar	Daepadar	God's Day before Adar
9th	Adar		Fire
10th	Aban	Avan	Water (Purity)
11th	Khwarshed	Khorshed	Sun
12th	Mah	Mohor	Moon
13th	Tir	Tishtar	Sirius (Dog Star)
14th	Goshorun	Gosh	Cow (sentient life)

(the third section focuses on moral qualities)

15th	Dae-pa-Mihr	Daepmeher	God's Day before Mihr
16th	Mihr	Meher	Fair-dealing
17th	Srosh		Harkening
18th	Rashn	Rashne	Justice
19th	Frawardin	Fravardin	Humanity
20th	Warharan	Behram	Victory
21st	Ram		Joy
22nd	Wad	Govad	Healthy Atmosphere

(the fourth section focuses on religious ideas)

23rd	Dae-pa-Den	Daepdin	God's Day before Den
24th	Den	Din	Inner Consciousness
25th	Ard	Ashishvangh	Blessings
26th	Ashtad		Virtue of Truth
27th	Asman		Sky and Shinning Universe
28th	Zam	Zamyad	Earth or Height
29th	Mahraspand	Mahrespand	Holy Word
30th	Anagran	Aneran	Endless Light

Five intercalary days at the end of the year are named for the five Gathas (Songs of Zoroaster):

1st	Ahunawad	Ahunavad	
2nd	Ushtawad	Ushtavad	
3rd	Spentomad	Spentomad	
4th	Vohukhshathra	Vohukhshathra	
5th	Vahishtoist	Vahishtoist	

*Month and day name spellings are based on transliterations from the Pahlavi language; alternate spellings are based on Persian forms.

Under both the Qadimi and Shahanshahi calendars, the holidays continued to progress through the seasons of the year. Early in the twentieth century, a reform was proposed to re-align the calendars with the seasons and to fix the new year on the spring equinox. Proponents of the new calendar hoped it would unite the Zoroastrians and establish a single time-keeping system. The proposed calendar was called the Fasli (seasonal) calendar.

The Fasli calendar, following the Gregorian model, added a day every four years. This practice kept it aligned with the solar year and maintained the seasonal ties between the natural year and Zoroastrian feasts and festivals. It met with mixed success. Some Zoroastrians embraced it as a way to ensure that holidays were observed on the "right" day; others denounced it as heretical. Rather than unite the Zoroastrians under one common calendar, the Fasli calendar became a third time-keeping system.

The three Zoroastrian calendars, Shahanshahi, Qadimi, and Fasli are all made up of the same twelve 30-day months with five Gatha days at the end of the twelfth month. The differences lie in the manner of reconciling the lunar pattern with the natural solar year. As a result, a single date on a Zoroastrian calendar has three equivalent days on the Gregorian calendar. For example, in 1996 C.E. the first day of the first month (Frawardin 1) fell on March 21 according to the Fasli calendar; it fell on July 18 according to the Qadimi calendar; and it fell on August 22 according to the Shahanshahi calendar.

TABLE 6.4. THE FIVE GAHS (WATCHES OF THE DAY)

First Watch
Ushahin (midnight to sunrise)

Second Watch
Hawan (sunrise to noon)

Third Watch
Rapithwin: from Farawardin 3 (Ardwahist) until Mihr 30 (Anagran)—(noon to 3:00 p.m.)

Second Hawan: from Aban 1 (Ohrmazd) until Farawardin 2 (Vohuman)—(noon to 3:00 p.m.)

Fourth Watch
Uzerin (3:00 p.m. to sunset)

Fifth Watch
Aiwisruthrem (sunset to midnight)

Zoroastrian Holidays

Daily

Private daily prayers include purification of the body, reciting specified prayers, observing physical gestures, and the ritual tying on of a ceremonial garment called a sudreh-kusti (a shirt-type garment that is tied with a cincture). Tradition mandates that this prayer cycle be done five times a day at the different gahs (watches) but many modern Zoroastrians perform them only twice a day or select to perform the rituals on specified days. Among more liberal Zoroastrians, the custom of wearing and tying the sudreh-kusti has been abandoned.

Annually

Frawardin

Nawruz (NoRuz; Nu Roz; Jamshed Navaroz; Patati)
Frawardin 1 (Ohrmazd)

Gregorian Equivalents for the years 1996–1999: Fasli—March 21; Shahanshahi—August 22; Qadimi—July 18

Nawruz, or the Zoroastrian New Year festival, is known by several names including Jamshed Navaroz, Patati, or the Day of Repentance. Zoroastrians who follow the Fasli calendar claim that the vernal equinox is the rightful day for beginning the new year. For other groups who observe the Shahanshahi and Qadimi calendars, the first day of the year progresses through the seasons, moving back 30 days every 120 years.

The tradition of marking the day with festivities has its roots in the belief that the festival was founded by Zoroaster who received his first revelation on the first day of the year. For all Zoroastrians, this festival serves as a bridge between the old and new year and the day emphasizes the themes of renewal, hope and joy.

A festive atmosphere prevails as adherents visit fire temples and offer prayers and sandalwood, begging pardon for any misdeeds committed knowingly or unknowingly. They exchange greetings, good wishes, visits, and presents. It is also a day of charity, so Zoroastrians give food, money, and clothes to the sick, needy, and poor.

Hordad Sal (Khordad Sal)

Frawardin 6 (Hordad)

Gregorian calendar equivalents for the years 1996–1999: Fasli—March 26; Shahanshahi—August 27; Qadimi—July 23

Hordad Sal is a celebration of the Prophet Zoroaster's birthday. It is typically observed with a Jashan ceremony.

Feast of Frawardignan

Frawardin 19 (Frawardin)

Gregorian equivalents for the years 1996–1999: Fasli—April 8; Shahanshahi—September 9; Qadimi—August 5

The Feast of Frawardignan is the day on which the month and day names coincide. Although most other month and day names refer to spiritual beings, Frawardin honors the spirits of people who are living, dead, and not yet living. On Frawardignan a special Jashan ceremony is performed in memory of people from the community who have died.

Ardwahist

Feast of Ardwahist

Ardwahist 3 (Ardwahist)

Gregorian equivalents for the years 1996–1999: Fasli—April 22; Shahanshahi—September 23; Qadimi—August 24

The Feast of Ardwahist is a sacred day because the same spiritual being rules over both the month and the day. Ardwahist is the spiritual being who is Truth and Righteousness; Ardwahist also presides over Fire.

Maidyozarem (Maidhyoizaremaya; Mid-Spring Feast)

Ardwahist 11–15 (Khwarshed—Dae-pa-Mihr)

Gregorian Equivalents for the years 1996–1999: Fasli—April 30–May 4; Shahanshahi—October 1–5; Qadimi—September 1–5

Maidyozarem is the first of six great feasts, called gahambars. The other five that are celebrated during the course of the year are Maidyoshahem (Tir 11–15), Paitishahem (Shahrewar 26–30), Ayathrem (Mihr 26–30), Maidyarem (Dae 16–20), and Muktad (Spendarmad 26–30 plus five Gatha days). The gahambar of Maidyozarem is linked to the creation of the sky. The spiritual being associated with it is Shahrewar, whose name means Desirable (or Benevolent) Dominion. Shahrewar presides over metals which are associated with the sky.

Traditionally the gahambars were joyous festivals that lasted five days and included activities such as intricate rituals, specific prayers, and the sharing of food. The type of Jashan ceremony performed during this and the other gahambars is called a Zinda-rawan. Part of the Jashan ceremony includes the recitation of a specific set of prayers called an afrinagan; a special gahambar afrinagan is used for the gahambar festivals. The term afrinagan is also used to refer to the container that holds the sacred fire during the ritual.

Hordad

Feast of Hordad

Hordad 6 (Hordad)

Gregorian Equivalents for the years 1996–1999: Fasli—May 25; Shahanshahi—October 26; Qadimi—September 26

The Feast of Hordad is a sacred day because the same spiritual being rules over both the month and the day. Hordad is the spiritual being who is Perfection or Health.

Tir

Maidyoshahem (Maidhyoishema; Mid-Summer Feast)

Tir 11–15 (Khwarshed—Dae-pa-Mihr)

Gregorian Equivalents for the years 1996–1999: Fasli—June 29–July 3; Shahanshahi—November 30–December 4; Qadimi—October 31–November 4

Maidyoshahem is the second of six great feasts, called gahambars. The other five that are celebrated during the course of the year are Maidyozarem (Ardwahist 11–15), Paitishahem (Shahrewar 26–30), Ayathrem (Mihr 26–30), Maidyarem (Dae 16–20), and Muktad (Spendarmad 26–30 plus five Gatha days). The gahambar of Maidyoshahem is linked to the creation of the waters. The spiritual being associated with it is Hordad whose name means Perfection or Health. Hordad presides over the waters.

Traditionally the gahambars were joyous festivals that lasted five days and included activities such as intricate rituals, specific prayers, and the sharing of food. The type of Jashan ceremony performed during this and the other gahambars is called a Zinda-rawan. Part of the Jashan ceremony includes the recitation of a specific set of prayers called an afrinagan; a special gahambar afrinagan is used for the gahambar festivals. The term afrinagan is also used to refer to the container that holds the sacred fire during the ritual.

Tiragan
Tir 13 (Tir)

Gregorian Equivalents for the years 1996–1999: Fasli—July 1; Shahanshahi—December 2; Qadimi—November 2

The observance of Tiragan, a celebration in honor of Tishtar, the Dog Star (Sirius), occurs during the gahambar of Maidyoshahem. It is a sacred name day on which the month and day names coincide. Zoroastrians believe that dogs belong to the good part of creation and that they serve as helpers of humankind. Dogs are also believed to have the ability to see spiritual beings. The festival's activities include splashing people with water.

Amurdad

Feast of Amurdad
Amurdad 7 (Amurdad)

Gregorian equivalents for the years 1996–1999: Fasli—July 25; Shahanshahi—December 26; Qadimi—November 26

The Feast of Amurdad occurs on the day on which the spiritual being Amurdad rules over both the month and the day. Amurdad is the spiritual being who is Immortality. Amurdad presides over the earth.

Shahrewar

Feast of Shahrewar
Shahrewar 4 (Shahrewar)

Gregorian equivalents for the years 1996–1999: Fasli—August 21; Shahanshahi—January 22; Qadimi—December 23

The Feast of Shahrewar occurs on the day when the spiritual being Shahrewar rules over both the month and the day. Shahrewar is the spiritual being who is Desirable (or Benevolent) Dominion. Shahrewar presides over metals.

Paitishahem (Patishahya; Feast of Bringing in the Harvest)
Shahrewar 26–30 (Ashtad–Anagran)

Gregorian Equivalents for the years 1996–1999: Fasli—September 12–16; Shahanshahi—February 13–17; Qadimi—January 14–18

Paitishahem is the third of six great feasts, called gahambars. The other five that are celebrated during the course of the year are Maidyozarem (Ardwahist 11–15), Maidyoshahem (Tir 11–15), Ayathrem (Mihr 26–30), Maidyarem (Dae 16–20), and Muktad (Spendarmad 26–30 plus five Gatha days). The gahambar of Paitishahem is linked to the creation of the earth. The spiritual being associated with it is Spandarmad whose name means Holy Devotion. Spandarmad presides over the earth.

Traditionally the gahambars were joyous festivals that lasted five days and included activities such as intricate rituals, specific prayers, and the sharing of food. The type of Jashan ceremony performed during this and the other gahambars is called a Zinda-rawan. Part of the Jashan ceremony includes the recitation of a specific set of prayers called an afrinagan; a special gahambar afrinagan is used for the gahambar festivals. The term afrinagan is also used to refer to the container that holds the sacred fire during the ritual.

Mihr

Feast of Mithra (Mithrakana)
Mihr 1 (Ohrmazd)

Gregorian equivalents for the years 1996–1999: Fasli—September 17; Shahanshahi—February 18; Qadimi—January 19

The Feast of Mithra is a lesser feast celebrated on the first day of the seventh month which coincides with the autumnal equinox in the Fasli calendar. Mithra is an alternate name for the spiritual being Mihr, who is charged with overseeing contracts and fair dealing. Mithra also had responsibility for avenging people who broke contracts or who did not deal fairly with others. According to some scholars, the Zoroastrian concept of Mithra served as the basis for the Roman god Mithra.

Mihragan

Mihr 16 (Mihr)

Gregorian equivalents for the years 1996–1999: Fasli—October 2; Shahanshahi—March 5; Qadimi— February 3

Mihragan is a sacred day because the month and day names coincide. The festival is associated with Mihr, the spiritual being presiding over justice. The celebration includes symbolic imagery of the ripening world before the expected resurrection at the end of time.

Ayathrem (Ayathrima; Bringing Home the Herds)

Mihr 26–30 (Ashtad–Anagran)

Gregorian Equivalents for the years 1996–1999: Fasli—October 12–16; Shahanshahi—March 15–19; Qadimi— February 13–17

Ayathrem is the fourth of six great feasts, called gahambars. The other five that are celebrated during the course of the year are Maidyoshahem (Tir 11–15), Paitishahem (Shahrewar 26–30), Maidyarem (Dae 16–20), and Muktad (Spendarmad 26–30 plus five Gatha days). The gahambar of Maidyozarem is linked to the creation of the plants. The spiritual being associated with it is Amurdad, whose name means Immortality. Amurdad presides over the earth.

Traditionally the gahambars were joyous festivals that lasted five days and included activities such as intricate rituals, specific prayers, and the sharing of food. The type of Jashan ceremony performed during this and the other gahambars is called a Zinda-rawan. Part of the Jashan ceremony includes the recitation of a specific set of prayers called an afrinagan; a special gahambar afrinagan is used for the gahambar festivals. The term afrinagan is also used to refer to the container that holds the sacred fire during the ritual.

Aban

Aban Parab

Aban 10 (Aban)

Gregorian equivalents for the years 1996–1999: Fasli—October 26; Shahanshahi—March 29; Qadimi— February 27

Aban Parab is a sacred name day on which the month and day names coincide. The celebration associated with it observes the birth of the waters. The spiritual being Aban, whose name means Water (or Purity), is the focus of ceremonies, prayers, and food offerings. Trips to the water are also often included.

Adar

Adar Parab

Adar 9 (Adar)

Gregorian equivalents for the years 1996–1999: Fasli—November 24; Shahanshahi—April 27; Qadimi—March 28

Adar Parab is a sacred name day on which the month and day names coincide. The celebration associated with it observes the birth of fire. People give thanks to Adar, the spiritual being who presides over fire, for supplying light and warmth. Traditions involve giving the household fire a rest by not cooking and offering special prayers. A portion of the *Avesta* (the Zoroastrian sacred writings) called the "Atash Niyayesh," which means Fire Litany, is also recited.

Dae

Feasts of Dae

Dae 1, 8, 15, and 23, (Ohrmazd, Dae-pa-Adar, Dae-pa-Mihr, and Dae-pa-Den)

Gregorian equivalents for the years 1996–1999: Fasli—December 16, December 23, December 30, and January 7; Shahanshahi—May 19, May 26, June 2, June 10; Qadimi—April 19, April 26, May 3, and May 11

The Feasts of Dae occur during the month of Dae on the days presided over by Dae, the name for the Creator aspect of Ahura Mazda. Each month contains four days dedicated to the Creator: the 1st, 8th, 15th and 23rd days. As a result, there are four name day feasts in the month of Dae on which the same spiritual being is presiding over both the day and the month.

Zarthastno Diso (Zardosht no Diso)

Dae 11 (Khwarshed)

Gregorian equivalents for the years 1996–1999: Fasli—December 26; Shahanshahi—May 29; Qadimi— April 29

The observance of Zardosht no Diso is a day set aside on which to remember the death anniversary of the Prophet Zoroaster. (Zardosht is the Parsi form of the prophet's name.) Traditionally, people made a special trip to one of the high fire temples. Currently there are eight high fire temples in India. Outside of India, a special Jashan ceremony reserved for commemorating sad historical events, called the Rawan, is performed. The afrinagan (a specific set of prayers to be recited during the Jashan) associated with Zardosht no Diso is called the Ardafravash.

Maidyarem (Maidhyairya; Mid-Year or Winter Feast)
Dae 16–20 (Mihr–Warharan)

Gregorian equivalent for the years 1996–1999: Fasli—December 31–January 4; Shahanshahi—June 3–7; Qadimi—May 4–8

Maidyarem is the fifth of six great feasts, called gahambars. The other five that are celebrated during the course of the year are Maidyozarem (Ardwahist 11–15), Maidyoshahem (Tir 11–15), Paitishahem (Shahrewar 26–30), Ayathrem (Mihr 26–30), and Muktad (Spendarmad 26–30 plus five Gatha days). The gahambar of Maidyarem is linked to the creation of cattle. The spiritual being associated with it is Vohuman, whose name means Good Mind.

Traditionally the gahambars were joyous festivals that lasted five days and included activities such as intricate rituals, specific prayers, and the sharing of food. The type of Jashan ceremony performed during this and the other gahambars is called a Zinda-rawan. Part of the Jashan ceremony includes the recitation of a specific set of prayers called an afrinagan; a special gahambar afrinagan is used for the gahambar festivals. The term afrinagan is also used to refer to the container that holds the sacred fire during the ritual.

Vohuman

Feast of Vohuman
Vohuman 2 (Vohuman)

Gregorian equivalents for the years 1996–1999: Fasli—January 16; Shahanshahi—June 19; Qadimi—May 20

The Feast of Vohuman is a sacred day because the same spiritual being rules over both the month and the day. Vohuman is the spiritual being who is Good Mind.

Spendarmad

Feast of Spendarmad
Spendarmad 5 (Spendarmad)

Gregorian equivalents for the years 1996–1999: Fasli—February 18; Shahanshahi—July 22; Qadimi—June 22

The Feast of Spendarmad is a sacred day because the same spiritual being rules over both the month and the day. Spendarmad is the spiritual being who is Holy Devotion. Spendarmad presides over the earth.

Muktad (Hamaspathmaidym; Coming of the Whole Group of Farohars; Farvardegan Days; Festival of all Souls; Parsi Remembrance of the Departed)
Spendarmad 26–30 (Ashtad–Anagran) plus five Gatha Days—Ahunawad; Ushtawad; Spentomad; Wohukhshathra; and Wahistotoisht

Gregorian equivalents for the years 1996–1999: Fasli—March 12–21; Shahanshahi—August 12–21; Qadimi—July 13–22

Muktad, the more popular name of Hamaspathmaidym, is the last of the six great feasts, called gahambars. The other five that are celebrated during the course of the year are Maidyozarem (Ardwahist 11–15), Maidyoshahem (Tir 11–15), Paitishahem (Shahrewar 26–30), Ayathrem (Mihr 26–30), and Maidyarem (Dae 16–20). The celebration of Muktad, is linked to the creation of mankind. The other five gahambars are each associated with a spiritual being created by Ahura Mazda, but Muktad is linked to the god himself.

According to tradition, the farohars (spirits of the righteous departed and also spirits of the unborn) return to earth at the end of the year and before the beginning of the new year. Zoroastrian homes are kept clean in order to receive the spirits as guests. People also ask the spirits for protection and blessings. During the last gah (watch) of the last day of Muktad, a special fire ceremony is performed to bid a final farewell to the spirits and prepare the way for the new year.

Muktad differs from the other gahambars in its duration. The first five are five-day festivals, but the Muktad observance lasts for 10 days. Historically, Muktad was also a five-day festival, but during the Sasanian period (226 C.E. to 651 C.E.) five days were added to the calendar for intercalary purposes. In order to avoid the problem of separating the Muktad festival from the beginning of the new year, the length of the Muktad observance was extended.

——— " ———

The Jasa-mê avanghe mazda prayer, an oath recited when a child is initiated into the Zoroastrian faith, declares...

I am a Mazda worshipper and a follower of Zarathustra

——— " ———

TABLE 6.5. ALPHABETICAL LIST OF ZOROASTRIAN HOLIDAYS

Holiday	Date(s)
Aban Parab	Aban 10
Adar Parab	Adar 9
Amurdad, Feast of	Amurdad 7
Ardwahist, Feast of	Ardwahist 3
Coming of the Whole Group of Farohars *see* Muktad	
Dae, Feasts of	Dae 1, 8, 15, and 23
Farvardegan Days *see* Muktad	
Feast of Amurdad *see* Amurdad, Feast of	
Feast of Ardwahist *see* Ardwahist, Feast of	
Feast of Bringing in the Harvest *see* Paitishahem	
Feast of Frawardignan *see* Frawardignan, Feast of	
Feast of Hordad *see* Hordad, Feast of	
Feast of Mithra *see* Mithra, Feast of	
Feast of Shahrewar *see* Shahrewar, Feast of	
Feast of Spendarmad *see* Spendarmad, Feast of	
Feast of Vohuman *see* Vohuman, Feast of	
Feasts of Dae *see* Dae, Feasts of	
Festival of all Souls *see* Muktad	
Frawardignan, Feast of	Frawardin 19
Hamaspathmaidym *see* Muktad	
Hordad, Feast of	Hordad 6
Hordad Sal	Frawardin 6
Jamshed Navaroz *see* Nawruz	
Khordad Sal *see* Hordad Sal	

Holiday	Date(s)
Maidhyairya *see* Maidyarem	
Maidhyoishema *see* Maidyoshahem	
Maidhyoizaremaya *see* Maidyozarem	
Maidyarem	Dae 16–20
Maidyoshahem	Tir 11–15
Maidyozarem	Ardwahist 11–15
Mid-spring feast *see* Maidyozarem	
Mid-summer Feast *see* Maidyoshahem	
Mid-year Feast *see* Maidyarem	
Mihragan	Mihr 16
Mithra, Feast of	Mihr 1
Mithrakana *see* Mithra, Feast of	
Muktad	Spendarmad 26–30 plus five Gatha Days
Nawruz	Frawardin 1
NoRuz *see* Nawruz	
Nu Roz *see* Nawruz	
Paitishahem	Shahrewar 26–30
Parsi Remembrance of the Departed *see* Muktad	
Patati *see* Nawruz	
Patishahya *see* Paitishahem	
Shahrewar, Feast of	Shahrewar 4
Spendarmad, Feast of	Spendarmad 5
Tiragan	Tir 13
Vohuman, Feast of	Vohuman 2
Winter Feast *see* Maidyarem	
Zardosht no Diso *see* Zarthastno Diso	
Zarthastno Diso	Dae 11

CHAPTER 7

Christianity and Post-Christian Movements

Overview

What Is Christianity?

Christianity, with believers in countries around the globe, is the largest of the world's religions. The reported number of followers varies depending on how the term "Christian" is defined and the method used for counting, but many estimates place the number between 1.7 and 1.9 billion people.

The word Christian refers to a follower of Christ. Christ is a title derived from the Greek word meaning Messiah or Anointed One. The Christ of Christianity is Jesus of Nazareth, a man born two thousand years ago in the region of Palestine. The precise explanation and understanding of who Jesus was and what it means to be a follower differ among the many Christian groups; however, the three main branches of Christianity (Roman Catholicism, Orthodoxy, and Protestantism) share several core beliefs and practices concerning the nature of Jesus and the actions required of his followers.

Christians believe that Jesus was both divine and human. A doctrinal concept called the Trinity is used by the largest branches of Christianity to provide an explanation of how one God exists in three distinct persons—Father, Son, and Spirit. The Father is equated with the Creator, the Son with Jesus, and the Spirit with the Holy Spirit (also called the Holy Ghost). The Spirit is described as a gift given to believers to provide guidance and strength for life on earth.

According to Christian teaching, Jesus was killed by Roman authorities using a form of execution called crucifixion (a term meaning he was nailed to a cross and hung from it until he died). After his death, he rose back to life. His death and resurrection provide a way by which people can be reconciled with God. In remembrance of Jesus's death and resurrection, the cross serves as a fundamental symbol in Christianity.

Christians view the world as God's creation and acknowledge his sovereignty. His work is opposed, however, by a resistant spiritual being called Satan, or the Devil. God has spiritual beings, called angels, who work in accordance with his wishes. Satan also has a cohort of spiritual beings called demons. The struggle between good and evil is defined as a spiritual battle that has consequences in the material world. Christians await the Second Coming of Jesus at which time the final judgement will occur and God's perfect kingdom will be instituted.

The Relationship between God and the Christian People

The Christian God is the same creator as the Jewish God. The basic difference between Judaism and Christianity is that Jews await the coming of a Messiah; Christians proclaim that the Messiah has already come in the person of Jesus Christ.

According to traditional Christian belief, people are created by God and given one life during which the consequences of their free choices determine their eternal destiny. Those who embrace the teachings of the Christian Church will be reconciled with God in heaven and rewarded after death; those who deny God will be punished in hell. The precise understanding of heaven and hell and a third alternate, an interim place called purgatory, are understood differently among the several branches of Christians.

People possess the freedom to obey or disobey God, but perfect obedience in all things is impossible because the first man, Adam, disobeyed God. This original sin was passed along to Adam's descendants—all of mankind. The impossibility of obeying God in all things is resolved by receiving supernatural help in the form of forgiveness, a doctrinal concept described as "salvation by grace." This salvation is accessed by placing one's faith in Jesus Christ, believing in his resurrection, and receiving assurance from the Spirit.

Authorities and Sacred Writings

There is no one central authority for all of Christianity. The Pope (the bishop of Rome) is the authority for the Roman Catholic Church, but other sects look to other authorities. Orthodox communities look to Patriarchs and emphasize doctrinal agreement and traditional practice. Protestant communities focus on individual conscience.

All three main branches of Christianity acknowledge the authority of Christian scriptures, a compilation of writings assembled into a document called the *Bible*. Methods of Biblical interpretation vary among the different Christian sects.

The *Bible* comprises two major segments called the *Old* and *New Testaments*. The *Old Testament* contains the 39 books of Jewish scriptures. These include the five *Books of Moses* (*Pentateuch*), books of history, poetry, wisdom, and prophecy. The *New Testament* includes an additional 27 books written by (or ascribed to) disciples of the first and second centuries. The oldest of these writings are letters ascribed to the Apostle Paul dating from about 65 C.E. Jesus did not write any of the *New Testament*. Details of his teachings and life are known from being recorded by his disciples.

The complete canon of *New Testament* writings was established in 367 C.E. and it includes:

- Four gospels. The word "gospel" means "good news." The *Gospels* tell about events of the life of Jesus with the most significant attention paid to the last week of his life. The first of the four (in their traditional order) is attributed to Matthew, an original disciple. The second, the *Gospel According to Mark*, is attributed to a follower known as John Mark who may have been a second-generation believer. Mark's *Gospel* is judged by many to be the oldest of the four, thought to have been written around 70 C.E. The third *Gospel*, *Luke*, was written by an associate of the apostle Paul. The last of the *Gospels*, *John*, is attributed to an original disciple.

- A book of history. *Acts of the Apostles* is attributed to Luke, the author of the third *Gospel*.

- Twenty-one *Epistles* (letters). The *Epistles* include thirteen letters attributed to the apostle Paul, one *Epistle* written to the Hebrews and traditionally associated with Paul although its authorship is unknown, and seven other letters ascribed to Peter, James, John and Jude.

- An apocalyptic book. *Revelation* was probably written about 96 C.E. It is ascribed to the apostle John.

Some Christians recognize an additional set of books, called the Apocrypha, which is a collection of Jewish writings found in the Greek version of Jewish scriptures, but not included in the Hebrew version. Other books exist which were written during the first and second centuries of the Christian era but were not included in the official canon either due to their limited circulation, lateness of composition, or questionable apostolic authority.

History of Christianity

Jesus, Called the Christ

The founder of Christianity was a Jewish man, Jesus, called the Christ (a term derived from the Greek word for Messiah). Jesus was born in the first decade B.C.E. in Bethlehem. He grew up in Nazareth, and died in approximately 29–30 C.E. after being arrested by Roman rulers and put to death by crucifixion, a common means of execution.

The birth of Jesus is recorded in two of the *Gospels*: *Matthew* and *Luke*. According to the *Gospels*, Jesus was born to a Jewish couple, Joseph and Mary, during the reign of the Roman Emperor Augustus and before the death of Herod the Great (approximately 4 B.C.E.). According to biblical accounts, after Jesus's birth the governor of Palestine, attempted to kill him by ordering a massacre of all Hebrew children under the age of two. Jesus's family escaped by fleeing to Egypt until the threat had passed. The slaughtered children, called the Holy Innocents, are remembered on a special day in the Christian calendar.

Very little is known about Jesus's childhood. His public ministry began when he was an adult. His work was preceded by a prophet known as John the Baptist. In approximately 28 C.E., John began proclaiming a message concerning the coming of the kingdom of God. He exhorted people to turn back to God and undergo a ritual of baptism, signifying repentance. According to Christian tradition, Jesus underwent baptism by John and afterward endured a time of temptation and testing in the wilderness. Shortly after these events John the Baptist was arrested, and Jesus himself began to carry the message proclaiming God's coming kingdom.

The precise duration of Jesus's ministry is unknown, but many estimates suggest that his public work lasted between one and three years. During his time, Jesus was a wandering teacher in the Palestine area. He taught in parables and spoke out against some practices of the Jewish authorities. Several different kinds of miraculous events were attributed to him including command over nature, physical healing, and the casting out of demons. Many people followed him, but twelve specially selected disciples were closest to him. These twelve were called apostles.

Jesus's earthly life ended when he was executed by Roman officials. The events surrounding Jesus's death occurred during the time of the Jewish celebration of Passover. The last meal he shared with his disciples was a Passover meal. The celebration and remembrance of this meal, in which Jesus identified his body and blood with the bread and wine, forms a focal point for most Christian worship.

According to Christian teaching, after Jesus's execution and death, his dead body was placed in a tomb. Three days later, or more precisely on the third day (Romans counted days inclusively), he rose from the dead. Following his resurrection, Jesus appeared to his disciples during a 40-day period after which he ascended into heaven.

The Beginning of the Christian Church

According to the book of *Acts*, after Jesus ascended into heaven, the disciples gathered in Jerusalem for the Jewish feast of Shavuot (also called the Feast of Weeks because it occurred seven weeks after Passover). Among Greek-speaking Jews the feast was called Pentecost because it fell 50 days after Passover. While they were gathered together, the disciples received the gift of the Holy Spirit. Many Christian denominations view the events at Pentecost as the birth of the Christian Church.

Following the giving of the Spirit, Jesus's disciples, who had been disheartened after his death, were revitalized. They began to proclaim Jesus's resurrection and to boldly preach his message despite being persecuted and even martyred.

Early practices of the first century Christians included fellowship, prayers, and the sharing of bread and wine. These three basic elements have remained a central part of practicing the Christian faith.

The first Christians were Jews who acknowledged Jesus as Messiah. They continued to follow the precepts of Judaism, read Jewish scriptures, follow Jewish laws, and meet at Jewish synagogues. In addition, however, they also met together to share bread and wine and celebrate Jesus's resurrection. These additional meetings were held on Sunday, the first day of the week, to coincide with the day of the resurrection.

The Spread of Christianity in the First Century

One prominent Jew who converted to Christianity following the death of Jesus was the apostle Paul. According to Christian teaching, Paul (previously known as Saul of Tarsus) originally persecuted believers. He was confronted by a vision of Jesus in which he was blinded. Three days later he was healed and given instruction in the Christian faith. Following a period of discipleship, Paul was sent out as a missionary, and under his ministry churches were founded in Asia Minor and Greece. One of the main themes in Paul's teachings was that a person did not have to become a Jew to be a Christian.

The Christian movement initially spread in urban centers throughout the Roman empire. It was introduced to areas outside the region of Palestine as Jews moved to avoid oppression. Jewish synagogues were often the first focal points of missionary efforts. Missionary activities were also made among non-Jewish people (called Gentiles). As a result the Christian community began to grow, first as a sect within Judaism and then as a separate religion.

Under Roman law, Jews held an exemption from the requirement of worshiping the Roman Emperor, but Christians, as followers of a new religion, did not enjoy this privilege. Because they refused to worship the Roman Emperor or recognize his divinity, they faced persecution. The apostles Peter and Paul were executed under orders from Emperor Nero between 54 and 68 C.E.

Christianity becomes Established as an Independent Religiou

In 70 C.E. the Romans destroyed the Jewish temple in Jerusalem. After the temple's destruction, Judaism became more focused on Rabbinic traditions and Christianity continued to evolve as an increasingly independent religion.

By the end of the first century, many Christian groups had grown from small gatherings to large assemblies. New forms of leadership structures emerged to give guidance to new converts and serve the needs of the rapidly expanding community. These positions included teachers, deacons, and bishops.

The persecution of Christians continued during the second century C.E. and intensified during the third as the Roman Empire faced ever-growing threats from invaders. Worship of traditional Roman gods was mandated and strictly enforced by Roman Emperors Decius (in the mid-third century C.E.), Diocletian (during the late third century C.E.), and Galerius (in the early forth century C.E.). Christians who refused to sacrifice to the Roman gods were imprisoned and often executed.

Many who suffered martyrdom are remembered on saint days in the calendars of several orthodox, catholic, and protestant sects. The basis of saint day remembrances is found in ancient Roman tradition. On the anniversary of a death, families would share a ritual meal at the grave site of an ancestor. This practice was adopted by Christians who began observing a ritual meal on the death anniversary of ancestors in the faith, especially martyrs. As a result, most Christian saint days are associated with the death of the saint. There are three important exceptions. John the Baptist, the Virgin Mary, and Jesus are honored on their nativities (birthdays).

Despite persecution, new converts continued to join the Christian ranks. By the end of the third century C.E., four cities had become important centers of Christianity: Rome, Antioch (in Syria), Alexandria (in Egypt) and Jerusalem. Bishops of these cities were charged with the responsibility of caring for the needs of the churches in the surrounding areas.

As the Roman Empire continued to decline, economic and social conditions deteriorated. Churches became more firmly established and provided necessary support to the poor, widows, orphans, and the sick. Some historians theorize that the attraction of social stability contributed to the spread of Christianity during an unstable time in history.

Emperor Constantine

Following the death of the Roman Emperor Galerius in 311 C.E. a new Emperor, Constantine, came to power. Constantine won a decisive military victory and attributed his success in battle to a god he called the "Unconquerable Son." Christian apologists convinced Constantine that the god responsible for his victory was the Christian God.

Although Constantine was not baptized until the end of his life, he became an advocate for Christianity. His Edict of Milan, issued in 313 C.E., ended the age of persecution by mandating the tolerance of Christianity. As a consequence of Constantine's advocacy, Christianity became the predominant religion of those in political power.

The Nicene Creed

Constantine also presided over the Council of Nicaea in 325 C.E. The council was a meeting of Christian leaders who defined Christianity and attempted to separate it from heresies. The Council of Nicaea produced a creed, known as the Nicene Creed, which is recognized by all major branches of Christianity as a foundational statement of doctrine.

Under continued pressure from invaders, Constantine moved the political capital of the empire from Rome to Byzantium (which was later renamed Constantinople). The church in each of these two major cities was presided over by a bishop. Because the political seat had been moved to Byzantium, the bishop in Rome (called the pope) became more powerful in both church and secular affairs. This shift aided the process by which the Papacy amassed its vast power.

The move ultimately led to the creation of a geographic division between the Eastern and Western branches of Christianity. The western branch of Christianity focused its efforts on attracting new converts in northern Europe and sought to establish political alliances to aid in guarding security. The first Frankish lord, Clovis, converted to Christianity in the fifth century. (The Franks ruled over an area currently occupied by Germany, France, and Italy.) A later Frankish ruler, Charlemagne, was made Emperor in 800 C.E. by the Roman Pope Leo III.

The Eastern practice of combining ecclesiastical and political power ultimately led to conflict. Nobles affiliated with the church in Rome had authority over unaffiliated nobles and the influence wielded by religious leaders brought more power to the pope in Rome.

Differences in the expression of Christianity also arose between the East and West. Western Christianity focused on the awesome holiness of God and developed precise rituals and a priestly class. In the east, practices focused on Christianity as a mystical experience and lay people retained more power. The mystical focus of the Eastern Church found its expression in a form of worship that used icons (images to be venerated as representations of the divine nature).

The Great Schism

As differences between Eastern and Western Christianity increased, tension also increased. Political power structures were challenged. Pope Leo IX (1048–54 C.E.) insisted that the Eastern people, who claimed to be representatives of Orthodox (correct) Christianity, shift their allegiance to him and the Catholic (Universal) Church. The Patriarch in Constantinople, Michael Cerularius, refused. In 1054 C.E., the Pope and Patriarch mutually excommunicated each other, an event called The Great Schism.

During the next century, Muslims rose in power in the East and Western Churches sent military aid. The campaigns were called the Crusades. The Crusaders of 1204 C.E. attacked Constantinople itself, ending efforts aimed at achieving reconciliation between the Eastern and Western branches of Christianity.

The Crusades, however, caused a renewed interest in religious expression in the West. As universities were developed and discussion of spiritual matters escalated, church officials became zealous in attacking heresy. The Inquisition was established and the power of the pope reached its zenith. Many important doctrines unique to Roman Catholicism arose during the thirteenth century.

These included the concept of transubstantiation (a doctrine meaning that the bread and wine used during the Eucharist actually became the body and blood of Christ) and the veneration of the Virgin Mary (Jesus's mother).

By the fourteenth century, however, authoritarian abuses and divisions within the Church hierarchy diminished the power of the pope. Between 1309 to 1377 the Roman popes moved from Rome to Avignon. At one time as many as three different men laid claim to the title Pope. The papacy was not reunified until the early fifteenth century.

The Reformation

Abuse of power and disunity within the Church helped plant the seeds for the coming reformation as some people sought a more personal, mystical experience. In the fourteenth century John Wycliffe, an English writer, advocated reforms including the translation of the *Bible* from Latin into the common languages of the people.

By the fifteenth century, the reunified Papacy had amassed tremendous political power. All priests in Europe received their authority from the Roman Pope. Only authorized priests were able to administer Church sacraments (which were baptism, confirmation, Eucharist, penance, holy orders, matrimony, and extreme unction). A person cut off from sacraments could not be assured of salvation and life after death. If a national ruler disobeyed the pope, an entire country would be placed under papal ban meaning that none of its priests could administer the sacraments. An individual who denied the authority of the Church could be excommunicated and refused the sacraments. These types of pressures over people led to protests which culminated in the Protestant Reformation.

Martin Luther (1483–1545), a German priest and professor at the University of Wittenberg, is often credited with beginning the Reformation. Luther opposed the Roman practice of selling indulgences (selling the remission of punishment from sin in order to raise money to build a cathedral). He believed that people received salvation as a result of their faith. Luther denied the authority of the Pope and church tradition, believing instead that the *Bible* was the only source of true doctrine and that it alone served as a guide for proper Christian conduct. Luther also asserted that priests did not have the power to save or condemn people but that such power belonged exclusively to God and that each person was individually responsible to God.

Other protestant leaders followed and the movement swept through Europe. The main thrust of Protestantism was the belief that Christianity needed to return to its original, Biblical state. The protestant legacy,

however, endowed the Church with an heritage of questioning authority and protesting abuses perpetrated by leaders. This willingness created conditions ripe for further splintering and the subsequent creation of progressively smaller and more numerous groups. As a result, by the late twentieth century there were more than 25,000 different Christian denominations.

Christianity Today

Christian Worship and Practices

Different groups of Christians worship in different ways. Some use elaborate rituals with prescribed prayers, others prefer informal gatherings. Some use music and dance; some worship in silence. Some meet in ornate cathedrals; some meet in private homes. Some use icons to focus their worship; some decry the use of icons as idolatry.

Most Christian worship, however, takes place within the context of a church. A "church" can refer either to a special building or to a faith community of Christians or to both. The purpose of the Church is to continue Jesus's mission until he returns at his anticipated second coming. Because Jesus's resurrection occurred on a Sunday, Sunday is the day on which many Christians meet for communal worship. Some sects, however, observe the Jewish Sabbath instead.

One of the central practices of Christianity, baptism, is a symbolic act that signifies dying with Christ and being raised to new life. Some Christians perform baptism by sprinkling or pouring water on candidates. Some groups practice baptism by total immersion, and others view baptism as a spiritual event rather than as a ritual performed with water. Some Christian groups baptize infants and children while others baptize only those old enough to make an informed decision.

Another practice common to most Christian groups is a ritual in which celebrants partake in a remembrance or reenactment of Jesus's last meal with his disciples. The celebration is known by different names including the Eucharist, Holy Communion, and the Lord's Supper. It involves the sharing of bread and wine. Specific means and frequency of the celebration vary among Christian sects.

Sects within Christianity

From its beginning as a sect within Judaism, Christianity spread throughout the world. Three aspects of the Christian faith made it especially suitable for global growth: Its message was available to everyone irrespective of their place of birth, race, or gender; it had a strong historic basis; and, it possessed the ability to adapt to new situations in diverse cultures.

There are three major divisions within Christianity: Catholicism, Orthodoxy, and Protestantism. Historically each group has believed that it held the exclusive representation of true Christianity. More modernly, many representatives from various segments of the global Christian community have expressed an opinion that none is exclusive and others may be viable, although the degree of the acceptance and the roster of accepted denominations varies considerably.

A fourth division also exists within modern Christianity. It comprises movements that were founded on Christian beliefs, practices, and traditions but that also incorporate non-traditional doctrines. Frequently these new doctrines result from revelations received by individual leaders outside the framework of Biblical knowledge. Among many traditional Christians, these extra-revelational sects may be called "cults."

Roman Catholicism

The word "catholic" is derived from the Greek word meaning universal. In some contexts, such as in ancient creeds, it refers to the universal Christian Church and encompasses all Christian believers. In the modern sense, however, "catholic" is often used as a synonym for Roman Catholicism.

Roman Catholicism is the largest branch of Christianity. An estimated 17 percent of the world's population is Roman Catholic—more than 950 million people. The Church claims an unbroken link to the apostolic days and specifically to the apostle Peter. The tradition of assuming that Christians in Rome held responsibility and authority over others dates back to the second and third centuries C.E.

The ultimate authority in Roman Catholicism is the Pope. His office is derived from his election as Bishop of Rome. Other leaders within the Roman Catholic Church are called Cardinals. They are appointed by the Pope and serve as the Church's Supreme Council. As of the early 1990s, there were 163 cardinals serving the Roman Catholic Church worldwide.

The Roman Catholic Church tends to place greater emphasis on doctrinal issues, traditions, the authority of the pope, veneration of saints, and the adoration of Mary than do churches within other Christian branches. The main worship service is called a Mass, which is a formal service comprising several parts that include chants, readings from the *Bible*, the recitation of specific prayers, an offertory, Holy Communion (Eucharist), and a benediction. The word mass comes from a Latin word meaning "sent"—a term used at the service's conclusion. There are two types of mass: High Mass and Low Mass. At High Mass most of the service is sung; at Low Mass, a simpler form of the service is used and its parts are read.

Protestantism

Protestant churches form the second largest major division within Christianity. Worldwide, Protestants number nearly 500 million people and represent about 25 percent of all Christians. Within Protestantism, however, there are thousands of denominations of varying sizes. Denominations tend to split into subsects over details such as the form of baptism, methods of government, and style of worship.

Many modern Protestant denominations have their roots in the fifteenth century European struggle to achieve freedom from the Roman Pope's authority. Four branches of Protestantism developed during the Reformation era: Lutheran; Calvinist (Reformed), Anabaptist, and Anglican. The label "Protestant" was derived from a protest signed by six German princes criticizing the Roman Catholic Church's withdrawal of tolerance toward Lutherans.

Lutherans trace their beginnings to Martin Luther, an Augustinian monk and theology professor. In the early 1500s Luther spoke out against abuses within the Roman Catholic Church, in particular against the practice of selling "indulgences" to help raise money to construct Saint Peter's Basilica in Rome (by purchasing indulgences, a person could escape punishments that resulted from his or her sins). Luther believed that a person's salvation was given by divine grace alone. In 1517 C.E. he published the *Ninety-Five Theses* with which he intended to help reform the errors he saw in the Roman Catholic Church. The Church, however, was not receptive to his views and Luther was excommunicated. Luther's ideas were published widely, and the Lutheran Church spread throughout northern Europe.

Calvinist churches (a group that includes Presbyterian, Congregational, and Reformed Churches) trace their beginnings to John Calvin, a sixteenth century French theologian who became established in Geneva, Switzerland. Calvin's writings helped further spread the Protestant movement.

Anglican Churches also joined the Protestant reformation in the sixteenth century. In 1534 C.E., King Henry VIII of England denied the Pope in Rome and assumed authority over the English Church himself. Some groups were dissatisfied, however, with the many Roman forms retained by the Anglicans (the official Church of England) and pressed for further reforms. Following the religious strife that ensued, some groups, such as the Puritans, left Europe to seek religious freedom in the New World.

Anabaptist groups were a more extreme form of Protestantism than the Anglicans, Lutherans, or Calvinists. They denounced all relationships between the Church and state and emphasized doctrinal reforms. The Anabaptist reforms ultimately led to the development of denominations such as the Mennonites, the Amish, and the Society of Friends (Quakers).

Orthodox

The third main branch within Christianity is the Orthodox Church. According to estimates, approximately 174 million people around the world belong to the Orthodox Church.

The word orthodox comes from a Greek term meaning "right-believing." Orthodox Churches are headed by patriarchs, who hold administrative jurisdiction in a territory. Unlike the Roman Catholic Pope, patriarchs make no claim to infallibility.

Orthodox Churches separated from Roman Churches in 1054 C.E. when the Patriarch in Constantinople and the Pope in Rome excommunicated each other. Differences between Orthodox and Roman Catholic Churches persist into the modern era. Unlike Roman and Protestant Churches, Orthodox Churches use icons in worship. Icons are painted pictures of Jesus, the Virgin Mary, the apostles, and saints that are intended to help worshipers feel a connection between themselves and others who have preceded them in the faith.

Other practices differentiate Orthodox Churches from Roman Catholic and Protestant Churches: Orthodox priests are permitted to marry (their Roman counterparts maintain a tradition of celibacy); Orthodox Churches tend to permit greater lay participation in missionary and educational work than do Roman Catholic Churches; infants are baptized by triple immersion and are immediately anointed with oil; and, eucharistic bread is leavened.

Orthodox Churches are traditionally associated with Eastern geographical areas. In the nineteenth and twentieth centuries, however, population movements led to the establishment of Orthodox communities in Eastern Europe, Africa, Asia and in the Americas. Many of the Churches within the Orthodox branch of Christianity carry names indicating their geographic origins such as Greek Orthodox, Russian Orthodox, Serbian Orthodox, Armenian Orthodox, and Syrian Orthodox.

Extra-Revelational Sects and Post-Christian Movements

Groups of Christians claiming to possess special knowledge have existed throughout the course of Christian history. As early as the second century, some groups claimed to possess special understanding. These people were called Gnostics (a word derived from the Greek word for knowledge). Marcion (in the second century) and Mani (who founded the Manichees in the third century) are both examples of founders of movements claiming to have received special knowledge apart from

the writings and traditions recognized by the main body of Christian believers.

In the modern era, extra-revelational sects and post-Christian movements include a vast array of groups with memberships ranging from a few individuals to millions. A few well-known examples of extra-revelational sects are the Church of Jesus Christ of Latter Day Saints (Mormons), Church of Christ, Scientist (Christian Science), the Holy Spirit Association for the Unification of World Christianity (Unification Church), and the Church of the New Jerusalem (who's members, called Swedenborgians, are disciples of the Swedish scientist, philosopher, and theologian, Emanuel Swedenborg.)

The inclusion of extra-revelational sects and post-Christian movements under the Christian umbrella may be seen by some as controversial; however, because these groups often see themselves as legitimate heirs to the Christian tradition, and because their holiday observances typically follow the calendar system used by other Christian groups, they are included here. Holidays associated with these groups, however, are not observed by other Christian sects.

The Church of Jesus Christ of Latter Day Saints (Mormonism) was founded by Joseph Smith in 1830. Smith claimed to have received visions from God and angelic visitations. According to Mormon teaching, Smith received a document called the *Book of Mormon* from an angel. Mormons hold the *Book of Mormon* and the *Bible* in equal esteem. Mormon teaching asserts that true Christian doctrine did not survive past the first generation of apostles.

The Church of Christ, Scientist (Christian Science) was founded by Mary Baker Eddy in the late nineteenth century. Eddy studied the *Bible* seeking information on healing, and the Church she founded grew out of her personal quest. Two documents written and revised by Eddy give direction and instruction: *Science and Health* (last revision in 1906) and *Manual of The Mother Church* (last revision in 1908). Christian Science teaches that healing is not a miracle but a natural working of spiritual laws.

The Holy Spirit Association for the Unification of World Christianity (Unification Church) has its roots in the early twentieth century in Korea. The Unification Church was introduced to the United States by the Rev. Sun Myung Moon. At first growth was slow, but in the 1970s the movement gained a rapid influx of converts. A document regarded as scripture, *Divine Principle*, presents revelation concerning the Messiah and church history. Unification teaching maintains that Jesus failed in his mission as God's Messiah and that a new Messiah must come. Many Unificationists believe that Moon fulfills the requirements of the second Messiah.

Christian Calendars

Hebrew Influences

Clearly visible within the Christian liturgical calendar are elements of both the Hebrew and Greek time-keeping systems. Most immediately recognizable, however, are the influences of the Hebrew calendar. The movable feasts within Christianity, such as Easter and Pentecost, have connections to Hebrew celebrations.

The Establishment of Sunday as a Meeting Day

The evolution of Christianity as a separate religion from Judaism is often misunderstood. The division between the two belief systems was not initially over the deity of Jesus of Nazareth and his position as the Messiah, as many people suppose; in fact, for the first fifty years that Christianity existed, it remained a movement within Judaism. Most Christians were Jews who believed that Jesus was the Messiah, and although many other Jews did not share the Christians' belief, the two groups continued to worship in the synagogues together.

Christians were only one of many sects within Judaism; others included the Sadducees, Pharisees, Essenes, Zealots, gnostics, and the "God-Fearers" (a group composed of Romans who lived a Jewish lifestyle without formal conversion—perhaps up to 20 percent of the Roman population). This diverse Jewish culture was fragmented in 70 C.E. following the Roman war.

After the Roman destruction of the Temple at Jerusalem, the surviving Hebrew rabbis argued that the disaster had been caused by "factionalism" and decided that unity was more important than individual expression. Thus, they merged the sects, drawing mainly from the Pharisaic tradition to create what is now known as normative or Orthodox Judaism. Christian Jews were invited to join this new, unified group, but the Christians decided not to merge because they could not accept the conditions and constraints of Orthodox Judaism. Jews and Christians continued to meet together in the synagogue on the Sabbath evening until about 80–85 C.E., when Christians began to form their own synagogues. At that point, they were no longer recognized as Jews under the Jewish and Roman law, and Christianity became illegal. More than two centuries passed before Christianity was legalized again.

While Christians continued to meet with other Jews in the synagogue for the Sabbath, they also observed their own special meetings on Sunday at sunrise to commemorate the resurrection of Jesus. Once they began to separate from the Jews, they slowly switched to Sunday mornings as their primary meeting time. The reasons for this change in meeting time were two-fold: First to remember the resurrection of Christ; second, to separate themselves more clearly from the Jews. This period marks the distinct point at which the two systems of belief moved in opposite directions, and it was here that the roots of longstanding resentments between the two groups began to grow.

Establishing Dates for the Easter Celebration

Initially, Christians celebrated the Jewish Passover as the anniversary of the Last Supper, and the Feast of the Resurrection (Easter) was observed on the first Sunday after the beginning of Passover. The Jewish Pentecost (Shavout or Feast of Weeks) was maintained as the anniversary of the New Covenant, when the Holy Spirit descended on the disciples.

By the second century C.E., the relationship between Judaism and Christianity had deteriorated so greatly that it became impossible for Christians to find out when Passover would be celebrated. The date for Passover was movable and the equation for its determination had not yet been made public. As a result, Christians began to determine the date of the Easter celebration according to the rules of their individual communities.

The Christian Churches east of Greece celebrated Easter on the fourteenth of Nisan (in the Jewish calendar) whether or not it was a Sunday. The Western Church, however, developed a more complex system to determine Easter's date and ensure that it was celebrated on a Sunday in the Passover week. To claim authority for the date established for Easter, both groups appealed to the *Gospels*. The *Gospel of John*, however, gives a different date for the crucifixion than the date given by the other *Gospels*. This inconsistency, coupled with the controversy over how the evening of the fourteenth day of the month should be calculated, produced a schism between the Eastern and Western Churches.

According to the Jewish religious definition, the full moon was the fourteenth day after the new moon irrespective of astronomical calculations. Defining the evening of the fourteenth day would, therefore, determine the date on which the Passover was celebrated. A group called the Quintodecimans counted the evening of the fourteenth as the one after the fourteenth day. The Quartodecimans claimed that it meant the evening following the thirteenth day, since sunset was the beginning of a new day. Supporters of the two points of view tended to fall along geographical lines: the Eastern Church supported the Quartodecimans, while the Western Church supported the Quintodecimans.

Date of Easter Established by the Council of Nicaea

In 325 C.E., Constantine summoned all the bishops to the first Ecumenical Council, in Nicaea, to settle the numerous differences that were cropping up and threatening the unity of the Church. It was also around this time that the seven-day week became common in the Roman Empire, and schoolchildren had to begin memorizing the names of the weekdays in order to know which day was Sunday—indicating how strong the influence of Christianity had become in a short period of time.

The Council of Nicaea passed policies on many issues facing the Christian Church; among the most pertinent of these was a system for determining the date of Easter. Even though disagreement has arisen over the interpretation of the rule, it has been used by Christians ever since.

Because Judaism and Christianity had become mutually exclusive religions, the Christian authorities wanted to ensure that Easter would never coincide with Passover. The rule for the date of Easter as declared by the Council of Nicaea was in agreement with the Quintodecimans. The Feast of the Resurrection should be celebrated on the first Sunday after (not on) the first full moon after March 21 (which was the date of the vernal equinox the year the council met). This full moon became known as the Paschal moon. In addition, the Council ruled that if the designated Sunday coincided with either Passover or the Easter Day of the Quartodecimans, the festival should be held seven days later.

The decision of the Council delighted the Western Church. The Eastern Church, on the other hand, decided to retain the Quartodeciman position, as did the Church in England. During the sixth century, however, Roman missionaries to England introduced the Western system which was adopted and is still followed.

The effort of the Church Fathers to avoid the coincidence of Easter with the Passover feast underscores how far Judaism and Christianity had diverged. The notion that the Last Supper was an extension of the Passover Feast seemed to have been forgotten. The Church Fathers also fixed Pentecost as the seventh Sunday (fiftieth day according to the Roman inclusive counting method) after Easter, just as the Jewish Pentecost is the fiftieth day after Passover.

A Formula for Determining the Date of Easter

The provisions of the Council of Nicaea later allowed the Church to devise a formula to calculate the date of Easter. There were two parts to the formula: dominical letters and golden numbers. The first part, dominical letters, was a system that would determine the day of the week on which any date of the year would fall. The golden numbers provided a method for calculating the dates of the full moon in any given year.

In order to determine what dates the Sundays in any given year would occur, the Church adopted a system similar to the one that had been used by the Romans to determine market days. For ecclesiastical use, the code gave what was known as the dominical letter.

The first seven letters of the alphabet, A through G, are each assigned to consecutive days beginning with the first day of the year. January 1 appears as A, January 2 as B, and so on through January 7 as G, January 8 as A, January 9 as B, et cetera. The letter given to the first Sunday in the year will be the letter of all the Sundays thereafter in the year. For example, if January 5 is the first Sunday, E will be the dominical letter for the year. The only exception to this is leap year. In this case, no dominical letter is assigned to February 29, but because it appears on the calendar like any other weekday, the series of letters changes by one after the intercalation. So if a leap year begins with the dominical letter E, it will change to the dominical letter F on March 1. In charts of dominical letters, leap years are designated with a double-letter notation such as EF.

To determine the date for the Easter observance, one would look at the dates between which Easter must be celebrated (March 22–April 25), identify the corresponding Sundays by using the system of dominical letters, and determine which of these Sundays meets the requirements for Easter: that it falls after the Paschal moon and does not coincide with the Passover or Quartodeciman celebrations. To find out if it falls after the Paschal moon, the system known as golden numbers was developed.

Golden Numbers

Golden numbers are based on a cycle much like the Metonic cycle. A nineteen-year chart was constructed that predicted the phases of the moon for each year in the period. The number cycle indicated which days within the range would be full moons.

The chart of dominical letters was then consulted to find out which days after the first full moon following March 21 were Sundays. The first Sunday to meet all of the requirements for Easter as laid down by the Council of Nicaea was then officially declared as the holiday.

Although the golden numbers were introduced in 530 C.E., the chart was constructed as if they had been accepted in the fourth century at the Council of Nicaea. The designers of the golden number system determined that the epoch of the era should fall when the New

Moon occurred on January 1. They determined this year to be the one preceding 1 C.E. Therefore to determine the golden number for any year one would divide the year by nineteen, then add one to the remainder of the quotient. If the result is zero, the golden number for the year is nineteen.

The origin of the name "golden numbers" dates to medieval times, but its exact derivation is uncertain. Some have suggested that they were named for the Greek name of the numbers within the Metonic cycle while others have conjectured that they were named after the gold color used for them in manuscript calendars.

Christian Movable Feasts

When the Council of Nicaea undertook the task of establishing a date for Easter, the Feast of the Resurrection had already been a movable feast for so long that it could not easily have been established as a fixed feast on the actual anniversary of the event. Some researchers theorize that the Church authorities may have made the holiday movable as a compromise to avoid controversy. Questions persisted about the actual date of the resurrection. Although the official teaching of the Roman Catholic Church was that the crucifixion occurred on April 7, 30 C.E., modern scholars and medieval tradition agree that the actual date was probably March 25, 29 C.E. (In fact, medieval Christians established March 25 as the feast day of St. Dismas, the "good thief" who died on the cross next to Jesus.)

Another possibility for the establishment of a movable date for Easter may have been that the Church leaders wanted to avoid having the Annunciation, a day commemorating Gabriel's announcement to the Virgin Mary that she would be the mother of the Messiah which is celebrated on March 25, and the crucifixion fall on the same date. If March 25 falls during Easter Week, the Feast of the Annunciation is celebrated a week or two later.

Based on the date of Easter, a series of "movable Feasts" developed. These begin with Shrove Tuesday and end with Corpus Christi. They also include Ash Wednesday, Palm Sunday, Maundy Thursday, Good Friday, Ascension Day, and Whitsunday (also known as Pentecost).

There are three movable feasts that do not depend on the date of Easter. The Sunday after January 6 is the Feast of the Baptism of the Lord. The last Sunday of the Roman Catholic liturgical year (it falls on the third or fourth Sunday in November) is the Solemnity of Christ the King. The Sunday within the eight day celebration period following Christmas (or December 30, if Christmas is on a Sunday) is the Feast of the Holy Family.

The Origins of Other Christian Holidays

Sunday, Passover, and Pentecost are the only Christian feast days mentioned by the prominent Church father, Origen, in the early third century. Other holiday traditions were quick to develop.

By the fourth century, Christians had become so numerous that the acts of persecution initiated by the Roman Emperor Diocletian a century before could no longer seriously endanger the movement. With the conversion of Constantine the Great in 312 C.E., Christianity became the official religion of the waning Roman Empire. This formal sanction spurred a massive evangelistic effort by Christians which resulted in the conversion of most inhabitants of the Empire and many barbarian groups on its outskirts.

To facilitate the acceptance of Christianity by pagans, the leaders of the Church instructed its missionaries to allow new converts to continue observing the festivals to which they were accustomed. Pope Gregory specifically instructed Augustine of Canterbury in the early seventh century that the only stipulation on the rule of acceptance was that a new meaning had to be assigned to the symbolism of the event which would bring it into line with Christian teachings.

One new festival the Church established about this time was Epiphany. The Alexandrian Church of Isis had long celebrated the day which became Epiphany as the day of Osiris's birth from the Virgin. The Mysteries of Isis originated under the Ptolemies as an Egyptian form of the Eleusinian Mysteries of Greece and had been imported into Rome by the first century B.C.E. For several centuries, the Alexandrian Church of Isis presented serious competition to the Christian Church in the Roman world. It was from the tradition of the Alexandrian Church that Christianity garnered the practice of having daily liturgical services in large ornate temples.

The worshippers of Mithras, a Persian god extremely popular among the Roman soldiers, had historically celebrated December 25 as the "Birthday of the Invincible Sun." In 273 C.E., the Christian Church established December 25 as the date of the Virgin Birth of their Invincible Son, and apparently about this time began emphasizing Christ as the Sacrificial Lamb as a substitute for the sacrificial bull of Mithraism.

Since December 25 had been established as the birthday of the Christ, the Council of Nicaea established March 25, nine months before, as the date of his conception or as the Feast of the Annunciation, the day when the angel Gabriel told Mary she had been chosen to be the mother of the Messiah. Similarly, the traditional date for the birth of Mary, September 8, determined the placing of the feast of Mary's Immaculate Conception on December 8. Each of these dates was originally a celebration of a Roman, Greek, or Egyptian deity.

Numbering Years from the Birth of Christ

In 463 C.E., Victorius of Aquitaine, who had been appointed by Pope Hilarius to undertake calendar revision, devised the Great Paschal period, also referred to as the Victorian period. The Great Pascal period was a combination of the solar cycle of 28 years and the Metonic 19-year cycle. This cycle brought the Full Moon back to the same day of the month every 532 years. In the sixth century, this period was used by Dionysius Exiguus to figure the date of Easter. Hence, it also became known as the Dionysian period.

Recognizing the profound impact of Christianity on the world, Dionysius used the cycle to define a new era, the Christian era, based on the birth of Christ. He took the year now called 532 C.E. as the first year of a new Great Paschal period and the year now designated 1 B.C.E. as the beginning of the previous cycle. In the sixth century it was the general belief that this

was the year of Christ's birth, and because of this, Dionysius introduced the concept of numbering years consecutively through the Christian era. Some scholars adopted Dionysius' practice early, but the B.C./A.D. dating method only came into wide use after its popularization in *The Ecclesiastical History of the English People* by the Venerable Bede of Jarrow (c. 673–735).

The Current Christian Liturgical Calendars

Many branches of Christianity follow similar calendars to mark the holy days of the year. The calendar focuses attention on special events in Jesus's life and also provides for the remembrance of many saints and historical events. It includes two types of dates: movable feasts which are typically established based on their relationship to the Feast of the Resurrection (Easter), and fixed holidays.

The Christian liturgical year begins in late November with a season called Advent. Advent is four weeks long and it provides a time during which Christians focus on preparing for Jesus birth. Advent is followed by Christmas and the Christmas season during which

---

TABLE 7.1. COMMON SEASONS AND MOVABLE FEASTS IN THE WESTERN CHRISTIAN LITURGICAL CALENDAR

Advent Season

The First through Fourth Sunday of Advent

Christmas Season

The Nativity of Our Lord (Christmas)
The First Sunday after Christmas Day
The Second Sunday after Christmas Day

Epiphany Season

The Epiphany
The First Sunday after the Epiphany:
The Baptism of Our Lord
The Second Sunday through the Eighth Sunday
   after the Epiphany
The Last Sunday after the Epiphany

Lenten Season

Ash Wednesday
The First through Fourth (or Fifth) Sunday
   in Lent

Compiled from Roman Catholic, Lutheran, and Anglican sources

Holy Week

Palm Sunday
Monday in Holy Week
Tuesday in Holy Week
Wednesday in Holy Week
Maundy Thursday
Good Friday
Holy Saturday

Easter Season

Easter Eve
The Sunday of the Resurrection, or Easter Day
The Second through Sixth Sunday of Easter
Ascension Day
The Seventh Sunday of Easter: The Sunday after
   Ascension Day
The Day of Pentecost: Whitsunday

The Season after Pentecost

The First Sunday after Pentecost:
   Trinity Sunday
The Second through the Twenty-seventh Sunday
   after Pentecost
The Last Sunday after Pentecost

TABLE 7.2. FIXED HOLIDAYS IN THE WESTERN CHRISTIAN LITURGICAL CALENDAR

November (after Advent begins)

30 . . . . . St. Andrew the Apostle

December

21 . . . . . St. Thomas the Apostle

25 . . . . . The Nativity of Our Lord Jesus Christ

26 . . . . . St. Stephen, Deacon and Martyr

27 . . . . . St. John, Apostle and Evangelist

28 . . . . . The Holy Innocents

January

1 . . . . . The Holy Name of Our Lord Jesus Christ

6 . . . . . The Epiphany

18 . . . The Confession of St. Peter the Apostle

25 . . . The Conversion of St. Paul the Apostle

February

2 . . . . . The Presentation of Our Lord Jesus Christ in the Temple

24 . . . . . St. Matthias the Apostle

March

19 . . . . . St. Joseph

25 . . . . . The Annunciation

April

25 . . . . . St. Mark the Evangelist

May

1 . . . . . St. Philip and St. James, Apostles

31 . . . . . The Visitation of the Blessed Virgin Mary

June

11 . . . . . St. Barnabas the Apostle

24 . . . . . The Nativity of St. John the Baptist

29 . . . . . St. Peter and St. Paul, Apostles

July

22 . . . . . St. Mary Magdalene

25 . . . . . St. James the Apostle

August

6 . . . . . The Transfiguration of Our Lord Jesus Christ

15 . . . . . St. Mary the Virgin, Mother of Our Lord Jesus Christ

24 . . . . . St. Bartholomew the Apostle

September

14 . . . . . Holy Cross Day

21 . . . . . St. Matthew, Apostle and Evangelist

29 . . . . . St. Michael and All Angels

October

18 . . . . . St. Luke the Evangelist

23 . . . . St. James of Jerusalem, Brother of Our Lord Jesus Christ, and Martyr

28 . . . . . St. Simon and St. Jude, Apostles

31 . . . . . Reformation Day (Lutheran)

November (before Advent)

1 . . . . . All Saints Day

This information was compiled from Roman Catholic, Lutheran, and Anglican sources. It includes Holy Days of Obligation, Red Letter Days, and Lesser Festivals. It omits Optional Feasts, Black Letter Days, and Commemorations.

TABLE 7.3. EASTERN ORTHODOX CALENDAR OF MOVABLE FEASTS

Holiday	Days Before Easter
Triodon	70
Saturday of Souls	57
Cheesefare	56
Second Saturday of Souls	50
Lent	48
St. Theodore	43
Sunday of Orthodoxy	42
Lazarus Saturday	8
Palm Sunday	7
Holy Friday	2

Easter

Holiday	Days After Easter
Saturday of Souls	39
Pentecost	49
All Saints	56

Jesus's birth is celebrated. Epiphany, in early January commemorates the manifestation of Jesus to the Gentiles (non-Jews). Lent is a season of introspection and penance in preparation for Easter. It concludes with Holy Week, a time during which events in the last week of Jesus's life are highlighted. The Easter season begins on Resurrection Sunday and lasts until Ascension Day, commemorating Jesus's ascension into heaven. The season of Pentecost begins with the celebration of the coming of the Holy Spirit. The longest season of the year, Trinity, completes the cycle.

Agnus Dei (Lamb of God): Agnus Dei is a representation of Jesus Christ as the Lamb of God, an allusion to the sacrificial lamb offered at Passover. According to the Gospel of St. John, upon seeing Jesus, John the Baptist said: "Behold the Lamb of God, which taketh away the sin of the world." (John 1:29, King James Version).

In this illustration, characteristic of depictions found in the Catacombs, the Agnus Dei stands on a mount and the four rivers of Paradise—the Gihon, the Tigris, the Euphrates, and the Pison—represent the four Evangelists and their gospels: the Gihon for St. Matthew; the Tigris for St. Mark; the Euphrates for St. Luke; and the Pison for St. John.

Christian Holidays

Weekly

Sunday

Many Christian groups observe Sunday as a day for communal worship. The practice of gathering on Sundays originated with the first generation of Christians, who were predominantly Jewish. In addition to meeting on the Jewish Sabath, they began meeting on Sunday in remembrance of Jesus's resurrection.

Many Christian ritual practices are drawn from Jewish sources. For example, the Jewish Passover Sedar forms the basis of a Christian ritual meal of bread and wine. Called by various names (such as Eucharist, Communion, Agape Lovefeast, and the Lord's Supper), the meal is often the focal point of Sunday services. It is observed in memory of Jesus's last meal with his disciples. Some sects observe this ritual on a weekly basis, others less frequently. To support and surround this ritual, Christians developed a host of other practices including singing hymns, offering prayers, reading portions of the sacred writings, and listening to teachings.

Quarterly

Ember Days
Four times a year

Ember Days are solemn observations occurring at the beginning of each of the natural seasons. Traditionally marked by three days of fasting, Ember Days are the Wednesday, Friday, and Saturday following the first Sunday in Lent, Whitsunday (Pentecost), Holyrood Day (September 14) and St. Lucy's Day (December 13). The weeks in which these days occur are called Ember Weeks, and the Friday in each of these weeks is known as Golden Friday.

The word "ember" derives from an old English word referring to the revolution of time. Some historians have suggested that the Ember Days originated with pagan purification rituals that occurred at the seasons of planting, harvest, and vintage. The notion of fasting on these days was instituted by Pope Calixtus I in the third century, but the dates of the fast varied until 1095 when they were fixed at their current times.

In 1969, the Roman Catholic Church replaced these days with days of prayer for various needs. The Anglican Communion dedicates these days to prayer for those in formal ministry and for contemplation of one's own role in lay ministry.

Annually

November

Advent

The Sunday closest to November 30 through December 24 in the Western Churches

November 15 through December 24 in the Eastern Orthodox Churches

Advent, the beginning of the Christian liturgical year, is the season of preparation for Christmas. In the West, it begins on the Sunday nearest St. Andrew's Day and ends on Christmas Eve. Because of the movable beginning date, the season can last from 22 to 28 days. The third Sunday of Advent is designated Gaudete Sunday by the Roman Catholic Church and the Anglican Communion. On this Sunday, the alter may be adorned with flowers and the purple vestments of the priests may be replaced by rose-colored garb.

The most common Advent customs in the United States have been imported from Germany. The Advent calendar and the Advent wreath are perhaps the best known. To help count the days before Christmas, parents often give children an Advent calendar that contains twenty-five flaps, one of which is opened each day between December 1 and December 24. The Advent wreath has become a part of many family devotional meditations during the season. It contains four or five candles which are lit in a special ceremony each Sunday of Advent and on Christmas day. Other Advent traditions include the German "Star of Seven," a special candle with seven braches which are lit in increasing numbers throughout the season and a European tradition of placing a branch from a cherry tree in water on the first Sunday of Advent so it will bloom on the last Sunday of Advent.

In the Eastern Orthodox tradition, the liturgical year begins on September 1, and Advent has a fixed beginning of November 15. A special name in the Eastern Orthodox Church for the Advent fast is Little Lent, because it is used as a time of meditation and preparation for Christmas like the Great Lent is for Easter.

St. Andrew's Day

November 30

St. Andrew, the brother of St. Peter, was the first apostle called by Jesus, but he is primarily known today as the patron saint of Scotland (though he was also chosen to be patron saint of Russia). According to tradition, St. Andrew went to Greece where he influenced the proconsul's wife to convert to Christianity. He was condemned to be crucified. Fastened to an X-shaped cross by cords rather than nails, he eventually died of thirst and starvation.

St. Andrew's association with Scotland began four centuries after his death when some of his relics were brought there. Some Scots continue the custom of wearing a "St. Andrew's cross" on November 30. The St. Andrew's cross consists of blue and white ribbons shaped like the letter X. The tradition for this form of a cross began no earlier than the 13th century.

St. Andrew's Day is also a major feast in Lapland and a time for weddings and meeting new people.

December

Mother Seton Day

December 1

Observed by the Sisters of Charity of St. Vincent De Paul as the anniversary of their founding by St. Elizabeth Ann Bayley Seton, a Staten Island native and the first American-born saint canonized by the Roman Catholic Church.

St. Nicholas's Day

December 6

Very little is known about St. Nicholas, except that in the fourth century he was the bishop of Myra in what is now Turkey. One of the legends surrounding him is that he saved three sisters from being forced into prostitution by their poverty-stricken father. This was accomplished by throwing three bags of gold into their room, thus providing each of them with a dowry. This may be the source of St. Nicholas's association with gift-giving.

On December 6 in the Netherlands, St. Nicholas, or *Sinter Klaas*, still rides into town on a white horse, dressed in his red bishop's robes. He is preceded by "Black Peter," a Satanic figure in Moorish costume who switches the bad children while the good are rewarded with candy and gifts. St. Nicholas is the patron saint of sailors, and churches dedicated to him are often built so they can be seen off the coast as landmarks.

The American Santa Claus, a corruption of "St. Nicholas," is a cross between the original St. Nicholas and the British "Father Christmas." The political cartoonist Thomas Nast created a Santa Claus dressed in furs and looking more like King Cole—an image that grew fatter and merrier over the years, until he became the uniquely American figure that adorns thousands of cards, decorations, and homes throughout the Christmas season. Although Americans open their gifts on Christmas or Christmas Eve, in the Netherlands, Switzerland, Germany, and some other European countries, gifts are still exchanged on St. Nicholas's Eve (December 5) or St. Nicholas's Day (December 6).

Immaculate Conception of Mary, Feast of the
December 8

This Roman Catholic observance is a holy day of obligation on which church attendance is required. It is classed as a solemnity. It honors Mary in view of her calling to be the Mother of Christ and in virtue of his merits. The day celebrates the belief that Mary was preserved from original sin beginning with the first moment of her conception and that she was filled with grace from the very beginning of her life. She was the only person, aside from Jesus, believed to be so preserved from original sin.

The present form of the Feast of the Immaculate Conception of Mary dates from December 8, 1854, when Pope Pius IX defined the dogma of the Immaculate Conception. An earlier feast of the Conception was observed in the East by the eighth century; in Ireland the feast dates to the ninth century. Centuries-old links also exist in other European countries. In 1846, Mary was proclaimed patroness of the United States under this title.

The Eastern Orthodox observance of this day falls on December 9.

St. Lucy's Day (Lucia Day; Luciadagen)
December 13

Lucia Day is a festival with Swedish origins which falls on the day of the winter solstice before the Gregorian reform. It is observed by Swedish-American communities in honor of Lucia, the Queen of Lights. Traditionally, the youngest daughter in the family dons a crown with lighted candles and wakes her parents to a breakfast of Lucia buns served in bed while the other children sing a hymn to Lucia.

Posadas
December 16–25

This feast of "The Lodgings" is celebrated in Hispanic communities to commemorate the journey of St. Mary and St. Joseph to Bethlehem. Folk plays in which children perform the roles of Mary and Joseph take place in the town. The children knock on doors and are turned away repeatedly until they finally find shelter in the parish church, at which point the community party begins. Another highlight of the celebration for the children is the breaking of the piñata which scatters gifts to those standing nearby.

St. Thomas's Day
December 21

St. Thomas the Apostle was dubbed "Doubting Thomas" because, after the Resurrection, when the other Apostles told him that they had seen Jesus, he wouldn't believe them until he had touched Jesus's wounds for himself. When the Apostles left Jerusalem to preach to the people of other nations, as Jesus had instructed them to do, tradition says Thomas traveled eastward toward India. In Kerala, the smallest state in India, the Malabar Christians (or Christians of St. Thomas) claim St. Thomas as the founder of their church. For them his feast day is a major celebration. Thomas is the patron saint of India and Pakistan.

The Roman Catholic Church celebrates St. Thomas's Day on July 3; the Eastern Orthodox Church on October 6.

Christmas Eve
December 24

The day before Christmas is a full or partial holiday in 29 countries, and in most of the United States. In central and northern Europe, Christmas Eve, rather than Christmas Day, is the occasion of the major family celebration, and some American families observe this custom as well.

A long-standing liturgical tradition of Christmas Eve has been the "Midnight Mass." Many parish churches, however, hold the service earlier than midnight so that entire families, including young children, can attend.

This day is celebrated in the Eastern Orthodox Churches as the feast day of Adam and Eve, the parents of the human race. There are some especially interesting Slavic customs on this day. One is that on Christmas Eve the house must be clean, all borrowed items returned, all tools put away, no lint or unfinished work exposed to sight, and no task started that cannot be finished before nightfall. Another is that at the beginning of the evening meal, the father of the family breaks wafers and distributes them to the family members with a kiss and a wish for a joyous feast. The parallels to the Jewish customs associated with the Passover Seder are obvious, and are a reminder of the Jewish origins of Christianity.

Another Christmas Eve custom, that of being especially kind to animals, was instituted by St. Francis of Assisi, who also introduced his Franciscan monks to the concept of a joyful Christmas carol (as distinguished from the solemn Christmas hymns), and who began the custom of setting up a "manger scene," with statues or other representations of the Holy Family, the angels, the Magi, the shepherds, and the animals. Some families place the Magi with their camels far away from the manger scene. Each day of Advent, the children in the home move the figures closer to the manger scene until, on Christmas Eve, they reach the manger. The manger itself is left empty until Christmas morning, when the statue of the Christ child is put in place to complete the story.

Although Christmas is observed by the majority of Christians, there are a few sects of Christianity that make a point of not observing Christmas or most other Christian holidays, often opting instead to harken back to the Hebrew roots of Christianity for their holidays. Among these groups are Adventist Churches, Jehovah's Witnesses, and various British Israelite communities. Since these groups usually use the Christian calendar, the dates of the holidays they celebrate are often different from the actual Jewish celebration of the same events.

Moravian Love Feast
December 24

The Moravian Love Feast began on a Christmas Eve during the eighteenth century. Count von Zinzendorf, who was visiting in Pennsylvania, noticed the parallel between the shelter they were in and the shelter where Jesus was born in Bethelehem. As a result, the location where they established their settlement was named Bethlehem.

The Love Feast is still celebrated by Moravians. It begins during the afternoon of Christmas Eve. Churches are decorated with evergreens and sweet buns and cookies are served to all the children in the congregation. The service closes with a candle ceremony using specially made beeswax candles. Other Moravian Christmas customs include a trombone choir, a musical Christmas Eve vigil, and the making of two types of special cookies which are cut into traditional shapes and used as tree decorations.

Christmas Day
December 25

Christmas is the day on which Christians celebrate the birth of Jesus Christ. The Roman Catholic Church designates it as a day of holy obligation on which members must attend services.

In the East, the birth of Jesus was originally commemorated on the Feast of Epiphany (January 6). By 354 C.E., the Christmas Feast had taken hold in the West on December 25, and since the fifth century, most Eastern Orthodox Churches have also celebrated the Nativity on December 25. Some Eastern congregations, called "Old Calendarists," still use the Julian calendar, however, and as a result they honor the birth of Christ on January 7, thirteen days later than its Gregorian calendar date. The Armenian Church continues to celebrate "Old Christmas" on January 6.

As with many traditions surrounding Christmas, the selection of December 25 as a commemoration of Jesus's birthday may be an example of the blending of Christian ideas and the pagan traditions they replaced. December 25 was the date of the Mithric observance of the "Birthday of the Invincible Sun." This also coincided with Saturnalia and the Winter solstice during the period when Mithraism was practiced in Rome. Since the day was already being kept as a holiday, Christians may have adjusted the symbolism of the day, declaring it the birthday of their "Invincible Son." According to events in the *Gospel of Matthew*, the date of Jesus's birth may actually have been much earlier in the year.

The word "Christmas" means "the mass of Christ." The term originated in the 11th century as a name for this feast. It was one of the most popular and universally celebrated holidays in Europe during the Middle Ages. During the Reformation, however, the celebration of Christmas began to decline in importance. Reformers engaged in complex doctrinal arguments in an attempt to prove the celebration of Christmas was unscriptural.

In some countries, the Protestant reforms brought about a ban of Christmas celebrations. By the time of the Restoration in 1660, however, the celebration of Christmas as a much more secular holiday was revived in these countries. In New England, Christmas remained outlawed until the mid-nineteenth century, and in Boston classes were held in the public schools on Christmas Day until 1870, with pupils who missed school that day being punished or dismissed. The mass immigration of Irish Catholics to New England brought about the reinstitution of Christmas celebrations.

In the calendar of the Roman Catholic, Lutheran, and Anglican confessions, Christmastide begins on Christmas Eve and continues until the Sunday after Epiphany. Christians generally attend services on Christmas Eve, and often on Christmas Day as well.

A vast number of non-religious customs are associated with Christmas in the United States. A traditional day of family gatherings, Christmas is often celebrated with a feast which typically includes such foods as turkey, goose or ham, yams, mince pies, and plum pudding.

The Christmas tree has become a standard symbol of the season in the United States. Each year, families decorate fresh cut or artificial evergreen trees in their homes. The tradition may have its roots in the sixteenth-century custom of decorating a "paradise tree" with apples in remembrance of Adam and Eve. Another theory about the origins of the Christmas tree date back to ancient pagan veneration of evergreen trees.

Other legends surrounding the origin of the Christmas tree abound. In one story, an eighteenth century saint, St. Boniface, convinced people to abandon the practice of sacrificing children around an oak tree. Instead, he urged that a fir tree be cut down for celebrations. Another legend involves St. Winfred, a missionary in Scandinavia during the eighth century. St. Winfred cut down an oak tree and miraculously a fir tree grew. As a result, the fir was declared holy, symbolic of endless life.

The Germans brought the idea of Christmas lights or candles to the United States (although they were not placed on trees until perhaps the eighteenth century). This practice, combined with the Irish custom of putting lights in the windows, led to the lighting of houses and Christmas trees. At first, candles were used but they were a fire hazard. In the twentieth century, electric lights came into use and proved to be much safer.

Other plants are used in traditional Christmas decorations as well. Mistletoe, for example, was used by Druids for healing and as a symbol of peace and reconciliation (hence the kiss under the mistletoe). Holly's green leaves and red berries in the midst of winter make it another evergreen symbol. Ivy is associated with midwinter carousing. Laurel wreaths, worn as a victory symbol by the Romans, are hung on front doors as a symbol of Christ's victory over the forces of darkness and death. Poinsettia was introduced from Mexico in the nineteenth century and is especially appealing because of its red and green coloring.

Another popular custom surrounding Christmas is the singing of carols. "Carols" were originally dance songs played on flutes. In current usage, carols are joyful songs of the Christmas season, typically focused on topics such as Christ's nativity, stars, or shepherds.

In many American homes, Christmas presents are wrapped and placed under the tree to be opened on Christmas Eve or Day. The Christian practice of gift giving is associated with the gifts brought to Jesus by the three Magi and may have originally taken place during Epiphany. In Europe, Epiphany is still the usual day for gift-giving. In Italy, presents are said to be brought by *La Befana*, a Fairy Queen or "Mother Witch" figure whose name appears to be a worn-down form of "epiphany."

Gifts are traditionally delivered to American children by Santa Claus. The name "Santa Claus" is derived from the Dutch name, *Sinter Klaas*, for Saint Nicholas. The popular concept of Santa is based on the immensely popular verse, "The Night Before Christmas," by Clement Moore, first published in the mid-nineteenth century.

Very sophisticated theological arguments are possible over the question of whether Santa Claus is still really a Christian saint because he has absorbed major characteristics of Hermes, Wotan, Thor, and various other pagan divinities. Another name for Santa Claus, Kris Kringle, was apparently derived from the German *Christkindel*, "Christ child," who is said to bring presents on Christmas Eve. Similar figures are Father Christmas (in England) and Knecht Rupprecht (Knight Rupert) in northern Germany.

Christmas, Twelve Days of
December 25 through January 5

The twelve days of Christmas are counted from Christmas to Epiphany. Epiphany was the traditional date for the visit of the Three Magi, and is still the traditional date for gift-giving in many parts of Europe, Mexico, and Latin America. Twelfth Night, the eve of the last day, marked the end of the Christmas season, usually by means of one last exuberant party. Because of Shakespeare's play *Twelfth Night*, the Twelfth Day of Christmas is generally observed as a festive occasion by actors. In many American homes, New Year's Day (rather than the Twelfth Day of Christmas) is considered the end of the holiday season.

St. Stephen's Day
December 26

On this day in about the year 35, St. Stephen became the first Christian martyr. The *New Testament* book of *Acts* records that Stephen was chosen by the Apostles as one of the first seven deacons of the church in Jerusalem. He was later denounced as a blasphemer by the Sanhedrin (the Jewish council in ancient Palestine) and stoned to death. St. Stephen is the patron saint of brick-layers.

In many countries, St. Stephen's Day is celebrated as an extra Christmas holiday. In England, it is known as Boxing Day. In Austria, priests bless the horses. In Poland tossing rice symbolizes blessings and recalls Stephen's stoning. And in Ireland, boys with blackened faces carrying a paper wren, go about begging and "hunting the wren." The hunting of the wren is most likely a carryover from an old belief that the robin, symbolizing the New Year, killed the wren, symbolizing the Old, at the turning of the year.

December 26, 27, and 28, otherwise known as St. Stephen's Day, St. John the Evangelist's Day, and Holy Innocents' Day, are considered examples of the three different degrees of martyrdom. St. Stephen's death is an example of the highest class of martyrdom, that is martyrdom in both will and deed. St. John the Evangelist, who showed that he was ready to die for Christ but was prevented from actually doing so, exemplifies martyrdom in will, but not in deed. And the children who lost their lives in the slaughter of the Innocents provide an example of the martyrdom in deed but not in will.

Flight into Egypt
December 26

On December 26, many congregrations within the Eastern Orthodox Church observe a remembrance of the holy family's flight to Egypt. According to the *Gospel of St. Matthew*, Herod (the reigning king in Palestine) wanted to seek out and kill Jesus. Joseph, the husband of Jesus's mother (Mary), was warned of the impending danger by an angel who instructed him to take the family to Egypt for safety and to remain there until Herod's death. (see HOLY INNOCENTS' DAY.)

St. John the Evangelist's Day
December 27

St. John the Evangelist, also called St. John the Divine, was thought to be not only the youngest of the Apostles but the longest-lived, dying peacefully of natural causes at an advanced age. Although he escaped actual martyrdom, St. John endured considerable persecution and suffering for his beliefs. He is said to have drunk poison to prove his faith (so he is the patron saint of protection against poison), been cast into a cauldron of boiling oil, and at one point banished to the lonely Greek island of Patmos, where he worked among the criminals in the mines. He remained healthy, vigorous, and miraculously unharmed throughout these trials and returned to Ephesus where it is believed he wrote the *Gospel According to John*. He is also believed to be the author of the *New Testament* book of *Revelation*, though some scholars disagree.

Holy Innocents' Day
December 28

Also called Innocents' Day or Childermas, this day is dedicated to the memory of the male children in Bethlehem who were slaughtered by King Herod in his attempt to kill the infant Jesus. The day has come to be considered unlucky; therefore, among those who observe it, few marriages or important ventures are consummated on this day.

January

Circumcision, Feast of the
January 1

This holiday is known by several different names throughout the Christian Church. Roman Catholics, who previously called it the Octave of the Birth of Our Lord, or the Circumcision of Jesus, now refer to the day as the Solemnity of Mary, the Mother of God. Episcopalians know the holiday as the Feast of the Holy Name of Our Lord Jesus Christ because it was on this day, according to Hebrew custom, that Jesus was given his name. Lutherans call it the Feast of the Circumcision and the Name of Jesus, while those in the Eastern Orthodox Church refer to the day as the Feast of the Circumcision of Our Lord. Some churches within the Eastern tradition continue to use the Julian Calendar for liturgical purposes and, therefore observe the holiday thirteen days later than the other branches of Christianity.

In the Roman Catholic Church, The Feast of the Solemnity supplants the former feast of the Maternity of Mary observed on October 11.

God's Day
January 1

God's Day is one of five major holidays celebrated by the Unification Church (the other four are True Parents' Birthday, Parent's Day, Day of All things, and Children's Day). The holiday was established in 1968 as a joyful commemoration of God's desire to bless his children. Unlike the other Unification holidays, God's Day always falls on a fixed day (January 1).

Unification holiday services are attended by invited participants. The ceremonies include ritual bowing, special prayers, a benediction, and the sharing of food. In preparation for the service, food gifts are set on elaborately prepared tables. The amount of food and its arrangement is related to a designated number having special significance. The True Parents (the Rev. Sun Myung Moon and his wife) preside over the service; in their absence pictures are hung behind empty chairs. Other holiday activities may include the giving of testimonies, sporting events, and participating in traditional Korean games.

Universal Week of Prayer
The first Sunday through the second Sunday in January

This custom, begun by the World Evangelical Alliance of London, England, in 1846, has been adopted and sponsored by the National Council of Churches. It is marked by interdenominational services in many American communities; these are held in the evenings, and move from denomination to denomination during the week.

Epiphany Eve
January 5 in Orthodox, Anglican, Protestant, and many Roman Catholic Churches

The Saturday between January 1 and January 7 in the Roman Catholic Church in the United States

Epiphany Eve is also known as Twelfth Night or Old Christmas Eve. One myth associated with this day is that of the Glastonbury Thorn. According to the Grail cycle of Arthurian legend, there is a blackthorn tree in Glastonbury, England, that grew from the staff of Joseph of Arimathea (the man who owned the burial site of Jesus). Each year on January 5, the Glastonbury Thorn is said to bloom.

This legend gave rise to an annual pilgrimage to Glastonbury and lent an illusion of credence to England's claim as the cradle of Christianity. King Henry II of England used the legends of the Grail cycle to assert the authenticity of England's apostolic succession as independent of Rome.

Epiphany
January 6 in Orthodox, Anglican, Protestant, and many Roman Catholic Churches

The Sunday between January 2 and January 8 in the Roman Catholic Church in the United States

A festival observed by Roman Catholic, Anglican, Lutheran, and Eastern Orthodox Churches on January 6 or, by Roman Catholics in the United States, on the Sunday between January 2 and 8. This feast, commemorates the manifestations of the divinity of Christ. It is one of the oldest Christian feasts, originating in the Eastern Church in the second century and antedating the Western feast of Christmas. Originally it commemorated the manifestations of Christ's divinity: in his birth, in the homage of the Magi, and at his baptism by John the Baptist. Later, the first two of these commemorations were transferred to Christmas when the Eastern Church adopted that feast between 380 and 430. The central feature of the Eastern observance now is the manifestation or declaration of Christ's divinity at his baptism and at the beginning of his public life.

The Epiphany was adopted by the Western Church during the same period in which the Eastern Church accepted Christmas. In the Roman Catholic service, commemoration is made in the Mass of the homage of the Magi, or astronomers, from the East, and of Jesus's first public "miracle" or "sign," the changing of water into wine at the wedding in Cana.

In the Orthodox Church, Epiphany is also associated with the Blessing of the Waters. On this day, in honor of the baptism of Christ, the baptismal water in each church is blessed and small bottles of holy water are distributed to the congregation. In the United States, a service is often held at the banks of a local stream or river which the priest blesses. All around the world, the tradition of diving into the river to retrieve crosses thrown there by the priest has been practiced for centuries. It is believed that those retrieving the crosses will be especially blessed.

Epiphany is also called the Feast of Kings, Twelfth Day, Twelfthtide, Three Kings' Day, or Day of the Three Wise Men.

Old Christmas Day
January 6

When the switch from the Julian to the Gregorian calendar was made in England, many people resisted the change because of emotional attachment to the previous system. One way in which people registered their dissatisfaction was to continue observing holidays according to the Julian calendar, placing them thirteen days later than their Gregorian counterparts. Old Christmas Day is one of these holdovers from the Julian system.

True Parents' Birthday
Approximately January 6

True Parents' Birthday is one of four major movable feasts observed by members of the Unification Church. (The other three are Parents Day, Day of All Things, and Children's Day). It is a day on which Unificationists celebrate the birthdays of their True Parents—the Rev. Sun Myung Moon and his wife. The date of the observance varies year to year based on the lunar cycle.

Holy Family, Feast of the
The Sunday after Epiphany

The Roman Catholic Church commemorates the Holy family of Jesus, the Virgin Mary, and St. Joseph on this day each year. As the model of the perfect family, they represent perfect holiness and virtue. The roots of the feast can be traced to the 17th century, and in 1921, Pope Benedict XV extended the Divine Office and Mass of the feast to the whole Church.

Baptism of the Lord, Feast of the
The Sunday following Epiphany

This feast was originally combined with Epiphany commemorating the manifestation of the divinity of Jesus at his baptism and the beginning of his public ministry. Although the Orthodox Church continues to observe this tradition, in 1961 the Roman Catholic Church set aside a separate holy day to recognize this event. The baptism of Jesus is observed by almost all Christian Churches on some date in January.

At first, the date for the Feast of the Baptism of the Lord was January 13, but in 1969, the date was fixed on the Sunday following Epiphany. Since many countries have moved the celebration of Epiphany from the traditional date of January 6 to the Sunday between January 2 and 8, the two holidays sometimes coincide.

In this case, the celebration of Epiphany takes precedence and the Feast of the Baptism is omitted.

Plough Monday
The first Monday after Epiphany

The origins of Plough Monday are thought to date back to the medieval custom of British farmers, or ploughmen, who would leave candles known as plough-lights burning in homage to the saints. Each year, the farmers would gather in town to collect money from the residents to buy the plough-lights. Although the adulation of the saints was quelled by the sixteenth-century Reformation, the festivities of the day continued.

By the nineteenth century, the day was filled with music, dancing, processions, and trick-or-treating by the local ploughmen. The trick-or-treat tradition included "The Bessy," a man dressed up as a buffoon in women's clothing, and "The Fool," a man wearing animal skins or a fur cap and tail, parading from door to door demanding money to fund their revelry. Another tradition was for the ploughmen to drag a beribboned plough from house to house, ploughing up the front yard of any homeowner who failed to financially sponsor the carousing.

These rural practices died out early in the twentieth century. The Church, however, continued to bless ploughs on Plough Sunday.

Death of George Fox
January 13

The death on January 13, 1691, of George Fox, founder of the Society of Friends, is observed worldwide by all Quaker Churches and Meetings.

Blessing of Animals
The Sunday nearest to January 17

The blessing of animals takes place in Catholic countries near the feast day of St. Anthony of Egypt, also known as Anthony the Abbot, the founder of monasticism and the patron saint of all four-footed beasts. (There are also some local blessings of animals on the feast of St. Francis of Assisi, whose love for animals is more well known.) Originally a day on which farm animals were blessed, the custom now extends to household pets, who are usually blessed at the church doors, but sometimes before the altar.

Birthday of Martin Luther King, Jr.
The third Monday in January

Observed as a holiday in most of the United States, usually on the third Monday in January. It is a political, rather than a religious, holiday; yet, its religious aspects cannot be ignored. King was a man of deep faith, and is regarded by millions as a modern-day saint much like Mahatma Gandhi. His accomplishments, and especially their foundation in King's Christian faith, are common topics for homilies in many Christian Churches in the United States, including Roman Catholic Churches, on the Sunday of that holiday weekend.

Conversion of St. Paul
January 25

Saul of Tarsus, a highly educated, devout Jew, was converted to Christianity on the road to Damascus not long after the death of Jesus Christ. Later he was known as Paul. Through his life, his teachings, and his writings, he became the most influential leader in the history of the Church. The Church believes he was beheaded in approximately 67 C.E. during Nero's persecution of Christians.

At one time the weather on this day was linked to predictions about the coming year. Fair weather on St. Paul's Day was said to presage a prosperous year; snow or rain an unproductive one. Clouds meant that many cattle would die, and a windy day was said to be the forerunner of war.

February

Presentation of Jesus (Purification of the Blessed Virgin Mary; Candlemas)
February 2

This day commemorates Jesus's presentation in the Temple which was in accord with the prescriptions of Mosaic Law and Mary's forty-day purification following the birth of her child. This presentation was also the occasion on which, according to the *Gospel of Luke*, Jesus was first publicly proclaimed as the Messiah by the prophets Anna and Simeon in the temple courtyard.

Also called the Feast of the Purification of the Blessed Virgin Mary, the holiday stemmed from a Jewish religious law that required a woman to abstain from sexual intercourse for forty days after the birth of a child and undergo a ritual purification bath at the end of that time.

The date set for this holiday was February 2, forty days after the celebration of Christmas which was fixed on December 25 in the fourth century. The feast was adopted earlier in the East than in the West and was celebrated by the Orthodox Church as a feast of Jesus rather than of Mary. The Roman Catholic Church, however, observed the holiday in honor of Mary until the calendar reform of 1969. At that time, the feast became known as the Presentation of Jesus in the Roman Catholic Church as well as in the Orthodox Church.

The secondary name for this holiday is Candlemas, which is derived from the day's tradition of blessing candles to be used for healing and other sacred practices during the year. The blessing of candles, which became popular in the eleventh century, emerged from Simeon's proclaimation of the baby Jesus as "a light for revelation to the Gentiles."

Arrival of Roger Williams in the New World
February 5

American Baptists celebrate the coming of Roger Williams to North America on February 5, 1631, when he arrived in the Massachusetts colony from his native Wales. Williams and four other men were later expelled from the colony for refusing to recognize the government's authority to prosecute religious offenses. The men and their families then established the colony of Rhode Island based on the principle of absolute religious liberty. The first Baptist congregation on the continent was established on Rhode Island.

Vartanantz Day
The Thursday preceding Ash Wednesday

This day marks the Armenian commemoration of the death of their patron saint, along with 1,036 other martyrs, during the war with Persia in 451 C.E.

Race Relations Sunday
The Sunday nearest February 12

This day is observed on the Sunday nearest Abraham Lincoln's birthday because of the role he played in freeing the slaves during the Civil War. Up until 1965 it was sponsored by the National Council of Churches, but since that time, sponsorship has been taken over by individual denominations. A number of Roman Catholic groups observe Race Relations Sunday as well, and some Jewish organizations observe it on the preceding Sabbath. Although it was originally conceived in 1924 as an opportunity to focus on improving relations among all races, the longstanding racial conflict between Whites and Blacks in the United States has made this the focal point in recent decades.

There are a number of other observances dealing with race relations at this same time in February. The NAACP (National Association for the Advancement of Colored People) was established on Lincoln's Birthday in 1909, and members of this organization combine the observance of Race Relations Sunday with their organization's founding and with the birthday of the black abolitionist and early human rights activist Frederick Douglass on February 7, 1817.

Carnival
Varying dates, beginning with Epiphany and ending with Shrove Tuesday.

In general, the carnival period is just before Ash Wednesday, the beginning of Lent. Its name is said to be derived from the Latin *carne vale*, "farewell to meat." Carnival is a time of revelry prior to the season of fasting during Lent.

Observed as a holiday in thirteen countries, Carnival varies in length from one to three days—usually the days just prior to Ash Wednesday. Some regions, however, begin the festivities soon after Epiphany, engaging in weekly or even daily parties, dances, and festivities, as in the German Fasching customs. The celebration in Haiti is the biggest holiday of the year. A particular characteristic of the Haitian Carnival is the construction of "lamayotes" or wooden boxes decorated with paint and tissue paper. Boys in Haiti place a surprise inside the boxes—usually a mouse, lizard, or bug. Dressed in masks and costumes during Carnival, the boys roam the streets, trying to coax people to pay a penny for a peek inside the box. Brazil's Carnival is a major holiday as well, lasting five days and drawing participants from all over the world to Rio de Janeiro. Massive parades, dance competitions, and other merrymaking fill the days with joyous activity.

The most renown Carnival in the United States is the Mardi Gras festival held each year in New Orleans. (See also MARDI GRAS).

Fasching
The three days preceding Ash Wednesday

This Shrovetide festival is celebrated in Austria and Germany (especially in Bavaria) with costumed balls and parades on Fasching Sunday, Rose Monday, and Shrove Tuesday, the three days before Ash Wednesday, and is usually preceded by several weeks of parties. It is similar to the Mardi Gras celebrations around the world.

Rose Monday
The Monday before Lent

Rose Monday, or Rosenmontag, occurs before Ash Wednesday and is celebrated in Germany and German-American communities as part of the Fasching or Carnival season. The German name Rosenmontag ("Roses Monday") takes its name from a mispronunciation of Rasen Montag ("Rushing Monday") or "live-it-up Monday"—an appropriate characterization of this day of celebration.

Birthday of Richard Allen
February 11

Richard Allen, founder of the African Methodist Episcopal Church (AME), is commemorated by members of that denomination on February 11, the date of his birth. Allen was born in 1760 and started the AME Church in 1816. He also served as its first bishop.

Mardi Gras
The Tuesday before Ash Wednesday

Mardi Gras is French for "fat Tuesday," which is the day before Ash Wednesday. More broadly, Mardi Gras refers to the pre-Lenten gala in New Orleans. The carnival is celebrated with a myriad of parades, costume balls, and pageantry beginning right after Twelfth Night, and concluding with the famous parade on Shrove Tuesday. Major Mardi Gras festivals also take place in other U.S. cities particularly in Louisiana, Florida, and Alabama.

Lent
Forty days before Easter (exclusive of Sundays) in the West

Seven weeks before Easter in the East (the dates of Easter in the Eastern and Western Churches do not coincide)

Lent is a period of introspection and penitence observed by Christians in preparation for the celebration of Easter. The tradition of prayer, fasting, and self-denial was initially practiced only for three days before Easter, beginning with Good Friday. In the late sixth century, however, the Lenten season, or Great Lent in the East, was established at forty weekdays by Gregory the Great (590–604 C.E.). The significance of the length of days may reflect the importance of the number forty in the *Bible*: Moses fasted for forty days on Mt. Sinai, the Israelites had wandered for forty years with few provisions, Elijah's fast lasted forty days, and Jesus went forty days without food after his baptism and prior to the onset of his public ministry.

Because of the tradition of abstinence during the Lenten season, festivals such as Carnival and Mardi Gras became popular as the last opportunity Christians had to engage in restricted activities and consume forbidden foods. Customarily, the three days beginning with the Sunday before Ash Wednesday are designated as the last day to eat a specific forbidden food. Sunday is Dairy or Cheesefare Sunday in the Eastern Church; Monday is Collop or Shrove Monday when the last of the meat in the house is eaten; Tuesday is Fat or Shrove Tuesday on which special, very rich pastries are baked and consumed.

Ash Wednesday
A movable observance, six and one-half weeks before Easter

In the Western Church, Ash Wednesday marks the beginning of Lent, a season of introspection and penitence for Christians as they prepare for Easter. Ash Wednesday was designated as the first day of Lent by Gregory the Great (590–604 C.E.) who extended the traditional three-day Lenten season to a penitential period of forty weekdays of fasting. The length of Lent is in memory of the forty-day fasts of Moses, Elijah, and Jesus.

Ashes, symbolic of penance, are blessed and distributed among the faithful. They are used to mark the forehead with the Sign of the Cross. The reminder, "Remember, man, that you are dust, and unto dust you shall return," or "Repent, and believe the Good News," is recited as the cross is drawn. The ashes used are typically made from burning palms used on the Palm Sunday of the previous year or from burning brushwood.

World Day of Prayer
The first Friday in Lent

World Day of Prayer was first suggested in 1887 by the Presbyterian Church in the United States. As its observance has spread to other demominations, the number of participants has grown. The United Church Women of the National Council of Churches assumes responsibility for organizing prayers and selecting a theme upon which women around the world focus as they join together in prayer. Prayer starts as the sun crosses the International Date line and travels westward around the globe.

Quadragesima
The first Sunday of Lent

This holiday is named for the Latin word "fortieth" because it falls forty days before Easter. There are three other numbered Sundays in the pre-Lent season: Quinquagesima ("fiftieth"), Sexagesima ("sixtieth"), and Septagesima ("seventieth"). Septagesima, therefore would be the first Sunday after Epiphany, and so forth until Ash Wednesday, when Lent begins. These three are no longer in general use; the days are now reckoned in relation to Epiphany.

St. Matthias's Day
February 24

St. Matthias was an apostle and martyr. The story of his selection to replace Judas Iscariot is found in the book of *Acts* (Acts 1:15–26). There is no historical record of his deeds or death, and some Christian historians believe he was martyred shortly after his election as an apostle.

March

Parents Day
Approximately March 1

Parents Day is one of four major movable feasts observed by members of the Unification Church. (The other three are True Parents' Birthday, Day of All Things, and Children's Day). It is a day on which Unificationists celebrate their origins and look forward to the restoration of humanity. The observance of Parents Day was initiated on March 1, 1960 by the Rev. Sun Myung Moon. The date on which the annual observance falls varies according to the lunar cycle.

Cheesefare Sunday (Meat Fare Sunday)
The Sunday before Lent

In the Orthodox Church, the second Sunday before the beginning of Great Lent is called Cheesefare Sunday or Meat Fare Sunday because it is traditionally the last day on which meat may be eaten until Easter. It is usually characterized by dancing, masquerading, and generally uninhibited behavior. At sunset, people attend an evening service during which the priest and congregation exchange mutual forgiveness for their sins. The last dish eaten on Cheesefare Sunday is usually eggs. Following custom, the last egg left over from the meal may be hung from a string in the middle of the ceiling. People sitting around the table hit it with their foreheads to get it swinging and then try to catch it in their mouths. Another variation of this game is to have someone hold a stick with an egg swinging from a string or thread on the end. People sit in a circle with their mouths open, trying to catch it. The saying, "With an egg I close my mouth, with an egg I shall open it again" refers to the hard-boiled Easter eggs that will mark the end of the Lenten fast.

Mothering Sunday (Carling Sunday; Laetare Sunday; Rose Sunday; Mid-Lent Sunday; Refreshment Sunday)
The fourth Sunday of Lent

During the seventeenth century, a custom of visiting the "Mother Church," the church in which a person had been baptized, developed among English Christians. On the same day, many people would visit their parents with a small gift for the mother of the family. In England, the gift was often a simnel or fruit cake with an almond paste topping. In Scotland, however, a carling (a pancake made of soaked peas fried in butter) was the traditional gift. Hence, this Sunday is also known as Carling Sunday.

There are many other names for this day. It is called Laetare Sunday because the Introit of the Roman Catholic Mass begins with the word "Rejoice" which is *laetare* in Latin; Rose Sunday because of the color of the vestments worn by the Priests and the blessing of the Golden Rose symbol; and Mid-Lent or Refreshment Sunday because of the brief intermission it offers in the Lenten season.

St. Patrick's Day
March 17

St. Patrick was born around 390 C.E. in Roman Britain. He was raised in the Christian faith but was kidnapped by pagan Irish raiders and sold into slavery when he was 16. During his time in Ireland, St. Patrick strengthened his Christian beliefs in spite of the Irish opposition, and when he gained his freedom, he returned to his home to train for the priesthood. Eventually he returned to the Irish people to share his faith with them, and he was highly successful in converting many to Christianity. The shamrock that has become a symbol of St. Patrick supposedly comes from his use of its three-part leaf to describe the Holy Trinity. St. Patrick later became the patron saint of Ireland.

The Feast of St. Patrick is celebrated by Roman Catholics, the Anglican Communion, and Lutherans on March 17. The city of Boston holds a St. Patrick's Day parade which dates back to 1737. New York City's parade is a major event for Irish-Americans and was started in 1762. Up to 125,000 participants march on the route which takes them past St. Patrick's Cathedral on Fifth Avenue in Manhattan.

Palm Sunday
The Sunday preceding Easter

Palm Sunday commemorates the day on which Jesus rode into Jerusalem greeted by a cheering crowd that had heard of his miracles. The people of Jerusalem saw Jesus as a leader who could free them from Roman rule, so they honored him by waving palm branches—a traditional symbol of victory—which they then spread in the street for him to ride over. Commemoration of this day began early in the history of the Church and was adopted by Rome in the ninth century when the blessing of palms was introduced. The use of palm leaves in a procession still marks the celebration of Palm Sunday; after the leaves are used for the procession, they are dried and burned to make the ashes for the next year's Ash Wednesday.

In the Roman Catholic Church, full liturgical observance includes the blessing of palms and a procession before the principal Mass of the day. The Passion, by Matthew, Mark, or Luke, is read during the Mass.

Annunciation of the Blessed Virgin Mary, Feast of (Annunciation of the Lord)
March 25 (or, if March 25 falls during Holy Week, April 1)

Formerly known as Annunciation of the Blessed Virgin Mary, this holiday commemorates the manifestation of the Archangel Gabriel to the Virgin Mary, announcing that she was chosen to be the mother of Jesus. Celebrated by the Roman Catholic, Anglican, Orthodox, and Lutheran Churches, the Annunciation usually falls during Lent, but moves to April 1 if March 25 falls during Holy Week. Christians in the middle ages believed the coincidence of the Annunciation and Easter on the same date was a bad omen.

The feast was instituted about 430 C.E. in the East. The Roman observance dates from the seventh century, when the celebration was said to be universal. It was traditionally called Lady Day in England and Ireland, where it was a quarter day (one of four days that were observed in conjunction with the solstices and equinoxes), and a date for paying rent.

March 25 is also observed as St. Dismas Day in honor of the "good thief" who was crucified with Jesus. It was to St. Dismas that Jesus said, "Today thou shalt be with me in Paradise." Some scholars have asserted that the date for commemorating St. Dismas may be the true date on which Jesus was crucified.

Maundy Thursday (Green Thursday; Shere [Sheer] Thursday; Paschal Thursday; Passion Thursday; Holy Thursday)
The Thursday before Easter

Maundy Thursday precedes Good Friday. It is also known as Green Thursday in Germany (from the practice of giving a green branch to penitents as a sign that their penance was completed), Shere or Sheer Thursday (meaning "free from guilt"), Paschal Thursday, Passion Thursday, or Holy Thursday. It commemorates Jesus's institution of the Eucharist during the Last Supper and has been celebrated by Christians since the middle of the fourth century.

The customary practice of ceremonial foot-washing in imitation of Jesus, who washed his disciples' feet before the Last Supper as a sign and example of humility and love, has been largely discontinued in Protestant Churches. The Roman Catholic Church and the Anglican Communion, however, still celebrate the rites of Maundy Thursday, but many modern customs may include handing out special coins known as "Maundy money" to the aged and the poor instead of foot washing. Also on this day, the sacramental Holy Oils, or chrism, are blessed.

The name "Maundy" probably comes from the Latin *mandatum*, or "commandment," referring to Christ's words after he washed the feet of his disciples: "A new commandment I give unto you, that you love one another as I have loved you." (John 13:34)

Good Friday
The Friday before Easter

The Friday before Easter is a major observance for all Christians. For Roman Catholics it is a privileged feast of Holy Week. Liturgical elements of the Roman Catholic ritual observance commemorate the Passion and Death of Christ by a reading of the Passion (according to the *Gospel of John*), special prayers for the Church and people of all ranks, the veneration of the Cross, and a communion service. The Solemn Liturgical Action takes place between noon and 3 P.M. This is the only day in the year on which the Eucharistic Liturgy is not celebrated in the Roman Rite.

In Catholic Churches and in some Anglican Churches, ceremonies on Good Friday often include the Stations of the Cross (or the Way of the Cross). The tradition of observing the stations of the cross began in the 15th century with the erection of memorial stations in devotion to the sights associated with Jesus's crucifixion. The Stations of the Cross are observed as groups of people pray and sing at each of the stations.

Although Protestant denominations allowed observance of this day to wane, a recent emphasis on the holy day has brought back its nearly universal acceptance. Between noon and three p.m., many churches hold special services called "Tre Ore" from the Italian for "Three Hours." During the service, the seven last words of Christ are meditated upon, and Jesus's procession to the cross may be acted out.

Greek Catholics observe the Ceremony of Platsenitis (the Winding Sheet) on Good Friday. During the ceremony, church elders carry a cloth depicting Jesus's dead body in a procession to a shrine where the priest places it in a symbolic tomb.

Holy Saturday (The Easter Vigil)
The Eve of Easter

In Catholic and Anglican Churches, a Saturday night service is observed the night before Easter. Rituals associated with Holy Saturday include the Easter Fire and the lighting of the Paschal Candle. The Vigil often begins with the church plunged into total darkness, the congregation listening to solemn, sometimes mournful music. Suddenly the rear doors are flung open, and the celebrant (the bishop, at a cathedral) enters, bearing the lit Paschal candle, and singing "Christ, our Light, the light of the world." The candles of those next to the aisle are lit from the Paschal candle, and the light is passed from one candle to the next, until the church is filled with light. The Paschal Candle is a special candle that symbolizes the body of Jesus. Following the lighting of the Paschal Candle, Alleluia is sung for the first time since it was discontinued on the third Sunday before Lent.

In Roman Catholic parishes, the Easter Vigil mass on Saturday night has become the liturgical focus of the Easter Triduum (which begins on Manudy Thursday). It is on this night that new adult converts are received into the Church, baptized, and receive their first communion.

In the Greek Church, the Solemn Easter vigil occurs at midnight when an outdoor procession, led by the priest, opens the church doors (symbolizing Christ's tomb) and declares Jesus's resurrection.

Easter (Resurrection Sunday)
The first Sunday after the first full moon on or following the vernal equinox (calculations differ between the Eastern and Western Churches. Easter falls between March 22 and April 25 in the West; between April 4 and May 8 in the East.)

Easter, the most important holiday of the Christian faith and one of the earliest observances of the Church, celebrates the Resurrection of Christ from the dead (Mark 16:1–7). The ceremonies, customs, and rituals surrounding this mystery extend from Easter Sunday until the feast of Pentecost fifty days later. Easter ends the forty-day fast of the Lenten season.

The week preceding Easter is called Holy Week, and it is the culmination of Lent, the period of introspection and penance. Holy Week begins with Palm Sunday, commemorating Christ's triumphal entry into Jerusalem one week before his crucifixion. Maundy Thursday is the traditional date of the Last Supper and Jesus's arrest. On Good Friday, Christians mourn the crucifixion and death of Jesus; and on Holy Saturday, his Resurrection is anticipated. Easter Sunday itself concludes the observances of Holy Week, and specifically completes the liturgical observances of the Easter Triduum, which begins on Holy or Maundy Thursday.

The determination of Easter's date has been a subject of continual debate and revision for most of the history of the Church. Since the date of Easter determines the dates of most movable feasts throughout the Christian year, variances in the celebration of these feasts occurring between different branches of the Church are often due to disagreements in the way Easter is designated.

In many churches, Easter services are held at sunrise. The Moravian Church observes a special Easter ceremony

in which worshipers gather in the pre-dawn hours to stand among grave markers and sing songs of faith and hope.

Many traditions have grown up around the celebration of Easter. One of these is the Easter egg. Long a symbol of new life, resurrection, and immortality in much of Europe, the egg was easily adopted by Christians as a part of the Easter iconography. The origin of coloring eggs is unclear because the practice is present in many traditions.

Another Easter tradition is the Easter Bunny. Each year, the Easter Bunny visits the homes of children, bringing colored eggs, candy, and gifts. The first record of a rabbit being associated with Easter dates to sixteenth-century Germany, although the custom may be even older. It is possible that both the Easter egg and Easter Bunny may have come from the ancient Teutonic goddess of spring and fertility, Eostre, from whom the English holiday derives its name. Another possibility is that the ancient Germanic goddess Ostara who was always accompanied by a hare inspired the tradition of the Easter Bunny.

Quasimodo Sunday
The Sunday after Easter

Also known as Low Sunday, Close Sunday, and Low Easterday, Quasimodo Sunday is named for the Introit of the Latin Mass recited on this day. It begins *Quasi modo geniti infantes*—"As newborn babes...." Quasimodo, the famous character in Victor Hugo's *The Hunchback of Notre Dame*, was named in honor of this day.

April

Founding of the Church of Jesus Christ of the Latter Day Saints
April 6

On April 6, 1830, Joseph Smith and the first five of his followers organized the Church of Jesus Christ of the Latter Day Saints under New York state law. This date is celebrated annually by members of the Church of Jesus Christ of the Latter Day Saints, by the Reorganized Church of Jesus Christ of the Latter Day Saints, and by the many small offshoot Mormon sects.

Salvation Army Founder's Day
April 10

Salvation Army posts and chapters worldwide commemorate the birthday of their founder, William Booth, on April 10, 1829, which is celebrated as the organization's birthday as well. The Salvation Army was established as a movement within Protestant Christianity, and it currently operates in over 80 countries. Organized in military fashion, the Salvation Army focuses on caring for people in need, working against poverty, and combating societal evils such as alcohol and drugs.

Lazarus Saturday (Saturday of Lazarus)
The Saturday before Palm Sunday

In Russia and in all Eastern Orthodox Churches, the Saturday before Palm Sunday (or Willow Sunday) is set aside to honor Lazarus, who was raised from the dead by Jesus. Pussywillows are blessed at the evening service in the Russian Orthodox Church, and the branches are distributed to the worshippers, who take them home and display them above their icons.

On this day in Greece, Romania, and the former Yugoslavia, one custom is for groups of children to carry willow branches from house to house, sing songs and act out the story of Christ raising Lazarus from the dead. In return, they receive gifts of fruit and candy. They believe the resurrection of Lazarus is symbolic of the renewal of spring, which is why the *Lazarouvane* (the celebration of St. Lazarus's Day in Bulgaria) focuses on fertility and marriage.

Birthday of Joseph Smith
April 24

The birthday of Joseph Smith, founder and first President of the Church of Jesus Christ of the Latter Day Saints, on April 24, 1805 is observed internationally by the six million members of the Mormon Church.

St. Mark's Day
April 25

Although he is often assumed to be one of the Apostles, Mark was too young at the time to be more than a follower of Jesus. He is known primarily as the author of one of the four *Gospels*, which biblical scholars believe is based on what he learned from his close friend and traveling companion, St. Peter. St. Mark the Evangelist is also associated with Venice, Italy, where the church bearing his name was built over the place where his relics were taken in 815 C.E.

In England, it was believed that if you kept a vigil on the church porch from 11 o'clock on St. Mark's Eve until one o'clock in the morning, you would see the ghosts of all those who would die in the coming year as they walked up the path and entered the church. Young girls believed that if they left a flower on the church porch during the day and returned for it at midnight, they would see a wedding procession, including an apparition of their future husband, as they walked home. Because it involved an all-night vigil,

St. Mark's Day eventually came to be associated with various forms of licentious behavior, which is why the parochial clergy in the Middle Ages decided that the day should be one of abstinence.

May

St. Philip and St. James's Day
May 1

St. Philip and St. James were both apostles and martyrs of the first century.

Day of All Things
Approximately May 1

Day of All Things is one of four major movable feasts observed by members of the Unification Church. (The other three are True Parents' Birthday, Parents Day, and Children's Day). It is a day on which Unificationists celebrate the restoration of the environment and cosmos. The observance of the Day of All Things was initiated on May 1, 1963 by the Rev. Sun Myung Moon. The date on which the annual observance falls varies according to the lunar cycle.

Family Week
Begins on the first Sunday in May

Protestantism, Roman Catholicism, and Judaism all observe Family Week. Although each faith celebrates this holiday in a manner unique to its own expression, the focal point for all three is the importance of religion in fostering strong familial bonds. Each congregation's members are encouraged to examine the manner in which they contribute to their family's religious life. Group discussions focus on social conditions having adverse effects on family life.

Family Week begins on the first Sunday in May and ends on Mother's Day. Some Christian families observe the Festival of the Christian Home.

A Family Day is also observed in many countries, particularly in some African nations. In Angola, the holiday falls on December 25; and in Nambia, December 26. South African families observe Easter Monday as Family Day.

Rogation Days
*Monday, Tuesday, and Wednesday preceding
Ascension Day*

These three days of prayer and fasting for the harvest have been observed in Europe since the Middle Ages. The tradition of praying for the crops was also intruduced to the United States and is observed by many churches on Rogation Sunday, the fifth Sunday after Easter. Since 1929, this day has also been known as Rural Life Sunday or Soil Stewardship Sunday.

In England, Rogation Days were a time when a procession of priests, prelates, and select parishioners walked the bounds of the parish. From these days, a tradition particular to rural England developed. The priests would drive young boys around the bounds of the parish by beating them with willow switches. The practice, known as "beating the bounds," served to both teach the boys the limits of the parish as well as purify their souls.

Ascension Day
Forty days after Easter

This holiday commemorates the ascension of Jesus back to heaven after his resurrection from the dead. It is celebrated forty days after Easter Sunday because the Biblical account in the *Acts of the Apostles* indicates that Jesus spent forty days with his disciples after his resurrection. During the forty days, he instructed them on how to carry out his teachings. Then, on the fortieth day, he took them to the Mount of Olives near Jerusalem and ascended to heaven as they watched.

According to oral tradition, the observance of this day is one of the oldest celebrations of the Christian Church, dating to 68 C.E. The first specific documentary evidence of the feast dates from early in the fifth century. Many churches traditionally observe the following Sunday as Ascension Sunday and structure their worship services around the Biblical account of Jesus's ascension.

Pentecost (Whitsunday)
Fifty days after the second day of Passover

Pentecost is a moveable celebration held on the seventh Sunday after Easter. According to St. Luke's account in the *Acts of the Apostles*, it was the day on which the Holy Spirit descended on the Apostles in a form likened to tongues of fire and accompanied by a sound like a rushing wind. According to Christian teaching, the Holy Spirit empowered St. Peter and the other believers with him to witness to Jews in Jerusalem. Three thousand conversions were reported in one day.

The name Pentecost comes from the word for fifty used by Greek-speaking Jews. It was the name of the celebration held fifty days after Passover. In England, Pentecost was called Whitsunday (Whit—"white"—Sunday) or Whitsuntide. As a traditional day for the baptism of new Christians, the name possibly derives from a reference to the white robes worn by converts. In some Anglican and Protestant Churches Pentecost remains a traditional day for baptisms and confirmations. In Roman Catholic Churches, Pentecost is marked by the wearing of red vestments.

Trinity Sunday
The first Sunday after Pentecost in the Western Church, the Monday after Pentecost in the Orthodox tradition (called Trinity Day)

Unlike other Christian observances, Trinity Sunday is not associated with any specific saint or historical event. Instead, it honors the Christian belief in one God with a triune nature. According to Christianity, there are three manifestations of God— Father, Son, and Holy Spirit. In Roman Catholic tradition, a votive Mass of the Most Holy Trinity dates from the seventh century, an Office was composed in the 10th century, and in 1334, Pope John XXII extended the feast to the entire Church.

Aldersgate Experience
The Sunday nearest to May 24

On May 24, 1783, John Wesley experienced a conversion while reading Martin Luther's preface to St. Paul's *Epistle to the Romans*. The incident occurred while he was with some friends in a house on Aldersgate Street in London. This event is commemorated by the Methodist Church on the Sunday nearest to May 24.

Corpus Christi (Feast of the Most Holy Body of Christ)
The Thursday after Trinity Sunday

In the Roman Catholic Church, this is a movable observance held in the United States on the Sunday following Trinity Sunday; elsewhere it is celebrated on the Thursday after Trinity Sunday. This holy day, celebrated in honor of the Eucharist, has been observed since the thirteenth century C.E. Originating at Liege, France in 1246, Corpus Christi festivities spread throughout the Church in the West under the guidance of Pope Urban IV in 1264. The Office for the feast was composed by St. Thomas Aquinas.

According to tradition, the celebration began after a young nun saw a vision of the moon with a part of it broken away. The interpretation of the vision maintained that the moon stood for the Church and that the break stood for the Eucharist, which was not being held in proper honor. An early Corpus Christi tradition involved carrying consecrated bread in a procession through the town. This later evolved into elaborate parades which are still conducted in many parts of Europe. Although the exuberant public veneration of the Eucharist has waned in the United States since the Second Vatican Council, many other nations still observe Corpus Christi day with public processions and liturgies in honor of the "Blessed Sacrament."

Sacred Heart of Jesus, Feast of the
The Friday after Corpus Christi

The Feast of the Sacred Heart of Jesus is recognized by the Roman Catholic Church as a solemnity "of the greatest importance." On this day, homage is paid to Christ's all encompassing love for humanity. Devotion to the Sacred Heart was introduced into the liturgy in the 17th century through the efforts of St. John Eudes, who composed an Office and Mass for the feast. It was furthered as the result of the revelations of St. Margaret Mary Alacoque after 1675 and by the work of Claude de la Colombiere, S.J. In 1765, Pope Clement XIII approved a Mass and Office for the feast, and in 1856 Pope Pius IX extended the observance to the entire Roman Catholic Church.

Feast of the Visitation (Visitation of the Virgin Mary to Elizabeth)
May 31 in the Roman Catholic and Protestant Churches

July 2 in the Anglican Church

This feast commemorates Mary's visit to her cousin Elizabeth, the mother of John the Baptist. After the Annunciation, Mary spent several months with her cousin Elizabeth in the mountains of Judea. Elizabeth reported that the baby in her womb (who would become John the Baptist, the precursor of Christ) literally leapt with joy when Mary approached. According to the doctrine of the Roman Catholic Church, this was the moment at which John the Baptist was cleansed from original sin and filled with heavenly grace.

The Feast of the Visitation is a feast of the Incarnation and is notable for its recall of the Magnificat, a canticle which acknowledges the unique gifts of God to Mary because of her role in the redemptive work of Christ. The canticle is recited at Vespers in the Liturgy of the Hours.

June

Birthday of Brigham Young
June 1

Brigham Young, second President of the Church of Jesus Christ of the Latter Day Saints and the leader who brought the beleaguered Mormons to refuge in Utah, was born on June 1, 1801. The date is honored by Mormon Churches worldwide.

Immaculate Heart of Mary, Feast of the
The Saturday following the second Sunday after Pentecost

This Roman Catholic memorial is observed as a day to honor Mary and obtain her intercession for "peace among the nations, freedom for the Church, the conversion of sinners, the love of purity, and the practice of virtue," according to Pope Pius XII's 1944 decree. Two years earlier, he consecrated the entire human race to Mary under this title. Devotion to Mary under the title of her Most Pure Heart originated during the Middle Ages, but was given great impetus in the 17th century by the preaching of St. John Eudes. A feast, celebrated in various places and on different dates, was authorized in 1799.

Children's Day
The second Sunday in June

Children's Day began as an observance in June 1856 at the Universalist Church of the Redeemer in Chelsea, Massachusetts. In 1868, it was formally adopted as the second Sunday in June by the Methodist Church. Currently it is still recognized on that date according to the calendar of the National Council of Churches.

In some Protestant Churches in the United States, Children's Day is marked as one in which children participate in special events during the service. Many other countries recognize a day on which children are allowed to participate in services, in government, and in various cultural and recreational activities. Children's Day is celebrated in Iceland (on April 24), Indonesia (June 17), Korea (May 5), Nigeria (May 27), and Turkey (April 23).

St. Barnabas's Day (Barnaby Day; Long Barnaby; Barnaby Bright)
June 11

St. Barnabas was a Christian in the first century. According to the Biblical account in St. Luke's *Acts of the Apostles*, he was one of the first to encourage and promote St. Paul.

Before England adopted the Gregorian calendar in 1752, St. Barnabas's Day (June 11) was the day of the Summer Solstice, the longest day of the year. This association gave rise to the old English jingle, "Barnaby bright, Barnaby bright, the longest day and the shortest night." It was a customary day for priests and clerks in the Church of England to wear garlands of roses and to decorate the church with them. Other names for this day were Barnaby Day, Long Barnaby, and Barnaby Bright.

Magna Carta Day
June 15

Although Magna Carta Day is not cited in any official church calendar, it is nonetheless a day of great significance for the notion of religious freedom. The day commemorates the signing of England's "great charter" on June 15, 1215 by King John. The document ensured certain rights to his noble subjects including the freedom of the Church of England from royal domination.

New Church Day
June 19

The anniversary of the founding of the Church of the New Jerusalem (New Church) on June 19, 1770, is commemorated by the disciples of the Swedish scientist, philosopher, and theologian, Emanuel Swedenborg.

Swedenborg taught that in 1757, a great judgment was passed in the spiritual realm, and the result was that the evil spirits were separated from the good and a new heaven was established. Jesus then called his apostles together and instructed them to preach the new doctrines to the new heaven, just as he had instructed them in the Great Commission seventeen centuries earlier. These cataclysmic events took place on June 19–20, 1757. In 1770, Swedenborg's disciples established the Church of the New Jerusalem.

In 1817, the General Convention of the New Jerusalem in the U.S.A. was founded in Philadelphia, Pennsylvania. American members of the New Church join with members worldwide in celebration of New Church Day.

Footwashing Day
On a Sunday in early summer

The practice of footwashing has its origins in the account of Jesus's Last Supper. According to the *Gospel of John*, Jesus washed his disciples' feet before their last meal together. Through his actions, Jesus entreated his disciples to show a similar love and humility to one another. Although originally performed during Maundy Thursday services, many American Protestant denominations practice the footwashing ceremony more frequently.

In some modern churches, footwashing has become a significant feature of the Eucharist. Congregations in the mountainous regions of Kentucky are particularly noted for this practice. Footwashing Day takes place only once a year, but is preceded by several weeks of preparation. When the day arrives, an elaborate ritual is practiced in which men and women are segregated and wash the feet of the members of the same sex. Children enjoy refreshments during the ceremony and, at its conclusion, all are invited to partake of a traditional meal.

Nativity of St. John the Baptist
June 24

It is unusual for a saint's day to commemorate his or her birth rather than death, but John the Baptist (who died in approximately 29 C.E.) and the Virgin Mary are two exceptions. Roman Catholics, Eastern Orthodox Christians, Anglicans, and Lutherans honor St. John on the anniversary of his birth; the Roman Catholic and Orthodox Churches commemorate his death as well, on August 29.

St. John the Baptist was Jesus's cousin, born to Zachariah and Elizabeth (a kinswoman of the Virgin Mary) in their old age. John was the one chosen to prepare the way for the Messiah. Roman Catholics believe that John was freed from original sin in his mother's womb when she was visited by Mary.

Until beginning his public ministry, John lived as a hermit in the wilderness where his diet consisted of honey and locusts. He preached repentance of sins and baptized many people, including Jesus. Because he denounced King Herod and Herod's second wife, Herodias, Herodias vowed revenge. Under her influence, Herodias's daughter, Salome, demanded the Baptist's head on a platter. The details of John's execution are recorded by the gospel writers.

Many St. John's Day customs date from pre-Christian times, when June 24 was celebrated as Midsummer Day. Celebrations in some areas still bear the hallmarks of the old pagan Summer Solstice rites, such as bonfires, dancing, and decorating with flowers. For the French in Canada, the Feast of the Nativity of St. John the Baptist is one of the biggest celebrations of the year, especially in Quebec. The San Juan Fiesta in New York City takes place on the Sunday nearest June 24 and is the year's most important festival for Hispanic-Americans.

St. John's Day (el Dia de San Juan) is a major holiday throughout Mexico. As the patron saint of waters, St. John is honored by decorating fountains and wells and by bathing in local streams and rivers. The bathing begins at midnight—often to the accompaniment of village bands—and it is customary for spectators to throw flowers among the bathers. In Mexico City and other urban centers, the celebration takes place in fashionable bath-houses rather than rivers, where there are diving and swimming contests as well. Street vendors sell small mules made out of cornhusks, decorated with flowers and filled with sugar cane and candy.

Wading or bathing in the water on St. John's Day is a tradition that many see as symbolic of John the Baptist's role in baptizing Jesus. In Puerto Rico, for example, San

Juan Day is observed by gathering at the beaches to eat, dance, drink, build bonfires, and bathe in the Caribbean. Over the years, the religious significance of the event has been overshadowed, and today bathing in the water is believed to bring good luck in the coming year.

Martyrdom of Joseph and Hyrum Smith
June 27

Joseph Smith, founder of the Church of Jesus Christ of the Latter Day Saints, and his brother Hyrum were lynched by a mob in Carthage, Illinois on June 27, 1845. The date is commemorated by the Church of Jesus Christ of the Latter Day Saints and the smaller Mormon Churches.

Blessing of the Shrimp Fleet
The last weekend in June

This traditional two-day gala in Bayou La Batre, Alabama celebrates the tiny town's major industries. Bayou La Batre is one of the top seafood producers in the nation, bringing in about $300 million annually. Boat building is the other major industry, producing about $400 million each year.

On the day of this celebration, the two industries join in the blessing of the fleet by the priest of St. Margaret's Roman Catholic Church. Fifty to one hundred festively trimmed boats parade down the bayou (which serves as the main street of the town). The ceremony originated in the late 1940s and attracts up to 25,000 people annually. Also included in the weekend's events are contests in oyster shucking, crab picking, gumbo making, and shrimp heading.

St. Peter's Day
June 29

St. Peter was one of Jesus's original twelve apostles. According to tradition, St. Peter and St. Paul were both martyred on June 29. For this reason their names have been linked in various observances around the world and the Eastern Orthodox Church celebrates the day as a combined day for Sts. Peter and Paul.

As the patron saint of fishermen, St. Peter's Day is celebrated in fishing villages and ports all over the world. Perhaps the largest American celebration takes place in Gloucester, Massachusetts, where St. Peter's Fiesta has been celebrated by the Italian-American fishing community for several decades. The life-sized statue of St. Peter donated by an Italian-American fishing captain in 1926 provides a focal point for the celebration, and the Sunday morning procession carrying this statue from St. Peter's Club to an outdoor altar erected on the waterfront is still the highlight of the two-day festival. The Mass that follows is usually celebrated by

the Roman Catholic archbishop of Boston, who also officiates at the Blessing of the Fleet that afternoon. Other festival events include fishing boat races, concerts, fireworks, and a "greasy-pole" contest in which competitors try to retrieve a red flag from the end of a well-greased spar suspended over the water.

In Malta, the feast of St. Peter and St. Paul is a harvest festival known as Mnarja. In Peru, the Dia de San Pedro y San Pablo is celebrated in fishing villages. Processions of decorated boats carrying an image of the saint are common, and sometimes a special floating altar is set up, with decorations made out of shells and seaweed. In Valparaiso, Chile, this sort of procession has been going on since 1682. In Trinidad fishermen first go out to catch fish to give to the poor and as they return, the Anglican priest blesses them and the sea. Then the partying begins. After the priest leaves, bongo and bele dances are done to honor St. Peter.

Sint Pieter (as he is called in Belgium) is honored each year on June 29 by Belgian fishermen, mariners, and others who are exposed to the dangers of the sea because he walked across the water to reach Jesus. The Blessing of the Sea ceremony is performed at Ostend, Blankenberge, and other seaport towns on the Sunday following the saint's day. After a special service is held, a procession of clergy, church dignitaries, and seamen carry votive offerings, flowers, and garlands down to the shore. Then the priests board the boats and go out to bless the waves.

July

Most Precious Blood, Feast of the
July 1

In the Roman Catholic Church, July is the month of the Most Precious Blood. During the month, many Christians venerate the blood of Jesus, which, they believe, possesses life-giving power. In 1849, Pope Pius IX established the festival on the first Sunday in July. Later, Pope Pius X moved the feast to the first day of July.

Birthday of Mary Baker Eddy
July 16

The birthday of Mary Baker Eddy (1821–1910), founder of Christian Science, is observed by Christian Science Churches worldwide.

Hill Cumorah Pageant
During July

The Hill Cumorah Pageant revolves around a Mormon play performed in July at Cumorah Hill, near Palmyra,

New York. The work recounts Joseph Smith's finding of the book engraved on golden plates that Mormons believe he translated as the *Book of Mormon*. The Pageant takes place over a nine-day period (excluding Sunday and Monday) beginning on the third weekend in July. The event involves as many as five hundred participants and attracts thousands of spectators. It is billed as the largest outdoor pageant in the United States.

Pioneer Day
July 24

On July 24, 1847, the first Mormon settlers arrived in the valley of the Great Salt Lake. Under the leadership of Brigham Young, they had traveled from Nauvoo, Illinois after the murder of Joseph Smith, the founder of their faith. The site of the original settlement is now Salt Lake City, Utah. Thousands of Mormon pioneers followed the original group, settling not only in Utah, but also in Idaho, Arizona, Nevada, Wyoming, and California. The anniversary of the founding of the Salt Lake City settlement is observed by Mormon Churches worldwide.

St. James's Day
July 25

The Apostle James the Great was martyred by Herod in 44 C.E. Also known as Santiago, he is the patron saint of Spain. His feast day is celebrated in the Western Church on July 25, the anniversary of the day on which, according to Spanish tradition, his body was miraculously discovered in Compostela, Spain, after being buried there for 800 years. A church was built on the site, which later became the town of Santiago de Compostela, once a popular place of pilgrimage. St. James's Day is still celebrated in Compostela with a week-long festival that features a mock-burning of the 12th-century cathedral and an elaborate fireworks display.

St. James's Day is celebrated by the Eastern Church on April 30.

Reek Sunday
The last Sunday in July

Reek Sunday is observed as a day on which Irish pilgrims ascend Croagh Padraig, the steep mountain in County Mayo named for Ireland's patron saint (St. Patrick).

Volunteers of America Founder's Day
July 28

Members of the Volunteers of America, an offshoot of the Salvation Army, honor the birth of their founder Ballington Booth who was born on July 28, 1859.

August

Feast of the Transfiguration (Transfiguration of Jesus)
August 6

This holiday commemorates the revelation of Jesus's divinity to Peter, James, and John on Mt. Tabor. According to the Biblical account recorded in three of the *Gospels*, Elijah and Moses appeared to Jesus and the three apostles during a visit to the mountain. The name "transfiguration" refers to changes in Jesus's physical appearance during the event. The story in *Matthew*, *Mark*, and *Luke* reports that Jesus's face shone, and his clothing became bright white. The feast, which is very old, was extended throughout the Church in 1457 by Pope Callistus III.

Assumption of the Blessed Virgin
August 15

Assumption Day, called the Feast of the Most Holy Mother of God in the Orthodox Church, is observed in honor of the belief that the body of the Virgin Mary, the mother of Jesus, did not suffer decay, but was translated into heaven upon her death. The belief was not official dogma of the Catholic Church until 1950 when Pope Pius XII endorsed it. It is, however, one of the oldest solemnities observed by the Church, dating back to at least the seventh century, when its celebration was already established in Jerusalem and Rome.

It is possible that Assumption Day is a Christianization of an earlier pagan harvest festival and, in some places, it is still called the Feast of Our Lady of the Harvest.

Marymass Fair
The third or fourth Monday in August

Marymass Fair is held in Irvine, Ayrshire, Scotland. It takes its name from the Feast of the Assumption on August 15, which coincides with Old Lammas Day and was celebrated locally by dances around bonfires. The fair, which dates back to at least the twelfth century, is famous for its horse races, believed to be the oldest in Europe.

Queenship of Mary
August 22

This Roman Catholic observance is classed as a memorial. It commemorates Mary as Queen of heaven, angels, and mankind. Universal observance of the memorial was ordered by Pope Pius XII in the encyclical *Ad*

Ceali Reginam, October 11, 1954. The original date of the memorial was May 31.

St. Bartholomew's Day
August 24

Saint Bartholomew was an apostle and martyr of the first century. In some places in Germany, the day's activities include pastoral activities, such as a shepherds' dance and a water-carriers' race in which contestants must balance a pail of water on their heads and pour it into a tub at the finish line.

Martyrdom of St. John the Baptist (Feast of the Beheading)
August 29

The Martyrdom of St. John the Baptist—also known as the Feast of the Beheading in the Eastern Ortho-dox Church—has been celebrated by Christians since the fourth century. The observance started at Sebaste (Samaria), where the Baptist was believed to have been buried.

St. John the Baptist was beheaded by King Herod af-ter denouncing Herod's marriage to Herodias, the wife of Herod's half-brother Philip (Luke 3:19,20), an illegal union according to Jewish law. Herodias's daughter by a former marriage, by legend called Salome, pleased Herod so much with her dancing that he swore to give her whatever she wanted. At her mother's urg-ing she asked for the head of John the Baptist on a platter (Matthew 14:3–12).

According to tradition, Herod, grief-stricken over hav-ing let himself be maneuvered into killing a good and innocent man, later had the head concealed within the palace walls to spare it any further indignities. The head remained there until after the discovery of the holy cross by St. Helena, an event which drew many pilgrims to Jerusalem. Two pilgrims found the head after St. John appeared to them in a vision.

African Methodist Quarterly Meeting Day
The last Saturday in August

This large annual gathering in Wilmington, Delaware, celebrates the establishment of the African Union Methodist Protestant Church (A.U.M.P.) in 1813, pop-ularly referred to as the "Mother Church" for African-Americans. The A.U.M.P. Church had its origins in the congregation of Wilmington's Asbury Methodist Church which had denied its black members the right to fully participate in services. Under the leadership of Peter Spencer, 41 members of Asbury's congregation broke away from the Church in 1805, establishing Wilmington's first black congregation.

In the early days of the Big August Quarterly, par-ticipants from Delaware and surrounding states, many of whom were slaves, gathered together. They would hear and deliver revival messages, sing gospel hymns, and reunite with friends and family. Although the size of the gathering has diminished since its beginnings, the Big August Quarterly has recently enjoyed a resur-gence of interest, and now offers an opportunity for participants to enjoy traditional cuisine and musical en-tertainment while mingling with fellow church members.

September

San Estevan, Feast of
September 2

This festival is the annual harvest dance and feast day in the Native American pueblo of Acoma, New Mex-ico. Acoma was established in the twelfth century and is the oldest continuously inhabited community in America. Home to roughly fifty year-round residents, Acoma Indians from nearby villages return annually for the feast day and celebration.

A Mass and procession begin the festivities as a stat-ue of San Estevan, the pueblo's patron saint, is taken from the church to the plaza. There, a variety of rit-ual dances are performed throughout the day.

Sante Fe Fiesta
The weekend after Labor Day

This festival combines religious and secular traditions in what is said to be the oldest such event in the United States. Dating to 1712, it recalls the early his-tory of Sante Fe, New Mexico.

The Spanish conquistadores were ousted from Santa Fe in 1680 by a Pueblo Indian revolt. The Spanish, led by Don Diego de Vargas, peacefully regained control in 1693. De Vargas had promised to venerate La Con-quistadora, the small statue of the Virgin Mary now enshrined in St. Francis Cathedral, if she granted them success. In fulfillment of that promise, de Vargas held the first procession in her honor in 1712.

The celebration begins with an early morning Mass on the Friday following Labor Day. After this, a grand procession takes place with figures representing Vargas and the fiesta queen, la reina, on horseback, leading the Caballeros de Vargas to the Plaza. On Friday night, a forty-four-foot fabric and wood effigy of Zozobra or Old Man Gloom is burned. Thousands of spectators shout "Burn him!" as the effigy pleads for mercy. Fire-works announce the end of Gloom; the crowds then proceed to the Plaza to embark on two days of danc-ing, street fairs, a grand ball, and a parade with floats satirizing local politicians. The fiesta ends on the following Sunday with an evening Mass of thanksgiving and a candlelight procession to the Cross of Martyrs overlooking Santa Fe.

Nativity of the Blessed Virgin Mary, Feast of the
September 8

The birth of the Virgin Mary is one of only three births celebrated by the Christian Church. (The births of John the Baptist on June 24 and Jesus on December 25 are the other two.)

The date of September 8 became widely accepted for this celebration during the seventh century although there seems to be no concrete evidence that this is the actual date of Mary's birth.

Coptic New Year
September 11

Members of the Coptic Orthodox Church, the native Christian Church in Egypt, celebrate the New Year on September 11 because it is the day on which the Dog Star, Sirius, reappears in the Egyptian sky, signalling the flooding of the Nile and the beginning of a new planting season. Church martyrs are also commemorated. Red vestments and altar clothes are used, and the red date serves as a food of special significance. Its red color signifies the martyrs' blood, the white meat symbolizes their purity of heart, and the hard pit represents their steadfast faith. The Coptic New Year is also celebrated outside of Egypt by people of Egyptian descent.

Triumph of the Holy Cross
September 14

This Christian feast commemorates significant events relating to the cross on which Christ was crucified. These events include: the 326 C.E. discovery of fragments of the cross by St. Helena, mother of Constantine; the consecration of the basilica which was constructed in honor of the cross nearly 10 years after St. Helena's discovery; and the recovery around 628 C.E. of a major portion of the cross that had been taken from Jerusalem by the Persians. The feast originated in Jerusalem and spread through the East before being adopted in the West. General adoption followed the building at Rome of the Basilica of the Holy Cross in Jerusalem, so called because it enshrined what was believed to be a major portion of the true cross.

Mary as Our Lady of Sorrows
September 15

This Roman Catholic memorial recalls the sorrows experienced by Mary in her association with Christ: the

prophecy of Simeon, the flight into Egypt (Matthew 2:13–21), and the three-day separation from Jesus (Luke 2:41–50). Also remembered are four incidents connected with the Passion: her meeting with Christ on the way to Calvary, the crucifixion, the removal of Christ's body from the cross, and his burial (Matthew 27:31–61; Mark 15:20–47; Luke 23:26–56; John 19:17–42). A Mass and Divine Office of the feast were celebrated by the Servites, especially in the 17th century. In 1817 Pope Pius VII extended the observance to the whole Church.

St. Matthew's Day
September 21

St. Matthew was an apostle, evangelist, and martyr of the first century. He is traditionally recognized as the author of the *Gospel* that bears his name.

Michaelmas (St. Michael and All Angels)
September 29

This Christian feast of St. Michael the Archangel is a traditional English quarter day, whose customs included bringing the herds down from the summer high pastures, eating roast goose, going back to school, and lighting bonfires. Many of these appear to be customs also associated with the fall equinox.

The Feast of St. Michael the Archangel on September 29 is observed by the Roman Catholic, Anglican, and Lutheran Churches, on the date when the first church in Italy was dedicated to him. It is a quarter day in England, and has always been associated with the opening of the Fall term at public schools and universities.

Also honored on this day are the other archangels, Raphael and Gabriel. Originally each archangel was commemorated on a separate day, but with the Roman Catholic calendar reform of 1969, the days were combined and moved to Michaelmas.

October

Children's Day
Approximately October 1

Children's Day is one of four major movable feasts observed by members of the Unification Church. (The other three are True Parents' Birthday, Parents Day, and Day of All Things.) It is a day on which Unificationists remember that all people have the potential to become members of the True Family which is headed by the True Father, the Rev. Sun Myung Moon. The observance was established on October 1, 1960 by Moon. The date on which it falls every year varies according to the lunar cycle.

Rally Day
During September or October

In liturgical Protestant Churches, Rally Day marks the beginning of the church calendar year. It typically occurs during the end of September or beginning of October. Participation in the day varies considerably among Protestant Churches. Some customs associated with it are: the giving of *Bibles* to children; promoting children from one Sunday school grade to the next; welcoming new members into the Church; and, the formal presentation of Church goals for the coming year.

Guardian Angels Day
October 2

Guardian Angels Day is a feast, classed as a memorial, observed by Roman Catholic Churches. It commemorates the angels who assist people in doing good and protecting them from spiritual and physical dangers. A feast in their honor celebrated in sixteenth-century Spain was extended to the whole Church by Pope Paul V in 1608. In 1670, Pope Clement X set October 2 as the date of observance. Earlier, guardian angels were honored liturgically in conjunction with the feast of St. Michael.

Mary as Our Lady of the Rosary
October 7

The Virgin Mary is commemorated on this Roman Catholic memorial day by recalling the mysteries of the Rosary which recapitulate the events of her life and the life of Christ. The feast was instituted to remember a Christian victory over invading Islamic forces at Lepanto on October 7, 1571, and was extended throughout the Church by Pope Clement XI in 1716.

St. Luke's Day
October 18

Saint Luke, a companion of St. Paul, is recognized as the author of two canonical works: one of the four *Gospels* and the book of the *Acts of the Apostles*.

St. Simon and St. Jude's Day
October 28

Because St. Jude is believed to have been martyred with St. Simon in Persia, where they had gone to preach Christianity, their feast is celebrated jointly on October 28, thought to be the date on which their relics were moved to old St. Peter's basilica. Aside from the fact that they were both apostles, little is known about Simon and Jude. The *New Testament* refers to "Judas, not Iscariot" to distinguish Jude the Apostle from the Judas who betrayed Jesus.

As the patron saint of hopeless causes, St. Jude's Day is observed particularly by students, who often ask for his help on exams.

Christ the King, Feast of
The last Sunday in October in the Roman Catholic Church

The last Sunday in August in the Protestant Church

Christians celebrate the kingship of Jesus over the earthly authority on this holiday. Pope Pius XI originally instituted the feast December 11, 1925. In 1937, the National Council of Churches designated the last Sunday in August for its celebration.

Reformation Day
October 31

On October 31, 1517, Martin Luther posted his ninety-five theses on the Wittenberg church door. His proposals were intended to spark discussion within the Roman Catholic Church about what Luther saw as doctrinal error; instead, he started one of the most influential and far-reaching movements in the history of Christianity—the Reformation. Luther's ideas swept across Europe, inspiring many to break from Rome and begin their own churches. The Protestant Churches that were a result of this event observe October 31 as the anniversary of their beginning. The Lutheran Church celebrates the Sunday prior to Reformation Day as Reformation Sunday.

November

All Saints' Day
November 1

All Saints' Day is observed by Roman Catholic, Anglican, and many Protestant Churches to honor all of the Christian saints, especially those who do not have their own feast days.

The celebration can be traced to the fourth century when groups of martyrs and other saints were honored on a common day, the first Sunday after Pentecost. Around 610 C.E., the Pantheon, a pagan temple at Rome, was consecrated as a Christian church for the honor of Our Lady and the martyrs. This event was celebrated annually on May 1. In 835 C.E., Pope Gregory IV combined the two celebrations and, in accordance with Pope Gregory I's policy of toleration for pagan tradition, moved the feast to November 1 to coincide with the pagan Festival of the Dead (see SAMHAIN).

Observed as a religious and national holiday in 36 nations of the world, All Saints' Day is a Holy Day of Obligation for Roman Catholics in the United States.

All Souls' Day
November 2 in the West

The three Saturdays prior to Lent and the day before Pentecost in the East

From the earliest days of Christianity, the faithful prayed for the dead. By the sixth century, Benedictine monasteries were holding a service on Pentecost to commemorate deceased members of the order. In 998 C.E., St. Odilo of Cluny moved the date of this memorial to November 2, which became the standard throughout the Christian Church. Although some Protestant Churches observe All Souls' Day, it is essentially a Roman Catholic, Anglican, and Orthodox holy day.

On All Souls' Day, many Christians honor their ancestors by visiting the graves of relatives. The evening of November 1 is often called All Souls' Eve and is observed by the decoration of family graves and lighting of candles as a remembrance of the dead.

Saints, Doctors, Missionaries, and Martyrs Day
November 8

Saints, Doctors, Missionaries, and Martyrs Day is observed by the Anglican Churches as a counterpart to the Roman Catholic feasts of All Saints and All Souls. The date was established in 1928 commemorate all unnamed saints.

Dedication of St. John Lateran
November 9

This Roman Catholic observance is classed as a feast and it commemorates the first public consecration of a church (the Basilica of the Most Holy Savior) by Pope Sylvester on November 9, 324 C.E. The church and the Lateran Palace were the gift of the Roman Emperor Constantine. Since the 12th century it has been known as St. John Lateran, in honor of John the Baptist, after whom the adjoining baptistery was named. The church was rebuilt by Pope Innocent X (1644–55), reconsecrated by Pope Benedict XIII in 1726, and enlarged by Pope Leo XIII (1878–1903). This basilica is highly regarded throughout the Roman Rite.

Birthday of Martin Luther
November 10

Martin Luther's birthday, November 10, 1483, is commemorated by Lutheran Churches and German Protestants.

Presentation of the Blessed Virgin Mary, Feast of the
November 21

Although no one is certain of the origin of this feast, the Greek Orthodox Church officially began celebrating the Presentation of the Blessed Virgin in the eighth century; the Roman Catholic Church instituted the observation later in the Middle Ages. The feast commemorates events related in the apocryphal *Book of James* of the presentation of the three-year old Mary in the Temple consecrating her to God's service.

Thanksgiving
The fourth Thursday in November

Thanksgiving Day in America traditionally commemorates the survival of the Pilgrims at the Plymouth, Massachusetts settlement. After their journey from England to North America, the settlers endured a terrible winter and an epidemic that threatened the existence of the colony. The Pilgrims were saved by native Indians who taught them how to plant crops in their new home; so, when the first bountiful harvest came in, the Pilgrims and Indians joined together to share in the goodness of the land.

Although many days of thanks have been declared and observed, the last Thursday in November was set aside by Abraham Lincoln as a day to remember the goodness of God to the United States. In 1939, Franklin D. Roosevelt changed this date to the fourth Thursday in November, although some states still observe the holiday according to Lincoln's proclamation.

Often, people attend church services on Thanksgiving morning. They may participate in a local parade, and then gather with family members for a meal usually consisting of stuffed turkey, mashed potatoes, yams, cranberry sauce, and pumpkin pie.

In Canada, Thanksgiving is normally celebrated on the second Monday in October, coinciding with Columbus Day.

Bible Sunday
The last Sunday in November

Bible Sunday is observed in many Protestant Churches in America as a day honoring the Christian Scripture.

——— " ———

The words of Jesus, according to St. John (John 14:6, King James Version):

"I am the way, the truth, and the life: no man cometh unto the Father, but by me."

——— " ———

TABLE 7.4. ALPHABETICAL LIST OF CHRISTIAN AND POST-CHRISTIAN HOLIDAYS

Holiday	Date(s)
Advent (Eastern)	November 15 through December 24
Advent (Western)	Begins the Sunday closest to November 30
African Methodist Quarterly Meeting Day . . .	The last Saturday in August
Aldersgate Experience . . .	The Sunday nearest to May 24
All Saints' Day	November 1
All Souls Days (Eastern)	The three Saturdays prior to Lent and the day before Pentecost
All Souls' Day (Western)	November 2
Annunciation of the Lord *see* Annunciation of the Blessed Virgin Mary	
Annunciation of the Blessed Virgin Mary . . .	March 25 (or April 1)
Arrival of Roger Williams	February 5
Ascension Day	Forty days after Easter
Ash Wednesday	A movable observance, six and one-half weeks before Easter
Assumption of the Blessed Virgin	August 15
Baptism of the Lord, Feast of the	The Sunday following Epiphany
Barnaby Bright *see* St. Barnabas's Day	
Barnaby Day *see* St. Barnabas's Day	
Bible Sunday	The last Sunday in November
Birthday of Brigham Young	June 1
Birthday of Joseph Smith	April 24
Birthday of Martin Luther King, Jr. . .	The third Monday in January
Birthday of Mary Baker Eddy . . .	July 16
Birthday of Richard Allen	February 11
Blessing of Animals . . .	The Sunday nearest to January 17

Holiday	Date(s)
Blessing of the Shrimp Fleet	The last weekend in June
Candlemas *see* Presentation of Jesus	
Carling Sunday *see* Mothering Sunday	
Carnival	Varying dates, between Epiphany and Shrove Tuesday
Cheesefare Sunday	The Sunday before Lent (Eastern)
Children's Day (Protestant)	Second Sunday in June
Childrens Day (Unification)	Approximately October 1
Christ the King (Protestant)	Last Sunday in August
Christ the King (Roman Catholic)	Last Sunday in October
Christmas Day	December 25
Christmas Eve	December 24
Christmas, 12 Days of . .	December 25 through January 5
Circumcision, Feast of the	January 1
Conversion of St. Paul . .	January 25
Coptic New Year	September 11
Corpus Christi	Thursday after Trinity Sunday
Day of All Things	Approximately May 1
Death of George Fox . .	January 13
Dedication of St. John Lateran	November 9
Easter (Eastern)	Movable; between April 4 and May 8
Easter (Western)	Movable; between March 22 and April 25
Easter Vigil *see* Holy Saturday	
Ember Days	Four times a year
Epiphany	January 6
Epiphany Eve	January 5
Family Week	Begins on the first Sunday in May
Fasching	Three days preceding Ash Wednesday
Feast of the Beheading *see* Martyrdom of St. John the Baptist	

TABLE 7.4. ALPHABETICAL LIST OF
CHRISTIAN AND POST-CHRISTIAN HOLIDAYS, Continued

Holiday	Date(s)
Feast of the Most Holy Body of Christ *see* Corpus Christi	
Feast of the Visitation	May 31 (July 2, Anglican)
Feast of the Transfiguration	August 6
Flight into Egypt	December 26
Footwashing Day	On a Sunday in early summer
Founding of the Latter Day Saints	April 6
God's Day	January 1
Good Friday	Friday before Easter
Green Thursday *see* Maundy Thursday	
Guardian Angels Day	October 2
Hill Cumorah Pageant	During July
Holy Family, Feast of the	Sunday after Epiphany
Holy Innocents' Day	December 28
Holy Saturday	The Eve of Easter
Holy Thursday *see* Maundy Thursday	
Immaculate Conception	December 8
Immaculate Heart of Mary, Feast of the	Saturday following the second Sunday after Pentecost
Laetare Sunday *see* Mothering Sunday	
Lent (Eastern)	Seven weeks before Easter in the East
Lent (Western)	Forty days before Easter (exclusive of Sundays)
Long Barnaby *see* St. Barnabas's Day	
Lucia Day *see* St. Lucy's Day	
Luciadagen *see* St. Lucy's Day	
Magna Carta Day	June 15
Mardi Gras	Tuesday before Ash Wednesday
Martin Luther, Birthday of	November 10
Martyrdom of Joseph and Hyrum Smith	June 27
Martyrdom of St. John the Baptist	August 29
Mary as Our Lady of Sorrows	September 15

Holiday	Date(s)
Mary as Our Lady of the Rosary	October 7
Marymass Fair	The third or fourth Monday in August
Maundy Thursday	Thursday before Easter
Meat Fare Sunday *see* Cheesefare Sunday	
Michaelmas	September 29
Mid-Lent Sunday *see* Mothering Sunday	
Moravian Love Feast	December 24
Most Precious Blood, Feast of the	July 1
Mother Seton Day	December 1
Mothering Sunday	Fourth Sunday of Lent
Nativity of St. John the Baptist	June 24
Nativity of the Blessed Virgin Mary	September 8
New Church Day	June 19
Old Christmas Day	January 6
Palm Sunday	The Sunday preceding Easter
Parents Day	Approximately March 1
Passion Thursday *see* Maundy Thursday	
Pentecost	Fifty days after the second day of Passover
Pioneer Day	July 24
Plough Monday	The first Monday after Epiphany
Posadas	December 16-25
Presentation of Jesus	February 2
Presentation of the Blessed Virgin Mary	November 21
Psachal Thursday *see* Maundy Thursday	
Purification of the Blessed Virgin Mary *see* Presentation of Jesus	
Quadragesima	First Sunday of Lent
Quasimodo Sunday	The Sunday after Easter
Queenship of Mary	August 22
Race Relations Sunday	The Sunday nearest February 12
Rally Day	During September or October
Reek Sunday	The last Sunday in July
Reformation Day	October 31

TABLE 7.4. ALPHABETICAL LIST OF
CHRISTIAN AND POST-CHRISTIAN HOLIDAYS, continued

Holiday	Date(s)
Refreshment Sunday *see* Mothering Sunday	
Resurrection Sunday *see* Easter	
Rogation Days	.Monday, Tuesday, and Wednesday preceding Ascension Day
Rose Monday	.The Monday before Lent
Rose Sunday *see* Mothering Sunday	
Sacred Heart of Jesus, Feast of the	.The Friday after Corpus Christi
Saint Philip and Saint James's Day	.May 1

Saints, Doctors,
  Missionaries, and
  Martyrs Day
	.November 8

Salvation Army Founder's Day	.April 10
San Estevan, Feast of	.September 2
Sante Fe Fiesta	.The weekend after Labor Day
Shere [Sheer] Thursday *see* Maundy Thursday	
St. Andrew's Day	.November 30
St. Barnabas's Day	.June 11
St. Bartholomew's Day	.August 24
St. James's Day	.July 25
St. John the Evangelist's Day	.December 27
St. Lucy's Day	.December 13
St. Luke's Day	.October 18
St. Mark's Day	.April 25

Holiday	Date(s)
St. Matthew's Day	.September 21
St. Matthias's Day	.February 24

St. Michael and
  All Angels
  see Michaelmas	

St. Nicholas's Day	.December 6
St. Patrick's Day	.March 17
St. Peter's Day	.June 29
St. Simon and St. Jude's Day	.October 28
St. Stephen's Day	.December 26
St. Thomas's Day	.December 21
Thanksgiving	.The fourth Thursday in November
Transfiguration of Jesus *see* Feast of the Transfiguration	
Trinity Day	.Monday after Pentecost
Trinity Sunday	.The first Sunday after Pentecost
Triumph of the Holy Cross	.September 14
True Parents' Birthday	.Approximately January 6
Universal Week of Prayer	.Begins the first Sunday in January
Vartanantz Day	.The Thursday preceding Ash Wednesday
Volunteers of America Founder's Day	.July 28
Whitsunday *see* Pentecost	
World Day of Prayer	.The first Friday in Lent

CHAPTER 8

Islam

Overview of Islam

What Is Islam?

The word Islam is an Arabic word. It means commitment or surrender. The central focus of Islam is a personal commitment and surrender to Allah, who is the god of Islam. According to Islamic belief, the name of the religion was bestowed by Allah himself. A person who follows Islam is called a Muslim. The word Muslim means one who surrenders or submits to Allah's will.

Islam was founded by Muhammad who was born around 570 C.E. and died in 632 C.E. Religious Islamic writers include the initials pbuh after every occurrence of Muhammad's name. For example the first sentence in this paragraph would have been rendered: Islam was founded by Muhammad (pbuh) who was born.... The initials stand for "Peace Be Upon Him."

Muhammad is considered a prophet, or messenger, of Allah. In all Islam recognizes 29 prophets including Adam, Abraham, Moses, and Jesus. Of these, Muhammad is considered the last and most important.

Islam is not just a religion of belief; it is a religion of action. Five specific deeds are required of followers; these are called *The Five Pillars of Islam*. They are:

1. *Shahadah*—confession of faith. Every Muslim is expected to publicly declare at least once in his or her life: "There is no God but Allah and Muhammad is his Prophet (some translations use slightly different words such as: Messenger, Servant, Slave, Apostle). The declaration must be made vocally and freely, without coercion, and with heart-felt assent.

2. *Salat*—prayer. Muslims are expected to pray at five specific times throughout the day: Before sunrise; early afternoon; late afternoon; after sunset; and before going to bed or before midnight.

Prayers involve specific recitations and postures, and they must be made facing in the direction of the Ka`bah in Mecca, Saudi Arabia. The Ka`bah is a cube-shaped structure that serves as Islam's central shrine.

3. *Sawm*—fasting. All Muslims who are physically able are expected to abstain from eating, drinking, smoking and sexual relations from dawn until sunset during the entire Islamic month of Ramadan.

4. *Zakat*—almsgiving. Every Muslim is expected to pay zakat. Zakat, originally a tax instituted by Muhammad to help the poor, is used to help spread Islam, pay debts, ransom captives, and support the holy war (called Jihad). In past times, Zakat was mandatory, and it was collected by governments. In more recent times zakat is treated as a voluntary charitable offering, but according to Muslim belief a believer's property is not "purified" or legitimate unless the zakat has been paid.

5. *Hajj*—pilgrimage. Every Muslim who is physically able and has the financial means to accomplish it is expected to make a pilgrimage to the Ka`bah in Mecca.

The Relationship between Allah and the Islamic People

The Islamic people worship a God called Allah. The name Allah is derived from the Arabic phrase *al-ilah* meaning "the god." Muslims believe people exist to serve Allah. Although Allah is compassionate and righteous, he is master; people are his servants. Serving Allah, however, is a fulfilling experience and does not equate with the humiliation suffered by the slaves of human masters.

Allah is one God, but he has 99 names which can be recited to the benefit of the person who recites them. Some of the names are: "The Great," "The Merciful," "The Disposer," and "Deity." In addition to their devotion to Allah, Muslims believe in a final judgement in which men will be raised to appear before Allah. They will be sent to live in paradise or hell according to their deeds. The Muslim concept of divine judgement also extends to the fates of nations. They believe that Allah's judgement upon nations plays out in the unfolding of history.

Islam also teaches that there are angels who are Allah's messengers. Angels are created beings made for the purpose of worshipping and serving Allah. Some of the angels rebelled, however, and these are demons. The chief of the demons is called Iblis (also Shiatan or Satan). Iblis tempts men to do evil things. The spiritual beings who serve Iblis are called jinn.

Authorities and Sacred Writings

The Qur'an

The *Qur'an* (also sometimes spelled *Koran* or *Alcoran*) is the holy book of Islam. According to Islamic belief, the *Qur'an* was given to Muhammad by Allah. Authorship of the *Qur'an* is attributed to Allah, and not to Muhammad; Muhammad merely received it. Muslims believe that because it originated with Allah, the *Qur'an* is infallible.

The word *Qur'an* comes from the word *qaraa* which in Arabic means to read or to recite. Initially the word *qur'an* was applied by Muhammad to refer to a revelation. Later, the term was broadened to refer to the book in which the revelations were recorded.

The *Qur'anic* messages were delivered to Muhammad by the chief of Allah's messenger angels, Jibril (also called Gabriel in Christian literature and sometimes spelled Jibreel). Jibril delivered the *Qur'anic* passages in pure Arabic, which is considered by Muslims to be the speech used by Allah and his angels. Because Muhammad could not read or write, he committed the recitations to memory and later dictated them to followers who memorized them and wrote them down. The entire text was delivered in this way over a 22-year period.

The authorized version of the *Qur'an* was compiled after Muhammad's death from oral and written sources in around 650 C.E. It consists of 114 chapters called suras. The shortest chapter contains 3 verses; the longest, 306. The text addresses a variety of topics including religious, social, commercial, and legal matters. It is poetic in nature. Muslims believe that the *Qur'an* transmitted to Muhammad is an exact copy of an original that exists in heaven; therefore, translations from the original pure Arabic into other languages are not permitted.

The Sunna and the Hadith

The Sunna refers to the "example of the prophet." Within it the collected remembrances of what Muhammad did or said regarding a number of issues not specifically addressed in the *Qur'an* are recorded. It covers the life of Muhammad and tells about activities within the early Islamic community.

The Sunna was transmitted orally until approximately the 9th century when it was set down in a standardized format. The *Hadith* is the book in which the Sunna is compiled. Different sects within Islam honor different canonical collections of *Hadith*. Those held by the Sunnis were compiled beginning in the 9th century C.E., and those held by the Shi`ites were compiled during the 10th and 11th centuries.

Although the *Hadith* is considered an important source of instruction, it is not considered infallible. Together, the *Hadith* and *Qur'an* form the *Shari`ah*, or law (or more literally "way").

The Ijtihad and Ijma

Two other sources of authority in Islam are the ijtihad and the ijma. Ijtihad refers to the opinion of a responsible individual. Its doctrinal use permitted an authorized person to use reasoning in establishing an appropriate response to a situation not covered in the *Qur'an* or *Hadith*. Some sects of Islam place strict limitations on the use of the ijtihad; others seek to expand its influence. The ijma, refers to the consensus of the Islamic community. It is reached through time as opinions are accepted or rejected by the community as a whole.

History of Islam

Pre-Islamic Conditions in the Arabian Peninsula

In the centuries before the founding of Islam, the Arabian peninsula consisted of a desert terrain which was inhabited predominantly by nomadic tribes. Several cultural centers had been established on the coastlines and around some oases, but between the cities wandering peoples followed the water. The harsh geographical conditions made the peninsula a place unconquered by foreign invaders but also not unified by its Arabian inhabitants.

The existing religious system included the worship of gods, goddesses, and other spirits often associated with water sources and other natural phenomenon. The establishment of shrines dedicated to the various gods and the performance of pilgrimages to important places was common. Over the pantheon, one deity ruled from afar. His name was Allah. Allah was not, however, intimately involved in the lives of the Arabian people.

One tribe, the Quraysh, settled in a valley near Mecca (also called Makkah or, more anciently, Macoraba). Mecca was home to a popular shrine called the Ka`bah, which consisted of a stone building that contains a black stone thought by some to be a meteorite. The many clans of the Quraysh tribe each erected shrines in the vicinity of the Ka`bah to their own preferred deity. The Quraysh flourished in Mecca due to its favorable position in relation to popular trade routes of the era. As a result, by the sixth century the tribe had become one of the strongest in the region. It was into this tribe that Muhammad was born.

Muhammad

The precise date of Muhammad's birth is unknown but most sources place it between 570 and 580 C.E. Muhammad's early life was difficult. His father died before his birth, his mother died when he was six, and his grandfather died when he was eight. He was raised by an uncle, Abu Talib, and served as an apprentice camel driver. During his time of service among the nomadic Bedouin people in the desert he learned the pure Arabic language, and other skills that would serve him later in life.

As a young adult, Muhammad went to work for a widow named Khadijah. At her suggestion, the two married. Their union resulted in six children: two sons who died during childhood, and four daughters who survived. One daughter, Fatimah, became the best known for her role in propagating the faith.

The Beginning of Islam

In 610 C.E., when Muhammad was about 40 years old he received a visionary revelation from God calling him to turn away from the polytheistic practices that predominated in the region and believe in one God, Allah. The revivalistic message focused on restoring the monotheism of Abraham (the Jewish patriarch). According to Islamic doctrine, Abraham was not a Jew by faith, but a man of pure faith that had been distorted throughout the centuries. Muhammad's "mission" was to restore proper worship at the shrine of the Ka`bah. After the first revelation, the prophetic messages continued coming to him over a period of 22 years until 632 C.E., the year of his death. Muhammad passed the messages along by preaching to those who would listen.

During the early years of Muhammad's proclamations, he had few followers. Although small in number they were devoted and played an important role in spreading Islam during its first century. They included his wife Khadijah, his cousin Ali (who was the son of the uncle who had raised him), two of Muhammad's friends, Abu Bakr and `Uthman, and a slave named Zaid.

The Hijrah

In accordance with his understanding of the messages he received from Allah, Muhammad preached against the traditional religious practices that were conducted at the Ka`bah. Serving the many pilgrims who came to the shrine, however, was a major industry in the city. As a result, Muhammad's preaching was resented by many of the people in Mecca. As Muhammad's preaching efforts intensified, they were viewed as a threat to the local economy. While his uncle and wife were alive, Muhammad was personally protected as a result of clan loyalties, but the persecution of his followers began.

Some of Muhammad's followers who lacked protection from powerful family members, emigrated to Ethiopia in Africa. These represented the first hijrah (or emigration), and their actions set the stage for the great Hijrah to Medina that was to follow. When Muhammad's uncle and wife both died in 620 C.E., he too was without family protection and began to suffer abuses at the hands of his contemporaries.

In 622 C.E. Muhammad and his followers left Mecca and traveled to a city called Yathrib which was located approximately 300 miles (480 km) to the northeast. Yathrib was selected because a delegation from it had invited Muhammad to come and serve as a political leader. Yathrib was later renamed Madina al-Nabi meaning City of the Prophet, and is modernly called Medina.

This movement, or emigration, was called the Hijrah (from the Arabic word hijrah meaning "flight"). It is the event that marks the beginning of the Islamic community (called the Umma), an event so important it serves as the epoch of the Islamic calendar. Islamic years are numbered with the designation of A.H. (anno hegirae, literally "in the year of the hijrah," or more simply in English, After Hijrah).

Wars Between Medina and Mecca

In Medina, Muhammad rose in power and gained many more followers.

After Muhammad became established in Medina, disputes arose between his followers and the residents of Mecca. Muslims, displaced economically in the agricultural community of Medina began raiding trading caravans from Mecca. Clashes between the two communities escalated.

In 624 C.E., two years after the hijrah, a force of approximately 300 Muslims defeated a large Meccan caravan of 950. The Muslims viewed their victory in the face of overwhelming numbers as a sign of Allah's favor. The event is remembered as the "Day of Discrimination."

By 630 C.E. Muhammad was strong enough to demand that Mecca be turned over to him and that its inhabitants convert from idolatry to Islam. When Muhammad captured Mecca he also captured the ancient shrine of the Ka`bah and rededicated it to Allah.

The Death of Muhammad

Muhammad died of a fever in 632 C.E. According to Islamic teaching, the end of his life signified the end of the prophetic era. Muhammad is sometimes called the Seal of the Prophets, signifying that no further prophets would come to the human race.

Abu Bakr

Following Muhammad's death, successors arose from among his followers to lead the Muslim people. They were called Caliphs (also sometimes spelled Khalifahs).

Abu Bakr, one of Muhammad's closest companions, was the first Caliph. One of the difficulties he faced was keeping the Islamic community unified. Muhammad had instituted the practice of collecting alms (called zakat) from the various tribes with which he had formed covenants. Some of these tribes felt that the covenant period ended with Muhammad's death, and that payments would be no longer due. Abu Bakr enforced the covenants on the basis that they had been made between the tribes and Allah, not Muhammad. By keeping the wavering tribes within the Islamic fold, the community remained intact.

Abu Bakr served as Caliph for two years. Another of his major accomplishments was overseeing the recording of the *Qur'anic* recitations.

Umar

Umar, another close companion of Muhammad, succeeded Abu Bakr. He served as Caliph for ten years from 634 until 644 C.E. when a servant assassinated him. In 639 C.E. Umar established the Islamic calendar and designated the epoch (year 1) as the year of the Hijrah. Umar also expanded the Muslim territory. Under his leadership the Muslims conquered Persia, Damascus and Jerusalem.

`Uthman ibn `Affan

`Uthman ibn `Affan, succeeded Umar as Caliph. He was selected on the basis of his conversion to Islam during Muhammad's early years in Mecca and close companionship with the prophet. `Uthman was also married to Muhammad's daughter Ruqayyah, and upon her death, he married another of the prophet's daughters, Umm Kulthum.

`Uthman's principal accomplishments included the production of an authorized version of the *Qur'an* and overseeing its distribution throughout all Islamic communities. In conjunction with this effort, `Uthman ordered the destruction of all unofficial versions of the *Qur'an*. This act angered some factions, and `Uthman's tenure as Caliph ended abruptly when he was assisanated in 656 C.E. by an Egyptian delegation.

Ali

Ali became the fourth Caliph. He was a son-in-law of Muhammad (married Muhammad's daughter Fatimah) and also a cousin of Muhammad. During his Caliphate, Ali moved the Islamic capital to an area in the territory now occupied by Iraq. He was assisanated in 661 C.E., and those who opposed him moved the Islamic capital back to the area occupied by present-day Syria.

Islamic Community Splits

The events following Ali's death led to a split in the Islamic community. Followers of Ali believed that only descendants of Ali had the right to be Caliphs. As a result, they disavowed the first three Caliphs who were companions of Muhammad and not his descendants.

The split resulted in the formation of two groups, who today comprise almost all Muslims: the Shi`ites, who hold to the doctrine of the House of Ali; and the Sunni, who recognize the legitimacy of the first three Caliphs and do not hold the House of Ali doctrine. Currently, the largest body of orthodox Muslims are Sunni.

Following Ali's death, his followers acknowledged the leadership of his son Husayn, the grandson of Muhammad. Husayn retained the Islamic capital in the Iraqi region of Kufa where Ali had located it.

Sunni Muslims did not recognize Husayn's authority. They acknowledged the leadership of Mu'awiya, a nephew of `Uthman—the third Caliph. Mu'awiya, founder of the Umayyad dynasty, established his capital in Damascus in Syria. A battle between Husayn's followers and the Umayyads occurred on Muharram 10, 680 C.E. Husayn and his followers were defeated, and Husayn was killed at Karbala. The day continues to be remembered by Shi`ites with fasting and mourning.

Rise in Islamic Power and Culture

Despite the differences between the two factions, the reach of Islam continued to spread. Muslims gained in religious influence and political power. Orthodox practices became established and further aspects of the law were defined.

During the eighth century, changes in political leadership brought the first influx of non-Arab followers. In 711 C.E. an Islamic army entered Spain and conquered the Iberian peninsula. Their advance was stopped by the French at the Battle of Tours in 732 C.E. To the east, the Arabian armies made their first advance toward the Indian subcontinent in 712 C.E. The Punjab and regions beyond were later annexed in the 11th and 12th centuries. As Islam rose in power, its influence spread, and Islamic communities emerged in northern Africa, Europe, Turkey, Persia, and the island nations of southeast Asia.

During the medieval centuries (generally considered the 9th through 13th centuries C.E.), Islamic culture also flourished. Academies were established in Baghdad and Cairo. Great strides were made in the area of the natural and social sciences, mathematics, and philosophy.

Shifts in Political Power

Islam's political power in Baghdad fell to the Mongols in 1258 C.E., and in the fifteenth century, the Muslims were ousted from Spain. These losses, however, were offset by growing power in Turkey and the rise of the Ottoman Empire. The Turkish army succeeded in carrying Islam into Eastern Europe, to areas currently occupied by the Balkan states, Albania, Bulgaria, and the former Yugoslavia. By the 17th century Islam was well established in a region that stretched from southeastern Europe, through the Near and Middle East, across the regions surrounding the Black Sea, and into India.

Toward the end of the Turkish Ottoman empire, increasing power in Europe led to colonialism. As a result, many Muslim lands lost their autonomy to Europeans, especially in India, Africa, and southeast Asia. This shift in political power led to much anti-Western sentiment.

Wahhabis

During the 18th century, reform movements within Islam began to surface. Some people believed that the loss of autonomy was a result of Allah's dissatisfaction with the Muslim community. One of the first of these efforts was Wahhabism.

In the 18th century Ibn `Abd al-Wahhab (c. 1703–1787) began a movement aimed at bringing social and moral reform to Islamic communities. He rejected the concept of ijma (consensus) and sought to purge non-Islamic influences from the Muslim community. He spoke out against luxuries such as music, dancing, gambling, and tobacco. Al-Wahhab also opposed the popular custom of saint veneration. He destroyed many tombs of popular Arabian saints and replaced them with unpretentious grave markers.

Additional Reforms

The emphasis on returning Islam to its fundamental roots in an effort to regain Allah's favor led to more revivalistic movements during the 19th and 20th centuries. Jamal al-Din al-Afghani (1838–1897) was a writer and an activist who traveled through Muslim territories urging revolution. Other reformers rose to prominence by promoting the concept of the jihad, or holy war. According to Islamic belief, although individuals should not be coerced into converting to Islam, armed force was an acceptable method of bringing about change in government structures. Once political institutions were transformed, the affected populations would be enabled to embrace Islam.

Islam Today

Muslims Around the World

During the early years of Islam, the faith spread throughout the Arabian Peninsula into regions that are today occupied by Saudi Arabia, Syria, Iraq, and Jordan. Contrary to popular opinion, however, Muslims are not just Arabs. Muslims—followers of Islam—are found in many different ethnic groups all over the globe.

According to some estimates there are more than one billion Muslims world-wide with major populations found in the Middle East, North and sub-Saharan Africa, Turkey, Central Asia, and Southeast Asia. In Europe and the United States, Islam is the second largest religious group (Christianity is the largest). Other countries with significant Muslim populations include France, Britain, West Germany, and Canada.

Worship

A Muslim house of worship is called a mosque (or *masjid*, an Arabic word meaning "place of prostration"). Because Islam does not allow images, mosques contain no representations of Allah or Muhammad. They are typically decorated in abstract patterns such as geometric figures, swirling designs that evoke feelings of infinity, or stylized calligraphic inscriptions of passages from the *Qur'an*.

The central feature of a mosque is the prayer hall in which Muslims gather to pray. Although private prayers may be offered in the mosque at any time, the largest gathering occurs on Friday afternoons. Because Muslims must face Mecca when they pray, one wall within the hall is decorated differently to provide the proper orientation. Other important components of the mosque include the minarets (exterior towers from which the call to worship is made), the minbar (a platform from which the leader may give instruction or teaching), and an area for performing ritual washing, called Wudu.

Services at the mosque begin with the call to worship made by a person called the muezzin. (In some modern countries, the call to worship may be made by a recording.) Although women are permitted to attend the Friday services, their presence is optional. Men are required to be present. A ritual washing of the body is performed before the prayers are offered. Prayers consist of a series of mandated recitations and postures.

Sects

Sunni

There are two main sects within Islam: Sunni and Shi`ite. Sunni are the majority (estimated at about 80 percent). They recognize the authority of the first three Caliphs, and they believe that the Sunna (example of the Prophet Muhammad) is interpreted through the consensus of the community.

Sunni Muslims recognize the validity of six collections of documents said to contain reports of Muhammad's actual words and deeds. These form the basis of their *Qur'anic* interpretations and governance of their communities.

Shi`ite

Shi`ite Muslims look to special teachers, called Imams. These individuals are believed to be inspired and to possess secret knowledge. Shi`ites, however, do not recognize the same line of Islamic leaders acknowledged by the Sunnis. Shi`ites hold to a doctrine that accepts only leaders who are descended from Muhammad through his daughter, Fatimah and her husband Ali. Many Shi`ite subsects believe that true Imams are errorless and sinless. They receive instruction from these leaders rather than relying on the consensus of the community.

The largest group of Shi`ites is called the Twelvers. The Twelvers believe that there were 12 infallible leaders beginning with Ali and continuing in a chain until the tenth century C.E. when the last disappeared. Twelvers expect the twelfth leader to return and bring justice to the world.

The Ismailis, another Shi`ite subsect, are one of the smallest groups within Islam. Their origins date back to an eighth century dispute over who was the legitimate successor to Jafar al- Sadiq, the sixth Imam. The Ismailis, who believe that the Imam is an incarnation of Allah, await the return of the seventh and last imam on Judgement Day. During the 12th century a small group of Ismailis, known as the Assassins, earned a reputation for attacking Sunni religious and political leaders (thus, their name entered the modern vocabulary). Modern Ismaili groups are centered in India, Pakistan, Iran, Yemen, East Africa, and Canada.

Sufism

Sufism, a mystical movement within Islam, originated in the 8th century among pious Muslims who wanted to focus on developing a meaningful inner spiritual life. They sought direct, ecstatic communion with Allah. Sufi practices were personal and spontaneous and included recitation and meditation which led to ecstatic experiences that produced intimate knowledge of Allah.

An early Sufi leader, al-Hallaj, was executed in Baghdad for heresy in 922 C.E. Later Sufis, however, were more successful in blending orthodox Islamic doctrine with their mystical pursuits. By the 12th century, Sufi brotherhoods, or schools, existed throughout the Islamic world. Founders of Sufi schools were called Shaikhs and they were regarded as saints. When a Shaikh died, his role would pass onto one of his followers. The Sufis often served the poor and sought to bring spiritual enlightenment to their followers.

There are three different categories of modern Sufi: traditional Muslims for whom Sufism represents an added focus of spiritual dimension in ritual worship; people who practice spiritual spontaneity and eschew rules and morals; and, those who seek ecstatic experiences with Allah.

TABLE 8.1. THE TWELVE ISLAMIC MONTHS
Muharram
Safar
Rabi al-Awwal
Rabi al-Thani
Jumada al-Ula
Jumada al-Akhira
Rajab
Sha`ban
Ramadan
Shawwal
Duh al-Qa`dah
Dhu al-Hijjah

❖ ❖ ❖

The Islamic Calendar

A Lunar Calendar

The *Qur'an* is the holy book of Islam, revealed through the Prophet Muhammad to his followers. Muslims believe that the *Qur'an* exists in Heaven with God, and that Muhammad transmitted a copy of it to his disciples. It is to this heavenly authority that the Muslims look for their calendar. In the *Qur'an* (IX, 36–37), Allah revealed to Muhammad that the calendar of Islam should be strictly lunar.

The Thirty-Year Cycle

The Islamic lunar calendar is based on a thirty-year cycle. It consists of twelve lunar months which alternate

---

TABLE 8.2. ISLAMIC HOLIDAY CYCLE

Muharram
1 . . . . . . .Awwal Muharram
10 . . . . . .Ashura
10 . . . . . .Yevmi Ashurer
10 . . . . . .Husayn Day

Safar
~ . . . . . .Mandi Safar
14-16 . . . . .Shah Abdul Latif Death Festival
18-19 . . . . .Data Ganj Baksh Death Festival

Rabi al-Awwal
12 . . . . . .Mawlid al-Nabi

Rajab
27 . . . . . .Laylat al-Miraj

Sha`ban
15 . . . . . .Shab-Barat

Ramadan
1-30 . . . . .Fast of Ramadan
27 . . . . . .Laylat al-Qadr
30 . . . . . .Lantern's Festival

Shawwal
1-3 . . . . . .'Id al-Fitr

Dhu'al-Hijjah
8-13 . . . . .Pilgrimage to Mecca (Hajj)
10 . . . . . .Al-'id al-Kabir
10-12 . . . . .'Id al-Adha

---

between twenty-nine and thirty days. The calendar operates on a thirty-year cycle in which an extra day is added to the last month of years 2, 5, 7, 10, 13, 16, 18, 21, 24, 26, and 29.

The eleven days which are added to the cycle compensate exactly for the .03059 days the moon gains in each average month of 29.5 days. Thus, the Islamic calendar stays perfectly in phase with the moon. However, because the Islamic year is 354 or 355 days long, it is about 11 days short of the solar year. As a result, there are about thirty-three Islamic years for every thirty-two solar years. This means that the months of the Islamic calendar pass through all the seasons every thirty-three years, and on the common civil calendar, Islamic festivals will seem to move backwards by 11 days from year to year.

The Epoch of the Muslim Era

The emigration of Muhammad is the epoch of the Muslim Era. In 622 C.E., Muhammad fled from Mecca to Medina, an event which is known as the Hijrah. The epoch of the Muslim Era is based on his arrival in the city of Medina. The era officially began at sunset on Muharram 1, 622 C.E. (which would have fallen on July 16 according to the Western civil calendar). In accord with the declaration in the *Qur'an*, the second caliph, Umar I, formally designated Muharram 1 to be the beginning of the year sometime during his reign (634–644 C.E.).

Throughout the Muslim world, the era of the Hijrah (A.H.) or Muslim Era is used privately, and many nations use it as the authorized method for reckoning time. Countries which officially recognize the Muslim Era include Saudi Arabia, Yemen, and the principalities of the Persian Gulf. In Egypt, Syria, Jordan, and Morocco, both Muslim and Common Eras are sanctioned.

Still other Muslim countries use a combination of the two systems. Around 1088 A.H. (1677 C.E.), Turkey, for example, designated March 1 as the New Year, adopted the solar year and Julian months, but kept the Muslim Era. In the nineteenth century, the Turkish Empire accepted the Gregorian calendar, and in the twentieth century, the Common Era.

Another country that adopted a combined system is Iran. During the reign of Reza Shah Pahlavi (1925–1942 C.E.), the solar year was incorporated into a calendar with Persian month names and the Muslim Era. March 21 is the beginning of the Iranian year. Thus, the Iranian year 1349 began on March 21, 1970.

Months, Weeks, and Days

Like the Hebrew month, the Islamic month begins when two witnesses report seeing the crescent of the new moon. Their claim is verified by a qudi (judge) and a mufti (interpreter of Muslim law). The mufti declares the beginning of a new month. Also like the early Hebrews, Muslims faced the problems of cloudy nights and poor communications which posed a hinderance to the timely and efficient declaration of a new month. Each town or community would assume responsibility for declaring the beginning of the month. This caused confusion because the months would start on different days from one location to the next. Eventually, albeit reluctantly, the majority of Muslims agreed to accept the ruling of Cairo as the official beginning of the month.

All Muslim calendars are composed of seven-day weeks and twenty-four hour days. The names for the days vary from place to place except for the weekly holy day, Al Jumah, "the day of gathering." In terms of the Western civil calendar, Al Jumah falls on Friday and marks the beginning of the Islamic week. Days in the Muslim system run from sunset to sunset to commemorate Muhammad's entrance to Medina which took place at sunset.

Tazia: A Tazia—a temporary structure representing Husayn's tomb or mausoleum—is carried in a procession on Husayn Day in commemoration of the fallen hero's death during the Battle of Martyrs. Husayn, the grandson and, according to Shi`ite belief, legitimate successor of Muhammad was killed on October 10, 680 C.E. (61 A.H.). Husayn represents a righteous person under persecution, and the Shi`ites draw inspiration from his example.

Islamic Holidays

Daily

Salat (Prayers)
Five times a day

Muslims are required to pray five times a day: just before sunrise, early afternoon, late afternoon, after sunset, and before retiring at night. Designated prayers are offered in units; each unit consists of specific postures, prayers and *Qur'an* recitations. The postures involve standing, genuflection, prostrations, and sitting. All prayers are offered facing in the direction of the Ka`bah in Mecca. Although these prayers are intended to be congregational and not private, individuals are not required to attend a mosque to participate in the daily prayers.

Tahajjud (Night Vigil)
After midnight

Tahajjud prayers are individual devotional prayers made after midnight. Unlike the mandated daily cycle of prayers, Tahajjud prayers are optional.

Weekly

Salat-ul-Jumu'ah (Friday Prayers)
Friday

Early afternoon prayers on Fridays typically represent the main Muslim gathering of the week. In addition to the regular prayers designated for the hour, a sermon (called a khutbah) or other form of teaching may be offered. Unlike weekly holy day observances in Christianity and Judaism where the entire day is marked by a cessation of regular activities, the Muslim Friday services take place during a pause in the regular workday pattern. The establishment of Friday as the day for special gatherings is based on the belief that Adam was both born and received into Paradise on Fridays.

Annual

Muharram

Muharram
First month of the Muslim calendar

Muharram was designated as the first month in the Islamic year by Umar, the second Caliph. At the beginning of a new year, Muslims set aside the sins of the past and determine to make a new start. The first and tenth days of the month (described below) have special significance.

Awwal Muharram (New Year's Day)
Muharram 1

Awwal Muharram is the Islamic New Year celebration. It is observed as a holiday in 19 countries. The day commemorates the flight of Muhammad from Mecca to Medina in 622 C.E. Muhammad's journey, called the Hijrah, came about as a result of hostility toward his teachings and the sparsity of converts in Mecca. In Medina, Muhammad was welcomed, and Islam gained a solid following. Because of the significance of this event, Muslims count their era from this date.

Ashura (Ashoora)
Muharram 10

Muhammad initially instituted the observance of Ashura as a mandatory two-day fast on Muharram 9 and 10, but later changed it to an optional single-day fast. It is still observed in this manner by Sunni Muslims. The fast falls during the first month of the Islamic year and may have been derived from the Hebrew fast of Yom Kippur.

The significance of the tenth day of Muharram is linked with several observances which vary among the different sects of Islam. Events associated with the day include: the creation of the heavens, land, and seas; the creation of Adam; the day of Noah's departure from the Ark after the great flood; the day Moses was saved from Pharaoh in Egypt; and, looking to the future, the tenth day of Muharram is the day on which Allah's final judgement will take place.

Yevmi Ashurer (Day of Sweet Soup or Porridge)
Muharram 10

Turkish Muslims celebrate Muharram 10 in memory of Noah's departure from the Ark onto Mount Ararat and God's covenant with Noah never to destroy the earth by flood again. Because they must share Allah's gifts with others, everyone makes ashurer, which is a sweet soup or porridge made of boiled wheat, dried currants, grain, and nuts, similar to that supposedly made by Noah and stored in the bins of the Ark. Each person invites his neighbors to come and share it at a designated time.

Husayn Day (Hosay Festival)
Muharram 10

Among Shi`ite Muslims, Muharram 10 is observed as Husayn Day (alternate spellings: Husain; Hussein) in honor of Husayn ibn Ali (son of Ali). Husayn, the grandson and, according to Shi`ite belief, legitimate successor of Muhammad was killed in a battle on October 10, 680 C.E. (61 A.H.). Husayn represents a righteous person under persecution, and the Shi`ites draw inspiration from his example.

The holy day of mourning includes fasting, praying, and the singing of elegies. Some Shi`ite communities also participate in reinactments of the battle and conduct processions in which Husayn's standard is carried. Passion plays called *ta'ziya* (a word that means consolation) are produced in Iran, Iraq, Pakistan, India and other areas with large Shi`ite populations.

In Trinidad and Tobago, however, where the remembrance of Husayn's death was first celebrated in 1884, the traditional procession of mourning has been mixed with various European, African, and Indian rituals to form a celebration that is far from somber. Called the Hosay Festival, the observance features popular processions held between February and March in the towns of St. James, Curepe, Tunapuna, Couva, and Cedros.

The festival in Trinidad and Tobago usually begins with a procession of flags symbolizing the beginning of the battle of Karbala, in which Husayn and his brother were killed. On the second day dancers wearing Tadjahs—small minaretted tombs made of bamboo, colored tissue, tinfoil, crepe paper, mirrors, and coconut leis—parade through the streets to the accompaniment of African drummers in a ritual that is reminiscent of Carnival.

The highlight of the festival occurs on the third night, when the large Tadjahs, some of which are six feet tall, are carried through the streets. There are also two moons, representing Husayn and his brother, carried by specially trained dancers. These large crescent-shaped structures are studded with sharp blades and carried on the dancers' shoulders. At midnight, the two moons engage in a ritual embrace to a chorus of cheers from the onlookers.

Safar

Mandi Safar
Occurs during the month of Safar

Mandi Safar is a Muslim bathing festival unique to Malaysia. The observance was originally believed to commemorate the last time Muhammad was able to bathe before his death. Muslims wearing bright colors visit beaches for a religious cleansing of the body and soul with water. There is no mention of the rite in the *Qur'an* (the Muslim holy book), and orthodox Muslims consider it nothing more than a picnic. It continues as a merry holiday. The best-known gathering places are the beaches of Tanjong Kling near Malacca and of Penang.

Shah Abdul Latif Death Festival
Safar 14–16

Shah Abdul Latif (1689–1752) was a Sufi poet who lived in Sind, Pakistan. He was one of the most beloved of Pakistan's mystic Sufi poet-musicians. He is best remembered as the author of the *Risalo*, a collection of romantic poetry in the Sindhi language. The heros and heroines in his work have become symbols of the oppression of Sind by foreign occupiers.

At Latif's death festival (called an "urs") a huge fair takes place outside the poet's shrine. There are wrestling matches (a popular entertainment in Sind), transvestite dancing, a circus, theater, and numerous food and souvenir booths. Inside the shrine the atmosphere is quiet, and there is devotional singing by well-known Sind groups. The main event of the urs is a concert at which the annual Latif Award is presented to the best performers.

Data Ganj Baksh Death Festival
Safar 18–19

Data Ganj Baksh, which means "He Who Gives Generously," was the name given to Syed Ali Abudl Hasan Bin Usman Hajweri (or Ali Hujwiri, or al-Hujwuri), a scholar and author who lived most of his life in Lahore, Pakistan, and died in 1072. He wrote *Kashful Majhab* (or *Kashf al-mahjub*), the oldest Persian treatise on Sufism. It is a text on the fundamentals of Sufism and it reviews Islamic mysticism, linking each famous master to a particular doctrine.

Ali Hujwiri is one of the most popular saints in Pakistan, and every day hundreds of pilgrims pray at the Mausoleum of Data Ganj Baksh in Lahore, Pakistan asking for blessings and favors. On his death festival (called an "urs"), thousands throng to the shrine for celebratory activities and prayers.

Rabi al-Awwal

Mawlid al-Nabi (Birthday of Muhammad; Bara Wafat)
Rabi al-Awwal 12

Mawlid al-Nabi, meaning birthday of the prophet, is not universally celebrated by all Muslims. Some Islamic communities refrain from participating in the festival because Muhammad himself did not celebrate his own

birth. The custom of celebration, however, dates back to the 10th century in Egypt. In India, the feast of Mawlid al-Nabi, or Bara Wafat, is celebrated with enthusiasm.

Muhammad was born on the twelfth day of Rabi al-Awwal, which in the Western calendar fell on April 12, 571 C.E. He was born at Mecca in Arabia, during a period of moral chaos and great corruption. Muhammad spent much of his time in prayer, meditation, and seclusion where he received revelations from Allah. For twenty-three years, from the time he was forty years old until his death, Muhammad succeeded in establishing a religion based on the revelations he had received, and brought a political cohesiveness to the Arab tribes that had not been previously experienced.

On the day of Mawlid, the Prophet's teachings are repeated, the holy *Qur'an* is read and recited, and religious meetings are held in the mosques. The devotees keep a night vigil, spending their time in prayer and reading the *Qur'an*. They invite friends and relatives to a feast and give donations to the poor.

Rajab

Laylat al-Miraj (Lailat al Miraj; Isra' and Mi'raj; Night Journey; Ascension of the Prophet)
Rajab 27

This celebration commemorates Muhammad's night journey to Jerusalem from Mecca in 620 C.E. and his ascension into heaven. According to the story, one night during the 10th year of his prophecy, the angel Gabriel woke Muhammad and traveled with him to Jerusalem on the winged horse, Burak. There he prayed at the site of the Temple of Solomon with the Prophets Abraham, Moses, Jesus, and others. Then, carried by Gabriel, he rose to heaven from the rock of the Temple Mount, where the Dome of the Rock sanctuary now stands. In heaven, Muhammad received instructions from Allah regarding the five daily prayers observed by all Muslims.

Muhammad's journey provided inspiration particularly to the mystical Sufis. In it, Sufis saw a foreshadowing of the possibility of the relationship between Allah and his servants in which the servant could experience an annihilation of self in order to experience the presence of Allah.

The holiday is observed by some Muslim groups as a festive gathering at which the story of Muhammad's experience is retold and food is shared. Other Muslims choose to not celebrate the occasion.

Sha`ban

Shab-Barat (Night of Forgiveness, Laylat-ul-Bara'h)
Sha`ban 15

Shab-Barat (or Shab-i-Barat) is the evening on which Muslims, especially Indian and Pakistani followers, entreat Allah for forgiveness of their dead. The devout often spend the night in mosques praying and reading the Qur'an. Muslims visit graveyards to pray for the souls of their friends and ancestors. Allah's mercy is celebrated by fireworks displays, the illumination of the outside of mosques, and provision of food for the poor.

This time is also known as Laylat al-Bara'ah, or the Night of Forgiveness. It is a time of preparation for Ramadan through intense prayer. Muslim belief indicates that this is the night on which destinies of the coming year are fixed and sins absolved.

Ramadan

Ramadan (Fast of Ramadan)
Ninth month of the Islamic lunar year

During the month of Ramadan, Muslims commemorate Muhammad's reception of the divine revelations recorded in the Qur'an. The Qur'an itself mandates this observance and provides explicit instructions for following the month-long fast which was first instituted in 2 A.H. (624 C.E.).

The first day of Ramadan occurs when the authorities in Saudi Arabia sight the new moon marking the ninth month. It is the holiest period during the Islamic year, and ends when the new moon is sighted for the next month. The Festival of Breaking Fast immediately follows the Fast of Ramadan, and is a time of rejoicing, gift-giving, and celebration.

During Ramadan, Muslims observe a strict fast from sunrise to sunset. The fast is one of the "Five Pillars" of the Islamic faith, and is considered a time of introspection and intensified devotion to Allah.

Each day, believers rise early and eat a light meal, called a Suhur, before dawn. They fast through the day, then after prayers they break the fast with an evening meal. In some places the end of the fast is announced by the firing of a cannon.

In addition to fasting food, Muslims abstain from sexual activity and alcohol during the daylight hours of Ramadan. Other things to be avoided during Ramadan include lying, promise breaking, and anger. In addition, an extra set of prayers, called the Tarawih, may be added to the fifth set of daily prayers. Although most Muslims are expected to fast during Ramadan, the Qur'an does make provisions to excuse those who are unable to fast due to reasons such as illness, pregnancy, and travel. Some pious Muslims elect to stay in the mosque for the last ten days of Ramadan.

Laylat al-Qadr (Night of Power; Night of Destiny; Night of Determination; Laylat il-Qader; Lailat Alqadr; Lelé-I-Kadir; Nuzulul Qur'an)
Ramadan 27

One night during the last ten days of Ramadan (most often Ramadan 27), is set aside for special attention. Known as the Laylat al-Qadr, or Night of Power, it marks the very first revelation of the Qur'an. It is observed by spending the night in worship. This night is believed to be the time when Allah establishes the events to occur in the coming year.

Islamic teaching states that Allah revealed the entire Qur'an (Muslim holy book) to Muhammad through a series of revelations. These began in 610 C.E. when the angel Gabriel first spoke to him. The revelations continued throughout the remainder of his life. Islamic children begin studying the Qur'an when they are very young, and they celebrate when they've read all 114 chapters for the first time. Many adults try to memorize the entire Koran.

According to custom, the night of Ramadan 26 is the precise date on which Muhammad received the first revelation of the Qur'an; however the common belief that this day occurred on the 26th or 27th day of Ramadan has no Islamic base. Some researchers speculate that the date originated in Manicheism where the death of Mani is celebrated on the 27th of the fasting month.

Lantern's Festival (Day of Light; Lai-Lai-Tu-Gadri)
Ramadan 30

Lantern's Festival, an observance originating in Freetown, Sierra Leone during the 1930s, occurs near the end of the month- long fast of Ramadan. The custom of parading with lanterns originated with a trader known as Daddy Maggay. The original lanterns where simple hand-held paper boxes, lit from within and mounted on sticks. They were carried through the streets of Freetown in celebration of the day Allah sent the Qur'an to earth (the twenty-sixth day of Ramadan, also known as the Day of Light, or Lai-Lai-Tu-Gadri).

As the years passed, the celebration—and the lanterns—grew larger. Heavy boots, originally worn as protection, came to be used to produce drum-like rhythmical beats on the paved streets since some Muslims

TABLE 8.3. ALPHABETICAL LIST OF ISLAMIC HOLIDAYS

Holidays	Dates	Holidays	Dates
Al-'id al-Kabir	Dhu al-Hijjah 10	Lailat Alqadr	
Ascension of the Prophet		*see* Laylat al-Qadr	
see Laylat al-Miraj		Lantern's Festival	Ramadan 30
Ashoora *see* Ashura		Laylat al-Miraj	Rajab 27
Ashura	Muharram 10	Laylat al-Qadr	Ramadan 27
Awwal Muharram	Muharram 1	Laylat il-Qader	
Bara Wafat		*see* Laylat al-Qadr	
see Mawlid al-Nabi		Laylat-ul-Bara'h	
Birthday of Muhammad		*see* Shab-Barat	
see Mawlid al-Nabi		Lelé-I-Kadir	
Data Ganj Baksh Death		*see* Laylat al-Qadr	
Festival	Safar 18-19	Mandi Safar	During the month of Safar
Day of Light			
see Lantern's Festival		Mawlid al-Nabi	Rabi al-Awwal 12
Day of Sweet Soup or		Muharram	First month of Muslim calendar
Porridge			
see Yevmi Ashurer		New Year's Day	
Eidul Adah		*see* Awwal Muharram	
see 'Id al-Adha		Night Journey	
Eidul Fitr *see* 'Id al-Fitr		*see* Laylat al-Miraj	
Fast of Ramadan	Ninth month of the Islamic lunar year	Night of Destiny	
		see Laylat al-Qadr	
		Night of Determination	
Feast of Breaking the Fast		*see* Laylat al-Qadr	
see 'Id al-Fitr		Night of Forgiveness	
Feast of Sacrifice		*see* Shab-Barat	
see 'Id al-Adha		Night of Power	
Hajj		*see* Laylat al-Qadr	
see Pilgrimage to Mecca		Nuzulul Qur'an	
Hosay Festival		*see* Laylat al-Qadr	
see Husayn Festival		Pilgrimage to Mecca	Dhu al-Hijjah 8-13
Husayn Day	Muharram 10	Sallah	
'Id al-Adha	Dhu al-Hijjah 10-12	*see* Al-'id al-Kabir	
'Id al-Fitr	Shawwal 1-3	Seker Bayram	
Id as-Saghîr		*see* 'Id al-Fitr	
see 'Id al-Fitr		Shab-Barat	Sha`ban 15
Isra' and Mi'raj		Shah Abdul Latif Death	
see Laylat al-Miraj		Festival	Safar 14-16
Lai-Lai-Tu-Gadri		Sugar Feast	
see Lantern's Festival		*see* 'Id al-Fitr	
Lailat al Miraj		Yevmi Ashurer	Muharram 10
see Laylat al-Miraj			

discourage using drums. Maggay's group was called bobo, the name for the distinctive beat. Neighborhood rivalries, based on competition in lantern-building, often erupted in violence. By the 1950s the Young Men's Muslim Association had taken over the festival in hopes of reducing the violence through better organization. The lanterns—which by that time were elaborate float-like structures illuminated from within and drawn by eight-man teams or motor vehicles—were divided into three categories for judging: Group A for ships; Group B for animals and people; and Group C for miscellaneous secular subjects. Prizes were awarded to the top three winners in each group, based on creativity and building technique.

Shawwal

'Id al-Fitr (Feast of Breaking the Fast; Eidul Fitr; Id as-Saghîr; Seker Bayrami; Sugar Feast; often referred to simply as Id—pronounced "Eid")
Shawwal 1–3

This three-day festival, also known as Breaking of the Fast, marks the end of the month-long fast of Ramadan. It begins when the new moon is first seen. It is a festival of thanksgiving, offering thanks to Allah for the blessing of enjoying the month of Ramadan.

'Id al-Fitr is a festival of great cheer, rejoicing, and festivity. Muslims wear their new or best clothes and shoes, and offer mass prayers in mosques or in specially designated spaces outside, called musallas. After prayers there is a religious lecture from an Imam and warm greetings. According to Islamic tradition, 'Id al-Fitr marks the last day during which a Muslim can pay the Zakat, or tribute.

In many Muslim communities around the world, the whole day of Id is spent in festivities and exchanging sweets, good wishes, and visits. Children often receive presents, and Id greeting cards may be sent. Many village squares have carnival rides, puppet shows, and candy vendors. In Indonesia, Thailand, and Malaysia, the festival is called Lebaran, or Hari Raya. In Turkey, where it is called the Candy Festival, or Seker Bayrami, children are given candy or money wrapped in handkerchiefs. In Pakistan the special treat associated with Id is saween, a spaghetti cooked in milk and sugar and sprinkled with almonds, pistachios, and dates. In the spirit of benevolence that characterizes the celebration, the poor and needy are also given food, money, and clothes.

In modern times it has become customary to have one's non-Muslim friends visit to foster understanding between different ethnic groups. Muslims in turn visit Chinese friends during Lunar New Year, Hindus during Dewali, and Christians at Christmas.

Dhu al-Hijjah

Pilgrimage to Mecca (Hajj)
Dhu al-Hijjah 8–13

At least once in a lifetime, every Muslim man or woman (if she is accompanied by a male protector) with the means and the opportunity to do so is expected to make a pilgrimage to Mecca, the city in Saudi Arabia where Muhammad was born. It is one of the Five Pillars (fundamental duties) of Islam, and must be performed during the special pilgrimage season. The *Qur'an* says the founder of this pilgrimage was Abraham. The pilgrims wear two sheets of seamless white cloth and perform elaborate rites at the Grand Mosque of Mecca and in the immediate vicinity. All together, the rites require about six days to complete.

The focal point of the pilgrimage is the Ka'bah, a fifteen-foot-high stone structure that stands in the center court of the Grand Mosque of Mecca. It consists of one room without windows and is shaped like a cube. Islamic tradition claims the Ka'bah was built by Abraham and Ishmael. In one corner of the court is the Black Stone, believed to have been brought by the angel Gabriel. The Black Stone serves as a symbol of eternity because of its durability, and pilgrims traditionally kiss it before entering the shrine. The Ka'bah represents a place where Allah's presence touches the world. It is kept covered with a dark cloth decorated with embroidery.

Pilgrims must perform specific rites during their pilgrimage. These include walking around the Ka'bah seven times, walking between two mounts near it seven times, marching to Mina (three miles away), marching to Arafat (another six miles), listening to instruction, marching back to the Ka'bah, offering a sacrifice, and walking around the Ka'bah a final time.

It is not uncommon for two million or more Muslims to participate in the pilgrimage, which has forced Saudi Arabia and other countries to explore new methods for freezing, preserving, and distributing the meat that is produced by so many sacrifices. At the end of the pilgrimage, it is customary to visit the tomb of Muhammad at Medina before returning home.

Returning pilgrims, wearing the green scarf of the Hajj, are met by family and friends who have rented taxis and decorated them with palm branches and the families' best rugs. The pilgrim's house has been decorated with palm-leaf arches and sometimes outlined with lights. In Kurdish and Egyptian villages, the doorways will also have designs suggesting the journey. A feast and party finish the welcome home. A person who has made the pilgrimage earns the right to use the title Hajji.

Al-'id al-Kabir (Sallah, Salah)
Dhu al-Hijjah 10

Al-'id al Kibar is the major Islamic festival marking the end of the Hajj or pilgrimage season. In Nigeria the festival is called Sallah (or Salah) where it is celebrated with pomp and ceremony. People throng together in their best regalia. Processions of nobles on horseback are led by the emir to the prayer grounds. After a prayer service, the emir, dressed in white and carrying the historic Sword of Katsina, is seated on a platform. Groups of men take turns galloping up, reining in so their horses rear up at the last moment, and salute the emir. He raises the sword in response. Later, there is entertainment by musicians, acrobats, jesters, and dancers. Niger and some other African countries also celebrate the day with elaborate festivities.

'Id al-Adha (Feast of Sacrifice; Eidul Adah)
Dhu al-Hijjah 10–12

This three-day festival commemorates Abraham's obedience to God in nearly sacrificing his son Ishmael. Muslims maintain that it was Ishmael who was the son of promise and thus it was Ishmael who was nearly sacrificed but saved by God at the last moment. (This contrasts with the Jewish and Christian accounts maintaining that Isaac was the son of promise and the object of the intended sacrifice.) Ishmael is believed to be the ancestor of all Arabs.

To commemorate the miraculous provision of a sacrifice in Ishmael's place, goats and rams are offered to Allah at this time. The sacrifice of a ram or goat also symbolizes that man's position in the creation is far higher than any beast, and any sacrifice, however great, is a small thing for the sake of Allah.

In India and Pakistan the festival is also known as Bakrid. Bakrid is observed by Muslims who go to the mosques in the morning to offer prayers to Allah, and then return home to sacrifice the animal at home. The cooked meat becomes part of the family meal which ensues. The holiday is traditionally a time of peace, charity, and goodwill. As part of this, many people reach out to the poor, needy, and sick with money and gifts.

CHAPTER 9

Baha'i

Overview of Baha'i

What Is Baha'i?

The Baha'i faith is one of the world's newest religions. It was founded during the nineteenth century by Baha-'Allah who claimed to be a Divine Messenger in a long line of prophets that included Abraham, Krishna, Moses, Zoroaster, Buddha, Christ, and Muhammad. The Baha'i theme is one of fulfillment: the great teacher, long-expected in other traditions, had arrived.

The central message of Baha'ism is unity of both people and religions. Baha'is believe that all the world's religions have been part of the revelation of one God. They also believe that there is only one human race and call for an end to prejudice based on sex, race, religion, ethnicity, and nationality. Other guiding principles include a quest for truth, a belief that religion should yield affection and love among all people, and an assertion that religious beliefs should conform to scientific principles and reason. Baha'is believe that with the establishment of their faith, the historical time had arrived when all the world's peoples would be united into a single global society.

The Relationship between God and the Baha'i People

The Baha'i faith teaches that there is one God, creator, all-powerful, and all-knowing. God is also unknowable. God chooses to reveal himself, however, through selected messengers who carry his instructions to people in different times and places. These revelations fit the needs of various people in varying circumstances and together form a progressive, but unified, revelation of God. Baha'is do not believe that the revelation made through Baha'Allah is the final expression of God, but only that it was made for the current age. They expect other revelations to be made in future ages.

According to Baha'i teaching, people were created for the purpose of loving, knowing, and serving God. The human soul is created at conception and after death it inhabits spiritual spheres. Baha'is do not believe in reincarnation.

Authorities and Sacred Writings

One of the most sacred books in the Baha'i collection is *Kitab al-aqdas* (Most Holy Book). It was written by Baha'Allah during the years he was imprisoned for his beliefs. The writing contains laws for the Baha'i community. Other works authored by Baha'Allah also have scriptural authority. These include *Kitab al-igan* (Book of Certitude) which examines the concept of progressive revelation and *The Seven Valleys and the Four Valleys*, a mystical work that examines spiritual growth.

In addition to the writings of Baha'Allah, Baha'is also include works by the Bab and Abd al-Baha in the canon of scripture. The writings of Shoghi Effendi, while not accorded the same status, are nevertheless thought to provide infallible guidance to the worldwide Baha'i community.

The governing body with authority over all Baha'is is the Universal House of Justice, headquartered in Haifa, Israel. Its members are chosen by election. Local bodies are likewise governed by councils whose members are elected. In the 1990s there were more than 18,000 such councils around the world.

History of Baha'ism

The Bab

The Baha'i faith developed from Islamic roots. Followers of Islam have not generated many new religions because of the threat of stern punishment for heresy. One of the most notable exceptions to this pattern is Baha'ism, which began within the Shi`ite branch of Islam.

During the eighteenth century, a religious seeker, Shaykh Ahmad, started a journey in search of the Mahdi, or "Promised One." The *Qur'an* mentions this person whom the Shi`ite Muslims believe will be the legitimate successor of Muhammad as the leader of Islam. Ahmad did not find the Mahdi, but passed his quest on to his successor, Sayyid Kazim, who in turn passed the quest on to his students, along with a revelation that would enable them to recognize the Mahdi.

Kazim's student Mulla Husain traveled to Shiraz in Persia (now Iran), where he met a young man, Sayyid Ali Muhammad, who fulfilled the requirements of the revelation. Sayyid Ali Muhammad (1819–1850) was a member of the Shaykhi subsect of the Shi`ite Islamic people. The Shaykhis were known for their anticipation of the appearance of a Divine Messenger. When Ali Muhammad's father died, he was raised by his uncle. He was known as a young man with excellent physical features and personal piety in respect to following the Islamic faith.

After sunset on May 22, 1844, Sayyid Ali Muhammad declared himself to be the Bab, the "Gate" of God. Followers of Baha'i date their era from this event.

Babism

Another 17 of Kazim's students arrived in Shiraz and, according to Baha'i teaching, spontaneously recognized the Bab. Afterwards, the Bab began to preach his message publicly and gathered a large following. He did not claim to be the Mahdi himself, but merely a messenger preceding the Mahdi, much as John the Baptist is portrayed in the Christian Gospels as being the forerunner of Jesus.

Following the declaration, eighteen disciples joined the movement and were disbursed throughout Persia and Turkistan to bring the news of the declaration to the people. The Bab traveled to Mecca and declared himself and his mission. Some people accepted his teaching but rulers in the more orthodox Muslim communities called him a heretic.

In 1848, the Bab officially broke with the Shi`ites and established an independent movement called Babism. In 1850, after a series of imprisonments, the Bab was put to death by firing squad along with one of his followers named Áqa Muhammad Ali.

Baha'Allah

One of the Bab's followers, Mirza Husayn Ali (1817–1892; also called Jinab-i-Baha) took up the mantle of leadership after the Bab's death. He similarly suffered persecution at the hands of the established Shi`ite leadership and was imprisoned in 1852 in Tehran. During his time in prison, Husayn Ali began to understand that he was the Mahdi of whom the Bab had spoken. In 1853, along with his family, Husayn Ali was deported to Baghdad. In 1863 he made the first revelation of himself to a small group of followers, family, and friends. He also assumed a new name, Baha'Allah, which means Glory of God. In the days immediately following, he revealed himself to more of the movement's followers.

Despite repeated imprisonments and persecutions, Baha'Allah continued to attract more followers. In 1868, he was exiled to Akka, a penal colony (modernly Acre, located in Israel), where he lived under house arrest until his death in 1892.

Abd al-Baha

After Baha'Allah's death on May 29, 1892, leadership passed to his appointed successor, his oldest son, Abbas Effendi (1844–1921). Effendi, who's birth on May 23, 1844 coincided with the Bab's declaration, took the name Abd al-Baha, which means "Slave of Baha."

During the first years of Abd al-Baha's leadership, he was under travel restrictions imposed by Turkish authorities. These were lifted in 1911 and he began the process of taking his message to the world. Abd al-Baha is credited with helping define and give shape to the faith. He advocated the adoption of one language for the world and believed in compulsory education for all.

Abd al-Baha died on November 28, 1921 and passed on the responsibility for leading the Baha'i people to his eldest grandson, Shoghi Effendi Rabbani (1899–1957).

Shoghi Effendi standardized organizational forms of leadership and began a world-wide crusade to spread the faith. When he died suddenly in 1957 without naming a successor, the Universal House of Justice (the organization's headquarters in Israel) was appointed as the ultimate authority for the Baha'i community.

Baha'ism Today

In only a century and a half, Baha'i evolved from a small movement into an independent world religion. By the closing decade of the twentieth century, there were an estimated 5 million Baha'is living in more than 200 countries and territories around the world.

Conflicts with the Islamic community continued, however. Although some Islam leaders officially recognized Baha'i's standing as a separate faith in 1925, much animosity remained. In the early 1980s when the Ayatollah Khomeini returned to Iran from exile in Paris, more than 100 Iranian Baha'i leaders were executed; thousands more fled the country.

Worship

Baha'i worship may be conducted in a home, meeting hall, or temple. The number nine, as the largest whole digit, is significant in Baha'i numerology. It represents unity and completion. To emphasize this concept, Baha'i temples are constructed with nine sides.

Congregational worship consists of regular gatherings, scripture readings, and prayer. Baha'is also practice individual devotion including prayer, meditation and pilgrimages to shrines in Acre and Haifa. Work done in service to others and the giving of monetary gifts are also considered forms of worship.

Sects within Baha'ism

The Baha'i community preaches a message of unity and prides itself on the absence of divisions within the faith. Several small groups, however, have separated themselves from the main body of the Baha'i.

One break occurred in the early twentieth century when Ibrahim Kheiralla combined Baha'i teachings with personal occultist beliefs. Abd al-Baha rejected the teachings, and Kheiralla formed an organization called the Behaists. The movement subsequently died out.

Other splinter groups with small, but active, memberships include three organizations who believe that leadership of the Baha'i faith passed from Shoghi Effendi to Mason Remey, an American Baha'i, rather than to the Universal House of Justice.

TABLE 9.1. ALPHABETICAL LIST OF BAHA'I HOLIDAYS

Holidays	Dates
Ascension of Abd al-Baha	November 28
Ascension of Baha'Allah	May 29
Ayyam-i-Ha	February 25 through March 1
Birth of Abd al-Baha	May 23
Birth of Baha'Allah	November 12
Birth of the Bab	October 20
Day of the Covenant	November 26
Declaration of the Bab	May 23
Martyrdom of the Bab	July 9
Naw-Ruz	March 20-21
Period of the Fast	March 2-20
Race Unity Day	Second Sunday in June
Ridvan, Feast of	April 21-May 2
World Peace Day	September 21
World Religion Day	Third Sunday in January

The Baha'i Calendar

A Solar Calendar

The Bab instituted many reforms of Islamic culture in his revelations. These laid the groundwork for establishing Baha'i as an independent religion. Turning away from the lunar Islamic calendar, he instituted a new solar-based time-keeping system. Its epoch was set at the year of his declaration, 1844 C.E. (or in the Islamic calendar, 1260 A.H.). The Baha'i designation is New Era (N.E.).

Nineteen Months

The Baha'i calendar contains nineteen months of nineteen days each. The month and day names each represent a characteristic of God and the same nineteen names are also used to delineate each day within the month. For example, the first month is Baha (Splendor) and second month is Jalal (Glory). The first day of each month is Baha and the second day of each month is Jalal. The combination of month and day forms a phrase such as "the Splendor of Splendor" and "the Glory of Splendor" (for the first two days of the first month) or "the Splendor of Glory" and the "Glory of Glory" (for the first two days of the second month. Other possible phrases in other months include "the Mercy of Light" (the sixth day of the fifth month) and "the Knowledge of Perfection" (the twelfth day of the eighth month). Table 9.2 lists the month and day names of the Baha'i calendar.

Nineteen months of nineteen days yields 361 days. Four intercalary days—five in leap years—are added to keep the calendar in phase with the solar year and the common calendar. These four or five days, called Ayyam-i-Ha, preceed the last month of the Baha'i year.

Weeks and Days

In addition to months and days, people of the Baha'i faith observe a seven-day week. Each of the week days also possesses a name. In a manner similar to the Western civil calendar in which the week days are observed concurrently with but separate from the days of the month, the Baha'i week days are acknowledged in order irrespective of the month days. The days of the Baha'i week are shown in Table 9.3.

Baha'i days begin at sunset. Therefore, a day begins on the "previous" day according to the common civil calendar. The last day of the week (Friday) is observed as a day of rest.

TABLE 9.2. THE BAHA'I MONTH AND DAY NAMES

Month Begins on Gregorian Date	Month/Day Number and Baha'i Name	Meaning
March 21	1. Baha	Splendour
April 9	2. Jalal	Glory
April 28	3. Jamal	Beauty
May 17	4. Azamat	Grandeur
June 5	5. Nur	Light
June 24	6. Rahmat	Mercy
July 13	7. Kalimat	Words
August 1	8. Kasmal	Perfection
August 20	9. Asma	Names
September 8	10. Izzat	Might
September 27	11. Mashiyyat	Will
October 16	12. Ilm	Knowledge
November 4	13. Qudrat	Power
November 23	14. Qawl	Speech
December 12	15. Masail	Questions
December 31	16. Sharaf	Honor
January 19	17. Sultan	Sovereignty
February 7	18. Mulk	Dominion
February 26	Ayyam-i-Ha	intercalary days
March 2	19. Ala	Loftiness

TABLE 9.3. THE BAHA'I WEEK

Day	Name	Meaning
Saturday	Jalal	Glory
Sunday	Jamal	Beauty
Monday	Kasmal	Perfection
Tuesday	Fidal	Grace
Wednesday	Idal	Justice
Thursday	Istijlal	Majesty
Friday	Istiqlal	Independence

Baha'i Holidays

Monthly

Nineteen-Day Feast
The first day of each of the nineteen months of the Baha'i calendar

The Baha'i calendar is organized into 19 months of 19 days each; these 361 days, plus a four-day intercalary period, make up the Baha'i year. A fifth day is added in leap years to keep the Baha'i dates fixed relative to the common calendar. On the first day of each month, the Baha'i community gathers for its Nineteen-Day Feast, which is restricted to confirmed members of the Baha'i faith. The Feast consists of three parts: a worship service; a town meeting for self-governance as a community; and a social occasion with feasting and celebration.

Annually

Naw-Ruz
March 20–21

Naw-Ruz is the Baha'i New Year's Day. It is observed from sunset to sunset on March 20 to 21.

The day also marks the end of the 19-day fast, from March 2–20, when people of the Baha'i faith abstain from food and drink from sunrise to sunset as a reminder that one's true nature is spiritual rather than material.

Ridvan, Feast of
April 21–May 2

During this twelve-day feast, Baha'is commemorate the 1863 declaration of Baha'Allah, the founder of the religion, as the Promised One or Mahdi. He is considered by his followers to be of the same stature as Abraham, Moses, Jesus, Muhammad, Buddha, Krishna, and Zoroaster. The first, ninth, and twelfth days of the feast are the most holy. On these days, work is suspended and believers participate in observing the celebrations of the day.

Baha'Allah's declaration took place in a garden he called Ridvan (or Paradise) located outside Baghdad. The full revelation of Baha'Allah's identity was made over a twelve-day period. On the first day of the process, he declared himself to his family and close friends. On the ninth day, news of his declaration spread and followers came to join him. Subsequently, he went out into the world with his message: he was the "promised one" prophesied by the Bab nineteen years earlier and would spread Baha'i to all the world. The main thrust of Baha'Allah's gospel was the unity of all religions and the kinship of all humanity. Throughout his life, Baha'Allah wrote over one hundred works which followers of Baha'i regard as sacred.

Declaration of the Bab
May 23

On May 23, 1844, Ali Muhammad revealed that he was the Bab, or gate, to the anticipated "Coming One" of all religions. With this declaration, the Baha'i faith was started. The Bab based his teachings on the *Qur'an*, but adopted a moderate interpretation of its meaning. Although the Bab maintained that he was simply the

forerunner of one who would be greater than himself (similar to John the Baptist as the precursor to Jesus in Christian doctrine), he attracted a significant following. His disciples were known as Babis and among them was Mirza Husayn Ali. In 1863, Ali revealed himself to be the Messiah of whom the Bab had spoken and assumed the title Baha'Allah.

The Declaration of the Bab is one of the nine holy days on which Baha'is suspend trade and commercial, industrial, and agricultural work.

Birth of Abd al-Baha
May 23

Abd al-Baha was born on the same night as the Declaration of the Bab, May 23, 1844. The Baha'i celebration commemorating the birth occurs in conjunction with the observance of the Declaration of the Bab. Abd al-Baha's birth on this date was significant because it fulfilled prophecies given by the Bab (Mirza Ali-Muhammad).

Ascension of Baha'Allah
May 29

Each year, followers of the Baha'i faith remember the death of Mirza Husayn Ali, known as Baha'Allah, by gathering together at 3:00 A.M. (the time of Baha'Allah's death) for prayers and occasional readings from Baha'i writings. The use of the term "ascension" connotes the rising of the spirit rather than the body to its heavenly dwelling. This is one of the nine holy days during the year on which Baha'is do not work.

Race Unity Day
The second Sunday in June

Observed by Baha'is worldwide, Race Unity Day was established in 1957 to focus attention on the problem of racial prejudice. Participants attend discussions and meetings to promote peace and universal recognition of the connection of all humanity.

Martyrdom of the Bab
July 9

In 1850, Ali Muhammad (known as the Bab) was executed by the Persian government. Threatened by the Bab's teachings of religious and social reform, the traditional political and religious powers were antagonistic toward the movement. The hostility between both powers culminated in the execution of the Bab.

Followers of Baha'i remember this event annually on July 9 by abstaining from trade and commercial, agricultural, and industrial work.

TABLE 9.4. BAHA'I HOLIDAY CYCLE

March
20-21 . . . . . .Naw-Ruz

April
23-May 2 . . .Feast of Ridvan

May
23 . . . . . . .Declaration of the Bab
23 . . . . . . .Birth of Abd al-Baha
29 . . . . . . .Ascension of Baha'Allah

June
~ . . . . . . .Race Unity Day

July
9 . . . . . . .Martyrdom of the Bab

September
21 . . . . . . .World Peace Day

October
20 . . . . . . .Birth of the Bab

November
12 . . . . . . .Birth of Baha'Allah
26 . . . . . . .Day of the Covenant
28 . . . . . . .Ascension of Abd al-Baha

January
~ . . . . . . .World Religion Day

February
25-Mar 1 . . .Ayyam-i-Ha

March
2-20 . . . . . .Period of the Fast

~ indicates a variable date

World Peace Day
September 21

The celebration of World Peace Day by the National Spiritual Assembly of the Baha'is of the United States is intended to call for and support leadership in world peace.

Birth of the Bab
October 20

On October 20, Baha'is honor the birth of their founder, Mirza Ali Muhammad, the Bab or "Gate" to God, in 1819; the Islamic date was Muharram 1, 1235 A.H. Baha'i grew out of a sect of Islam, called Shaikiya, which taught that a human intercessor between Allah and man was necessary. Ali Muhammad claimed to be this intercessor, or gate, and began teaching a more moderate form of Islam that advocated toleration of other beliefs and fewer restrictions on its adherents.

Birth of Baha'Allah
November 12

On November 12 Baha'is celebrate the 1817 birth of their Persian-born teacher and Messiah of their faith. Born Mirza Husayn Ali, he was a follower of Ali Muhammad, or the Bab. The Bab founded a religion called, Babism, focused on the belief that a Messiah was coming. The expectancy of Babism was fulfilled in Ali.

In 1863, Ali announced that he was the Messiah for whom the Babis were waiting. He changed his name to Baha'Allah, and began teaching social and religious reform. Although many of his doctrines were based on Islam, some major teachings of the *Qur'an* (such as polygamy, slavery, and the notion of the holy war) were rejected. Baha'Allah also placed a strong emphasis on the equality of the sexes.

The subsequent leader of Baha'i, Abbas Effendi, spread the faith around the world through his missionary journeys. Followers of Baha'i observe the Birth of Baha'Allah as one of the nine holy days on which they refrain from work.

Day of the Covenant
November 26

On this date each year, Baha'is celebrate the Covenant set forth in Baha'Allah's last will and testament. The Covenant established religious freedom for followers of Baha'i by insisting that the kingdom of God depends on the freely given assent of Baha'is to the doctrines of their faith and the authority of Baha'Allah's legitimate successor (whom he designated as his son, Abd al-Baha).

Ascension of Abd al-Baha
November 28

The third Baha'i leader, Abbas Effendi (called Abd al-Baha) was the eldest son of Mirza Husayn Ali (called Baha'Allah). His death on November 28, 1921 is commemorated annually.

The term "ascension" in the name of the holiday (Ascension of Abdu'l l-Baha) connotes the rising of the spirit to its heavenly dwelling. It does not imply the rising of the body.

World Religion Day
The third Sunday in January

In 1950, the National Spiritual Assembly of the Baha'is of the United States established this day as a holiday to focus world attention on the harmony of all religions. The Baha'i maintain that all religion is intended to create unity, ease suffering, and bring about peace. Everyone should, therefore, work together to accomplish these goals. People gather in homes, or hold public meetings and panel discussions to observe the day.

Ayyam-i-Ha
February 25 through March 1

Ayyam-i-Ha consists of intercalary days inserted between the eighteenth and nineteenth months of the Baha'i calendar. These days are a time of charity, gift-giving, rejoicing, and hospitality in preparation for the Baha'i fast days during the nineteenth month.

Period of the Fast
March 2–20

During the nineteenth month, the last month of the Baha'i year, Baha'is observe a fast in which adherents refrain from eating and drinking from sunrise to sunset. The fast ends at the spring equinox in the northern hemisphere and with the autumnal equinox in the southern hemisphere. Although believers abstain from food, the focus of the fast is on abstaining from desires that hinder them from serving god. Children, the sick, travelers, and pregnant and nursing women are excused from the rigors of fasting.

CHAPTER 10

Hinduism

Overview of Hinduism

What Is Hinduism?

The word Hindu is derived from the Sanskrit term Sindhu (or Indus) which meant ocean or river. It referred to people living in the Indus valley in the Indian subcontinent. Many scholars regard Hinduism as the oldest living religion.

Hinduism has no founder, many gods, and several scriptures. It is a religion of diversity within an established tradition founded on writings called the *Vedas*. It encompasses a multitude of sects who venerate selected gods or goddesses (or their consorts or children) in any one of their various or multiple manifestations. Although Hindu adherents practice their faith differently and venerate different gods, they share a similar view of reality and look back on a common history.

Some concepts that are part of the Hindu heritage include transmigration of the atman (a concept similar to that of the self, soul, or spirit) and karma. Transmigration of the atman, also called reincarnation, means that a person's atman goes through a succession of lives. Depending on the form of Hinduism, previous lives may include animals and even plants. The cycle of rebirths, called samsara, continues without end until spiritual purity is achieved. Upon reaching this level of perfection, the person's atman is liberated from samsara and becomes one with Brahman, the ultimate universal reality. The term moksa is used to describe the achievement of freedom from samsara.

The means by which perfection and liberation are achieved vary among different groups of Hindus but they focus on the elimination of karma. Karma is produced by a person's actions in life. Good actions lead to the accumulation of good karma; bad actions lead to the accumulation of bad karma. A person's karma determines several features of their next rebirth: what level of society (caste) they will be born into, how long their life will be, and what experiences they will encounter. Good and bad karma, however, both lead to rebirth. To become freed from karma, a Hindu must attain a level of detachment in which no karma is accumulated or follow a precise code of conduct that eliminates karma.

To eliminate karma, some Hindus practice yoga, a system of mental and physical disciplines in which a heightened state of consciousness is sought through attention to body posture, breath control, and focused mental concentration. Others may follow a path of devotion to one of many personal gods or goddesses. Some stress the importance of specific actions, deeds, or occupations. Other Hindus seek the attainment of secret knowledge learned from a teacher, called a guru. Many Hindus recognize four separate stages of life: during the first stage a youth begins to study under the guidance of a guru; the second stage involves duty to family and the community; during the third stage detachment is sought; and the fourth stage prepares for what lies beyond the current life.

From the concepts of karma and rebirth a belief in social stratification, called the caste system, developed. The caste system is a hierarchical organization that governs many things about a person's life including occupation and marriage partner. Hindu tradition teaches that castes were originally established according to skin color, but later they came to represent stations in life. The highest class (called the Brahmins) comprises priests, scholars, and professionals. The next level, the Ksatriyas consists of rulers and soldiers. The third level, the Vaishyas, are merchants and farmers. The lowest class, the Sudras, are peasants and servants. Within these four major groups there exist approximately 3,000 subcasts.

The Relationship between the Gods and the Hindu People

The Hindu pantheon includes many gods—more than 33 million according to some estimates. Some of these are held in higher esteem than others.

Over all the gods, Hindus believe in one absolute high god or universal concept. This is Brahman. Although he is above all the gods, he is not worshipped in popular ceremonies because he is detached from the day to day affairs of the people. Brahman is impersonal. Lesser gods serve him, and because they are more intimately involved in the affairs of people, they are the gods that are venerated.

The most honored god in Hinduism varies among the different Hindu sects. Three of the most popular are Visnu, Siva, and Sakti. Some Hindus consider these three different gods; some consider them different expressions of the same god.

Visnu is a good, benevolent god. Laksmi, the goddess of fortune, is his wife. He is known through his ten incarnations (called avataras). These are:

- Matsya, the Fish, who saved the first man from the flood
- Kurma, the Tortoise, upon whose back Mount Mandara rested when the ocean was churned so the gods could look for lost ambrosia
- Varaha, the Boar, who rescued the earth after a demon threw it into an ocean
- Narasimha, the Man-Lion, who killed the demon Hiranyakasipu
- Vamana, the Dwarf, who freed the earth, air, and sky from the dominion of demons
- Parashu Rama, Rama of the Axe
- Rama, King of Ayodhya, hero of the epic *Ramayana* who freed Sri Lanka by killing the demon Ravana
- Krishna, a mischievous but beloved manifestation, whose dialogue with Arjuna is presented in the *Bhagavad Gita*
- Buddha, the founder of Buddhism, the last avatara in history
- Kalkin, an awaited savior—an expected incarnation of the future who will bring judgement to the earth and restore the golden age

Of these, the two primary incarnations of Visnu were as Rama and as Krishna. Some Hindus believe that Jesus of Nazareth, and Muhammad were also incarnations of Visnu. In this way they create a unification of all religions.

Siva represents destruction and regeneration. He has a dual aspect of good and bad and is often accompanied by evil spirits. To his followers, he is loving. Although Siva represents death, in death is rebirth and renewal. He is associated with storms and has authority over diseases and healing herbs. Siva can often be recognized in artistic renditions of him by his blue neck. In the *Rig Veda* he is called Rudra. Other names by which he is known are Pashupa (Protector of Cattle), Sambhu, and Sankara.

Sakti, the wife of Siva, is a mother goddess. She has both benevolent and horrifying aspects. Her forms are Durga (also known as Kali) and Parvati (also known as Uma). Durga is a harsh form that in the past was worshipped with blood sacrifices, both animal and human. Parvati is a mild form of the goddess, a beautiful, passionate lover and virtuous wife.

Other major Hindu gods include Brahma, Ganesa, Indra, Skanda, and Hanuman. Brahma is not the same as the universal Brahman. Brahma, however, is the creator god, credited with fabricating the earth. Saraswati is his consort. She supervises the work of musicians, writers, and students. Ganesa is a son of Siva, a deity with an elephant head and human body who helps remove obstacles. According to legend, after Ganesa's head was turned to ashes, Siva took the head of Indra's elephant to give to Ganesa. Indra is a warrior god credited with saving the world from the cosmic serpent. Skanda, another son of Siva, is often portrayed with six heads. Hanuman, a monkey god, was Rama's helper. He is considered a guardian. In his honor, monkeys are protected in India.

Authorities and Sacred Writings

The Vedas

Hinduism has no priesthood or hierarchical structure. Hindus acknowledge the authority of a wide variety of writings but there is no single, uniform canon. The oldest of the Hindu writings are the *Vedas*. The word "veda" comes from the Sanskrit word for knowledge. The *Vedas*, which were compiled from ancient oral traditions, contain hymns, instructions, explanations, chants for sacrifices, magical formulas, and philosophy.

The *Rig Veda* is a collection of 1028 hymns to the Vedic gods and goddesses. It dates from approximately 1500–1200 B.C.E. and is the oldest surviving literature for any of the world's living religions. The *Rig Veda* is also the oldest surviving literature in any of the Indo-European languages. Other Vedic works include the *Sama Veda* (hymns for chanting), the *Yajur Veda* (for sacrifices), and the *Atharva Veda* (incantations and sacrifices.)

Ritual and philosophy books based on the four *Vedas* are *Brahmanas* and *Aranyakas*. *Brahmanas* dates between 800–600 B.C.E. It provides a commentary on the *Vedas* and explains Vedic mythology. *Aranyakas* dates from approximately 600 B.C.E.

The *Upanisads* are also books in the Vedic tradition. They consist of doctrinal texts written between 800–300 B.C.E. and include dialogues between a teacher and student or between sages. The discussions focus on ritual, commentary, and philosophy.

The Epics

Another set of sacred books include the *Great Epics* which illustrate Hindu faith in practice. The *Epics* include the *Ramayana* the *Mahabharata*, and the *Bhagavad Gita*.

The *Ramayana* (which means Romance of Rama) presents a story about Visnu in his avatara of Prince Rama. The tale recounts his exploits and the rescue of his wife after she is taken captive by a demon. The epic story contains seven books and comprises 24,000 verses. Its central focus is on human virtues.

The *Mahabharata* (which means War Poems of the Bharata) is a compilation of legends that present accounts of a civil war among the potential heirs to an ancient kingdom. It is the longest epic, comprising 18 books, called parvas, and totaling 100,000 verses. The central focus of the *Mahabharata* is on human virtues and vices.

The *Bhagavad Gita* (which means Song of God) is the fourth book of the *Mahabharata* and is perhaps the most widely read of all the Hindu scriptures. It contains a sermon delivered by Krishna to warriors preparing for battle. The shortest of the three Hindu epics, it consists of 700 verses in 18 chapters. Important elements in the *Bhagavad Gita* include the worship of Krishna as an incarnation of Visnu, a discussion of the nature of atman and Brahman, ways to achieve moksa (freedom from the cycle of rebirth), comparative philosophies, and the moral and religious duties of the different castes.

Law Codes, Puranas, and Tantras

Other sacred books include the *Law Codes* and the *Purnas*. The *Law Codes* offer societal regulations. The *Manyu-Smriti* (Laws of Manu) was developed around 100 B.C.E. It provides comprehensive laws governing things such as marriages, funerals, the duties of kings, and caste regulations. The *Puranas* are verses dating from 500–1000 C.E. that further develop classical Hindu mythology and provide genealogies for various gods and heros.

The *Tantras* comprise a set of writings dating from about the seventh century to the 14th century C.E. They focus on feminine power and include information about spiritual matters, disciplines, and rituals to harness sensual energies for the attainment of moksa.

History

The Aryan People

Modern Hinduism is based on the beliefs of people who established themselves in the Indus Valley (northwestern region of the Indian subcontinent) between 2500 and 1700 B.C.E. Called the Aryans, they were taller and of lighter skin than the native population. The word Aryan is derived from Sanskrit and it means "noble people." Most of the information available about the ancient Aryans comes from the Hindu sacred books.

The Caste System

The Aryans lived in semi-nomadic tribal groups, each with its own warrior chief called a rajah. The people were divided among three castes: priests, leaders and soldiers, and common people. A lower fourth class, called the Sudras, consisted of dark-skinned, non-Aryan indigenous people. Around the time of the first millennium B.C.E. a fifth group of "untouchables" was added to the four-fold caste system. Called Pariahs, people so classified were non-Aryans who were kept in impoverished conditions and obligated to do jobs deemed unclean such as tanning leather and handling dead animals.

The strictures of the caste system and abuses perpetrated by those of the highest caste led to discontent. Between 400–500 B.C.E. several religious movements separated from Hinduism to become distinct religions. Two of the most notable were founded by Gautama Buddha (Buddhism) and Mahavira (Jainism). Although Jainism never acquired a sufficient number of followers to pose a threat to traditional Hinduism, Buddhism won many converts including the leader of the Indian empire, Chandragupta Maurya (c. 321–297 B.C.E.).

Rather than abandon the caste system, however, Hindu society enlarged it. Beginning around 300 B.C.E. the original divisions underwent a series of subdivisions based on occupational groups. The presence of numerous individual groups, called jatis, increased the segregation between people at all levels of society.

Societal Changes

Asoka, the last emperor of the Maurya dynasty died in 232 B.C.E. and the era that followed was marked by turbulence and conquest. By the end of the second century B.C.E., the Indian empire had diminished in power and new kingdoms had gained prominence in the northern regions of the Indian subcontinent. During the uncertain times of the era, people returned to their ancient beliefs, revitalized their complex legal system, and empowered the Brahmin (priestly) caste.

The Gupta dynasty dates from approximately the fifth century C.E. It marked a time when both Buddhism and Hinduism flourished in India, but Hindu practices began to prevail. The role of Hindu priests, under the emperor's patronage, was elevated. The practice of venerating a particular god or gods rose, primarily in the southern portion of the region and with particular emphasis on Visnu and Siva. The bhakti movement, which is marked by devotion to gods and saints, traces its beginnings to this era in southern India. Its spread into other regions occurred slowly, reaching northern India during the eleventh century.

Different Schools of Hinduism

During the following centuries, Brahminical forms of Hinduism rose in popularity. Elaborate temples were built and dedicated to the gods, particularly to Visnu and Siva. Worship of gods increased as literature helped spread knowledge of them. Different schools of Hinduism also began to differentiate themselves.

Sankara, born in 788 C.E. was a philosopher, mystic, and poet. Some believed him to be an incarnation of Siva. Sankara founded the Advaita Vedanta school of Hinduism and taught that the physical world was an illusion; the only true reality was Brahman. He also believed that the human soul and Brahman were merged into oneness when moksa was achieved. His views emphasized the unity of Brahman (the universal reality) and atman (the human soul).

Contrasted with Sankara's teachings are those of Ramanuja (1017–1137 C.E.). Ramanuja founded a school of Hinduism called Vishisht Advaita. He believed that the physical world was not an illusion and that a person's soul was not identical with Brahman. He promoted individual devotion as the proper way of worshipping.

Madhva (1197–1280) started the Dvaita school of Hinduism. He believed that Brahman and atman were different and remained separate even after a person achieved release from the cycle of rebirth.

Foreign Influences

Beginning with the 13th century, Hindu society came in more frequent contact with other cultures. The Muslim Moghul dynasty became established in the northwestern part of the Indian subcontinent. By the sixteenth century, contact with European culture, particularly Christianity, technology, and education, brought new ideas about social reforms.

British rule, established in 1757 in Calcutta brought further reforms to ancient practices including changes in child marriage laws, the lessening of caste distinctions, and the abatement of some of the human misery associated with the lower casts and "outcastes."

Social and Religious Reforms

Ram Mohan Roy (1772–1833) was a social reformer who advocated an educational system and the abolishment of sati (the practice of burning a widow on her husband's funeral pyre). Roy also founded the Brahmo Samaj (Congregation of Brahman) which emphasized humanism and promoted the belief that faith should be founded on reason.

Another Hindu reformer of the nineteenth century, Ramakrishna (1836–1886) believed that god could be found through any religion and that all religions were merely different paths to the same ultimate reality.

One of the best known figures during the years before India's independence was Mahatma Gandhi (1869–1948). Born Mohandas Karamchand Gandhi, he was given the title Mahatma which means "great soul." Gandhi's religious focus was based on the *Bhagavad Gita* from which he developed the belief that the intention of life was for purposeful action. He advocated non-violence and non-cooperation with foreign rulers. He promoted the cause of the "untouchables" and called them "Harijan" (Children of God). Gandhi's vision and efforts helped create the Independent Republic of India in 1947. (Discrimination on the grounds of "untouchability" was outlawed in India in 1950.)

Gandhi was assassinated on January 30, 1948. Some Hindus believe he was an avatara (incarnation) of Visnu.

Hinduism Today

The Hindu People

Although the largest population of Hindu people exists in India, significant numbers of Hindus also live in Africa, Europe, Latin America, North America, and in the Pacific Islands. Population estimates vary widely from 400 million or 500 million to over one billion.

Hindu Worship

Temples and shrines are common throughout India. Typically they contain an image which is called a murti. For some Hindus the murtis are representative of concepts. For others, the murtis are actual gods. They are bathed, dressed, and carried in processions. Music and dances are provided for their entertainment. Festivals celebrate special events or reenact mythic legends.

In the temples, worship is typically not congregational (although in some places a form of congregational worship does exist). Priests, who are specialists in the performance of specific rituals, make offerings on behalf of the worshippers. Typical offerings are of flowers, food, or money which the worshipper gives to the priest to offer to the god. A token portion of the offering may be returned. Individual worshippers perform other rituals such as walking around the murti. Prayers and bowing may be performed. A mantra may be recited. Mantras are believed to represent a god in sound. The "om" syllable that is often chanted represents Brahman. Some temples are built in conjunction with a body of water (either natural or constructed) where worship often involves bathing.

The act of worship is called a puja. It can occur in a private home or in a temple. One of the most important aspects of Hinduism is individual worship which is conducted in private homes. Most houses devote either a room or a portion of a room as the family shrine which contains an image of the god the family serves. Worship includes anointing the image or representation of the god, lighting incense, placing flowers, reciting sacred texts, and meditation.

Hindu Sects

Hindu sects are called sampradayas. Initiation into a sampradaya often involves wearing some kind of identifying mark, learning a mantra (sacred verbalization), following a particular guru, and applying devotion to a specific god or goddess. Some of the most popular sampradayas are Vaishnava (devotees of Visnu), Saivite (devotees of Siva), Rama Cults (devotees of Rama), and Krishna Cults (devotees of Krishna).

Vaishnavas

Vaishnavas are devotees who honor Visnu as the supreme god in the Hindu pantheon. Many Visnu sampradayas appeared between the fifth and twelfth centuries C.E. and attracted people from the lower castes.

The Sri Vaishnavas, considered to be among the oldest of the Viashanava Sampradayas, claim that Visnu and his wife, Laksmi, founded their sect which is marked for its personal worship of the god and goddess. Another Vaisnava sect, the Nimbarki Sampradayas hold a doctrinal position describing the similarities and differences between the human atman and the divine.

Saivites

Saivites are devotees of Siva. The first Siva sects appeared during the first and second centuries C.E. They focused on the manifestation of Siva as Pashupa, (Protector of Cattle). During the following centuries other Siva sects developed. Some worshipped the ambiguous deity by indulging in wine and performing ritual sexual intercourse. By the seventh century, the worship of Siva had assumed a less controversial nature and included elements such as meditation and penance. Worship of the "linga," a symbolic representation of Siva's phallus, continues to play an important role in honoring Siva.

Rama Cults

Rama Cults first appeared during the centuries of Muslim incursion into traditionally Hindu lands (beginning in the eighth century, but with its main push beginning in the eleventh century). Many Rama cults tended to elevate Rama to the position of supreme deity rather than merely as a manifestation of Visnu.

Krishna Cults

Madhwaguariya Samparadayas, a subsect of Vaishnavas, honor Krishna and worship him through the recitation of his name. The Hare Krishna movement, well known in the United States, has its roots in Madhwaguariya Samparadaya.

Caitanya, a scholar from Bengal who was born during the 15th century, became a follower of Krishna. He assumed the name Krishna Caitanya, which means "he whose consciousness is Krishna." He sought moksa (liberation from the cycle of rebirth) through the adoration of Krishna and the constant repetition of his name. After several centuries and through generations of followers the movement became established in the United States in 1966 as the International Society for Krishna Consciousness (ISKCON). The sect attained popularity through its association with singer George Harrison of The Beatles.

Krishna: One of the most popular avataras of Visnu.

The Hindu Calendars

Many Methods of Measuring Time

There is no single Hindu calendar. Various Hindu sects define the month differently. The varying definitions of the lunar month caused a division in the Hindu religion. The boundaries of the contending groups seem to fall along geographical lines. In northern India, the lunar month begins with the full or waning moon, while Hindus in the south of India measure the month from the new or waxing moon.

The confusion caused by the use of two methods of measuring the month has resulted in the celebration of holidays on different dates by the Visnu and Siva sects of Hinduism. This happens because the waxing half of the month (from the new to the full moon) falls in the same month in both regions, but the waning half falls in different months. Therefore any festivals that take place in the waning half of the month can fall up to thirty days apart in the north and south.

Common Components

Despite regional differences, the Hindu calendars share some common components. To make the two systems as compatible as possible, Hindus number the two halves of the months separately. The months are divided into two periods of approximately fifteen days called pakshas, or "fortnights," in which the days are numbered from one to fifteen. Each of the days in the fortnight is consecrated to a deity in the Hindu pantheon.

The calendars contain both solar and lunar aspects. The solar component is based on a sidereal year (not the tropical year used in the West). The sidereal year marks a complete orbit of the earth around the sun by observing the precise positioning of stars; the tropical year is based on the progression of the sun from equinox to equinox.

By relying on sidereal calculations, the Hindu calendar months perfectly correspond to the signs of the zodiac. Month names among the Hindu calendars vary according to the dialects of the regions, but the names of the astrological signs are consistant throughout the country.

TABLE 10.1. DAYS OF THE HINDU FORTNIGHT

Day	Name	Consecrated to
1	Pratipada	Brahma
2	Dvitiya	Vidhatr
3	Tritiya	Visnu
4	Chaturthi	Ganesa or Yama
5	Pañcami	Moon
6	Shashti	Karttikeya
7	Saptimi	Indra
8	Ashtami	Sakti or the Vasus
9	Navimi	Sakti or the Serpent
10	Dashami	Dharma
11	Ekadashi	Visnu or Rudra
12	Dvadashi	Sun
13	Trayodashi	Siva
14	Chaturdashi	Ganesa or Yama
15	Purnima —full moon	Devas
15	Amavasaya —new moon	Devas

TABLE 10.2. THE HINDU YEAR

Season	Month Names	Gregorian Equivalents
Vasanta		Spring
	Vaisakha	April-May
	Jyestha	May-June
Grisma		Summer
	Asadha	June-July
	Sravana	July-August
Varsa		Rains
	Bhadrapada	August-September
	Asvina	September-October
Sarad		Autumn
	Kartika	October-November
	Margasira	November-December
Hemanta		Winter
	Pausa	December-January
	Magha	January-February
Sisira		Dews
	Phalguna	February-March
	Caitra	March-April

The solar months are based on the celestial movement of the sun and stars along the ecliptic. A new month begins when the moon enters a new celestial sign. Each month and sign has an arc of 30° along the ecliptic, but the months vary in actual length between 27 and 32 days.

A Lunar Component

Like many other religious calendars, the Hindu calendars also have a lunar component. The Hindu lunar calendar consists of twelve 30-day months with one month intercalated about every three years. Whenever two new moons occur within one solar month (months based on the zodiacal signs), the intercalary lunar month is added. The normal month in which the two new moons occurred has "nija" added to the end of its name. The intercalated month is named for the normal month but "adhika" is added to the end. The normal months of the Hindu lunar calendar are named for the solar month in which they begin.

Hindu Eras

In addition to marking the passing of lunar and solar months and years, Hindu mythology describes long eras called yugas. The current era, called the Kali Yuga, began in 3102 B.C.E. It is considered to be the most decadent of the Yugas.

There are four Yugas which begin with perfection and go through successive stages of deterioration. After the fourth yuga, the Kali Yuga, time is interrupted while the cosmos is recreated and begins again. A cycle of four Yugas, called a Maha Yuga, lasts 4,320,000 years. According to some Hindu belief systems, 1,000 Maha Yugas comprises one day in the life of the creator, Bramha.

TABLE 10.3.
THE LENGTH OF THE YUGAS
(HINDU AGES)

Kruga Yuga	1,728,000 years
Treta Yuga	1,296,000 years
Dwapar Yuga	864,000 years
Kali Yuga	432,000 years

TABLE 10.4. THE HINDU HOLIDAY CYCLE

Dates	Holidays
Vaisakha—Waxing (April-May)	
1	Vaisakhi
1–10 days	Pooram
3	Akshya Tritiya
3	Parasurama Jayanti
3–24	Chandan Yatra
5 or 10	Sankaracarya Jayanti
9	Janaki Navami
14	Narasimha Jayanti
Jyestha—Waxing (May-June)	
6	Sithinakha (Cake Festival)
8	Jyestha Ashtami
10	Ganga Dussehra
11	Nirjala Ekadashi
Jyestha—Waning	
1–15	Snan Yatra
13	Vata Savitri
Asadha—Waxing (June-July)	
2	Ratha Yatra
11	Hari-Shayani Ekadashi
15	Guru Purnima
Sravana—Waxing (July-August)	
3	Hariyali Teej
5	Nag Pancami
7	Tulsidas Jayanti
11	Putrada Ekadashi
15	Narieli Purnima
15	Raksa Bandhana
15	Jhulan Latra
Sravana—Waning	
1–15	Sravani Mela
11	Kamada Ekadashi
14	Ghanta Karna

(continued on next page)

TABLE 10.4. THE HINDU HOLIDAY CYCLE, continued

Bhadrapada—Waxing (August-September)

~ . . . . .Tirupati Festival
~ . . . . .Onam
3 . . . . .Haritalika Teej
4 . . . . .Ganesa Caturthi
5 . . . . .Rishi Pañcami
14 . . . . .Anant Chaturdashi

Bhadrapada—Waning

6 . . . . .Halashashti
8 . . . . .Janmashtami
8 . . . . .Radha Ashtami
14–Asvina . . . . . . .Indra Jatra

Asvina—Waxing (September-October)

~ . . . . .Laksmi Puja
1–10 . . . . .Durga Puja
10 days . . . . . . .Dasain
10 . . . . .Dussehra
15 . . . . .Sharad Purnima
15 . . . . .Kojagara
15 . . . . .Valmiki Jayanti

Asvina—Waning

1–14 . . . . .Pitra Visarjana Amavasya

Kartika—Waxing (October-November)

~ . . . . .Kartika Snan
~ . . . . .Skanda Shashti
1 . . . . .Govardhan Puja
2 . . . . .Bhaiya Duj
6 . . . . .Surya Shashti
11 . . . . .Devathani Ekadashi
15 . . . . .Kartika Purnima
15 . . . . .Puskar Mela

Kartika—Waning

4 . . . . .Karwachauth
5 days . . . . .Tihar
13 . . . . .Dhan Teras
14 . . . . .Narak Chaturdashi
15 . . . . .Dewali

Margasirsa—Waxing (November-December)

11 . . . . .Gita Jayanti
11 . . . . .Vaikuntha Ekadashi
15 . . . . .Dattatreya Jayanti

Margasirsa—Waning

8 . . . . .Bhairava Ashtami
11 . . . . .Vaitarani

Pausa—Waning (December-January)

8 . . . . .Rukmini Ashtami
12 . . . . .Swarupa Dwadashi

Magha—Waxing (January-February)

~ . . . . .Makar Sankranti
3 days . . . . .Pongal
3–12 days . . . . . .Thaipusam
        (Thai Poosam)
5 . . . . .Vasant Pañcami
8 . . . . .Bhishma Ashtami
15 . . . . .Magha Purnima
15 . . . . .Minakshi Float Festival

Magha—Waning

4 . . . . .Sakata Chauth
15 . . . . .Mauni Amavasya

Phalguna—Waxing (February-March)

11 . . . . .Amalaka Ekadashi
14 . . . . .Holi
15 . . . . .Dol Purnima

Phalguna—Waning

14 . . . . .Mahasivarati

Caitra—Waxing (March-April)

~ . . . . .Gangaur
1 . . . . .Gudi Parva
1 . . . . .Ugadi Parva
1–9 . . . . .Vasanta Navaratra
7 . . . . .Caitra Parb
8 . . . . .Sitala Ashtami
8 . . . . .Ashokashtami
9 . . . . .Ramanavami
10 days . . . . . . .Panguni Uttiram
10 days . . . . . . .Caitra Purnima
15 . . . . .Hanuman Jayanti

~ indicates a variable date

Hindu Holidays

Semi-monthly

Ekadashi
Eleventh day of each waxing and waning moon

Ekadashi is the Hindi word for "eleventh." In all, 24 Ekadashi (eleventh-day) fasts are observed during the course of a year, but some are of relatively greater importance. (See also AMALAKA EKADASHI, DEVATHANI EKADASHI, HARI-SHAYANI EKADASHI, KAMADA EKADASHI, NIR-JALA EKADASHI, PUTRADA EKADASHI, and VAIKUNTHA EKADASHI.) Each Ekadashi is held in honor of a different Hindu legend and has specific religious duties associated with it.

On all Ekadashi fasts, rice eating is prohibited because a demon is said to dwell in rice grains on the eleventh day. According to Hindu legend, a demon was born of the sweat that fell from Brahma's head. Brahma sent it to inhabit the rice grains eaten by people on Ekadashi and to become worms in their stomach.

Every 210 Days

Galungan
Every 210 days

Galungan is a Bali Hindu festival commemorating the Balinese New Year. The ten-day event is celebrated throughout the Indonesian island province of Bali every 210 days. (The Balinese festival calendar follows a 210-day cycle.) The Balinese religion mixes traditional Balinese thought with Hindu practices and beliefs.

During the festival, Balinese believe that the gods come to earth. Small thrones are set up in temples as symbolic seats for the gods to occupy. Activities include rituals; cock-fights (a combination of sport and gambling); offerings of foods, fruit, and flowers made to the temple by the women; and card games, music, and dancing.

Annual Holidays

Vaisakha (April-May)

Vaisakhi (The Hindu New Year; Baisakhi)
First day of the waxing half of Vaisakha, April 13

The Vaisakhi festival marks the beginning of the Hindu New Year. It derives its name from the Hindu month of Vaisakha. On this day early in the morning people bathe in sacred rivers such as the Ganges, pools, or wells, then dress in festive clothes, and visit shrines and other places of worship to offer prayers. It is also customary to exchange gifts.

This northern Indian festival is also observed in Punjab with special enthusiasm and fervor. The people of Punjab perform special dances, sing folk songs accompanied by rolling drums, exchange greetings, and enjoy feasts and merrymaking.

Vaisakhi marks the beginning of a month-long bathing tradition held during Vaisakha. The pilgrimage to the only shrine of Badrinath, in the Himalayas, also commences from this day. Many Hindus believe that charities done during Vaisakha are especially meritorious; thus, people generously give money, grains, and other items to the poor and the Brahmans. Observers of Baisakhi also fast, chant the glories of the Lord, and practice other pious activities.

Pooram
During Vaisakha

One of the most spectacular festivals of southern India, this is a 10-day celebration in Trichur, Kerala, dedicated to Siva. People fast on the first day of the festival and the rest of the days are devoted to fairs, processions, and fireworks displays. The highlight of the pageantry comes when an image of the deity Vadakkunathan (Siva) is taken from the temple and carried in a procession of richly caparisoned elephants. The Brahmans riding them hold colorful ceremonial umbrellas and whisks of yak hair and peacock feathers. The elephants lumber through the pagoda-shaped gateway of the Vadakkunathan temple and into the village while drummers beat and pipers trill. Fireworks light the skies until dawn.

Akshya Tritiya
Third day of the waxing half of Vaisakha

Observance of Akshya Tritiya consists of both fasting and festivities. "Akshya" literally means undecaying or exempt from decay. The piety and devotions done on this day are believed to never decay and to secure permanency.

On Akshya Tritiya, a fast is observed and Visnu, along with his consort Laksmi, is worshipped with holy Ganges water, tulsi leaves (basil), incense, flowers, lamps, and new clothes. Brahmans are given food in charity. Bathing in the Ganges or other waters is considered a sign of devotion.

Also on this day, the passes of Sri Badrinarain in the Himalayas open after the long, snowy winter. Devotees worship Badri with food offerings in their homes and temples.

Akshya Tritiya is also believed to be the first day of Satya-Yuga, the "golden age."

Parasurama Jayanti
Third day of the waxing half of Vaisakha

According to Hindu mythology, Parasurama (Rama with an Ax) destroyed the evil Ksatriya kings and princes 21 times, including the thousand-armed warrior, Arjuna. Parasurama became manifest in the world in the beginning of the Treta Yuga (the second age). Parasurama Jayanti (Parasurama's birthday) is observed with fasting, austerities, and prayer. It is also a day to worship Lord Visnu, of whom Parasurama is believed to be the sixth incarnation. To Hindus, Parasurama represents filial obedience, austerity, power, and brahmanic ideals.

Chandan Yatra
Beginning on the third day of the waxing half of Vaisakha and lasting twenty-one days

On each of this festival's twenty-one days, images of Hindu deities are taken out in procession to nearby water tanks, where they are rowed in decorated boats to the accompaniment of music and dance. This summer festival is celebrated at Puri, Orissa, Bhubaneshwar, Baripada, and Balanga.

Sankaracarya Jayanti
Fifth day (southern India) or tenth day (northern India) of the waxing half of Vaisakha

This birth anniversary celebration honors Adi Sankaracarya, one of the greatest saint-philosophers of India who symbolizes India's cultural and emotional integrity and unity. Sankaracarya, believed to be an incarnation of Siva, revived Brahmanism and took Vedanta philosophy to new heights. Historians believe he lived between 788 and 820 C.E., but Hindu tradition places him in 200 B.C.E.

Sankaracarya was a native of Malabar in the Indian state of Kerala. He worked many miracles and died at the age of 32. He is the reputed author of many original philosophical works and commentaries on the Upanisads, Vedanta Sutras, and *Bhagavad Gita*. He has been called the "Vedanta Guru," and his philosophy is equally accessible to both the learned and the layman. He composed many popular hymns, and urged people to devote themselves to God in any of his forms and incarnations. The Hindu custom is that Sankaracarya Jayanti is a fit occasion to study his works, to fast, to meditate, and to rededicate oneself to the service of the Lord.

Janaki Navami
Ninth day of the waxing half month of Vaisakha

Sita, heroine of the Hindu epic poem *Ramayana* whose name means "furrow," is supposed to have sprung on this day from a furrow plowed by King Janaka in a field. Janaka took her up and raised her as his own child. She is also called A-Yonija, "not born from the womb." She was actually the goddess Laksmi in human form, incarnated in the world to bring about the destruction of Ravana and other demons. Many Hindus believe that she reflects the idealized Indian woman as an embodiment of self-sacrifice, purity, tenderness, fidelity, conjugal affection, and other virtues. Some believe that Sita appeared in Janaka's field on the eighth day of the waning half of Phalguna (February-March), and they fast on that day.

Narasimha Jayanti
Fourteenth day of the waxing half of Vaisakha

According to Hindu mythology, this is the day on which Visnu appeared as the Narasimha, or Man-Lion, to free the world from the demon king, Hiranyakasipu. Hiranyakasipu had forbidden prayer and worship to Hari (Visnu), and substituted worship and prayer to himself. He was very much annoyed to discover his own son Prahlada was an ardent devotee of Visnu, and tortured Prahlada to convert him, but the child remained unmoved in his devotion to the god. The king tried to kill Prahlada by trampling him under elephants, by throwing him down precipices, and by other means, but without success.

One day Hiranyakasipu was so enraged that he rushed to kill Prahlada with his own sword, asking the child, "Where is your savior?" Instantly Visnu stepped out of a nearby pillar in the form of Narasimha, half lion, half man, and tore Hiranyakasipu to pieces.

On this day, people fast, meditate on Narasimha, and seek his grace to have devotion like that of Prahlada. To Hindus, Narasimha symbolizes the omnipresence of god, his deep concern and love for the devotees, and the victory of good over evil. People often demonstrate the sincerity of their devotion by giving cows, grains, gold, robes, and other goods to the poor and the Brahmans as acts of charity on this day.

Jyestha (May-June)

Sithinakha (Cake Festival)
Sixth day of the waxing half of Jyestha

On this day Hindus honor the birth of the god Kumara (also known as Skanda) the god of war. Kumara was the first-born son of Siva. He has six heads because he was nursed by the Karttikas, six women who as stars comprise the Pleiades. For this reason he is also called *Karttikeya* meaning "son of Karttikas." The six heads also represent the six senses (including extrasensory perception). He also has a large following under the name *Subrahmanya*, meaning "dear to the Brahmanas."

Most Hindus observe this day with a ritual purification bath followed by processions to the temples to honor Kumara. It is also considered a good opportunity to clean out wells and tanks. According to tradition, the snake gods are off worshipping on this day, so it is safe to enter their habitats.

In Nepal, eight different kinds of cakes, made from eight different grains, are offered to Kumara on his birthday, and for this reason Sithinakha is sometimes referred to as the Cake Festival. Lotus-shaped windmills are often set on rooftops at this time, to symbolize the end of bad times and the onset of holier days.

Jyestha Ashtami
Eighth day of waxing half of Jyestha

Jyestha Ashtami is celebrated by the people of Khir Bhawani in Kashmir in honor of their patron goddess, also named Khir Bhawani. People come from the adjoining hill areas to assemble at the shrine, offer prayers and worship at the foot of the goddess, and sing hymns and songs in praise of Bhawani. Khir (rice boiled in milk) is prepared as a food offering. The beautiful marble shrine overlooks a pool formed by spring waters, which change color from rosy red, turquoise green, lemon pale, sky blue, milky white, or pure white. It is located 25 kilometers from Srinagar, and 5 kilometers from Ganderbal and is visited by hundreds of Kashmiri Hindus daily.

Ganga Dussehra
Tenth day of the waxing half of Jyestha

According to Hindu mythology, the Ganges River in India originally flowed only in heaven. In the form of a goddess, Ganga, the river was brought down to earth by King Bhagiratha in order to purify the ashes of his ancestors, 60,000 of whom had been burned under a curse from the great sage Kapila. The river came down reluctantly, breaking her fall on the head of Siva so that she wouldn't shatter the Earth. By the time she reached the Bay of Bengal, she had touched the ashes of the 60,000 princes and fertilized the entire region.

Ganga Dussehra commemorates the Ganges' descent to earth in Hashta Nakhsatra. Literally the word Dussehra means "that which takes away ten sins." People get up early in the morning and go to the Ganges to bathe in holy waters. When the Ganges is inaccessible, they bathe in some nearby tank, pool, river, or the sea, chanting "Har Har Gange! Har Har Gange!" thus invoking the Ganges and offering her prayers and worship. At places where the Ganges flows, such as Rishikesh, Hardwar, Garh Mukteshwar, Prayag, and Varanasi, its banks are overcrowded with worshipers. Many Hindus believe that a bath in the Ganges on this day is of great religious merit and washes away all sins.

The very name of the Ganges is sacred to Hindus. Samples of its waters are kept within sealed pots in Hindu homes where, some believe, the water remains unpolluted even if it is kept for many years. Holy Ganges water thus kept is used on sacred days to sanctify places and is given to a dying person with tulsi leaves (basil) to facilitate the soul's peaceful separation from the body.

Nirjala Ekadashi
Eleventh day of the waxing half of Jyestha

Nirjala Ekadashi is a complete fast; even water is not taken. Because the month of Jyestha is very hot and the day is long, observing a fast without water is an extreme act of pious austerity. Both men and women observe the fast and offer puja (worship) to Visnu to ensure happiness, prosperity, and forgiveness of transgressions and sins. Pancamrata is prepared by mixing together milk, ghee (clarified butter), curds, honey, and sugar. It is then offered to the image of Visnu, which has been draped in rich clothing and jewels, with a fan placed beside it. Hindus meditate on Visnu as the Lord of the Universe and worship the deity with flowers, lamps, water, and incense. In the evening worshippers venerate Visnu while holding durva grass in their hands. The night is spent in meditation and prayer.

Some Hindus believe that faithful observance of the fast and other rituals on this day ensures happiness, salvation, longevity and prosperity. Clothes, grains, umbrellas, fans, and pitchers filled with water are given in charity to the Brahmans according to the ability of the giver.

Snan Yatra
Full-moon day of Jyestha

On this occasion, a grand bathing festival is held in Orissa. Images of the Lords Jagannatha, Balabhadra, Subhadra, and Sudarshan are brought in a grand procession to the bathing platform for their ceremonial baths. With the recitation of mantras from the Vedas, 108 pots of consecrated waters are poured upon the deities. Then, the deities are ceremonially attired before they retire into seclusion for fifteen days. It is an occasion of great rejoicing and merrymaking.

Vata Savitri
Thirteenth day of the waning half of Jyestha

The fast of Vata Savitri is generally observed on this date, but at some places it is observed on the full moon of Jyestha. It is meant only for married women, who keep this vow for the sake of the longevity and well-being of their husbands.

Asadha (June-July)

Ratha Yatra
Second day of the waxing half of Asadha

Ratha Yatra is a festival honoring Jagannatha, Lord of the Universe, a form of Krishna. It is celebrated throughout India but the biggest festival commemorating it is held at the Jagannatha Temple in Puri in Orissa, one of the largest Hindu temples in India. During the festival, wooden images of Jagannatha, Balabhadra (his brother), and Subhadra (his sister) are taken in procession in three huge chariots or carts that look like temples and are called *raths*. The main chariot carrying Jagnnath measures 45 feet high, 35 feet square, and is supported by 16 wheels, seven feet in diameter. At the termination of the ceremony the chariot is disassembled and its materials used to manufacture religious relics.

The images go from the Jagannatha Temple to be bathed at Gundicha Mandir, a temple about a mile away; the gods are installed there for a week before being brought back to the Jagannatha Temple. This is a popular festival because all castes are considered equal, and everyone has to eat the food prepared by low caste men at the shrine.

The festival of Puri is famous worldwide, and thousands of devotees participate in this spectacular event. The imposing twelfth-century Jagannatha shrine, 60 kilometers from Bhubaneshwar, is situated on Nilachala mountain. It is one of the four great Hindu holy places (the others being Badrinath, Dwarka, and Rameshwaram). For a devout Hindu, a pilgrimage to Jagannatha Puri is a lifelong ambition. Many Hindus believe that a three-day sojourn to Puri will free a pilgrim from future births and deaths.

Hari-Shayani Ekadashi
Eleventh day of the waxing half of Asadha

Hari-Shayani Ekadashi is the day when Lord Hari (Visnu) retires to sleep on the bed of Shesha Nag in the Ksirsagar. According to a popular Hindu religious belief, Hari slumbers during the four months of the rainy season, which begins on the 11th of the waxing fortnight of Asadha. The rainy season is known as "Chaturmas," and during this period such activities as marriage and the thread ceremony are prohibited.

Guru Purnima (Vyasa Purnima; Asadha Purnima)
Full-moon day of Asadha

The purnima, or full moon day, of Asadha is set apart for the veneration and worship of the Guru. In ancient days students received their education in Ashrams and Gurukuls. The students would worship their teachers on this day, pay their fee, and give them presents according to their means and capacity. Devotees and disciples fast and worship their gurus to seek their blessings.

The day is also known as Vyasa Purnima because Rishi Vyasa was a great guru. Vyasa (or Veda-Vyasa), the son of Rishi Parashar and Satyavati, is also known as Krishna Dwaipayna. He is said to have compiled the four Vedas, the *Mahabharata*, and the 18 Puranas.

Sravana (July-August)

Sravani Mela
During Sravana

Festivities associated with this festival include a grand fair, held in Bihar at Deoghar. Throughout the month, devotees pick up water from the holy Ganges at Sultanganj, carry it on their shoulders to Deoghar, and offer it on linga (phallic symbol of Siva).

Hariyali Teej (Tij; Green Teej; Teej; Hari Tritiya)
Third day of the waxing half of Sravana

On this day women of all ages make merry. Daughters and daughters-in-law are given gifts. Swings are hung in the houses and gardens, and the women enjoy them throughout the day. The preparation of sweets is also a highlight in each home. Hariyali Teej is celebrated on a large scale in Uttar Pradesh and especially in Braj Mandal.

Nag Pañcami (Bhratri Panchami)
Fifth day of the waxing half of Sravana

Nag Pañcami is a Hindu festival celebrated throughout India and Nepal. It is dedicated to the sacred serpent, Ananta, on whose coils Hindus believe Visnu rested while he was creating the universe. According to Hindu belief, snakes can bring wealth and rain, and unhappy ones can cause a home to collapse. Cobras and snakes are worshipped with milk, sweets, flowers, lamps, and sometimes sacrifices. Images of snake deities painted on walls or made from silver, stone, or wood are bathed with milk and water, then they are worshipped with the reciting of mantras. Worshippers observe a fast on this day, but the Brahmans are fed. In return for their piety, people are assured protection against snake bites in the future. One particular custom associated with Nag Pañcami is that digging in the earth is prohibited, because serpents live underground (which is believed to be the netherworld), and digging may hurt or annoy them.

Because snakes are also worn by Siva, hundreds of snakes are released at the Indian Siva temples in Ujjain, where Siva lived after destroying a demon, and in Varanasi, considered the religious capital of the Hindu faith. In Jodhpur, India, huge cloth Nagas, or "cobras," are displayed.

Nag Pañcami is also observed as Bhratri Panchami, and some Hindu women fast and worship snakes to guard their brothers against snake-bites.

Tulsidas Jayanti
Seventh day of the waxing half of Sravana

According to Hindu belief, the saintly poet Tulsidas was contemporary with Akbar the Great. He was born to Brahman parents but was orphaned. St. Narharidas, after receiving instructions from God in a dream, raised and educated Tulsidas. Tulsidas married and started living the life of a householder, but chance words of his wife awakened his ardent devotion to God, and he became a sanyasi and began to live at Varanasi. There he wrote his well-known *Ramacharitra Manas* and a dozen other books. His masterpiece *Ramayana* was written in the language of the common people for their benefit and is revered by devout Hindus. His example of sanctity and the magic of his writings have had a far-reaching impact for the spiritual uplifting of the masses—comparable to the teachings of hundreds of gurus. He and his works are so greatly revered that tradition regards him as Valmiki reborn.

Many Hindus believe that Tulsidas died on the same day that he was born; on that day, a fast is kept, and works of charity are done. The *Ramayana* is read and recited, Brahmans are fed, and Lord Rama, along with his consort Sita and devotee Hanuman, is worshipped with great religious fervor. In literary and social circles, discussions, lectures, seminars, and symposiums are organized on Tulsidas' teachings, life, and works.

Putrada Ekadashi
Eleventh day of the waxing half of Sravana

Putrada Ekadashi is observed by couples without children in order to produce a son. Some Hindus believe that fasting and piety on this day will ensure conception of a boy while also destroying the sins of the aspirants. Like other Ekadashis, it is dedicated to Visnu.

A fast is observed, Visnu is worshipped and meditated upon, and the Brahmans (priests learned in the Vedas and sacred religious lore) are fed and given robes and money. At night the aspirants sleep in the room where Visnu was worshipped. In addition, they are encouraged to observe Kamada Ekadashi in the waning half of the month of Sravana. Kamada Ekadashi is known as the wish-fulfilling Ekadashi.

Narieli Purnima
Full moon day of Sravana

Narieli Purnima is celebrated in order to appease the fury of the sea god Varuna. Marking the end of the monsoon season, it is primarily observed by sailors, fishermen, and others living in the coastal areas of south India, who offer coconuts to the sea on this occasion. If the sea happens to be far away, this ritual may be carried out at a nearby water source.

Raksa Bandhana (Brother and Sister Day; Avani Avittam)
Full-moon day month of Sravana

The word "Raksa" means protection, and as a ritual of protection, Hindu women and girls tie a thread bracelet around their brothers' wrists to guard them against evil during the ensuing year. Sisters also feed their brothers with sweets, dried fruits, and other delicacies. The brothers give their sisters gifts of money, clothes, and other valuable things and promise to protect them in return.

Priests and Brahmans also tie threads around the wrists of their patrons to receive gifts. They recite a mantra or sacred formula to charge the thread with the power of protection.

In southern India, the day is called Avani Avittam. A holy thread is charged and a libation of water is offered to the ancestors and rishis. The new thread is worshipped with saffron and turmeric paste before being worn, and the old one is discarded in the water. The day is specially significant for a Brahman boy who has recently been invested with a holy thread to remind him of its religious significance. Vedas are also read and recited on this day.

Jhulan Latra
Full moon day of Sravana

In Orissa, a festival of Lord Jagannatha is celebrated. In a lavishly decorated swing, Lord Jagannatha is asked to relax to the accompaniment of music and dance. The celebration is particularly observed in the Jagannatha temple at Puri and other shrines for a week preceding the Sravana Purnima (full moon). The full-moon day of the month marks the festival's culmination.

Kamada Ekadashi
Eleventh day of the waning half of Sravana

The Kamada Ekadashi is known as the wish-fulfilling Ekadashi. Like other Ekadashis, it is dedicated to Visnu.

Ghanta Karna (Festival of Boys)
Fourteenth day of waning half of Sravana

This day commemorates the death of Ghanta Karna, or "Bell Ears," a monster who wore jingling bells in his ears so that he'd never have to hear the name of Visnu. In Hindu mythology he caused death and destruction wherever he went, until a god in the form of a frog persuaded him to leap into a well, after which the people clubbed him to death and dragged his body to the river to be cremated.

Also known as the Festival of Boys because young boys play a primary role in the celebration of Ghanta Karna's death, this day is observed in Nepal by erecting effigies at various crossroads and making passersby pay a toll. After they've spent the day collecting tolls and preparing for the Ghanta Karna funeral, the boys tie up the effigy with a rope and throw it in the river. Sometimes the effigy is set on fire before being thrown in the water. Young girls hang tiny dolls on the effigy of Ghanta Karna to protect themselves from the monster.

Children also sell iron rings on this day and use the money to buy candy. It is believed that those who have iron nails in the lintels of their homes or are wearing an iron ring will be protected from evil spirits in the coming year.

Bhadrapada (August-September)

Tirupati Festival
Ten days during Bhadrapada

A grand festival, held at Tirupati, the seat of Lord Venkteshwara, a manifestation of Lord Visnu. The festival lasts for ten days and during it devotees congregate to seek Lord Venkteshwara's blessings for material and spiritual gains.

The shrine at Tirupati, one of the richest temples in the world, is situated on the seven Tirumala hills, which correspond to the seven hoods of the snake god Adishesha, who forms the bed of Visnu in the cosmic ocean. Because of these seven picturesque hills, Venkteshwara is also known as the "Lord of the Seven Hills."

Tirupati is considered an essential pilgrimage center for every devout Hindu. It is tradition that devotees, whether men or women, shave their hair off as a votive offering for a vow fulfilled. Parents bring their very young children to perform their first tonsure (the act of clipping the hair) at the feet of the Lord.

Onam
Four days in the Malyalan month of Chingam (August-September)

According to legend, Bali was permitted by Vamana (the fifth incarnation of Visnu) to visit his lost kingdom and subjects once a year; this visit is celebrated by his devotees on Onam. To welcome their ancient king Bali, the people of the Indian state of Kerala tidy up their houses and environs, decorate the houses with flowers and leaves, and arrange grand feasts and many types of amusements. The spectacular snake-boat races mark the crowning glory of these games.

A clay image of Vamana is worshipped on this day in temples and houses, and youngsters are given gifts by the elders. On the second day of the festivity, Bali is believed to visit his kingdom in Kerala. Bali is also called Mahabali, and his capital was Mahabalipuram, near Madras.

Haritalika Teej
Third day of the waxing half of Bhadrapada

Observed by Hindu women, the Haritalika fast honors the goddess Parvati and her consort Siva, and their statues are worshipped ritually. Parvati, the daughter of Himalaya and Mina, desirous of having Sankara (Siva) as her husband, performed extraordinary feats of magic and thereby married him. From that day onward married women have worshipped the divine couple, keeping a strict fast to ensure their conjugal happiness and prosperity. Unmarried girls fast to gain suitable husbands of their choice. Brahmans receive charity, unmarried girls are fed, and aspirant women tell the story of Haritalika among themselves and break their fast in the evening. The next morning the sun is worshipped and offered water.

Ganesa Caturthi (Ganesha Chaturthi; Ganesha Chata)
Fourth day of the waxing half of Bhadrapada

This lively Hindu festival honors Ganesa, the elephant-headed god of prosperity, wisdom, learning, prudence, success, and power. He is also known as Vighnesha, or remover of obstacles. Ganesa is propitiated at the start of every activity, whether it be a journey, marriage, initiation, house construction, writing of a book or even a letter.

Hindus generally believe that Ganesa is a great scribe and learned in religious lore and scripture. It was Ganesa who, at the dictation of the seer Vyasa, wrote the *Mahabharata*. He is also the Lord of Ganas, Siva's hosts. Ganesa bears a single tusk; holds in his four hands a shell, a discus, a goad, and a lotus; and is always accompanied by his mount, the rat. Ganesa is a great lover of sweets and fruits.

On Ganesa Caturthi, the images of Ganesa are worshipped with sweet balls, water, new clothes, incense, flowers, scent, betel leaf, and naivaidyas (food offerings). His mantra is repeated as he is meditated upon and worshipped. Food offerings are later distributed as charity. Brahmans are fed and given gifts. Clay figures of Ganesa are worshipped during this festival and then immersed in sea, river, pool, or some other water. Around Bombay, a spectacular week-long festival ends with the immersion of Ganesa's sculpted likeness in the waters at Chowpatty Beach to ensure well-being on both land and sea. In Maharashtra this festival is observed with great religious fervor, pomp, and gaiety, and Ganesa statues are taken out in grand processions before immersion in the sea. In Nepal the day, called Ganesha Chata, celebrates a bitter dispute between Ganesa and the moon goddess. Therefore, the Nepalese try to stay inside on this night and close out the moonlight.

Rishi Pañcami
Fifth day of the waxing half of Bhadrapada

The Sapta Rishis, (seven seers, or mental sons of Brahma) are honored on this day with piety and acts of devotion. The seven are: Bhrigu, Pulastya, Kratu, Pulaha, Marichi, Atri, and Vasistha. Although the day is primarily observed by women, a man can also participate for the well-being and happiness of his wife.

An earthen or copper pitcher filled with water is sanctified with cow dung and an eight-petalled lotus is made on it. After the pitcher is installed on an altar, the seven seers are worshipped with betel leaf, flowers, camphor, and a lamp. Devi Arundhati, the wife of Rishi Vasistha (a model of conjugal excellence) is also worshipped along with the seven sages.

Anant Chaturdashi
Fourteenth day of the waxing half of Bhadrapada

On this day, Hindus worship and meditate upon Visnu. A fast is observed and fruits, sweets, and flowers are offered to Visnu in worship. An unrefined thread colored in turmeric paste and having 14 knots is also tied on the upper right arm while meditating. Hindus believe that this ensures protection against evil and brings prosperity and happiness.

According to Hindu belief, the Pandava princes in exile observed this fast on the advice of Krishna to regain their lost kingdom and prosperity. As a result, they defeated the Kauravas and regained their kingdom, wealth, reputation, and happiness.

Halashashti (Balarama Shashti)
Sixth day of the waning half of Bhadrapada

Halashashti is a festival commemorating the birth of Krishna's older brother, Balarama. Balarama's weapon was a plough, so it is also the day on which the farmers and peasants of India worship the hala, or plough. They apply powdered rice and turmeric to the plough's iron blade and decorate it with flowers. A small piece of ground is sanctified and plastered with cow dung. In it, a small pool of water is created. Branches of plum, fig, and other fruit trees are then planted.

In observance of the day, some Hindu women fast to ensure happiness, prosperity, and longevity of their sons. Only buffalo milk and curds are eaten. Unmarried girls observe the Chandra Shashti on this day, and their fast is terminated by the rising of the moon.

Janmashtami (Krishnastami; Krishna's Birthday)
Eighth day of the waning half of Bhadrapada

Janmashtami, one of the most important Hindu festivals, commemorates the birth of Krishna, the eighth avatara (or incarnation) of Visnu. The birthday of Krishna, the direct manifestation of Visnu himself, is celebrated in all parts of India with great enthusiasm. Krishna's life is described in great detail in the *Puranas*. He is known as "the supreme universal spirit, the supreme dwelling, the eternal person, divine prior to the gods, unborn, omnipresent."

The Janmashtami celebrations start with an early morning bath in sacred waters and prayers. The climax occurs at midnight with the rising of the moon, which signifies Krishna's divine birth. A strict fast is kept and broken only after the birth of Krishna at midnight. The piety and fast observed on this day ensure the birth of many good sons, and salvation after death.

Temples and homes are decorated, and scenes depicting Krishna's birth and his childhood pranks are staged with both animate and inanimate models. The Krishna child's image is put into a richly decorated swing and rocked with tender care all day. At night, after the birth, a small image of toddling Krishna is bathed in the Charnamrita, amidst the chanting of hymns, blaring of the conches, ringing of bells, and joyous shouting of "Victory to Krishna!"

In Mathura, where Krishna was born, there are performances of Krishna Lila, folk dramas depicting scenes from Krishna's life. In the state of Tamil Nadu, oiled poles called "ureyadi" are set up, a pot of money is tied to the top, and boys dressed as Krishna try to shinny up the pole and win the prize while spectators squirt water at them. In Maharashtra, where the festival is known as Govinda, pots containing money and curds and butter are suspended high over streets. Boys form human pyramids climbing on each others' shoulders to try to break the pot. These climbing games reflect stories of Krishna, who as a boy loved milk and butter so much they had to be kept out of his reach.

In Nepal, a religious fast is observed on Krishnastami, and Krishna's temple at Lalitpur is visited by pilgrims. People parade in a procession around the town and display pictures of Krishna.

Radha Ashtami
Eighth day of the waning half of Bhadrapada

Radha Ashtami celebrates the birth of Radha, an incarnation of Laksmi. Some Hindus believe that Radha, the favorite mistress and consort of Krishna during his Vrindavana days, is a symbol of the human soul drawn to the ineffable god Krishna, or the pure divine love to which the fickle lover returns.

On this day, after early morning baths, the image of Radha is bathed in Panchamrita, and then richly adorned and ornamented before being offered food and worship. A fast is kept on this day and charity distributed.

Indra Jatra
Beginning the end of Bhadrapada until early Asvina

Indra Jatra is the most important festival of Nepal, combining homage to a god with an appearance by a living goddess. The festival, lasting for eight days, is a time to honor the recently deceased and to pay homage to the Hindu god Indra and his mother Dagini so they will bless the coming harvests. It also commemorates the day in 1768, during an Indra Jatra ("jatra" means "festival"), that Prithwi Narayan Shah (1730–1775) conquered the Katmandu Valley and unified Nepal.

Legend says that Indra, the god of rain and ruler of heaven, once visited the Katmandu Valley in human form to pick flowers for his mother. The people caught him stealing flowers. Dagini, the mother, came down and promised to spread dew over the crops and to take those who had died in the past year back to heaven with her. The people then released Indra and they have celebrated the occasion ever since.

Before the ceremonies start, a 50-foot tree is cut, sanctified, and dragged to the Hanuman Dhoka Palace in Katmandu. It represents Siva's linga, the phallic symbol of his creative powers and shows he has come to the valley. As the pole is erected, bands play and cannons boom. Images of Indra, usually as a captive, are displayed, and sacrifices of goats and roosters are offered.

Three gold chariots are assembled in Basantpur Square, outside the home of the Kumari, the living goddess and vestal virgin. The Kumari is a young girl who was selected to be a goddess when she was about three years old, and she will be replaced by another girl when she begins to menstruate. Two boys playing the roles of the gods Ganesa and Bhairab emerge from the Kumari's house to be attendants to the goddess. Then the goddess herself appears in public for the first time, walking on a carpet so her feet don't touch the ground. The crowds go wild. The king bows to the Kumari, and the procession moves off to the palace where it stops in front of the 12-foot mask of the Bhairab. This is the fearsome form of Siva in Nepal and is displayed only at this time. The Kumari greets the image and rice beer pours from its mouth. Those who catch a drop of the beer are blessed, but even more are those who catch one of the tiny live fish in the beer.

In the following days the procession moves from place to place around Katmandu. Masked dancers perform every night at the Hanuman Dhoka square dramatizing each of the earthly incarnations of Visnu. On the final day of the festival the great pole is carried to the river.

Asvina (September-October)

Laksmi Puja
During Asvina

The annual festival in honor of the Hindu goddess Laksmi is held in the autumn, when Hindus of all castes ask for her blessings. Lights shine from every house, and no one sleeps during the celebrations.

Laksmi is traditionally associated with wealth, prosperity, and good luck. In later Hindu literature, she appears as the dutiful wife of the god Visnu and is typically portrayed massaging his feet while he rests on the cosmic serpent, Shesa. She remains a popular Hindu goddess in India, where she is worshipped especially by merchants, who ask her to grant them wealth and success.

Durga Puja (Festival of Victory)
During the waxing half of Asvina

This Hindu festival of the Divine Mother is a ten-day holiday in India honoring the ten-armed Durga, wife of Siva. Also known as the Festival of Victory, Durga Puja honors Durga's conquest of the demon Mahisasura.

On the first lunar day of the waxing half of Asvina, an earthen pitcher, filled with water and its mouth covered with green leaves and an earthen lid, is installed with an invocation of Ganesa, the god of learning and wisdom. A clarified butter lamp (ghee lamp) is always kept burning before the installed pitcher during the celebration. Durga is then invoked and worshipped with ceremonial rites. Daily readings of the *Durgasaptasati, Devi Bhagvat Purana,* and *Devi Mahatmya* sections of the *Markandeya Purana* are part of the celebrations as well. Unmarried girls below the age of ten are also worshipped and given gifts during these nine days. The aspirants sleep on the ground and keep a strict fast all these days. On the final day of the festival, people wear young barley sprouts in their hair and visit older relatives to seek a blessing.

In Bengal, Durga Puja is celebrated with great excitement and festivity. Huge puja (worship) pavilions with ten-armed Durga figures are constructed for this purpose. Durga, the beautiful but fierce goddess, rides her lion, killing the demon Mahisasura. She holds in her hands the gods' special weapons: Visnu's discus, Siva's trident, Varuna's conch shell, Agni's flaming dart, Vayu's bow, Surya's quiver, Indra's thunderbolt, Kubera's club, and a garland of snakes from Shesha. During the celebrations music, dance, drama, and poetry are performed. The images of the goddess Durga are taken on the final day in triumphal processions to the river, where they are ceremonially immersed.

Dasain
During the waxing half of Asvina

This ten-day festival commemorating the *Ramayana* epic in which the benevolent gods overcome the evil demons is observed throughout the Hindu world. In Nepal it is the most important festival of the year.

The Nepalese participate in many special activities and ceremonies to commemorate the victory of the goddess Durga over the evil demon Mahisasura. Houses are cleaned; swings and ferris wheels are set up in villages; joyful religious ceremonies are conducted daily; and hundreds of animal sacrifices are performed because Durga is believed to be a bloodthirsty goddess. In return, the people ask Durga to protect them through the following year.

The last day of the festival is a day of visiting older relatives to receive a blessing. In some towns, masked dances and processions consisting of priests carrying wooden swords symbolic of Durga's victory are held.

Dussehra (Dashara; Vijay Dashami)
Tenth day of the waxing half of Asvina

This Hindu festival celebrates Rama's victory after a ten-day struggle against Ravana (king of the demons) as told in the epic story of the *Ramayana*. Rama is worshipped, prayed to, and meditated upon to obtain his blessings and favor. In the past, kings often marched their forces against their enemies on this day.

During the ten days of the celebration, the battle is reenacted in puppet shows and in traditional plays. In addition, elaborate and joyous processions depicting various scenes of the *Ramayana* in the form of tableaus take place through bazaars and main streets. On the last day of the festival, huge mannequins representing Ravana, his brother Kumbhakrna, and his son Meghnatha are stuffed with brilliant fireworks, raised at various open grounds, and set afire. This climactic event marks the termination of the festival.

Sharad Purnima
Full moon day of Asvina

The Hindu moon god, Hari, is honored on this day. Hari is also the lord of herbs, seeds, Brahmans, waters, and Naksatras (or Constellations). Some Hindus believe that on Sharad Purnima, amrit (an elixir) is showered on the earth by moonbeams.

A custom associated with Sharad Purnima is the collection of amrit. Khir, milk thickened with rice and mixed with sugar, is prepared in the temples and homes, and offered to Hari amidst the ringing of bells and chanting of hymns. The mixture is kept in the moonshine all night so that it may absorb the amrit falling from the moon. At night the moon god is worshipped and offered food. The next morning the khir is given to the devotees.

Kojagara
Full moon day of Asvina

The word "Kojagara" is a combination of two terms, "Kah" and "jagara," which means "who is awake?" It is an exclamation of the goddess Laksmi, who descends to the earth this night, and blesses with wealth and prosperity all those who are awake. Hence, the night is spent in festivity and various games of amusement to honor the goddess. It is a harvest festival and is celebrated throughout India. Laksmi is worshipped and a night vigil is observed.

Valmiki Jayanti
Full-moon day of Asvina

This festival celebrates the birthday of the Ai Kavi (the "first Poet") Valmiki, whom Hindus believe to be the author of the Sanskrit *Ramayana*. A contemporary of Rama, the hero of the *Ramayana*, Valmiki himself is represented as taking part in some of the scenes he relates. He received the banished Sita into his hermitage and educated her twin sons Kusha and Lava. The invention of the "Shloka" (epic meter) is attributed to Valmiki.

Valmiki received his name because when immersed in meditation he allowed himself to be overrun with ants

135

like an anthill. Members of many disadvantaged Indian classes claim they are descended from Valmiki. On his birthday he is worshipped and prayed to, and his portraits are taken out in gay processions through the main bazaars and streets.

Pitra Visarjana Amavasya (Pitra Paksha)
During the waning half of Asvina

This fourteen-day ceremony is a time for honoring ancestors by making special offerings of food and water, especially khir (rice boiled in milk) to deceased relatives by their surviving family members. These sacrifices, called Sraddha, symbolically supply the dead with strengthening nutriment after the previous funeral ceremonies have endowed the ethereal bodies. One Hindu belief is that until Sraddha has been performed, the deceased relative is a restless, wandering ghost and has no real body. Only after the Sraddha does he attain a position among the Pitris, or Divine Fathers, in their blissful abode called Pitri-Loka.

Brahmins (priests, members of the highest Hindu caste) are often invited to partake of these special foods in the belief that they will ensure that the offerings reach the souls of departed family members. According to custom, a Sraddha is most desirable and efficacious when done by a son, so the eldest son or senior member of the family typically performs the rituals associated with this festival. On the last day of the fortnight, called Amavasya (the new moon), oblations are offered to all ancestors whose day of death is unknown.

Kartika (October-November)

Kartika Snan
During Kartika

Among the 12 months of the year, some are regarded as especially holy and sacred, and as such they are most suitable for acts of piety. These are Vaisakha (April-May), Kartika (October-November), and Magha (January-February).

Throughout the month of Kartika, the early morning bath in a sacred river, stream, pond, or at a well is considered highly meritorious. On the sacred rivers like the Ganges and Yamuna, a month-long bathing festival is held. Some people set up tents along the river banks for this purpose, and at the termination of the festival return to their distant homes. During the month, aspirants observe strict continence, have regular early morning baths in the sacred streams, take a single simple meal every day, and spend their time in prayer, meditation, and other acts of piety and devotion.

Hindu women in villages and towns get up early in the morning and visit the sacred streams in groups, singing hymns, and after their baths visit the nearby temples. They fast and hang lamps in small baskets from the bamboo tops of their homes or on the river banks. These sky lamps are kept burning through Kartika to light the path of departed souls across the sky.

Tulsi leaves offered to Visnu in Kartika (October-November) are said to please him more than the gift of a thousand cows. The Tulsi plant is sacred and cultivated specially in homes and temples. It is considered the wife of Visnu and shown according respect. It is offered daily puja (worship) by Hindu women in the evening with lamps. Tulsi leaf is put in the mouth of a dying person along with Ganges water to facilitate an easy departure. Hindus believe that watering, cultivating, and worship of the Tulsi plant ensures happiness. When its leaves are put into any water, it becomes as holy as Ganges water.

Since Tulsi is Visnupriya (beloved of Visnu), their marriage is celebrated on the 11th day of the waxing half of the month of Kartika (October-November). On this day the image of Visnu is richly decorated and then carried to the place where the Tulsi plant is grown, and the marriage ritually solemnized. Fasting is also observed on this day.

Skanda Shashti
During the Tamil month of Tulam (October-November)

Skanda, the second son of Siva, is also known as Karttikeya or Subramanya. According to Hindu mythology, Siva cast his seed into fire, and it was afterwards received by the Ganges, which "gave birth" to him. The boy was fostered by the Karttikas (Pleiades) and has six heads. He was born for the purpose of destroying Taraka, a demon whose austerities had made him a formidable opponent to the gods. The festivities of Skanda Shashti celebrate Taraka's defeat.

In south India there are six holy places associated with Skanda's life and work. At these places Skanda Shashti is celebrated with great fervor, and thousands of devotees congregate at each temple to seek the lord's blessings. Hymns are sung, psalms chanted, people fed, and scenes from his life dramatized. The festivity begins six days before the Shashti. Lord Subramanya is worshipped during these days, and devotees make pilgrimages to different Subramanya shrines. A common Hindu belief is that the devotion observed on this day ensures success, prosperity, peace, and happiness.

Govardhan Puja
First day of the waxing half of Kartika

Govardhan Puja is celebrated in northern India on the day following Dewali. The day is associated with an event of Krishna's life where he lifted the Govardhan

Mountain (in Vrindavana) on his little finger for seven days to protect the cows and people of Vrindavana against the deluge of rain sent by the enraged Indra, god of the heavens and rains. People by the thousands from all over India visit, worship, and circumambulate Mount Govardhan on this day. Those who cannot come to Vrindavana worship at home with great devotion and give gifts to Brahmans. Cows and bulls are also decorated and worshipped.

Bhaiya Duj (Yama Dvitiya)
Second day of the waxing half of Kartika

Celebration of Bhaiya Duj honors the affection between brothers and sisters. Married women invite their brothers to their homes, apply turmeric or sandal paste tilaks on the men's foreheads, tie a colored thread round their right wrists, pray for their prosperity and longevity, and then feed them sweets and other delicacies. In return the women receive valuable gifts. Unmarried girls do so at their parent's homes.

Bhaiya Duj is also called Yama Dvitiya in commemoration of the affection between Yama and his sister Yami. Sisters observe a strict fast and pray to Yama for their brother's longevity, good health, and happiness. Yama's sister, Yami (also known as Yamuna) is also worshipped.

Surya Shashti
Sixth day of the waxing half of Kartika

Observance of Surya Shashti includes a continual three-day fast for married Hindu women with children. Women participating in the fast abstain from taking even water, yet they worship the sun with offerings of food and water and keep a night vigil.

The next day the aspirant women bathe before sunrise, worship the rising sun, and break their fast. Brahmans are also fed and given gifts on this day. Hindu women believe that the fast and piety observed on this day ensure the good health, longevity, and happiness of their children and husbands.

Devathani Ekadashi
Eleventh day of the waxing half of Kartika

Devathani Ekadashi is a rural festival observed with much jollity in the countryside. It celebrates the waking of Visnu. Hindus believe that Visnu's eventually triumphant battle with the great demon Shankhasura was so exhausting that he and the other deities went to sleep for a period of four months. Each year, Visnu slumbers from the 11th day of the waxing half of Ashadha (June-July) till the tenth day of the waxing half of Kartika (October-November), then awakes on the 11th day. During the months of sleep, ceremonies such as marriages or the thread ceremony are not observed.

On Devathani Ekadashi Hindu women fast, worship Visnu, and sing hymns in praise of various gods and goddesses around a fire. New products from the fields, including sugarcane and waternuts, may be eaten for the first time. From this day onward marriages and other ceremonies can be held.

Kartika Purnima
Full moon day of Kartika

Hindus celebrate Kartika Purnima in honor of the day when Visnu incarnated himself in a fish form called the Matsya Avatara. The reason he appeared as a fish was to save Vavaswata, the seventh Manu and the progenitor of the human race, from destruction by a deluge. Charities done and piety observed on this day are believed to earn high religious merit. Bathing in the Ganges, or in other holy water, is considered to be of special religious significance. People fast, practice charities, and meditate on the gods.

It is also believed that Sankara killed the demon Tripurasura on this day, for which he is also called Tripurari. Siva is worshipped on this occasion and giving a bull (Siva's mount) as a gift to a Brahman is thought to be of great religious significance. Big cattle fairs are also held at various places.

Puskar Mela
Full moon day of Kartika

A camel fair and one of the best known of the Hindu religious fairs (melas) is held annually at Puskar, the place where it is said a lotus flower slipped out of Lord Brahma's hands. Water sprang up where the petals fell and created the holy waters of Puskar Lake. A temple to Brahma on the shore of the lake is one of the few temples in India dedicated to Brahma. Puskar is in the state of Rajasthan, a vast desert area dotted with oases and populated with wild black camels.

Karwachauth
Fourth day of the waning half of Kartika

Karwachauth is observed by married Hindu women in order to ensure prosperity, sound health, and their husband's longevity. Married women keep a strict fast and do not take even a drop of water. They get up early in the morning, perform their baths, and wear new and festive clothes.

Siva, Parvati, and their son Karttikeya are worshipped with ten Karwas (the small earthen pots with spouts) filled with sweets. The Karwas are given to daughters and sisters along with gifts. At night, when the moon appears, the women break their fast after offering water to the moon. The story of Karwachauth is told and heard among the women. Sometimes a Brahman priest tells this story and receives gifts in return. Married women receive costly gifts from their husbands, brothers, and parents on this occasion. They touch the feet of their mother-in-law and other elderly women of the family and seek their blessings.

Tihar
During the waning half of Kartika

A five-day Hindu festival in Nepal that honors different animals on successive days. The third day of the festival is the most important day because the goddess Laksmi visits every home that is suitably lit for her. It is known throughout India as Dewali (see below).

On the first day of the festival, offerings of rice are made to crows, thought to be sent by Yama, the god of death, as his "messengers of death." The second day honors dogs, since in the afterworld dogs will guide departed souls across the river of the dead. Dogs are fed special food and adorned with flowers. Cows are honored on the morning of the third day; they, too, receive garlands and often their horns are painted gold and silver.

The fourth day is a day for honoring oxen and bullocks, and it also marks the start of the new year for the Newari people of the Katmandu Valley. On the fifth day, known as Bhai Tika, brothers and sisters meet and place tikas (dots of red sandalwood paste, considered emblems of good luck) on each other's foreheads. The brothers give their sisters gifts, and the sisters give sweets and delicacies to their brothers and pray to Yama for their brothers' long life. This custom celebrates the legendary occasion when a girl pleaded so eloquently with Yama to spare her young brother from an early death that he relented, and the boy lived.

Dhan Teras (Dhanvantri Trayodashi)
Thirteenth day of the waning half of Kartika

Two days prior to Dewali, Dhan Teras, or Dhanvantri Trayodashi, is observed with great mirth and rejoicing. Dhanvantri, the physician of the gods, who appeared at the churning of the ocean, is worshipped on this day, especially by physicians. He is the father of Indian medicine, and Ayurveda is attributed to him. He is also called Sudhapani, because he appeared from the ocean carrying nectar in his hands.

People rise at dawn, bathe, don new robes, and fast. In the evening, an earthen lamp is lit before the door of every house and the fast broken. It is considered an auspicious day to purchase new utensils.

Narak Chaturdashi
Fourteenth day of the waning half of Kartika

The day after Dhan Teras is celebrated as Narak Chaturdashi. It is dedicated to Yama, the god of Naraka or Hell. Bathing at dawn on this day is considered of great religious merit; in fact, some texts assert that Hindus believe those who bathe on this day after sunrise have their religious merit destroyed. Therefore, the devout rise early in the morning to bathe.

After the bath, libations are offered to Yama three times to please and appease him. The hope of those who sacrifice is that he may spare them the tortures of death. A fast is observed and in the evening lamps are offered to Yama. Some Hindus believe that piety observed on this day in honor of Yama liberates them from the possible tortures of hell.

Dewali (Divali; Deepavali; Festival of Lights)
Fifteenth day of the waning half of Kartika

Dewali, or the Festival of Lights, is an important and popular festival which marks the New Year and is celebrated throughout India. Hindus believe that this great festival of lights symbolizes the human urge to move toward the light of truth from the darkness of ignorance and unhappiness. The climax of the five-day festival falls on the last day of the waning half of Kartika.

The customs observed during Dewali are associated with several legends. One myth says that on this day Laksmi, the goddess of wealth and good fortune, roams about and visits the houses of people. Therefore people clean their homes and businesses, decorating them lavishly as they prepare to welcome the goddess. It also commemorates the triumph of Rama over Ravana, the ruler of Sri Lanka who had stolen Rama's wife. Also on this day, Krishna is said to have killed the demon of Narkusura.

A few days before the festival, houses are whitewashed and cleaned. The courtyards, the gates, and the place of worship are decorated with flowers and intricate colored paperwork. The theme of illumination serves as one of the festival's primary features, and at night people place earthen lamps and candles on the edges of roofs and windows and along rivers and driveways. According to custom, these lights help the goddess Laksmi find her way to houses to distribute her gifts of prosperity. The word "dewali," from which the festival derives its name, means "a row or cluster of lights."

Dewali is celebrated with gift exchanges, fireworks, and festive (typically vegetarian) meals. Sweets are prepared and exchanged, and people ask forgiveness of one another for any wrongs committed. In the evening, Laksmi is worshipped.

Margasirsa (November-December)

Gita Jayanti
Eleventh day of the waxing half of Margasirsa

Gita Jayanti honors the birthday of the Bhagavad Gita, a Sanskrit poem relating a dialogue between Krishna and Arjuna found in the Hindu epic *Mahabharata*. Some texts assert that on this day Krishna taught Arjuna the sacred lore of the *Gita* on the battlefield of Kurukshetra, and thus made available to the whole human race the Song Celestial. The day is celebrated by reading and reciting passages from the *Gita* and by holding discussions on its philosophical aspects. It is also a day on which Hindus fast, worship Krishna, and resolve to put more effort into their study of the *Gita*.

The *Gita* has been a great source of strength, inspiration, and wisdom to Hindus through the centuries. Many Hindus believe that the *Gita*, as a voice of the Supreme, is not merely scripture, but a great song of universal spiritual uplifting, always to be studied and pondered, for it illumines the path to perfection and purity, which can be followed even while doing one's worldly duties. It urges all to perform actions while remaining united with God at heart.

Vaikuntha Ekadashi
Eleventh day of the waxing half and the eleventh day of the waning half of Margasirsa

Vaikuntha Ekadashi is celebrated in southern India. Devotees observe a fast, keep vigil the whole night, and have meditation sessions. A gateway in the temple is thrown open on this day for aspirants to pass through, signifying their entrance into heaven or vaikuntha.

Dattatreya Jayanti
Full-moon day of Margasirsa

Dattatreya Jayanti, observed all over India, is a celebration in commemoration of Dattatreya's birth. Dattatreya, son of Rishi Atri and Anusuya, is identified with Brahma, Visnu, and Siva, for it is believed that portions of these deities were incarnated in him.

One legend explains that Anusuya was an exceptionally devoted and virtuous wife. The wives of Brahma, Visnu, and Siva decided to test her virtue by sending their husbands, disguised as beggars, to ask her to give them alms while in the nude. Anusuya avoided the trap by transforming them into babies and suckling them. When her husband returned from his morning bath and discovered what had occurred, he turned the babies into one child with three heads and six hands. The wives begged for their husbands' return, and when Anusuya restored them to their original forms, Anusuya, Rishi Atri, and their son Dattatreya

were blessed. Dattatreya had three sons, Soma, Datta, and Durvasa, to whom a portion of the divine essence was also transmitted.

On Dattatreya Jayanti people rise early in the morning and bathe in sacred streams. They fast and spend the day in meditation, prayer, and worship. They meditate on the life of Dattatreya and read sacred works attributed to him, which include *Avadhuta Gita* and *Jivanmukta Gita*. The image of Dattatreya is worshipped with flowers, lamps, incense, and camphor, and the aspirants resolve to follow in Dattatreya's footsteps.

Bhairava Ashtami
Eighth day of the waning half of Margasirsa

Bhairava is a manifestation of Siva: a terrifying character worshipped to obtain success, prosperity, the removal of obstacles, and recovery from illness. One of the Bhairava's characteristics is that he punishes sinners with a danda (staff or rod); thus, he is also called Danda-pani. Another of Bhairava's names, Swaswa, comes from the legend that he rides a dog. "Swaswa" means "He whose horse is a dog."

On Bhairava Ashtami, people worship Bhairava and his mount with sweets and flowers. The dogs are fed milk, sweets, and other such delicacies. At night, aspirants keep vigil and spend the time telling stories of Bhairavanath. Dead ancestors are offered oblations and libations.

Vaitarani
Eleventh day of the waning half of Margashirsha

Aspirants observe a fast and other prescribed rituals. In the evening a black cow is worshipped. She is bathed in fragrant water, sandal paste is applied on her horns, and food is offered to her. Brahmans are also given gifts of food, clothes, and a cow made of either gold or silver.

A cow is worshipped and offered food on this day because the river Vaitarani (the Hindu Styx) can only be crossed with the aid of a cow. The river, said to be filled with all kinds of filth, blood, and moral offenses must be crossed by departed souls before the infernal regions can be entered. Many Hindus believe that a cow given to Brahmans transports the dead over the river. Thus, cows are given in charity to Brahmans when there is a death in the community.

Pausa (December-January)

Rukmini Ashtami
Eighth day of the waning half of Pausa

Vaishnavite Hindus believe that Rukmini was born on this day. Rukmini was Lord Krishna's principal wife and queen. She bore him a son, Pradyumna. According to the *Harivansha Purana*, she was sought in marriage by Krishna, with whom she fell in love, but her brother Rukmin had betrothed her to Sisupala, king of Chedi. On her wedding day, as she was going to the temple, Krishna saw her, took her by the hand, and carried her away in his chariot. They were pursued by Sisupala and Rukmin, but Krishna defeated them, took her safely to Dwarka, and married her.

On Rukmini Ashtami a strict fast is observed by both married and unmarried women, and married women are honored. Rukmini, Krishna, and Pradyumna are worshipped. A Brahman priest is also fed and given dandakshina on this day. Middle-class Hindus believe that observance of this fast ensures conjugal happiness and prosperity, and also enlists the help of Rukmini in finding good husbands for unmarried girls.

Swarupa Dwadashi
Twelfth day of the waning half of Pausa

The vow of Swarupa Dwadashi is observed by women desiring physical beauty, happiness, and healthy children. On the preceding day (the Ekadashi, which is the eleventh day), aspirant women ritually tell stories relating to Lord Visnu. On Dwadashi they keep a strict fast, place an image of Visnu in a vessel full of sesame, and worship it. Afterward, oblations are offered in the fire, Brahmans are fed and given charity, and the fast is broken.

Magha (January-February)

Makar Sankranti (Magh Sankranti; Uttarayana Skranti)
During the Hindu month of Magha; commences upon the sun's entrance into Capricorn, at the winter solstice, on or about January 14

This three-day Hindu festival, generally falls around January 14 according to the Gregorian calendar. It is celebrated as Pongal in the south (see below), but in the north it is observed as Makar Sankranti or Uttarayana Sankranti. The beginning of the period, when the sun travels northward, is considered highly favorable for activities.

On this day Hindus bathe in the Ganges and other holy streams. At Ganga Sagar, where the Ganges enters the sea, a grand fair and festival is held. Devotees in large numbers reach Sagar Island in boats, and bathe there.

Makar Sankranti is a very significant day. The first batch of corn from the new harvest is cooked and offered to the Sun and other deities. The poor are fed and given clothes and money. In the morning, people offer libations to their dead ancestors and visit temples.

In Assam this day is called Magha Bihu or Bhogali Bihu, the festival of feasts. Bonfires are lit, and the round of feasts and fun continues for about a week.

In Nepal the celebration of the sun's movement back toward the Northern Hemisphere is called Magh Skranti. The Nepalese people visit holy bathing spots during their festival. Some actually bathe in the shallow water, but the weather is usually chilly and most are content to splash water on their hands and faces and sprinkle it on their heads. People also spend the day sitting in the sun and massage each other with mustard oil, which is also used by mothers to bless their children. Foods traditionally served on this day include *khichari,* a mixture of rice and lentils; sesame seeds; sweet potatoes; spinach; and home-made wine and beer. Traditional gifts for the priests are a bundle of wood and a clay fire pot.

Pongal
During Magha; mid-January

Pongal is a three-day festival in honor of the sun, earth, and the cow. The celebration takes place in southern India on Sankranti and marks the beginning of the sun's northern course. This occasion for rejoicing and merrymaking takes place when the sun passes to Capricorn from Sagittarius.

The first day is Bhogi-Pongal, the Pongal of joy. On this day, people exchange visits, sweets, and presents, and enjoy a leisurely day. The second day is dedicated to the sun. As part of the traditional celebration, people rise early in the morning, and the woman of the house puts rice to boil in milk, which makes a sweet treat. As soon as the rice begins to simmer, the family shouts together, "Pongal! Pongal!" ("It boils!"). The sweet rice is then offered to Surya, the sun god, and a portion of it is given to the cows. The family then enjoys the treat as well. On this day of the festival, people often greet one another with the phrase "Has it boiled?" to which the response is "Yes, it is boiled."

The third day, Mattu Pongal, is the Pongal of the cows. Cows and oxen are worshipped and proudly paraded around the village. Their horns are painted in various colors, and garlands of leaves and flowers are hung around their necks. On this day the cows are allowed to graze anywhere they like, without any restraint.

Thaipusam (Thai Poosam)
Three to 12 days in Magha

Thaipusam marks the birthday and victory of the Hindu god Subrahmaniam (known as Lord Murugar) over the demons. It is a time of penance and consecration to the god, usually involving self-mortification in a test of mind over pain. The dramatic festival is celebrated in India, Malaysia, Sri Lanka, Singapore, South Africa, Mauritius, and elsewhere.

In Malaysia, the festival is a public holiday in the states of Perak, Penang, and Selangor. In Georgetown, Penang, a statue of Subrahmaniam—covered with gold, silver, diamonds, and emeralds—is taken from the Sri Mariamman temple along with his consorts, Valli and Theivanai. It is placed in a silver chariot and carried in a grand procession to his tomb in the Batu Caves near the capital city of Kuala Lumpur. The statue is carried up 272 steep steps and placed beside the permanent statue kept there. The next day about 200,000 people begin to pay homage, while movies, carrousels, and other entertainments are provided for their amusement.

Among the Tamil people of Mauritus, devotees, both male and female, abstain from meat and sex during the sacred 10 days before the festival. Each day they go to the temple (kovil) to make offerings. In Port Louis, at Arulmigu Sockalingam Meenaatchee Amman Kovil, Murugar and his two consorts are decorated differently each day to depict episodes in the deity's life.

On the eve of the Tamil celebration, devotees prepare the kavadees (wooden arches on wooden platforms) and decorate them with flowers, paper, and peacock feathers. They may be built in other shapes, such as a peacock or temple, but the arch is most common. The next morning, priests pour cow milk into two brass pots and tie them to the sides of each kavadee. Fruits, or jagger (a coarse, brown sugar made from the East Indian palm tree), may also be placed on the platform. Then religious ceremonies are performed at the shrines to put the bearers in a trance. When ready, penitents have their upper bodies pierced symmetrically with vels, the sacred lance given to Lord Subrahmaniam by his mother, Parvati; some also have skewers driven through their cheeks, foreheads, or tongues. The procession then begins, with the devotees carrying the kavadees on their shoulders. Some penitents draw a small chariot by means of chains fixed to hooks dug into their sides; some walk to the temple on sandals studded with nails. Groups of young men and women follow, singing rhythmic songs. Each region may have 40 to 100 kavadees, but in places like Port Louis there may be 600 to 800. At the temple, the kavadee is dismounted, the needles and skewers removed by the priest, and the milk in the pots is poured over the deity from head to foot. The penitents then go out and join the crowds. Some believe carrying the kavadee washes away sins through self-inflicted suffering; others say the kavadee symbolizes the triumph of good over evil.

Vasant Pañcami
Fifth day of the waxing half of Magha

This Hindu festival honors Saraswati, goddess of learning, eloquence, and the arts. During this holiday season, people wear bright yellow clothing to represent the mustard plant whose blossoms herald the coming of spring. The day of Vasant Pañcami is celebrated with music, dancing, and kite-flying.

In West Bengal, Saraswati is known as the goddess of speech, learning, wisdom, fine arts, and sciences. She is credited with the invention of the Sanskrit language and the Devnagari script. Celebrations of Vasant Pañcami in West Bengal include a procession in which images of her graceful figure are carried to the river for a ceremonial bath, and books and pens are placed at her shrine.

Bhishma Ashtami
Eighth day of the waxing half of Magha

On this day, Bhishma is offered libations with barley, sesame, flowers, and Ganges water.

In Hindu mythology Bhishma was the son of King Shantanu. The king decided he wanted to marry a beautiful young maiden named Satyavati, but her parents would not permit it because Bhishma was heir to the throne. This meant that if King Shantanu and Satyavati had sons, the boys could not inherit the kingdom. To allow the marriage to go forward, Bhishma vowed never to marry, nor have children of his own, nor to accept the crown. Shantanu then married Satyavati, and she bore him two sons.

The two sons died without producing any offspring, but Satyavati had two grandchildren by a son who had been born before she married the king. Bhishma ended up raising these two and taking charge of the training of their children, who were known as the Kauravas and the Pandavas.

In the battle that was eventually fought between the two groups of offspring, Bhishma sided with the Kauravas. According to Hindu mythology, he was so badly wounded during the fighting there was barely a space of two fingers' width on his body that had not been pierced by an arrow. He did not die immediately, however, because he had been allowed to choose the time of his death. He waited on his death-bed of arrows for 58 days. As he waited to die, Bhishma delivered many religious discourses. He later became the model for modern ascetics who lie on nail-studded beds. Bhishma is considered a great example of self-denial, loyalty, and devotion.

Magha Purnima
Full moon day of Magha

Magha is one of the four most sacred months and Hindus believe that bathing in the Ganges on the purnima (full moon day) is of high religious merit. When the Ganges is not accessible, one may bathe in any holy stream, river, tank, or pond. Fasting is also observed and charities are done. Early in the morning, libations are offered to dead ancestors, and clothes, food, and money are given to the poor. Gifts are also given to Brahmans according to one's means and capacity.

Minakshi Float Festival
Full moon day of Magha

The Float Festival is celebrated at Madurai, which is famous for its majestic Minakshi Temple. Minakshi is the fish-eyed goddess, and it is another name of Parvati. The major part of the Minakshi temple was built during the reign of Tirumala Nayak (1623–55), whose birthday falls on Magha Purnima.

On this day, images of Minakshi and Lord Sundareshwara (Siva) are mounted on floats and taken to Marriamman Teppakulam, Sarovar, east of Madurai. The deities are displayed on richly decorated and illuminated floats that are drawn back and forth across the water to the accompaniment of music and devotional songs. Afterwards they are returned to Madurai.

The waters on which the deities are displayed are confined in a pool called a tank which is fed by underground channels from the river Vaigai. A shrine stands on an island in the center of the tank. It was built in 1641 by King Tirumala Nayak. The float festival is very popular, and thousands of pilgrims and devotees from all parts of India congregate to see it.

Sakata Chauth
Fourth day of the waning half of Magha

Ganesa is honored with a fast on this day, believed to be the day of his birth. The fast is observed by both men and women. After the early morning bath, a pitcher and Ganesa statue are installed and worshipped with sweets and balls made of jaggery and sesame seeds. The moon god and Rohini are also worshipped ritually and offered food. At night, with the rising of the moon, the fast is broken. The moon is worshipped and offered water (arghya). The day-long fast is believed to ensure wisdom, a trouble free life, and prosperity.

Mauni Amavasya
Fifteenth day of the waning half of Magha

The month-long bathing and fasting associated with the month of Magha ends with the observance of Mauni Amavasya, when Lord Visnu is worshipped and the peepal tree (*Ficus religiosa*) circumambulated. A complete silence is observed. If the day falls on Monday, then its auspiciousness increases.

Hindus believe that piety and devotion on this day at Prayag, the place where the Ganges, Yamuna, and Saraswati are confluent, is highly meritorious. Aspirants come and live there for a full month and practice prescribed rituals and ceremonial sacrifices known as "Kalpa-Vas." Through the entire month, religious discourses and services are held for aspirants. Observers take one simple meal a day or ingest only fruit and milk.

Phalguna (February-March)

Amalaka Ekadashi
Eleventh day of the waxing half of Phalguna

On Amalaka Ekadashi the Alma tree (*Emblica officinalis*) is worshipped. Hindus believe in taking a respectful attitude toward all things, whether trees or beasts, rivers or deities, animate or inanimate, because the one Universal Spirit pervades all. It is this concept of God or Reality that underlies the worship of trees. In addition, according to Hindu thought, Visnu lives in the Alma tree.

An Alma tree is ceremonially bathed and watered and then worshipped. A fast is observed and Brahmans are given gifts. Amalaka Ekadashi also marks the beginning of the Holi festival.

Holi (Holika Dahan)
Fourteenth day of the waxing half of Phalguna

Holi is one of the four most popular festivals in India, observed by all Hindus without any distinction of caste, creed, status, or sex. It celebrates the burning of Holika, an evil sorceress who once tormented all of India and marks the end of winter and the advent of the spring season. The two-day festival is most notable for the freedom and loss of inhibition practiced by the people.

On the first night of the festival, a bonfire is constructed in the evening. Before the fire is lit, a worship ceremony is performed in which water and grains are offered, then people dance around the fire. Throughout the evening, images of Holika are burned, drums are pounded, horns are blown, and people shout.

The next day many people interact by splashing colored water and throwing colored powder on their friends, relatives, neighbors, and even passersby. Noisy and colorful processions are made through the bazaars and streets. Other people celebrate the day with songs, music, floral decoration, and by splashing perfumed water. Sweets and visits are exchanged, and cold drinks prepared at home are served liberally. People forget all enmity and embrace each other, with warmth and love, and renew their friendship. New corn is baked and eaten on this day for the first time in the season.

There are several myths about the origin of the festival of Holi. According to one Puranic myth, an evil king, Hiranyakasipu, had a good son, Prahlada, who was sent by the gods to deliver the people from the oppressive rule of the king. This angered the king so greatly that he ordered the death of the child. The sister of the king was an evil witch named Holika, who claimed to be impervious to fire. So to kill Prahlada, Holika snatched the child and jumped into a great bonfire. Prahlada, however, was rescued from the flames by Krishna and it was Holika who was destroyed. Holi commemorates this event and symbolizes the triumph of good over evil.

Dol Purnima
Full moon day of Phalguna

Dol Purnima is a Bengali festival dedicated to Krishna. An image of Krishna, richly adorned and smeared with colored powder, is taken out in procession in a swinging cradle decorated with flowers, leaves, colored clothes, and papers. The procession proceeds forward to the accompaniment of music, sounding of conch shells, trumpets, and shouts of "Jai!" (victory).

Dol Purnima is also significant because it is the birthday of Chaitanya Mahaprabhu (1485–1533), also known as Gauranga, the Vaishnava saint who popularized modern Sankirtana. Followers of the Chaitanya School of Vaishnavism believe Chaitanya himself was a manifestation of Krishna.

Mahasivarati (Great Night of Siva; Siva Chaturdashi of Phalguna)
Fourteenth day of the waning half of Phalguna

Mahasivarati is a major Hindu festival marked by worship services at all temples where Siva is honored throughout India. Devotees by the thousands collect at Siva shrines and spend the entire night practicing devotion and piety, meditating, and reading and reciting Siva scriptures. The linga (phallic) symbol of Siva is worshipped with Ganges water, milk, curds, honey, and clarified butter (ghee). Betel leaves, dhatura fruit, aak, and flowers, are also offered to Siva.

Special puja (worship) celebrations are held at Varanasi, Tarkeshwar, Baidyanath, Walkeshwar, Rameshwaram, and Ujjain. At Pashupatinath in Nepal a grand celebration is held and adherents keep a strict fast and do not take even a drop of water.

According to Hindu teaching, Siva is a great and powerful god, one of the Hindu Trinity. As Mahadeva, he is worshipped by various gods including Brahma and Visnu. He is Mahakala the destroyer dissolving everything into nothingness, but also, as Sankara, restores and reproduces that which has been destroyed. His linga (phallus) symbolizes this reproductive power. As a Mahayogi, or great ascetic, he combines in himself the highest perfection of austere penance and abstract meditation. In this form he is a naked ascetic, digambra "clothed with the elements." He is also called Chandrashekhra, "Moon Crested"; Girisha, "Mountain Lord"; Mahakala, "Great Time"; Pashupati, "Lord of the Beasts"; and Vishwanath, "Lord of the Universe."

Caitra (March-April)

Gudi Parva
First day of the waxing half of Caitra

Gudi Parva, or Padva, marks the beginning of preparations for the Hindu New Year, and is mainly celebrated in Maharashtra on Caitra Pratipada. People arise early in the morning, tidy up their houses, have baths, and wear festive and new clothes. Women decorate their houses, a silk banner is raised and worshipped, and then greetings and sweets are exchanged.

Ugadi Parva
First day of the waxing half of Caitra

Ugadi Parva is a Hindu festival that ushers in the New Year for the inhabitants of Andhra. On this day, people visit one another, enjoy feasts, and wear new clothes. The festive day begins with ritual bathing and prayers, and continues late into the night. Some Hindus believe that both Brahma's creation of the world and Lord Visnu's first incarnation as Matsya (the fish) occurred on this day. Brahma is especially worshipped on this day.

Vasanta Navaratra
Nine nights preceding Ramanavimi during the month of Caitra

Navaratras are observed twice a year. Vasanta Navaratra occurs in the Hindu month of Caitra (March-April), preceding Rama Navami; the second Navaratra fast occurs in the month of Asvina (September-October) preceding Dussehra. The name of the fast means "nine nights." The purpose of Navaratra is to propitiate the goddess Durga and to seek her blessings. The methods by which Navaratra is kept vary regionally.

Caitra Parb
Eight days prior to the full-moon day of Caitra

Caitra Parb is a festival held by the tribes in Orissa, India. It starts eight days before the Purnima (full moon). Throughout the celebrations people fast, dance, and hunt. Heads of the families pay homage to their forefathers in the presence of the "Jani," or village priest, and every member of the family attends in festive new costumes. Animal sacrifice is a main feature of the festival, which also signals the beginning of the mango season.

Sitala Ashtami
Eighth day of the waxing half of Caitra

Sitala Ashtami is a festival honoring the Hindu goddess Sitala. She is the goddess of smallpox and her blessings are invoked for protection against the disease. Sitala is depicted as roaming the countryside riding an ass. She is identified with the devil or Durga in her role as the goddess of smallpox. On this day, which is either a Monday or Friday, Hindu women visit the Sitala shrine in the morning, and offer rice, homemade sweets, cooked food, and holy water mixed with milk. At several places colorful fairs are held on this occasion near the shrine of Sitala and there is a lot of merry-making, songs, dance, feasting and brisk buying and selling.

Ashokashtami
Eighth day of the waxing half of Caitra

This festival of Lingaraja at Bhubaneshwar is based on the Car Festival of Jagannatha at Puri, also known as Ratha Yatra. The protege of Lingaraja is taken out in a giant wooden chariot to the Rameshwar temple, about two kilometers from the Lingaraja temple, and returned after four days. Ashokashtami is a major local festival witnessed by thousands of devotees and spectators.

Ramanavami (Ram Navami; Rama Navami)
Ninth day of the waxing half of Caitra

The Hindu festival of Ramanavami celebrates the birth of Rama, who was the first son of King Dasaratha of Ayodhya. According to Hindu belief, the god Visnu was incarnated in ten different human forms, of which Rama was the seventh. He and his wife, Sita, are venerated by Hindus as the ideal man and wife. Because Rama is the hero of the great religious epic poem, the *Ramayana*, Hindus observe his birthday by reciting stories from it. They also flock to the temples, where the image of Rama is enshrined, and chant prayers, repeating his name as they strive to free themselves from the cycle of birth and death.

In Ayodhya, the birth place of Rama, great celebrations are held; the temples are decorated, the *Ramayana* is read and recited, and a fair is held. At other places icons of Rama, along with Sita and Hanuman, are richly adorned and worshipped, and other acts of devotion and piety are observed. Chanting the holy name of Rama and lectures and discourses on Rama's life and teachings are common features of the celebrations. People take vows to devote themselves more to their spiritual and moral evolution on this occasion. Many Hindus believe that Ram-Nam is a great magic formula (mantra) that should be repeated, recited, and meditated upon frequently.

Panguni Uttiram (Meenakshi Kalyanam)
Ten days including the full moon day of Caitra

The full moon day of Caitra is the day on which the Hindu god Siva married the goddess Meenakshi at Madura, Indonesia. The 10-day Hindu festival that follows also celebrates the marriage of Subrahmanya to Theivanai, adopted daughter of Indra.

Panguni Uttiram is a popular festival in Malaysia, where the worship of Subrahmanya is widespread. There are fairs on the temple grounds and processions in which Hindu gods and goddesses are carried through the streets in chariots. In Kuala Lumpur, Subrahmanya and his consort are taken from the Sentul temple in an elaborately decorated chariot through the city streets. Free meals are served throughout the day to visitors.

In Singapore, Panguni Uttiram is a two-day festival held at the Sri Veeramakaliamman Temple. There is a procession of Subrahmanya on the first day, and special pujas (worship ceremonies) are held at the temple on the second day. At Bukit Mertajam, a fire-walking ceremony is held.

In India, the festival is known as Meenakshi Kalyanam. Garlands, marigolds, and other offerings presented at the temple are devoted to Meenkashi in Madurai. Figures representing the god and his wife are then adorned with ceremonial robes and later carried in chariots.

Caitra Purnima
Ten days in Caitra

In southern India, Caitra Purnima is also considered sacred to Chitra Gupta. On this day, Chitra Gupta, Yama's assistant, is worshipped. Some Hindus believe that it is Chitra Gupta who maintains the accounts of good and bad actions in this world, and that people are rewarded or punished accordingly hereafter. At Kanchipuram, near Madras, the image of Chitra Gupta is taken out in a procession and devotees bathe in the holy waters of the River Chitra, which flows from the nearby hills.

Hanuman Jayanti
Full-moon day of Caitra

The monkey-god Hanuman is worshipped all across India, either singularly or together with Rama because he played a central role in the great Hindu epic the *Ramayana* in which he helped Rama rescue his wife Sita from the demon Ravana. Hanuman is depicted in the form of a monkey with a red face who stands erect like a human.

On his birth anniversary (jayanti), Hanuman is celebrated with great religious fervor. People visit Hanuman's shrines, fast, offer prayers and puja (worship), and read the *Ramayana* and the Hanuman *Chalisa*. Statues of Hanuman are given new coats of vermillion mixed with clarified butter and then richly decorated. Fairs are sometimes held at places near the shrines.

Hanuman is regarded by Vaishnavites as one of the greatest embodiments of strength, speed and agility, learning, and selfless service to Lord Rama. On Hanuman Jayanti, Vaishnavites observe a strict fast, meditate on Hanuman and his lord Rama, practice charity, and spend the day repeating his glories and adventures.

Gangaur
Two weeks after Holi

Gangaur is primarily an eighteen-day Hindu women's festival that begins the day after Holi and culminates two weeks later. It is a great local festival in Rajasthan, but is also celebrated in many parts of northern India.

During the festival both married women and unmarried girls worship the goddess Gauri (the most fair and benign aspect of the goddess Durga, the consort of Siva) with durva grass, flowers, fruits, and bright brass pots filled with fresh water. The married women seek Gauri's blessings for conjugal happiness, while the unmarried pray for a suitable handsome husband and future marital prosperity.

On the final day of the Gangaur festival, Hindu women keep a strict fast, worship the goddess, wear colorful clothes and ornaments, and exchange sweets. The wooden or earthen images of the goddess are taken through the main streets and bazaars in procession with decorated elephants, camels, horses, chariots, dancers, and musicians.

Every 12 Years

Kumbha Mela (Pitcher Fair)
Every 12 years on a date calculated by astrologers (1989, 2001, ...)

The Kumbha Mela festival is marked by mass immersion rituals by Hindus near the city of Allahabad (the ancient holy city of Prayag) in north-central India. Millions of pilgrims gather to bathe at the confluence of the Ganga (Ganges) and Yamuna Rivers, which is also where the mythical river of enlightenment, the Saraswati, flows. The bathers wash away the sins of their past lives and pray to escape the cycle of reincarnation. Sadhus (or holy men) carry images of deities to the river for immersion. The most ascetic sadhus, naked except for loincloths and with their faces and bodies smeared with ashes, go in procession to the waters, escorting images borne on palanquins. The Ganges is not only a sacred river but is the source of all sacred waters. The junction of the three rivers at Allahabad is

called the "sangam" and is considered by some to be the holiest place in India.

The mela (a word that means "fair") is thought to be the largest periodic human gathering in the world. During its duration a vast tent city appears, temporary water and power lines are installed, and ten pontoon bridges are laid across the Ganges. Movies of Hindu gods and heroes are shown from the backs of trucks, and plays recounting Hindu mythology are performed. Merchants lay out all manner of goods.

The story behind the mela is that Hindu gods and asuras (or demons) fought for a Kumbha (or pitcher) carrying amrit, the nectar of immortality. The god who seized the Kumbha stopped at Prayag, Hardwar, Nasik, and Ujjain on his way to paradise. The journey took 12 days (longer than earthly days), and therefore the mela follows a 12-year cycle.

A purification bathing ceremony called the Magh Mela is also held each spring in Allahabad. It is India's biggest yearly religious bathing festival. Although the Magh Mela attracts about a million people, the Kumbha Mela dwarfs it.

Masi Magham
full moon day February-March

The Masi Magham festival is observed every 12 years during the full moon in February or March, although a smaller festival takes place annually. Hindus flock to Kumbakonam, in southern India, to bathe in the Maha-Magha tank, where the waters of nine holy rivers are said to be mixed: the Ganges, the Yumma, the Godavari, the Saraswati, the Narmada, the Cauvery, the Kumari, the Payoshni, and the Sarayu. Bathing in the sacred tank (or pool) purifies them of their sins.

The Masi Magham festival is also a time for gift-giving, particularly in support of charitable institutions. One way of measuring the size of one's gift to the poor is to give one's weight in gold, a custom known as Tulabhara. Sometimes the gold collected in this way is used to renovate the 16 temples that have been built over the years near the site of the sacred tank.

In Malaysia, the Masi Magham is a two-day festival celebrated by the Chettiyar (a Tamil merchant caste) community in Malacca. The image of Subrahmanya, a Hindu god, is taken in procession to the temple known as Sannasi Malai Kovil, formerly the home of a famous ascetic who had the power to heal. Oratorical contests are held and dramas are staged at the temple. At the end of the day, the statue is taken back through the streets of Malacca to Poyyatha Vinayagar Kovil, where it remains for another year.

TABLE 10.5. ALPHABETICAL LIST OF HINDU HOLIDAYS

Name	Dates	Name	Dates
Akshya Tritiya	Third day of the waxing half of Vaisakha	Dol Purnima	Full moon day of Phalguna
Amalaka Ekadashi	Eleventh day of the waxing half of Phalguna	Durga Puja	During the waxing half of Asvina
Anant Chaturdashi	Fourteenth day of the waxing half of Bhadrapada	Dussehra	Tenth day of the waxing half of Asvina
Asadha Purnima *see* Guru Purnima		Festival of Boys *see* Ghanta Karna	
Ashokashtami	Eighth day of the waxing half of Caitra	Festival of Lights *see* Dewali	
Avani Avittam *see* Raksa Bandhana		Festival of Victory *see* Durga Puja	
Baisakhi *see* Vaisakhi		Ganesa Caturthi	Fourth day of the waxing half of Bhadrapada
Balarama Shashti *see* Halashashti		Ganesha Chata *see* Ganesa Caturthi	
Bhairava Ashtami	Eighth day of the waning half of Margasirsa	Ganesha Chaturti *see* Ganesa Caturthi	
Bhaiya Duj	Second day of the waxing half of Kartika	Ganga Dussehra	Tenth day of the waxing half of Jyestha
Bhishma Ashtami	Eighth day of the waxing half of Magha	Gangaur	Two weeks after Holi
		Ghanta Karna	Fourteenth day of waning half Sravana
Bhratri Panchami *see* Nag Pañcami		Gita Jayanti	Eleventh day of the waxing half of Margasirsa
Brother and Sister Day *see* Raksa Bandhana		Govardhan Puja	First day of the waxing half of Kartika
Caitra Parb	Eight days prior to the full-moon day of Caitra	Great Night of Siva *see* Mahasivarati	
Caitra Purnima	Ten days in Caitra	Green Teej *see* Hariyali Teej	
Cake Festival *see* Sithinakha		Gudi Parva	First day of the waxing half of Caitra
Chandan Yatra	Beginning on the third day of the waxing half of Vaisakha	Guru Purnima	Full-moon day of Asadha
		Halashashti	Sixth day of the waning half of Bhadrapada
Dasain	During the waxing half of Asvina	Hanuman Jayanti	Full-moon day of Caitra
Dashara *see* Dussehra		Hari Tritiya *see* Hariyali Teej	
Dattatreya Jayanti	Full-moon day of Margasirsa	Hari-Shayani Ekadashi	Eleventh day of the waxing half of Asadha
Deepavali *see* Dewali		Haritalika Teej half of Bhadrapada	Third day of the waxing
Devathani Ekadashi	Eleventh day of the waxing half of Kartika	Hariyali Teej	Third day of the waxing half of Sravana
Dewali	Fifteenth day of the waning half of Kartika	Hindu New Year *see* Vaisakhi	
Dhan Teras	Thirteenth day of the waning half of Kartika	Holi	Fourteenth day of the waxing half of Phalguna
Dhanvantri Trayodashi *see* Dhan Teras		Holika Dahan *see* Holi	
Divali *see* Dewali		Indra Jatra	Beginning the end of Bhadrapada until early Asvina

TABLE 10.5. ALPHABETICAL LIST OF HINDU HOLIDAYS, continued

Name	Dates
Janaki Navami	Ninth day of the waxing half month of Vaisakha
Janmashtami	Eighth day of the waning half of Bhadrapada
Jhulan Latra	Full moon day of Sravana
Jyestha Ashtami	Eighth day of waxing half of Jyestha
Kamada Ekadashi	Eleventh day of the waning half of Sravana
Kartika Purnima	Full moon day of Kartika
Kartika Snan	During Kartika
Karwachauth	Fourth day of the waning half of Kartika
Kojagara	Full moon day of Asvina
Krishna's Birthday see Janmashtami	
Krishnastami see Janmashtami	
Kumbha Mela	Every 12 years on a date calculated by astrologers
Laksmi Puja	During Asvina
Magh Sankranti see Makar Sankranti	
Magha Purnima	Full moon day of Magha
Mahasivarati	Fourteenth day of the waning half of Phalguna
Makar Sankranti	Commences upon the sun's entrance into Capricorn, at the winter solstice
Masi Magham	Every 12 years on the full moon in February or March
Mauni Amavasya	Fifteenth day of the waning half of Magha
Meenakshi Kalyanam see Panguni Uttiram	
Minakshi Float Festival	Full moon day of Magha
Nag Pañcami	Fifth day of the waxing half of Sravana
Narak Chaturdashi	Fourteenth day of the waning half of Kartika
Narieli Purnima	Full moon day of Sravana
Narasimha Jayanti	Fourteenth day of the waxing half of Vaisakha
Nirjala Ekadashi	Eleventh day of the waxing half of Jyestha
Onam	Four days in the Malyalan month of Chingam
Panguni Uttiram	Ten days including the full moon day of Caitra
Parasurama Jayanti	Third day of the waxing half of Vaisakha

Name	Dates
Pitcher Fair see Kumbha Mela	
Pitra Paksha see Pitra Visarjana Amavasya	
Pitra Visarjana Amavasya	During the waning half of Asvina
Pongal	During Magha (mid-January)
Pooram	10 days during Vaisakha
Puskar Mela	Full moon day of Kartika
Putrada Ekadashi	Eleventh day of the waxing half of Sravana
Radha Ashtami	Eighth day of the waning half of Bhadrapada
Raksa Bandhana	Full-moon day month of Sravana
Ram Navami see Ramanavami	
Rama Navami see Ramanavami	
Ramanavami	Ninth day of the waxing half of Caitra
Ratha Yatra	Second day of the waxing half of Asadha
Rishi Pañcami	Fifth day of the waxing half of Bhadrapada
Rukmini Ashtami	Eighth day of the waning half of Pausa
Sakata Chauth	Fourth day of the waning half of Magha
Sankaracarya Jayanti	Fifth day (south) or tenth day (north) of the waxing half of Vaisakha
Sharad Purnima	Full moon day of Asvina
Sitala Ashtami	Eighth day of the waxing half of Caitra
Siva Chaturdashi of Phalguna see Mahasivarati	
Sithinakha	Sixth day of waxing half of Jyestha
Skanda Shashti	During the Tamil month of Tulam
Snan Yatra	Full-moon day of Jyestha
Sravani Mela	During Sravana
Surya Shashti	Sixth day of the waxing half of Kartika
Swarupa Dwadashi	Twelfth day of the waning half of Pausa
Teej see Hariyali Teej	
Thai Poosam see Thaipusam	

TABLE 10.5. ALPHABETICAL LIST OF HINDU HOLIDAYS, continued

Name	Dates
Thaipusam	.Three to 12 days in Magha
Tihar	.During the waning half of Kartika
Tij *see* Hariyali Teej	
Tirupati Festival . . .	.Ten days during Bhadrapada
Tulsidas Jayanti . . .	.Seventh day of the waxing half of Sravana
Ugadi Parva	.First day of the waxing half of Caitra
Uttarayana Skranti *see* Makar Sankranti	
Vaikuntha Ekadashi .	.Eleventh days of the waxing and waning halves of Margasirsa
Vaisakhi	.First day of the waxing half of Vaisakha (about April 13)

Name	Dates
Vaitarani	.Eleventh day of the waning half of Margashirsha
Valmiki Jayanti	.Full-moon day of Asvina
Vasant Pañcami . . .	.Fifth day of the waxing half of Magha
Vasanta Navaratra . .	.Nine nights preceding Ramanavimi during the month of Caitra
Vata Savitri	.Thirteenth day of the waning half of Jyestha
Vijay Dashami *see* Dussehra	
Vyasa Purnima *see* Guru Purnima	
Yama Dvitiya *see* Bhaiya Duj	

CHAPTER 11

Jainism

Overview of Jainism

What Is Jainism?

The Jains are an ascetic religious community with roots in Hinduism. The religion originated around the same time Buddhist thought developed. Jains believe in a sequence of reincarnations: Animals must become human; women must become men; and lay people must become monks in order to attain salvation from the world. Salvation, called mokhsa, is attained by liberating the soul from the contamination of matter (karma). This liberation results in omniscience and bliss for eternity.

One of the fundamental doctrines of Jainism is the separation of living matter (called jiva) and non-living matter (called ajiva). In order to achieve freedom from karma, Jains must completely avoid harming any living thing and practice perfect asceticism. Three concepts govern the affairs of the Jain people. These are known collectively as the Triratna (Three Jewels) and consist of right faith, right knowledge, and right conduct.

The primary focus of the religion is on nonviolence and asceticism. Jains believe that all life is sacred and that cruel actions darken the soul and thwart the ability to achieve freedom from karmic matter. Some Jains wear cloths across their mouths to keep them from accidentally destroying insect life. Some carry brushes to help remove insects from their path and are strict vegetarians. Some Jains eschew even simple farming on the basis that tilling the soil can harm small living things. Monks vow to abstain from killing, stealing, lying, sexual activity, and possessing personal property.

The name Jain comes from the Sanskrit word, Jinas, which means Conquerors. The conquerors honored by the Jains are people who have overcome and won enlightenment. The name Jinas also applies specifically to 24 spiritual guides from history and the legendary past who are collectively called the Tirthamkaras (which means ford-markers). Each of the Tirthamkaras achieved liberation, and by his model taught others how to do the same.

Jainism teaches that the universe is eternal—it was not created, it has no beginning, and will have no end. It passes through cycles during which civilizations rise and fall, men attain large size and life-spans lengthen. In each cycle, 24 Tirthamkaras appear. The last (24th) Tirthamkara was Vardhamana Mahavira who lived about the same time as Buddha. Precise dates for his life and death vary among the different Jain sects and scholarly research. Some place the date of his death in 527 or 510 B.C.E., others in the middle of the fourth century B.C.E. Mahavira taught a path of passionless detachment and, according to Jain teaching, upon his death achieved omniscience (knowledge of all things).

The Relationship between the Gods and the Jain People

There is no personal god in Jainism. Although several deities from the Hindu pantheon are recognized, they take a subordinate position to the 24 Tirthamkaras.

The first Tirthamkara to appear in the current cycle of degenerative ages was Risabha. The timing of his birth, placed him at a point in the era that was closer to an idealistic age. Risabha is credited with establishing the first Indian emperor, founding human social conventions (such as marriage), and developing the caste system. According to tradition, he lived more than 600,000 years.

Historical evidence exists for the lives of only the last two Tirthamkaras, Parsva and Mahavira. Parsva, the twenty-third Tirthamkara, lived approximately 250 years before Mahavira. Jains believe that his disciples joined with Mahavira. Jains thus believe that Mahavira did not found a new religion, but that he provided guidance to a tradition that was already established.

In addition to the Tirthamkaras, some sects of Jains also venerate heavenly beings called yaksas (male) and yaksis (female). Some of these have similarities with Hindu gods and others serve as protectors, guardians, or servants of the Tirthamkaras and the Jain community.

Sacred Writings

The two main sects of Jains acknowledge different canons of scripture. The Svetambara sect established the canon of writings it considered as scripture through a series of councils that culminated in the sixth century. The complete canon currently contains 45 texts. The Digambara sect, not represented at the councils, independently established their own canon. The Digambara scriptures, called the *Puranas* are based on oral traditions not recognized by the Svetambaras.

Both sects acknowledge that the original writings, called purvas, were lost. Their efforts at establishing canonical lists of writings is aimed at recovering portions of the original writings that were preserved in other texts and traditions. The types of documents include rules for conduct and doctrinal dissertations. One important document, the *Kalpa Sutra*, dates from the second century B.C.E. The *Kalpa Sutra* describes the lives of the Jinas, and it is often recited at major festivals.

Other books of Jain writings, while not considered sacred, have been influential. These texts include historical narratives, religious and moral teachings, medicinal and other secular sciences, and poetry. Other important writings include commentaries and biographies of Jain monks.

History

Jainism began during the sixth century B.C.E. partly as a revolt against exploitation by the highest of the Hindu castes (the priestly, or Brahmin, caste). Its founder, Vardhamana Mahavira, lived in the sixth century B.C.E. (although some accounts also place him in the fourth or fifth centuries B.C.E.). The designation Mahavira is a title rather than a given name; it means Great Hero.

Mahavira was born in northern India into a Hindu family of the warrior caste. He was trained in the tradition of a spiritual guide named Parsva, who Jains consider the 23rd Tirthamkara. Mahavira is revered as the twenty-fourth Tirthamkara.

According to Jain teaching, Mahavira's mother Trisala (also known as Priyakarini) had a series of miraculous dreams heralding his birth and signifying his importance. Beginning at the age of 30, he followed a path of austerity for more than 12 years. Mahavira then achieved enlightenment and became a Jina (conqueror)

while meditating under an Ashoka tree after two and a half days of fasting. After his enlightenment, Mahavira gave away all his wealth and possessions.

Accounts of Mahavira's life after his enlightenment vary among the Jain sects. According to some, he also stripped himself of all his clothes and went naked afterwards. Other Jains believe that Indra (a goddess from the Hindu pantheon) presented him a white robe to wear.

Mahavira lived 30 years after his enlightenment and gathered many disciples. At the age of 72 he died and attained mokhsa (liberation from the material world). Although the account of specific events of Mahavira's life, especially those that occurred after his enlightenment, are a point of division among the two major sects of Jainism, both recognize the same set of the five most important phenomenon from his life: his conception; his birth; his renunciation of the world; his enlightenment; and his attainment of nirvana.

After Mahavira's death, one of his disciples, Indrabhuti, received enlightenment and became a leader in the Jain community. Another of his disciples, Gosala, left the bounds of the tradition and established a sect called the Ajivika, which enjoyed a small following for several centuries and then eventually died out.

About 200 years after Mahavira's death, a council was held to establish official Jain doctrines. Consensus was not achieved, and ultimately the events that transpired during the century following the council led to the development of separate Jain sects in distinct geographic areas. The two sects were called the Digambaras and the Svetambaras. Other councils held in subsequent centuries were predominantly represented by members of the Svetambara sect and focused on establishing the canon of Jain scripture.

Although never a majority faith in India, the Jains developed into a sizable and well-respected community. Between the eleventh and sixteenth centuries, elaborate shrines were constructed in several cities. Two temples on Mount Abu in Rajasthan are among the best known and continue to be important places of pilgrimage.

Jainism Today

The Jain People

There are approximately four million Jains worldwide. The largest Jain community is in western India centered in Uttar Pradesh, Mysore, Madhya Pradesh, and Maharashtra. Other smaller communities exist in the United Kingdom, Canada, and the United States. In North America there are an estimated sixty Jain centers affiliated with Jain Associations in North America (JAINA).

The Jain community retains many of the characteristics organized by Mahavira. In India, it consists of four ranks of members: monks, nuns, lay men, and lay women. Many communities outside India, however, do not have monks and nuns.

Worship

Jain temple activity is not considered worship in the traditional sense. It is more closely associated with contemplation. Images of the Tirthamkaras, called murtis, serve as the focal points in Jain temples to assist laypeople in their worship. Worship includes making offerings to the images by pouring a specially prepared solution (which is often made from milk, curds, clarified butter, sugar, and flowers) over the image and then washing it with pure water. In addition to bathing the images of the Tirthamkaras, worshippers wave lamps, and sing devotional hymns.

Sects

There are two main sects of Jainism, each with its own texts. They differ primarily in the areas of discipline and practice rather than in areas of belief.

Digambaras

Digambaras ("sky-clad" sect) are the dominant form of Jainism in southern India. They believe that total nudity is required of monks (although current Indian law requires that Digambara monks wear a loincloth in public). This prohibition of clothing for monks extends into worship as well. Digambaras believe that images of the Jinas should not be clothed.

Digambaras claim the possession of oral teachings passed down from Mahavira and subsequently preserved in their writings. One belief that separates Digambaras from other Jains is the position that only men can achieve liberation from the cycle of rebirths. Another unique belief centers on the life of Mahavira following his enlightenment. According to Digambara understanding, after Mahavira experienced enlightenment he did not become involved in human relationships or routine activities such as eating, drinking, or talking. They believe that he lived solely on divine provisions.

Svetambaras

The Svetambaras ("white-clad" sect) represent the dominant form of Jainism in northern India. They believe that, because of the current condition of the universe, it is not practically possible for monks to be naked. In accordance with this belief, Svetambaras worship images of the Jinas which they also cover with clothes and adorn with jewelry.

Svetambara Jains possess written texts which they claim were based on Mahavira's original teaching. They believe that men and women alike can achieve liberation from the cycle of rebirths and that the nineteenth Tirthamkara, Malli, was female. In contrast with the Digambaras, Svetambaras believe that, after his enlightenment, Mahavira continued interacting with other humans and teaching them.

Sthanakvasins

Sthanakvasins emerged as a subsect of the Svetambaras during the seventeenth century. They differentiated themselves in how worship was practiced. The Sthanakvasins have no temples and do not worship before images.

TABLE 11.1
NAMES OF THE TWENTY-FOUR TIRTHAMKARAS

NAME	EMBLEM
1. Rishabha *or* Adi-nātha	Bull
2. Ajita-nātha	Elephant
3. Sambhava-nātha	Horse
4. Abhinandana-nātha	Monkey
5. Sumati-nātha	Curlew
6. Padmaprabha	Red Lotus
7. Supārsva-nātha	Svastika
8. Chandraprabha	Crescent
9. Pushpadanta *or* Suvidhi-nātha	Dolphin
10. Sitala-nātha	Wishing Tree
11. Sreyamsa-nātha	Rhinoceros
12. Vasupujya	Buffalo
13. Vimala-nātha	Boar
14. Ananta-nātha	Bear
15. Dharma-nātha	Spiked-headed Club
16. Santi-nātha	Deer
17. Kunthu-nātha	He goat
18. Ara-nātha	Fish
19. Malli-nātha	Waterpot
20. Muni-suvrata	Tortoise
21. Nami-nātha	Blue Lotus
22. Nemi-nātha	Conch
23. Parsva-nātha	Serpent
24. Mahavira *or* Vardhamana	Lion

Jain Adaptation of the Hindu Calendar

A Lunar Calendar

The Jain calendar has many similarities to the version of the Hindu calendar observed in Northern India. Jains observe the beginning of the month at the full moon. This means that the first fortnight is waning. Hindus in Southern India typically mark the beginning of the month at the new moon and the first fortnight is waxing. The Jain and Hindu month names are the same (although spelling varies; for ease of identification the spelling standardization used for the Hindu month names in this text has also been applied to the Jain month names).

Unlike their Hindu neighbors, however, Jains observe a different new year. The Hindu new year occurs in the spring (on or about April 13, according to the solar rather than lunar calendar). Jains begin the new year in the autumn with their version of the Dewali festival commemorating the liberation (achievement of Nirvana) of their founder, Nataputta Mahavira.

Mahavira's achievement of Nirvana (at his death) in 527 B.C.E. also serves as the epoch for the Jain calendar. Dewali 1997 C.E. will begin the year 2524 V.N.S. (Vira Nirvana Samvat).

Cyclical Eras

The Jain concept of how time cycles through progressive and regressive eras also differs from that of the Hindus. Jains believe that a complete cycle of time consists of twelve separate units. Of these, six represent deteriorating conditions and six represent improving conditions. The third and fourth units of both half-cycles represent times when neither extreme predominates. Only during these units can the Tirthamkaras be born.

Currently, the earth is experiencing the fifth unit in the declining part of the time cycle. Risabha, the first Tirthamkara of the current age, is said to have been born during the third unit; Mahavira was born at the close of the fourth. Each of the last two units in the declining half-cycle has a duration of 21,000 years.

TABLE 11.2.
THE JAIN CALENDAR

Month Names	Gregorian Equivalent
Kartika	October-November
Margasira	November-December
Pausa	December-January
Magha	January-February
Phalguna	February-March
Caitra	March-April
Vaisakha	April-May
Jyestha	May-June
Asadha	June-July
Sravana	July-August
Bhadrapada	August-September
Asvina	September-October

TABLE 11.3.
THE JAIN HOLIDAY CYCLE

Dates	Holidays
Kartika, waning	
15	Dewali
Pausa, waning	
10	Birth of Parshvanath
Caitra, waxing	
13	Birth of Mahavira
Vaisakha, waxing	
3	Aksaya Trtiya
Asadha, waning and waxing	
~	Caturmas begins
Sravana, waning and waxing	
~	Caturmas continues
Bhadrapada, waning	
13	Paryushan
Bhadrapada, waxing	
5-13	Dasa Laksana Parvan
14	Anata-Chaturdashi
~	Caturmas ends

~indicates a variable date

⬧ ⬧ ⬧

Annual Holidays

Kartika

Dewali
Fifteenth day of the waning half of Kartika

The Jains celebrate Dewali as Lord Mahavira's day of final liberation (the achievement of Nirvana) and as the anniversary of Swamy Sayananda Saraswati's salvation experience. Also commemorated on this day is the entrance of the great Swami Rama Tirtha into his final jal-samadhi. At great Jain shrines like Pavapuri in Bihar, and Girnar in Gujarat, special puja (worship) festivals are held, sacred scriptures read and recited, and Lord Mahavira worshiped. Additionally, Lakshmi, goddess of wealth and good fortune, is honored by many Jains on this day.

Dewali also serves as the beginning of the new year in the Jain calendar.

Pausa (December-January)

Birth of Parshvanath
Tenth day of the waning half of Pausa

The birth of Parshvanath, an Indian teacher who lived approximately 250 years before Mahavir, is commemorated by Jains. Jains believe that Mahavir did not establish a new religion, but that he gave guidance to one that was previously established.

Caitra (March-April)

Birth of Mahavira (Mahavir Jayanti)
Thirteenth day of the waxing half of the Hindu month of Caitra

Jains celebrate the birth of Vardhamana Jnatiputra, called Nataputta Mahavira (Mahavira means Great Hero), a sixth century B.C.E. religious reformer and founder of Jainism.

Jain pilgrims from all over India congregate at the ancient Jain shrines at Girnar and Palitana in Gujarat and at Mahavirji in Rajasthan. Pawapuri and Vaishali in Bihar are the other such centers. A grand festival is held at Vaishali, Mahavira's birthplace, and it is known as Vaishali Mahotsava.

Chariot processions with the images of Mahavira are taken out, rich ceremonies in the temples are held, fasts and charities are observed, Jain scriptures are read, and at some places fairs are held.

Vaisakha (April-May)

Aksaya Trtiya
Third day of the waxing half of Vaisakha

Svetambaras Jains honor a fast on Aksaya Trtiya. According to Jain teaching, the first Tirthamkara observed a fast and after fasting was given some sugar cane juice to break the fast. This holiday commemorates his fast.

Asadha

Caturmas
June through September

Jains observe a retreat during the rainy season in India. It involves a curtailment of travel. Some speculate that the tradition has its basis in Jain concern about unnecessarily killing many small insects that come out during the season. This season is also marked by frequent fasting.

Bhadrapada

Partyshana Parva (Paryushan; Pajjo-Savana)
Thirteenth to the fifth day of the waning half of Bhadrapada

Paryushan is a Svetambara (white-clad) Jain festival that lasts eight days. It takes place during the rainy season and is marked by recitations from the *Kalpa sutra* (Jain sacred writings) including the section that describes the birth of Mahavira.

The festival signifies a man's emergence into a new world of spiritual and moral refinement from that of a gross and depraved world. The ten cardinal virtues cultivated during this festival are forgiveness, charity, simplicity, contentment, truthfulness, self-restraint, fasting, detachment, humility, and continence. During the festival all of the virtues are lectured upon by the Jain saints and their cultivation stressed.

During this celebration devout Jains fast, eating only once a day; worship the Tirthamkaras; and try to take in the qualities and virtues of the great Jain saints and preachers. This is also an occasion of self-analysis and criticism. Jains ask one another for forgiveness during this festival for offenses done knowingly or unknowingly, helping to restore lost relations and friendships. On the final day of the festival people can confess their sins and receive pardon. This is traditionally done by exchanging letters and cards with friends and family members. At the end of the festival, an image of one of the Tirthamkaras (Jinas) is carried in a procession.

Dasa Laksana Parvan (Time of the Ten Characteristics)
Fifth to thirteenth day of the waxing half of Bhadrapada

Dasa Laksana Parvan is a Digambara (sky-clad) Jain observance similar to the Svetambara festival of Paryushan. It typically occurs later during the rainy season and may last ten days instead of eight. The scripture readings focus on different portions of the holy text describing the ten characteristics to which Jains aspire. The ten characteristics are: forbearance, gentleness, uprightness, purity, truth, restraint, austerity, renunciation, lack of possession, and chastity.

Anata-Chaturdashi
Fourteenth day of the waxing half of Bhadrapada

Anata-Chaturdashi is a day of special worship observed by Digambara (sky-clad) Jains to mark the end of the Dasa Laksana Parvan festival. Many places observe it with special temple processions.

TABLE 11.4. ALPHABETICAL LIST OF JAIN HOLIDAYS

Holidays	Dates
Aksaya Trtiya	waxing Vaisakha 3
Anata-Chaturdashi	waxing Bhadrapada 14
Birth of Mahavira	waxing Caitra 13
Birth of Parshvanath	waning Pausa 10
Caturmas	June through September
Dasa Laksana Parvan	waxing Bhadrapada 5–13
Dewali	waning Kartika 15
Mahavir Jayanti *see* Birth of Mahavira	
Pajjo-Savana *see* Partyshana Parva	
Partyshana Parva	waning Bhadrapada 13–5
Paryushan *see* Partyshana Parva	
Time of the Ten Characteristics *see* Dasa Laksana Parvan	

CHAPTER 12

Sikhism

Overview of Sikhism

What Is Sikhism?

Sikhism is an independent faith that, in some ways, resembles both Islam and Hinduism, but is not directly associated with either. Similar to Hindus, Sikhs believe that the human soul progresses through a series of births and rebirths and that its ultimate salvation occurs when it breaks free from the cycle. Sikhs, however, reject the Hindu pantheon and do not participate in bathing rituals. Instead they worship one God who they believe is the same God of all religions, including Allah of Islam. Unlike Muslims, however, they shun fasting and pilgrimages.

Sikhism developed during the fifteenth century in India. The word Sikh comes from the Sanskrit word *shishya* meaning disciple. The faith is also sometimes called Gurmat, which means "the Guru's doctrine." Sikhs believe that God was the original guru and that he chose to reveal his message to the first Sikh Guru, Nanak. Sikhs believe that their gurus were prophets sent by God to lead people into truth. They emphasize equality among people of different castes, practice Kirat Karni (a doctrine of laboring), and follow the precepts of charity.

The Sikhs can be distinguished from their Hindu neighbors by the distinctive turbans they wear. The largest population center of Sikhs is in the Punjab area of northwestern India. Many members of the faith hope they will eventually win sovereignty.

The Relationship between God and the Sikh People

For Sikhs, God is a personal creator with whom people can have individual relationships. God is eternal, without form, and indescribable, but he is willing to reveal himself in visible ways. He is present everywhere in creation and in the human heart. According to Sikh teaching, religious rituals of both the Hindu and Islamic faiths serve only to keep their adherents bound in the reincarnation cycle. Sikhs call God Nam (literally "Name"). Other names by which he is known are Akal Purakh (the Eternal One) and Raheguru (Wonderful Lord).

Service to God is one of the primary human tasks. It may be performed by reading from the Sikh sacred writings, by helping maintain a house of worship, or by assisting in the preparation and service of a meal (called a Langar) that traditionally follows a Sikh worship service. God may also be served by offering hospitality to anyone irrespective of their caste or religion.

Authorities and Sacred Writings

The Sikh holy scriptures are called the *Guru Granth Sahib* (*Guru* means Teacher or Lord; *Granth* means book; *Sahib* means revered). A more ancient name is *Adi Granth*, which means first or original book. The *Guru Granth Sahib* was compiled by the fifth Sikh Guru, Arjan, and revised by Gobind Singh, the tenth Guru. It contains hymns composed by the gurus.

On special occasions such as festivals and certain ceremonies the *Guru Granth Sahib* may be read continuously in its entirety, a process that takes about 48 hours. Such a complete reading is called an Akhand Path. On other occasions, such as at weddings and funerals, parts of the book may be read. These partial, non-continuous readings are called Sidharan Paths.

Within the Sikh temple (called a gurdwara), the *Guru Granth Sahib* is displayed on a special platform called a Palki. It is elaborately arranged with embroidered cloths and set on special cushions. At night it is moved to a room of rest.

Two other important, but non-canonical Sikh books, are the *Dasam Granth* (book of the Tenth) and the *Nit nem.* The *Dasam Granth* consists of a collection of writings including popular prayers, devotional hymns, biographical narratives, and poetry attributed to the Tenth Guru, Gobind Singh. The *Nit nem* is a collection of sacred songs excerpted from the *Guru Granth Sahib*. It is used primarily in homes for private worship. When not in use, it is honored by keeping it wrapped in cloth.

Sikhs do not have an established priesthood. Gobind Singh abolished the Sikh priesthood because he believed that priests would become egocentric and corrupt. Although individual gurdwaras may employ specially trained people to care for the *Guru Granth Sahib*, all Sikhs are free to read from their holy scriptures either in the temple or in their homes.

In addition, there is no one person to whom all Sikhs look for guidance in religious matters. The Sikh community is called the Panth, and collective decisions may be made by the Panth for the entire community. The Shiromani Gurdwara Parbandhad Committee, whose members are elected, provides guidance for all the gurdwaras in the Punjab. Individual local gurdwaras elect their own committees to oversee local matters.

History

Guru Nanak

Sikhs originated with Guru Nanak who was born in Talvandi (which is now located in Pakistan) in 1469 C.E. Talvandi was later renamed Nankana Sahib in his honor. Although born into a Hindu family, Nanak was influenced by Islamic teachings, particularly those of the Sufis (a mystical sect within Islam).

According to Sikh teaching, Nanak began to ask questions about spiritual matters at the age of five. As a young man, he sought out the company of holy men and wandering ascetics. Then, at the age of 30 he had a mystical experience with God in which he received a mission to teach people about God and how to practice devotion.

Nanak's teachings combined elements from both the Islam and Hindu faith systems. He advocated reforms such as the abolition of idol worship and caste regulations. He promoted liberalized social practices and preached the name of God as a potent means of spiritual realization. Nanak also encouraged his followers to work hard and pursue normal family relations.

Nanak traveled throughout India, toward each of the four compass points, to proclaim his message to both Hindu and Islamic audiences. His companions included Mardana, a Muslim musician, and Bala, a Hindu peasant. Upon the approach of his death, Nanak appointed one of his disciples to succeed him as Guru.

Successive Gurus

Under the supervision of ten successive gurus, Sikh doctrines developed over a two-hundred-year period. Upon the death of a guru, religious leadership passed to the person considered to be the most worthy candidate. The first four gurus were unrelated; the last six were from the same family.

The second Sikh guru, Angad (1504–1552), began to follow Nanak after being inspired by the divine message he received upon hearing one of Nanak's hymns being sung. Angad is remembered for his work to consolidate Nanak's followers, for compiling and writing hymns, and for building temples.

The third guru, Amar Das (1479–1574), converted from Hinduism to Sikhism when he was 60 years old. He devoted the remaining years of his life to serving Angad, and at the age of 73 was appointed to be his successor. Amar Das reorganized the Sikh community into units called manjis and instituted the custom of assembling the entire community for special occasions. Amar Das is also remembered for initiating communal meals (based on a tradition originating with Nanak) and teaching on the equality of mankind. He appointed Ram Das to be his successor.

Ram Das (1534–1581), the fourth Sikh guru, was a son-in-law of Amar Das. His name was originally Bhai Jetha but upon his appointment as Guru it was changed to Ram Das which means "God's Servant." The focal points of his teachings were sincere worship, hard work to earn one's living, and charity. Ram Das also spoke out against the Hindu practice of sati (burning a widow on her husband's funeral pyre), and he championed the right of widows to remarry. In addition, Ram Das established Amritsar as a place of worship. He is credited with beginning preparations for the eventual construction of the Sikh Golden Temple. Ram Das appointed his youngest son to succeed him.

Arjan (1563–1606) was the fifth guru. Although he is best remembered for building the Golden Temple at Amritsar, he also oversaw the construction of gurdwaras in other places including Taru Taran, Kartarpur, and Sri Hargobindpur. In addition, Arjan compiled hymns and teachings of the previous gurus into the *Adi Granth*, which later became the *Guru Granth Sahib*, the Sikh sacred scriptures.

Although the events of his life were important, his death marked a turning point in Sikh history. In 1606, Argan was taken captive by the Mughal Emperor Jehangir. (The Mughal dynasty ruled over portions of India between 1526 and 1858.) After five days of torture, Arjan was put to death for refusing to convert to Islam. Arjan submitted to the ordeal peacefully, but he left instructions for his successors to take up arms to defend the innocent.

The Beginning of the Sikh Militaristic Tradition

Har Gobind (1595–1644), Arjan's only son, became the sixth guru. Under his leadership the Sikhs began the militaristic tradition with which they are currently associated. It is said that Har Gobind wore two swords, one signifying spiritual power and the other worldly power. He trained a small army and created the Nishan Sahib (the Sikh's national flag). The Nishan Sahib is triangular in shape with an orange (or saffron) background. The emblem shows two kirpans (swords), a khanda (a double-edged sword) and a circle that symbolizes the unity of God.

In 1609, Har Gobind built the Akal Takhit, which means "throne of the divine." The building in Amritsar faces the Golden Temple and serves as the Sikh high court. It also provides a nightly resting place for the copy of the *Guru Granth Sahib* that is used in the Golden Temple. Important decisions for the entire Sikh community are made at Akal Takhit. The building was destroyed in a military action in 1984 but was subsequently rebuilt.

Har Raj (1630–1661), the seventh guru, was raised to his office when he was fourteen years old. He retained a small army and taught that the hymns of the Gurus should not be changed. He also taught against the show of miraculous power, which he felt was contrary to God's will.

Har Krishan (1656–1664), the youngest son of Har Raj, became the eighth guru when he was only five years old. He fell ill with smallpox at the age of eight. Before his death, he named his great uncle (a son of Har Gobind) to be his successor.

The ninth guru, Tegh Bahadur (1621–1675), was appointed guru at the age of 43. He was martyred at the age of 54. He death resulted from fighting against the Mughals and refusing to convert to Islam. A gurdwara was erected to mark the place of his death in Delhi. After Tegh Bahadur died at the hands of invaders, Sikhs focused more intently on building their military.

The Last Human Guru

The tenth, and last of the human Gurus, Gobind Singh (1666–1708) was established in his position when only nine years old. His life was marked by constant fighting against Mughal armies. He died in 1708 after being stabbed by an assassin. He is best remembered for founding the Khalsa and installing the *Adi Granth* (which became the *Guru Granth Sahib*) as perpetual guru to the Sikh community.

The Khalsa

The Khalsa is a spiritual brotherhood with military significance open to all baptized Sikhs. Its members wear the "Five Ks":

- *kesh*, uncut hair (Sikhs believe that because growing hair is natural it should not be cut off from the body);

- *kangha*, a comb which holds the hair in place;

- *kirpan*, a dagger (symbol of self-defense and the fight against evil);

- *kara*, a steel bracelet (it is worn on the right wrist, the steel represents strength; the round shape symbolizes continuity);

- *kachh*, an undergarment (part of the military uniform that also symbolizes sexual restraint).

Members of the Khalsa also abstain from beef, pork, alcohol, tobacco, hemp, and opium.

According to Sikh teaching, the Khalsa was created by Gobind Singh in 1699 on Baisakhi Day when the Sikhs were assembled at Anandpur (approximately 175 miles east of Amritsar) for a festival. During the gathering, Singh brandished his sword and asked if any among those assembled were prepared to die for the religion and for their leader. When one man came forward, he was taken into a tent with the guru. The guru came back out of the tent with blood on his sword and again asked if anyone was willing to die for him and for the Sikh faith. Another man came forward. The process was repeated five times. After the fifth man entered the tent, all five were presented—alive—to the crowd. They were wearing special uniforms and earned the title Panj Pyares (five beloved ones). These five were the first five members of the Khalsa, a brotherhood of people willing to give their lives for their faith.

Sikhism after Gobind Singh

After Gobind Singh's death other leaders emerged within the Sikh community but no single person stood as a sole spiritual leader. One of the most well-known Sikh leaders was Ranjit Singh (1780–1839). He lead Sikh defiance against British attempts to conquer the Punjab along with the rest of India.

Eventually, however, the Punjab did fall. In 1849, the British annexed the Punjab area, and recruited Sikhs into the British army. This action paved the way for Sikh migration into other British lands including Hong Kong and Singapore and eventually to other countries such as the United States and Canada.

During the latter part of the nineteenth century and the early part of the twentieth century many Sikh struggles were focused on the effort to define Sikh identity and achieve autonomy. In 1870, the Singh Sabha was established to help schools in the Punjab and to increase the strength of the people through education and knowledge of literature.

The Struggle for Autonomy

In 1919 following World War I, British rulers in India controlled Sikh houses of worship and other shrines. They issued orders forbidding Sikhs to assemble for the celebration of Baisahki because they feared an uprising. The Sikhs did assemble and were subsequently attacked. In the fighting that followed, more than 1,500 people were killed. In 1925, the Gurdwaras Act placed oversight of Sikh holy places under the Indian Government.

British rule ended in 1947, and India was divided into separate countries. Part of the Punjab, the Sikh homeland, became part of Pakistan which was under Islamic rule. As a result, many Sikhs emigrated to India and to other parts of the world. The struggle for Sikh self-rule continued unresolved into the later part of the twentieth century.

Sikhism Today

The Sikh People

An estimated 16 million Sikhs live around the world, the vast majority of them dwelling in northwestern India. The largest Sikh population outside India is in Britain. Other substantial Sikh communities exist in the United States and Canada with smaller population centers in Singapore, Hong Kong, Thailand, East Africa, Iran, Malaysia, Fiji, and Australia.

Worship

Sikhs participate in family worship and attend temples called "gurdwaras." The word gurdwara means "guru's door," or more figuratively, "house of God." Temples do not contain images; they contain the Sikh sacred scripture, the *Guru Granth Sahib*, which is revered and kept on a cushion under a canopy.

Worship is traditionally conducted in the Punjabi language, although in places outside of India, part of the service (such as some of the hymns and prayers) may be conducted in English. A granthi (reader) serves as the custodian of the *Guru Granth Sahib*.

In India, Sikh temples are open to worshippers all day long but typically two daily services are held, one in the morning and another in the evening. They consist of singing or recitation and the distribution of Karah parshad, a consecrated food made from flour, clarified butter and sugar. The Karah parshad symbolizes equality. Outside India where Sikh communities are smaller, services are held on a weekly basis.

Sikh temples also provide free food to all people who come, including members of the Sikh community, visitors, and travelers. Every Gurdwara contains a community kitchen called a Langar (which means kitchen of the guru) where the meal is prepared.

True worship, however, is not marked by attendance at the gurdwara but by a lifestyle. Sikhs also consider an upright manner of living and personal love and devotion to God as forms of worship.

Sects

During the 19th century two Sikh offshoots developed. Primarily in response to British rule, they both focused their efforts on holding fast to the Sikh national identity.

Nirankari

The name Nirankari means worshippers of the Formless One. They were founded by a former Hindu, Dayl Das (1783-1853). The Nirankari emphasized the centrality of the *Guru Granth Sahib* in naming and marriage ceremonies but they also honored another book, the *Hukam-nama* (Book of Ordinances). Most Nirankari Sikhs are centered in eastern Punjab.

Namdhari

The Namdhari (Name-bearing) sect was founded by Baba Balak Singh (1816-1884) in the 19th century. Singh instituted new baptismal rituals and promoted strict disciplines. He emphasized the centrality of the gurus' teachings, advocated adherence to religious authorities, and denied the perpetual authority of scripture. Unlike other Sikhs who believe that Gobind Singh appointed the *Guru Granth Sahib* as guru, the Namdharis believe Gobind Singh went into hiding and that Baba Balak Singh, as the twelfth guru, was his successor.

———— " ————

"Without praise of the Almighty, Darkness shalt prevail in one's mind."

—Guru Nanak

———— " ————

Sikh Gurupurab Calendar

A Lunar Calendar

The Sikh calendar is a lunar calendar that is based on the moon's movement from one zodiac sign into the next rather than on the phase of the moon. The dates of some festivals, however, are based on the phase of the moon. The beginning of a new month is called the Sangrand. It is announced in the Sikh house of worship (gurdwara) but it is not a festival day.

Sikh festivals are marked on a special calendar called the Sikh Gurupurab Calendar. A Gurupurab is a date commemorating births, deaths (and martyrdoms), or other important events associated with the lives of the ten Sikh human gurus or with the Sikh scriptures, the *Guru Granth Sahib*. The Gurupurab Calendar also notes the anniversary dates of historic incidents that are important to the Sikh faith.

The Sikh Gurupurab Calendar begins with the month of Chait (March–April). The Sikh New Year celebration, however, falls on the first day of the second month, Basakh.

Intercalations

The Sikh lunar calendar, called the Bikrami calendar, consists of twelve months averaging 29½ days. This yields a year that is approximately eleven days shorter than the solar year. To keep the lunar calendar in line with the solar seasons, the Sikh calendar intercalates an extra lunar month whenever two new moons occur within the same solar month. The thirteenth lunar month then takes the name of the solar month in which it falls. The names of the regular twelve lunar months are listed in the *Guru Granth Sahib*.

Calendar Reform

The solar component of the Bikrami calendar does not correspond exactly to the natural solar year. Every seventy years a discrepancy equal to one day accrues. Two calendars have been developed that would accurately match the natural solar year. The Nanakshai Calendar is based on Guru Nanak's birth and the Khalsa Calendar is based on the founding of the Khalsa. Some Sikh groups hope that calendar reform can occur by the year 1999 C.E. marking the 300th anniversary of the Khalsa.

TABLE 12.1. THE SIKH CALENDAR

Month Name	Gregorian Equivalent
Chait	March–April
Basakh	April–May
Jaith	May–June
Har	June–July
Sawan	July–August
Bhadro	August–September
Asun	September–October
Katik	October–November
Magar	November–December
Poh	December–January
Magh	January–February
Phagan	February–March

TABLE 12.2. SIKH HOLIDAY CYCLE

Basakh

Baisakhi (Birth of the Khalsa)

Jaith

Martyrdom Anniversary of Guru Arjan

Har

Birthday of Guru Har Krishan

Asun

Installation of Sri *Guru Granth Sahib*
Birthday of Guru Ram Das

Katik

Divali (Diwali)
Guru Nanak's Day (Guru Parab)

Magar

Martyrdom Anniversary of Guru Tegh Bahadur

Poh

Guru Gobind Singh's Birthday
Lohri

Magh

Maghi

Phagan

Hola Mohalla

⊞ ⊞ ⊞

Sikh Holidays

Weekly

Diwan (Weekly Worship)
Often on Sunday, but some Sikh communities choose other days of the week

Sikhs observe a weekly gathering at their gurdwaras (houses of worship). These gatherings include prayers, reading from their holy scriptures, the *Guru Granth Sahib*, and singing or reciting hymns. A teaching or sermon based on the scripture readings is often given.

After the service, Sikhs share a communal meal called a langar. The meal is served to all, including non-Sikhs, free of charge and irrespective of caste distinctions. The tradition of serving a communal meal was instituted by the first Sikh guru, Guru Nanak and promoted into general acceptance by the third guru, Guru Amar Das.

Annually

Basakh (April/May)

Baisakhi (Birth of the Khalsa)
At the beginning of the Hindu New Year, usually April 13

This Sikh celebration of the New Year coincides with the spring harvest. Unlike other Sikh festivals that are observed in accordance with the lunar calendar, the date for Baisakhi is set in accordance with the solar calendar and usually falls on April 13.

The observance of the Baisakhi holiday was first instituted by Guru Amar Das, the third Sikh Guru, in 1567. At a Baisakhi gathering in 1699 under the leadership of the tenth Guru, Gobind Singh, the Sikh brotherhood of the Khalsa was formed. As a result, the day is also marked as the birth of the Khalsa, and it is a traditional day on which initiates are baptized into the Khalsa.

Other traditions associated with Baisakhi include visiting gurdwaras (houses of worship) for prayers and the singing of hymns, changing the wrappings on the flag post at the gurdwaras, and participating in parades. In addition, a large fair is held at the Golden Temple in Amritsar, the central shrine of Sikhism.

Jaith (May/June)

Martyrdom Anniversary of Guru Arjan
During Jaith

Guru Arjan was the fifth Sikh Guru and the first martyr. Jehangir, the Emperor of the Mughal Empire, unsuccessfully sought to have Guru Arjan convert to Islam. After five days of torture, Arjan was put to death in 1606. Although Arjan accepted his death peacefully, he left instructions for his successor, his son Har Gobind, to permit the Sikhs to take up arms to protect the innocent. The anniversary of Arjan's death is remembered with services in the gurdwaras (houses of worship) and with readings from the *Guru Granth Sahib* (Sikh scriptures).

Har (June/July)

Birthday of Guru Har Krishan
During Har

Har Krishan was the eighth of the ten human Sikh Gurus. He is sometimes called the "Child Guru" because he was only five years old when he succeeded his father and assumed the position of Guru. Har Krishan served as Guru for only three years. He died from smallpox at the age of eight. The anniversary of his birth, or Gurupurab, is celebrated with services in the gurdwaras (houses of worship) and with readings from the *Guru Granth Sahib* (Sikh scriptures).

Asun (September/October)

Installation of Sri Guru Granth Sahib
During Asun

Three days before his death in 1708, Guru Gobind Singh selected his successor. Rather than choosing a human follower, as had been done by his predecessors, he selected the Sikh scriptures, the *Adi Granth*. The *Adi Granth* was renamed the *Guru Granth Sahib* and became installed as the eleventh, perpetual Guru to the Sikhs.

The anniversary of the installation of the *Guru Granth Sahib* is observed with ceremonies in the gurdwaras (houses of worship). These often include readings, singing of hymns, lectures, and the distribution of free meals. A continuous reading of the entire *Guru Granth Sahib* that takes approximately three days to complete may also be conducted. The installation anniversary is also a popular day for Sikhs to rededicate themselves to their faith.

Birthday of Guru Ram Das
During Asun

Guru Ram Das, the fourth Sikh Guru, was the son-in-law of the third Guru (Amar Das). Upon his selection to succeed his father-in-law his name was changed from Bhai Jetha to Ram Das meaning "God's Servant." The Gurupurab commemorating his birth is celebrated in Sikh gurdwaras (houses of worship) with prayers, the singing of hymns, and with readings from the *Guru Granth Sahib* (Sikh scriptures).

Katik (October/November)

Divali (Diwali)
During Katik

Divali is a Sikh adaptation of the Hindu celebration Dewali. It features an assembly in Sikh temples, called gurdwaras. The origin of the Sikh observance of the festival dates to the sixteenth century C.E. when Guru Amar Das declared that all Sikhs should gather together to receive the Guru's blessing on the Hindu celebration of Divali.

Some historical events served to make the date more auspicious. In 1577, the foundation for the famous Golden Temple at Armritsar was laid on Divali. In 1619 the temple was illuminated on Divali to provide a special homecoming to Guru Har Gobind when he returned to Amritsar following his release from jail. Sikhs continue the tradition of illuminating the Golden Temple on Divali. Lights are also used to decorate homes and businesses, and the Divali celebration often includes a fireworks display.

Guru Nanak's Day (Guru Parab)
On the full moon day in Katik

The festival celebrates the birth of Guru Nanak, the founder of Sikhism. He was followed by nine other Gurus, in succession, under whom Sikhism gradually developed. Many of Nanak's hymns form part of the *Guru Granth Sahib* (the Sikh scriptures).

Guru Nanak was born in 1469 at Talwandi (about 45 km away from Lahore), now known as Nankana Sahib. At Nankana Sahib there is a beautiful shrine and a holy tank. On Guru Parab, a grand fair and festival is held.

The birth of Nanak is also observed in other parts of India and in other Sikh communities around the world. Frequently the celebration will cover a three-day period beginning two days before the designated date. During the first two days a ceremony called an Akhand Path begins. The Akhand Path is an uninterrupted, continuous reading of the entire *Guru Granth Sahib*. The reading is timed so that it ends on the birthday celebration day. Other activities include prayers, lectures, singing of hymns, processions, and the distribution of free meals.

Magar (November/December)

Martyrdom Anniversary of Guru Teg Bahadur
During Magar

Guru Tegh Bahadur (a name that means "brave sword") was ninth of the ten human Sikh gurus. He was put to death by the Mughal Emperor Aurangzeb for refusing to convert to Islam and for participating in a revolt against the Mughals. The anniversary date of his martyrdom is honored with services in the gurdwaras (houses of worship) and with readings from the *Guru Granth Sahib* (Sikh scriptures).

Poh (December/January)

Guru Gobind Singh's Birthday
During Poh

Guru Gobind Singh was born in 1666 at Patna. He was the tenth and last of the human gurus. Instead of appointing a human successor, Gobind Singh installed the Sikh scriptures, the *Guru Granth Sahib*, to be eternal Guru to the Sikh community.

Singh's birth is celebrated by Sikhs in India and around the world. The festivities are similar to those that mark the birth of Guru Nanak, the first Sikh guru. They also often include the three-day-long, continuous reading of the *Guru Granth Sahib* called the Akhand Path ceremony.

Lohri
During Poh

The festival of Lohri marks the end of winter. Bonfires are lit, and people dance and sing folk songs around the fire. Traditional sweets are made of sesame, ground nuts, and puffed rice. Lohri is celebrated in cities, towns, and villages alike, with great enthusiasm and merrymaking. It is a traditional time for unmarried women to pray for a happy marriage.

Magh (January/February)

Maghi
During Magh

This Sikh observance commemorates an event that occurred during the seventeenth century when Guru Gobind Singh struggled against the Mughal army at

Anandpur. Forty of his followers who fought against the Mughal army were killed. The forty were blessed by the Guru and he proclaimed that their actions had enabled them to achieve liberation from the cycle of rebirth.

Maghi is a day that honors these men, now called the Forty Immortals. Sikhs observe the holiday by visiting gurdwaras (houses of worship) and listening to the recitation of sacred hymns.

Phagan (February/March)

Hola Mohalla
During Phagan

The observance of Hola Mohalla (a term that means "attack and counter-attack") was instituted in 1700 C.E. by Guru Gobind Singh. He assembled the Sikhs in Anandpur to take part in military exercises so that they would be prepared to fight for their defense if necessary.

Sikhs celebrate the day with a three-day festival that includes fairs and carnival processions. Demonstrations of horsemanship and swordsmanship along with traditional children's games are typical features of the event. In addition to games of physical skill, Sikhs also enjoy presentations of singing and poetry reading.

TABLE 12.3. ALPHABETICAL LIST OF SIKH HOLIDAYS

Holidays	Dates
Baisakhi	Usually April 13
Birthday of Guru Har Krishan	During Har
Birthday of Guru Ram Das	During Asun
Divali	During Katik
Diwali *see* Divali	
Guru Gobind Singh's Birthday	During Poh
Guru Nanak's Day	At the full moon in Katik
Guru Parab *see* Guru Nanak's Day	
Hola Mohalla	During Phagan
Installation of *Sri Guru Granth Sahib*	During Asun
Lohri	During Poh
Maghi	During Magh
Martyrdom of Guru Arjan	During Jaith
Martyrdom of Guru Tegh Bahadur	During Magar

CHAPTER 13

Buddhism

Overview of Buddhism

What Is Buddhism?

Buddhists believe that earthy human life is characterized by suffering and ceaseless change. The cause of suffering is found within the individual person who has desires. Buddhists teach that suffering can be overcome by reaching a level of detachment or enlightenment (called bodhi) and thereby achieving nirvana. The word nirvana means "blown out." It implies that desire has been extinguished and that a changeless state which is the true reality has been attained. Buddhists believe that this level of selflessness is true bliss because it is devoid of all suffering and discontentment. Nirvana can only be attained through developing moral attributes, meditating, and gaining wisdom.

The term samsara refers to the continual cycle of birth and death to which a person is bound by karma. Karma is the entity that binds a self to its former existences, its present existence, and its future existences; it comes from deeds. Bad deeds produce bad karma, called papa karma. Papa karma leads to sickness, poverty, an untimely death, and rebirth as a demon, ghost, animal, or resident of hell. Good deeds produce good karma, called punya karma. Punya karma leads to a long life, good health, prosperity, and rebirth into one of twenty-two heavenly realms. To live as a god in heaven, however pleasurable, is not the ultimate goal. Buddhists seek to escape the samsara cycle and reach nirvana.

To eliminate desire and attain nirvana, Buddhists follow a path called The Middle Way, avoiding both the extremes of hedonism (self-centered participation in unrestrained sensual delights) and asceticism (self-denial). The Buddhist path involves an effort of the self, which is comprised of the body, feelings, perception, impulses, and consciousness. The Buddhist concept of self does not include a component similar to the Christian "soul" or Hindu "atman."

Both monks and laity play important roles in the pursuit of nirvana. Monks provide teaching and inspiration; lay people honor and support the monks. To help people in their quest for nirvana, the Buddhist community comprises three resources, called the Triratna (or Three Jewels): (1) Buddha, who found enlightenment and taught it to others; (2) dharma, teaching about truth; and (3) samgha, the local assembly of monks. (Samgha can also refer to the entire Buddhist community of monks, nuns, and laity.)

The Buddha's dharma refers to his doctrinal position. It is summarized in a statement called The Four Noble Truths. The truths are: (1) there is suffering; (2) suffering results from desire; (3) the way to end suffering is to end desire; and (4) the Eightfold Path shows the way to end suffering.

The Eightfold Path consists of (1) right view or right understanding; (2) right thoughts and aspirations; (3) right speech; (4) right conduct and action; (5) right way of life; (6) right effort; (7) right mindfulness, and (8) right contemplation.

The Relationship between Buddha and the Buddhist People

Buddha is not a god. There is no personal god in Buddhist teaching. There is no ultimate principle or reality that upholds or animates the material world. Buddha is viewed as a human who achieved nirvana. Each individual Buddhist seeks to follow the Buddha's example and reach nirvana, a pure state of being.

Some Buddhists believe that Gautama, who is called Buddha, was a unique person, the only Buddha. Others believe he is not the only Buddha but that there were other Buddhas in previous ages; some expect that at least one more future Buddha will come.

There are many paths to nirvana. Some Buddhists focus their energies on meditation and self-understanding;

some believe that actions and good deeds lead to nirvana; others believe that the true path is found through the worship of one or more of the Buddha's manifestations.

Authorities and Sacred Writings

Books

Different sects of Buddhism acknowledge different canons of sacred writings but they draw on the same basic traditions. Scriptures of the Mahayana Buddhists, written in Sanskrit, date back to the first century B.C.E. The Theravada Buddhist scriptures, called the Pali Canon (because they are written in an ancient dialect related to Sanskrit known as Pali) are believed by adherents to contain Gautama's actual words.

The *Tripitaka* (Sanskrit) or *Tipitaka* (Pali) is the foundational document for Buddhist scriptures. The title means "three baskets" and it contains three separate volumes (with slightly different titles for Theravada and Mahayana Buddhism). The first basket, called "Basket of Discourses" and the second, "Basket of Discipline," contain similar information for the two main branches of Buddhism. The third, "Basket of Higher Teachings," deals with monastic discipline, theories of the self, reincarnation, and philosophy. For each branch of Buddhism, its content reflects the specific doctrines of the sect. A list of selected Buddhist scriptures for both Theravada and Mahayana Buddhism is given in Table 13.1.

TABLE 13.1. BUDDHIST SCRIPTURES

Theravada Buddhism
Tipitaka ("Three Baskets"):
    Sutta Pitaka ("Basket of Discourses)
    Vinaya Pitaka ("Basket of Disciplines")
    Abhidhamma Pitaka ("Basket of Higher Teachings")
Milinda-panha ("Questions of Milinda")
Visuddhi-magga ("The Way of Purification")

Mahayana Buddhism
Tripitaka ("Three Baskets"):
    Sutra Pitaka ("Basket of Discourses")
    Vinaya Pitaka ("Basket of Disciplines")
    Abhidharma Pitaka ("Basket of Higher Teachings")
Prajna-paramita Sutras ("Perfection of Wisdom Discourses")
Sad-dharma-pundarika Sutra ("Sutra of the Lotus of the True Dharma"
Sukhavati-vyuha ("Vision of the Pure Land")

For some Buddhists, canonical texts exist only in ancient languages and translation is forbidden. For others, translation is an on-going process. Other Buddhist groups view the canon as still open and new teachings may yet be added.

Samgha

The Buddhist community, called a samgha, is made up of laypeople and monks (or monks and nuns). Monks typically live a life of abstinence, abstaining from both sexual activity and material possessions. Monks vow to maintain celibacy and are permitted to own only eight prescribed items (a robe, an alms bowl, a belt, a razor, a needle, a filter with which to strain water, a staff, and a toothpick). Laypeople give offerings to provide food, shelter, and clothing for the monks. Monks spend their time studying, meditating, and teaching.

History

The Buddhist tradition began in India with the teachings of a wandering monk named Siddhartha Gautama who later became known as the Buddha (a title that means "Enlightened One").

Gautama was born about 563 B.C.E. according to Mahayana Buddhist traditions and many Western scholars. Theravada Buddhists give the date 624 B.C.E. Both agree that he was born to royal parents in Lumbini Grove—an area that is modernly located in Nepal in the foothills of the Himalayas between India and Tibet.

Several legends surround his birth. According to one legend, when Gautama was conceived his mother saw a white elephant—a sign that he would be special. His mother died shortly after his birth. His father tried to protect him from suffering because astrologers had predicted that the young Gautama could be a great ruler, but if he saw suffering he would become a religious leader instead.

Gautama was raised in luxuriant surroundings and protected from the sufferings of the world. On an excursion into the countryside, however, he met a meaningful series of people: a diseased man, an aging man, and a corpse. From these Gautama understood the suffering of illness, the suffering of growing old, and the fact that death was the ultimate end of life. He also saw a fourth person, a religious beggar, who radiated peace and joy. This experience led to Gautama's decision to become a wandering ascetic.

At the age of 29, Gautama renounced his princely life, his wife, and his infant son to search for a path that would offer relief from universal human suffering. For six years he practiced severe austerities, including eating very little and nearly starving. He came to realize that self-mortification would not provide a solution to the problem of suffering. He sat down under a tree, now called the Bodhi tree (or Bo Tree), and in accordance with a dream, he waited there for enlightenment.

Gautama's Enlightenment

During his time under the tree he was tempted by a demon named Mara. Mara tried to distract him from his quest for enlightenment first by enticing him with temptations and then by attacking. After several unsuccessful attempts, Mara left. Many Buddhists interpret the temptation in psychological terms and see the assault as the surfacing of impurities that had still been in Gautama's mind.

Afterwards, while sitting in deep meditation, Gautama achieved enlightenment, or awakening. The basis of his enlightenment was the understanding that desire lay at the root of human problems and suffering. Gautama's enlightenment occurred at Bodh Gaya in 528 B.C.E. (589 B.C.E. according to Theravada texts).

The experience of enlightenment accorded Gautama a new title, the Buddha (Enlightened One). The Buddha's first sermon was delivered to five companions, and it detailed the Four Noble Truths and the Noble Eightfold Path (Table 13.2).

In the years that followed, Buddha laid down rules of ethics, condemned the Hindu caste system, and promoted the equality of men and women. Buddha's teachings emphasized that the aim of religion was to free oneself of worldly fetters in order to attain enlightenment. The Buddha trained large numbers of disciples to continue his work before his death in 483 (or 544) B.C.E. Four important places in the life of the Buddha—where he was born, Bodh Gaya, the place of enlightenment, Deer Park where he delivered his first sermon, and the place of his death—all located in the Ganges Valley in northern India are important pilgrimage sites for modern Buddhists.

After Buddha's Death

In the first few centuries after the Buddha's death, the Buddhist community established its identity. Communities of monks developed and created regulations to govern monastic life. The first efforts at memorizing (and later recording) the Buddha's words were made.

During the third century B.C.E. an Indian leader, Asoka (the last ruler in the Indian Maurya Dynasty) converted to Buddhism from Hinduism and became an example of an ideal ruler. He embraced Buddhist teachings because of remorse over the human suffering caused by his military conquests. Under his patronage the monks were upheld, ancient burial mounds

were renovated, and new ones were built. The burial mounds, called stupas, served to honor kings and great religious leaders of the past. He also established government ministries to help the impoverished rural population. According to legend, Asoka sent his son and daughter as missionaries to Sri Lanka where they established a Buddhist Samgha (community).

According to Buddhist legend, King Devanampiyatissa of Sri Lanka was chasing a deer in the forest of Mihintale when someone called out his name. He looked up and saw a figure in a saffron-colored robe standing on a rock with six companions. The robed figure was the holy patron of Sri Lanka, Arhat Mahinda, the son of Emperor Asoka of India. Mahinda converted King Devanampiyatissa and the royal family, and they in turn converted the common people. Mahinda, who propagated the faith through works of practical benevolence, died in about 204 B.C.E.

The spread of Buddhism by missionary efforts continued in other regions as well. During the third century B.C.E., Buddhism reached southeast Asia, an area that remains predominantly Theravada Buddhist. Buddhism reached China during the first century B.C.E. where the faith commingled with existing Taoist philosophies. The resulting form of Chinese Buddhism focused more on human relationships than did other forms of Buddhism.

TABLE 13.2.
THE FOUR NOBLE TRUTHS AND THE EIGHTFOLD PATH

The Four Noble Truths

1. There is suffering.

2. Suffering results from desire.

3. The way to end suffering is to end desire.

4. The Eightfold Path shows the way to end suffering.

The Eightfold Path

1. Right view or right understanding

2. Right thoughts and aspirations

3. Right speech

4. Right conduct and action

5. Right way of life

6. Right effort

7. Right mindfulness

8. Right contemplation

The practice of making images of the Buddha (called rupas) also began during the first century B.C.E. Some common features of the popular statues were long ear lobes, representing spiritual wisdom, and wheel patterns on the feet, signifying one who restarts the wheel of teaching.

During the first century of the common era, another movement within Buddhism developed. It focused veneration on a Buddha called Amitabha, the celestial Buddha. According to Mahayana texts, Amitabha established a heaven (celestial home) for people who wished to be reborn there. The paradise he created, called the Pure Land, was devoid of suffering, aging, and death. People who were reborn into the Pure Land could benefit from Amitabha's teaching and gain sufficient merit to step up into nirvana. Under traditional Buddhist teaching, being born into a heavenly realm did not lead to nirvana. Descent back to earth in a human form was the only path by which nirvana was attainable. In addition to creating the Pure Land, Amitabha provided the means by which people could attain it. The simple expression of faith through the recitation of a formulaic prayer offering homage to Amitabha Buddha assured a follower a place in the Pure Land.

Buddhism was introduced to Korea during the fourth century C.E. and reached Japan during the sixth century C.E. In Japan, it commingled with existing Shinto beliefs resulting in many forms of Buddhism that focused on personal experience and intuition. In the eighth century, Buddhism was introduced to Tibet where it blended with traditional folk beliefs giving rise to a unique form in which leaders are seen as incarnations of earlier leaders. By the ninth century, Buddhism, in its many forms, had spread throughout the entire Asian continent.

Buddhism Today

The Buddhist People

Buddhism, a diverse faith, has a long, 2500-year history and a global presence. During the late twentieth century, it claimed an estimated 500 million followers. Most of these were located in Asia, but other places around the world, including North America and Europe, had significant populations. In some countries, Buddhism was the official national religion. These included Sri Lanka, Burma, and Thailand.

Worship

Buddhist people do not worship Buddha in the same sense that other religions worship gods. Buddha was not a god, but a person who attained enlightenment. Worship in the sense of acknowledging the worth-ship of Buddha involves laying flowers in front of his images, lighting incense, and making offerings. Some forms of Buddhism practice prostration as a form of showing respect and developing proper humility. Some Buddhists may pray to the Buddha within themselves.

Buddhist temples typically have a statue of Buddha. The statues show Buddha in a traditional pose with specific hand gestures, called mudras. The mudras represent different aspects of enlightenment.

The central religious act in Buddhism is meditation for the purpose of bringing a kind of stillness that helps the person understand what is deep within himself and the reality around him. Buddhists recognize eight levels of meditation, the first four of which involve differing levels of consciousness. The other four levels operate at a plane at the karmic level above consciousness. Some Buddhists may also use pictures called yantras or thangkas as an aid to help focus visually during meditation.

Sects

As Buddhism developed, different schools emerged. The two major traditions within Buddhism, Mahayana and Theravada, developed as a result of a doctrinal dispute among followers of the Buddha (Siddhartha Gautama) after his death. Many Buddhists acknowledge the veracity of different paths and do not judge the correctness of one path in comparison with others. Other Buddhists, however, make distinctions of preference among the many paths.

Mahayana

The term Mahayana means "Great Vehicle." It connotes the ability to carry many passengers beyond suffering to nirvana. Mahayana is the largest sect of Buddhism and it offers many different paths.

One of the distinctions between Mahayana and Theravada Buddhism is in the concept of a bodhisattva. Mahayana Buddhists use the term to refer to someone who is capable of becoming enlightened and for whom certain vows are required. These vows include being generous, virtuous, patient, energetic, meditative, and wise. People who become bodhisattvas are worshipped as saints and they are able to help others attain enlightenment. For Theravada Buddhists, Bodhisattva refers to the Buddha during his many lives before he achieved enlightenment or to the expected Maitreya Buddha of the future.

Buddhism in the West has generally been of the Mahayana tradition, which emphasizes the universal presence of the "Buddha-nature" rather than the historical person of the Buddha himself. According to Robert S. Elwood in his *Religious and Spiritual Groups in Modern*

America, the Buddha-nature is an "ontologizing of the Buddha's enlightenment experience. It is the true nature of reality, which he lets irradiate his being at that moment." Followers of this faith believe that the Buddha-nature can be realized whenever one lets go of the fear of separateness and allows himself (or herself) to become one with all. To aid the believer in this release, followers are encouraged to envision the universe as filled with Buddhas and Bodhisattvas who are projections of the enlightened self. These figures are a psychological creation rather than individuals of historical actuality. The essential character of this group is reflected in the abstract quality of its holidays. When these are contrasted with traditional Theravada holidays, which center on the person of Buddha, the difference between the two groups is apparent.

Theravada

Theravada is the oldest form of Buddhism. The name means "Way of the Theras." The "Theras" are senior monks. It is the most conservative sect of Buddhism, and its adherents assert that its traditions are the most accurate representation of the Buddha's teaching. Mahayana texts pejoratively call it the "Little Vehicle" (Hinayana) because it limits the number of those who can achieve nirvana to the monks.

One of the most distinctive practices of Theravada Buddhism is the honoring of "arhats." The term "arhat" is somewhat analogous to "saint." It refers to a person who followed the Eightfold Path and reached spiritual perfection.

Temple worship is more important in Theravada Buddhism than in Mahayana Buddhism. Temples, more akin to the Western notion of a monastery, provide a place where monks live as well as a shrine where rituals are carried out. In Theravada Buddhism, meditation was historically done by monks, but more recently meditation centers for people from other walks of life have been established.

Tibetan Buddhism

Tibetan Buddhism is a form of Mahayana called Vajrayana ("Diamond Vehicle"). It combines traditional Buddhist thought with ancient Chinese folk beliefs and incorporates evil spirits, magic, and the spirits of nature.

Tibetan Buddhists also venerate Avalokiteshvara, a Bodhisattva whom they believe is incarnated in the Dalai Lama. The Dalai Lama is held in such esteem that he is considered the fourth jewel of Buddhism (the traditional three are the Buddha, the Buddha's doctrine, and the Buddhist community).

One form of worship unique to Tibetan Buddhism involves the use of a mandala, which is a geometric representation used as a focal point for meditation. Its design, often consisting of a square within a circle, offers a complex pattern of detail upon which to focus. Tibetan Buddhists also recite mantras, which are sacred sounds believed to have magical qualities and the ability to open the mind to higher levels of consciousness. Mantras may also be written on paper that is attached to a wheel. When the mantra is chanted the wheel is turned; this is believed to release its power.

Political events of the twentieth century have had an impact on Tibetan Buddhism. Tibet was invaded by the Chinese in 1949, and the Dalai Lama has been in exile since 1959 when he and many of his ministers along with approximately 100,000 Tibetans escaped across the Himalayas. The Dalai Lama has lived since then in exile in Dharmsala, India. Today there are some 80,000 Tibetans in India, 30,000 in Nepal, and 3,000 in Bhutan. Much of the Tibetan culture has been suppressed, but festivals are still observed in a modest way in Tibet and by Tibetans in exile.

Chinese Buddhism

Buddhism was introduced to China in the first two centuries of the common era but did not begin to find popular acceptance until the fourth century. The merging of traditional Chinese philosophies and Buddhist philosophies led to the creation of schools of Buddhism in which compatible beliefs merged. The Tiantai school of Buddhism, which asserts that many skillful means can lead people to enlightenment, was compatible with the ancient Chinese belief that the harmony of different things was good. Buddhism continued to thrive in China along with Confucianism, Taoism, and other folk religions, until the Cultural Revolution (1966–1976) sought to suppress religious expression.

Japanese Buddhism

There are many Japanese Buddhist schools and sects based on the Mahayana tradition.

Tendai Buddhism, introduced into Japan from China around the ninth century C.E., focused on attaining salvation from the world through meditation and faith. Followers of Tendai obscured the difference between Buddhas and bodhisattvas. They also incorporated rituals and secret teachings into their practices. From Tendai Buddhism, many other sects developed.

Shingon Buddhism (which means "True Word") uses symbol, ritual, and sacred mantras to express the mystery at the heart of the universe. One of the principles in Shingon is that an individual's own Buddha nature is identical with the Buddha's teaching. It was introduced to Japan during the ninth century C.E. from China and became popular among Japan's warrior class, the samurai. The central focus of Shingon is on the Buddha of Infinite Light and it also incorporates the veneration of other gods.

Pure Land Buddhism is the largest Buddhist school in Japan. It is also called Jodo-shu. It involves a faith in Amitabha Buddha (Buddha of Boundless Light). Practitioners believe that salvation can come from repeating Amitabha's name. The form of Pure Land Buddhism practiced in the United States is the form that comes closest to the traditional Western understanding of religion. The basis for the Pure Land doctrine is that salvation comes from a transference of merit from the Buddha to an unworthy follower. Emphasis is placed on the importance of family and community involvement. A celebration of Amitabha is observed by this sect on the fifteenth day of each month. Another type of Pure Land Buddhism, True Pure Land (Jodo Shinshu), emphasizes that faith is expressed in passivity.

Nichiren Buddhism is a Japanese nationalistic form of Buddhism marked by heightened devotion to Buddha, doctrine, and scripture. It is named for its founder who studied Tendai Buddhism in the middle thirteenth century C.E. Nichiren denounced practitioners of Pure Land Buddhism and Zen Buddhism for placing their trust in anything but the *Lotus Sutra*. In homage to the sacred text, he developed a mantra, which Nichiren followers chant.

Zen Buddhism

Zen Buddhism is a Japanese form of Buddhism with roots in Ch'an Buddhism in China. Because it was popularized during the 1960s by the counterculture movement in the United States, it is perhaps better known to Westerners than many other forms.

Unlike the highly esoteric and ethereal Mahayana system, Zen advocates strict asceticism as a means to achieve freedom from the individual self. The theory is that extreme self-denial builds a tension that can be used to break through to an instant revelation of oneness. The ability to achieve enlightenment suddenly is unique to Zen.

Zen adherents seek to develop their own intuition. One type of Zen teaching employs koans. Koans are questions asked by a teacher designed to evoke insight from the student. Their use dates back to the twelfth century.

Zen meditation is often performed while doing simple tasks or walking. These simple steps are designed to help keep the seeker from falling asleep or from developing muscle cramps. The aim of Zen meditation is enlightenment from within.

TABLE 13.3.
BUDDHIST HOLIDAY CYCLE

Dates	Holidays
January	
1–3	Oshogatsu
~	Chinese New Year
February	
~	Losar
~	Monlam
March	
1–14	Omizutori Matsuri
~	Magha Puja
20 or 21	Spring Higan
April	
~	Vesak
13–14	Songkran
May	
~	Poson
~	Sanghamitta Day
June	
~	Airing the Classics
~	Esala Perahera
July	
~	Hemis Festival
6	Birthday of the Dalai Lama
~	Waso
13–15	Obon Festival
~	Marya
August	
15	Floating Lantern Ceremony
September	
2	Shinbyu
~	Vatsa
23 or 24	Autumnal Higan
October	
5	Bodhidharma Day
November	
19	Tazaungdaing
~	Festival of Lights
December	
8	Rohatsu

NOTE: Dates marked with a ~ are variable. They are placed in their approximate sequence.

Buddhist Adaptations of Regional Calendars

Based on Hindu Roots

Buddhism is derived from Hinduism in much the same way that Christianity is derived from Judaism. As a reform of Hinduism in India, Buddhism did not meet with great success. In fact, at one point, it became virtually extinct as a separate movement, only to be reintroduced into the country in the 1950s when the Dalai Lama fled to India for sanctuary after the Chinese annexation of Tibet. However, Buddhism bears the marks of its Hindu ancestry in its time reckoning systems. Similarities between the two calendars include the lunar and astrological base and intercalations.

Buddhists and Hindus also hold similar views on the cyclical character of time. Buddhists view time as an extension of the ever-repeating sequences in nature: day follows day; the moon waxes and wanes; the seasons repeat year after year. In Buddhist history, there is no story of the first creation or ultimate destruction of the universe, only a cycle of expansion, decline, and rest.

A Variety of Lunar Calendars

Because Buddhist calendars are not associated with a specific civil calendar, the variances among geographical locations are even more pronounced than differences in Hindu calendars. For example, the method for determining the date of the new year is not uniform among Buddhist sects. Some Buddhist calendars begin the new year, Wesak, with the full moon in Taurus, which is believed to be the date of the Buddha's birth, enlightenment, and passing on. In contrast, the Tibetan Buddhists, whose calendar has been heavily influenced by the Chinese calendar, begin their new year at the full moon nearest to the midpoint of the sign Aquarius. In Vietnam, the new year, called Tet Nguyenden, begins at the new moon in Capricorn.

Development of Regional Calendars

As Buddhism spread outside of India following the death of the Buddha (Siddhartha Gautama) around 483 B.C.E., the two dominant traditions, Mahayana and Theravada, became prominent in separate regions. The Theravada tradition predominated to the east of India; to the West, the Mahayana tradition was established. Also around the same time, Alexander the Great, who ruled some parts of India where Buddhism was practiced, exported Buddhist teachings to the West.

From the northwestern part of India, Buddhism spread into Tibet where it became amalgamated with the native magical and Tantric traditions. It also spread to China and Japan, becoming integrated with the existing systems of Confucianism, Taoism, and Shintoism.

Each of these regions developed different holidays and calendars. Holidays honoring diverse manifestations of the Buddha, such as the Medicine Buddha, became a part of some calendars. The Buddha of Boundless Light, or Amitabha, is honored by followers of Pure Land Buddhism and is celebrated on the fifteenth day of each month. In the United States, some popular Zen Buddhist holy days are observed. Also, many religious festivals of the new host lands became incorporated into the Buddhist calendar. One such festival is the Chinese Ch'ing Ming, or Festival of Pure Brightness. This ancient Chinese observance, held in honor of the dead, has become an established Buddhist holiday in China.

Dates for Buddhist Holidays

For convenience, the holidays listed in this book are shown in Gregorian months. Where practical, notations about their order in terms of lunar cycles are also given. Although some Buddhist communities follow the fixed dates that appear on the Gregorian calendar, many others calculate holiday dates on the basis of a lunar calendar. There is, however, no single lunar calendar that serves as a model for all Buddhists. In practice many of the holidays listed are observed on different and widely varying dates. Month names in the Buddhist calendar also vary considerably depending on the community, nation of origin, and type of Buddhism.

The procession of the Sacred Tooth in Sri Lanka.

⊞ ⊞ ⊞

Buddhist Holidays

Weekly

Uposatha Days

The Theravada Buddhist tradition of weekly festivals developed out of the customary monks' practice of gathering at every new moon and full moon. Although Uposatha gatherings at the full moon and new moon are still the most important, gatherings at quarter moons are also observed. On the Uposatha days, lay people come to the temples, make offerings to the monks, and venerate the image of Buddha.

Monthly

Jizo Ennichi
Twenty-fourth day of each month

It is customary for Japanese Buddhists to express their devotion to Ksitigarbha Jizo on the twenty-fourth day of each month in a devotional practice known as Jizo Ennichi.

Ksitigarbha Jizo is a Bodhisattva, or "Buddha-to-be," who is highly regarded by Buddhists in Japan as well as in China, where he is known as Ti-t'sang. Among Japanese Buddhists, Ksitigarbha is known for helping children, women in labor, and the wicked. He is also believed to play a role in receiving and welcoming the faithful when they die. He is usually depicted in monk's robes, holding a staff with six rings in his right hand (symbolizing the six dimensions of existence in the realm of desire) and an orb or pearl in his left hand whose symbolic meaning is not known. His statue is most often found outside the temple, where he can guide both the dead and the living. Shrines in his honor are often set up along the roadside, since he protects travelers as well.

Annual

January

Oshogatsu (Ganjitsu; Japanese New Year's Day)
January 1–3

This Japanese New Year's Day celebration is also known as the "festival of festivals." Government offices, banks, museums, and most businesses are closed during its duration from January 1 through January 3.

Preparations begin in early **December, when** cities start decorating the streets with **pine and plum** branches, bamboo stalks, and ropes **festooned with paper.** Small pine trees with bamboo **stems attached,** representing longevity and constancy, **are traditionally** placed in the home. For weeks before **the New Year** celebration, people clean house and **purchase new** clothes for their children, exchange **gifts and pay off** personal debts.

On New Year's Eve, many people **don traditional** kimonos and walk through the **streets as they** visit shrines. The ancient tradition **of tolling the great** bells in the Buddhist temples at **midnight ends the day** of celebration. Priests strike the **bells 108 times as a** reminder of the 108 human **frailties or sins in Buddhist** belief. At the end of the **bell tolling ceremony,** the impure desires of the old **year have been driven** away.

New Year's Day celebrations **begin early, at four a.m.** with the practice of worshiping **in four directions.** Traditionally, the Japanese emper**or looked in all four di**rections asking for peace and **abundant crops during** the coming year. Other New **Year's Day traditions** include saying prayers at the **household altar and eat**ing specially prepared food. **Often the New Year's** Day repast includes such specialties **as mochi (steamed rice** pounded into small round **cakes), herring roe,** black beans, dried chestnuts, porgy, **and prawns.**

Chinese New Year
*Typically between January 21 **and February 19**; first day of the first full moon*

The Chinese New Year is a **festival involving family** celebrations, ancestor respect, **religious duties, and** celebration. It is a 14-day festi**val and each day has a** special significance.

On the first day family me**mbers present new year** wishes to one another and **also offer prayers to their** ancestors. The youngest child **in the family wears a** special cap depicting the eig**hteen Buddhist saints.** On the second day, new year **wishes are given to neigh**bors. Other days of the festival **feature visiting friends,** going from house to house, **receiving rice cakes and** fruit, and holiday pageants. **The New Year** celebrations culminate on the fourteenth **day when decorated lanterns** made in a variety of colors **and shapes are attached** to fir branches and hung **over doors to attract pros**perity. Costumes, masks, **plays, and parades are com**monly part of the celebration.

February

Losar (Tibetan New Year)
Usually in February, the date determined by Tibetan astrologers in Dharmsala, India

Tibetans observe a form of Buddhism known as Lamaism, Lama Buddhism, or Tibetan Buddhism, which involves belief in evil spirits, magic, and the spirits of nature. Many of the traditions surrounding the celebration of Losar, or the New Year, are associated with these beliefs.

Prior to the new year, houses are whitewashed and thoroughly cleaned to chase away bad memories from the old year; a little dirt from the house is saved and thrown in a crossroads where spirits are believed to dwell. On the last day of the old year, the monks ceremoniously drive out evil spirits. In one such ritual, the monks dressed in grotesque masks, wigs, and exotic robes, perform a dance portraying the struggle between good and evil.

On the first day of the new year, people place water and offerings on their household shrines early in the morning. The three-day celebration is a time of hospitality and merrymaking, with feasts, dances, and archery competitions. Although much of the Tibetan culture has been suppressed since the Chinese invasion in 1950, the festivals are still observed in a modest way in Tibet and by Tibetans in exile.

Tibetan exiles in India celebrate Losar by flocking to the temple in Dharmsala where the Dalai Lama lives. On the second day of the new year, he blesses people by touching their heads and giving them a piece of red and white string. People tie the blessed string around their necks as a protection from illness.

In Bodhnath, on the eastern side of Katmandu, Nepal, crowds of Tibetan refugees visit the stupa to watch lamas perform rites. Copper horns are blown, there are masked dances, and a portrait of the Dalai Lama is displayed.

Monlam (Prayer Festival)
Usually begins in February; fourth through twenty-fifth day of the first lunar month of the Tibetan calendar

Monlam is a great Tibetan festival that follows the Losar, or New Year, celebration. Started in the fifteenth century by Tsongkhapa, the reformist monk, the festival ensures that the new year will be successful and prosperous. In the past, celebrants thronged to Lhasa's famous Jokhang Monastery where monks created enormous butter sculptures of Buddhist heroes. A procession around the Barkor, the old city of Lhasa, carried a statue of Maitreya, the future Buddha.

Celebration of the festival ceased when the Chinese denounced religious observances in 1959, but it was revived in 1986 and has been practiced since on a smaller scale.

March

Omizutori Matsuri (Water Drawing Festival)
March 1–14

The Omizutori Matsuri has been observed at the Buddhist Todaiji Temple in Nara (Akita Prefecture) in Japan since the twelfth century. This time of meditative rituals is characterized by the drone of devotees reciting sutras and the sound of blowing conchs echoing from the temple. The climax of the festival occurs on March 12 when young monks in the gallery of the temple shake off burning pieces from pine-branch torches. Observers attempt to catch the sparks, believing them to have supernatural power against evil.

The Water Drawing ceremony commences at 2:00 A.M. on March 13. Ancient music plays as monks carry buckets to a well and the first water drawn for the year is offered to the Buddha. The monks then perform a dramatic fire dance to the beating of drums which signals the end of the festivities.

Magha Puja (Maka Buja, Full Moon Day; Four Miracles Assembly)
~March 6; Full moon night of the third lunar month

Magha Puja commemorates Buddah's meeting with 1,250 of his followers. The day is sometimes called the Four Miracles Assembly because of the four miracles that occurred during the auspicious meeting. These miracles were: (1) all the disciples were enlightened; (2) the meeting was not predetermined; (3) all disciples independently arrived at Veluvan Monastery in Rajagriha, India, by coincidence; and (4) the samgha, brotherhood of monks, was established.

The day is remembered by bringing offerings to the temple when the full moon is visible. The offerings often include items such as candles, incense, and lotus. Other activities associated with the day include sermons, chanting, and freeing captive birds and fish. After sunset, monks lead followers in walking three times around the chapels of monasteries. Each person carries flowers, glowing incense, and a lighted candle in homage to the Buddha. In Laos, the ceremonies are especially colorful at Vientiane and at the Khmer ruins of Wat Ph near Champasak.

Spring Higan
March 20 or 21

Higan is the seven-day period surrounding both the spring and autumnal equinoxes when day and night are of equal length. The word means the "other shore," and refers to the spirits of the dead reaching Nirvana after crossing the river of existence. Thus, Higan celebrates the spiritual move from the world of suffering to the world of enlightenment and is a time for remembering the dead, visiting, cleaning, and decorating their graves, and reciting sutras (Buddhist prayers). A week of Buddhist services is observed in Japan. A similar observance is held at the autumnal equinox.

April

Vesak (Wesak; Buddha's Birthday; Waicak, Vesakha Puja; Buddha Jayanti; Phat Dan Day; Buddha Purnima; Full Moon of Waso; Vixakha Bouxa; Feast of the Lanterns)
April 8; or the full moon day of the Hindu month of Vaisakha

Vesak is the holiest of Buddhist holy days. In Theravada Buddhist countries, it marks three anniversaries: Buddha's birth, his enlightenment, and his death, or attaining of Nirvana. In Japan and other Mahayana Buddhist countries, it commemorates Buddha's birth and the other two anniversaries are usually observed on separate days—the enlightenment on December 8, and the death on February 15. Vesak is a public holiday in many countries, including Thailand, Indonesia, Korea, and Singapore. In addition to the popular name of Vesak (or Wesak), it is known by many other names including Waicak, Vesakha Puja (Thailand), Buddha Jayanti (Nepal and India), Phat Dan Day (Vietnam), Buddha Purnima (India), Full Moon of Waso or Kason (Burma), Vixakha Bouxa (Laos), and sometimes it is called the Feast of the Lanterns.

The celebration differs from country to country, but in general activities are centered on Buddhist temples, where people gather to listen to sermons by monks. In the evening, there are candle-lit processions around the temples. Homes are also decorated with paper lanterns and oil lamps. In honor of the virtue of showing kindness to all living things, some countries practice a tradition of freeing caged birds on this day. In some areas, food booths are set up along streets. In Burma, people water the Bodhi tree with blessed water and chant prayers around it.

Lumbini, the isolated birth place of the Buddha (prince Siddhartha Gautama), is one of the most sacred pilgrimage destinations for Buddhists, especially on Vesak.

A stone pillar erected in 250 B.C.E. by the Indian emperor Asoka designates the birthplace, and a brick temple contains carvings depicting the birth. Another center of celebration in Nepal is the Swayambhunath temple, built about 2,000 years ago. On Vesak it is constantly circled by a procession of pilgrims. Lamas wearing colorful silk robes dance around the stupa (temple) while musicians play. On Vesak, the temple's collection of mandalas (geometrical and astrological representations of the world) and rare embroidered religious scrolls called "thangkas" are displayed.

Sarnath, India, is the place where the Buddha preached his first sermon. A big fair and a procession of relics of the Buddha highlight the Vesak celebrations there. Bodh Gaya (or Buddh Gaya) in the state of Bihar is also a site of special celebrations. It was here that Siddhartha Gautama sat under the Bodhi tree, attained enlightenment, and became known as the Buddha, meaning the "Enlightened One."

Songkran (Pi Mai; Thai Buddhist New Year)
April 13–14; during the sixth or seventh moon of the Thai calendar

The Thai Buddhist New Year takes place in the spring. The festivities surrounding the day take place over a three-day period (April 12–14) and are religious as well as secular. In the religious ceremonies, images of the Buddha are bathed in water and, like the Hindu Holi festival from which the tradition is derived, people splash each other with water as they walk through the street. Respect is shown to older people, however, as the young honor them by sprinkling water on their hands or feet rather than splashing them indiscriminately.

May

Poson (Dhamma Vijaya; Full Moon Day)
May-June; full moon day of the Hindu month of Jyestha

The Poson festival celebrates the bringing of Buddhism to Sri Lanka (formerly Ceylon) where it is second in importance only to Vesak (the celebration of Buddha's birth). While the holiday is celebrated throughout Sri Lanka, the major ceremonies are at the ancient cities of Anuradhapura and Mihintale. There, historical events involving Arhat Mahinda (the holy patron of Sri Lanka who was a convert to Buddhism from Hinduism and the son of Emperor Asoka of India) are reenacted, streets and buildings are decorated and illuminated, and temples are crowded. In Mihintale, people climb to the rock where Arhat Mahinda delivered his first sermon to the king. An important part of the festival is paying homage to the branch of the Bodhi Tree brought to Sri Lanka by Mahinda's sister, Sanghamitta. This is the tree that Gautama sat under until he received enlightenment and became the Buddha.

Sanghamitta Day
May or June; full moon day of the Hindu month of Jyestha

In Sri Lanka, the Buddhist community commemorates an event from 288 B.C.E. Princess Sanghmtita (daughter of India's Emperor Asoka) presented King Devanamipiyatissa with a sapling from the Bo Tree under which Buddah received enlightenment. The sapling was planted in Anuradhapura and is currently reputed to be the oldest documented tree in existence. It is a popular place of pilgrimage.

June

Airing the Classics
June or July; sixth day of the sixth lunar month

Buddhist monasteries in China observe the sixth day of the sixth lunar month by examining the books in their library collections to make sure that they have not been damaged. It commemorates the time when the boat carrying the Buddhist scriptures from India was upset at a river crossing, and all the books had to be spread out to dry. Setting aside a special day for "Airing the Classics" is important in tropical climates, where books are more susceptible to mold and insects.

Esala Perahera
June or July; full moon day of the Hindu month of Asadha

In Sri Lanka, the temple at Kandy has a relic reputed to be a tooth of the Buddah. The Esala Perahera celebration originated in the fourth century when the king of Kandy declared that the tooth be paraded annually so people could honor it. During the festival a decorated elephant carries the tooth out of the temple while actors, dancers, and other elephants form a parade. Each successive night of the nine-day festival more participants join the parade.

Hemis Festival
Usually in June or July

This three day Buddhist festival occurs at the Hemis Gompa (monastery) in the mountainous northern Indian state of Ladakh. The festival celebrates the birthday of Guru Padmasambhava, the Indian Buddhist mystic who introduced Tantric Buddhism to Tibet in the eighth century. Tradition says he was a native of Swat (now in Pakistan), an area noted for magicians.

The ceremonial aspects of the day include dancers in elaborate robes and heavy masks swirling to the music of symbols, drums, and pipes as they enact the battle between good and evil spirits. Fairs are set up around the monastery where local artisans sell their crafts.

The highlight of the festival is the Devil Dance of the monks. Demon dancers are costumed as satyrs, many-eyed monsters, fierce tigers, or skeletons, while lamas portraying saints wear miters and opulent silks and carry pastoral crooks. These good lamas, ringing bells and swinging censers, scatter the bad lamas, as they all swirl about to the music of cymbals, drums, and 10-foot-long trumpets. The dance is a morality play, a battle between good and evil spirits, and also expresses the idea that a person's helpless soul can be comforted only by a lama's exorcisms.

July

Birthday of the Dalai Lama
July 6

The Dalai Lama is the spiritual and political leader of Tibet and Tibetan Buddhism. The observance of the Dalai Lama's birthday is always held on July 6. The birthday is observed today by exiles in India with incense-burning ceremonies to appease the local spirits, family picnics, and traditional dances and singing.

The name Dalai means "ocean," and it was given to the ruling lama in the sixteenth century by the Mongol leader Altan Khan. The title suggests depth of wisdom. The present Dalai Lama, who was enthroned in 1940 at the age of five, is the latest in the line that began in the fourteenth century. Each Dalai Lama is believed to be the reincarnation of the preceding one, and when a Dalai Lama dies, Tibetan lamas search throughout the country for a child who is his reincarnation.

Waso (Buddhist Rains Retreat; Buddhist Lent)
Three months beginning around July 23

The rainy season of three months is traditionally a time of retreat for Buddhist monks. The practice may have begun in order to keep the monks, who typically wandered around the countryside, from walking on rice plants during the critical part of their growing season.

In observance of Waso, monks stay in monasteries and their followers bring offerings of food and gifts. The permitted gifts, however, must be items from among a list of only eight things a monk is permitted to own (a robe, an undergarment, a belt, a begging bowl, a water strainer, a blade, a needle, and a mat.)

TABLE 13.4. ALPHABETICAL LIST OF BUDDHIST HOLIDAYS

Holidays	Dates
Airing the Classics	Sixth day of the sixth lunar month in the Chinese calendar
Autumnal Higan	September 23 or 24
Birthday of the Dalai Lama	July 6
Bodhidharma Day	October 5
Buddha Jayanti *see* Vesak	
Buddha Purnima *see* Vesak	
Buddha's Birthday *see* Vesak	
Buddha's Enlightenment *see* Rohatsu	
Buddhist Lent *see* Waso	
Buddhist Rains Retreat *see* Waso	
Chinese New Year	First day of the first full moon (typically between January 21 and February 19)
Dhamma Vijaya *see* Poson	
Esala Perahera	Full moon day of the Hindu month Asadha
Feast of the Lanterns *see* Vesak	
Festival of Lights	Twenty-fifth day of the tenth Tibetan month
Festival of the Dead *see* Obon Festival	
Floating Lantern Ceremony	August 15
Four Miracles Assembly *see* Magha Puja	
Full Moon Day *see* Magha Puja	
Full Moon Day *see* Poson	
Full Moon of Waso *see* Vesak	
Ganden Ngamcho *see* Festival of Lights	
Ganjitsu *see* Oshogatsu	
Hemis Festival	Usually in June or July
Ho Khao Slak *see* Vatsa	
Japanese New Year's Day *see* Oshogatsu	
Losar	Usually in February, the date determined by Tibetan astrologers
Magha Puja	Full moon night of the third lunar month in the Chinese calendar

Holidays	Dates
Maka Buja *see* Magha Puja	
Marya	Third day of waning half of the Hindu month of Sravana
Monlam	Fourth through twenty-fifth day of the first lunar month of the Tibetan calendar
Obon Festival	July 13–15 or August 13–15
Omizutori Matsuri	March 1–14
Oshogatsu	January 1–3
Phat Dan Day *see* Vesak	
Pi Mai *see* Songkran	
Poson	Full moon day of the Hindu month of Jyestha
Prayer Festival *see* Monlam	
Rohatsu	December 8
Sanghamitta Day	Full moon day of the Hindu month of Jyestha
Shinbyu	September 2
Songkran	April 13–14; during the sixth or seventh moon of the Thai calendar
Spring Higan	March 20 or 21
Tazaungdaing	November 19
Thai Buddhist New Year *see* Songkran	
Tibetan New Year *see* Losar	
Toro Nagashi *see* Floating Lantern Ceremony	
Vatsa	Three months beginning around September 22
Vesak	April 8; or the full moon day of the Hindu month of Vaisakha
Vesakha Puja *see* Vesak	
Vixakha Bouxa *see* Vesak	
Waicak *see* Vesak	
Waso	Three months beginning around July 23
Water Drawing Festival *see* Omizutori Matsuri	
Wesak *see* Vesak	

The months in the Waso season are considered a time of restraint and abstinence. Weddings are not celebrated, and people try to avoid moving to new homes. Many young men enter the priesthood just for the retreat period. As a result, many ordinations take place. The new young monks have their heads shaved and washed with saffron. Then they are given yellow robes. Many lay people attend the monasteries for instruction.

The end of the Lenten season is marked with a joyful celebration. Lamps and lights are used in homes for three days; processions to pagodas occur in the evening. From the full moon that marks the end of the Lenten season until the next full moon, is a traditional time to bring new robes to monks. Each community may set aside a special day on which the offering of robes is presented.

Obon Festival (Festival of the Dead)
July 13–15 or August 13–15

The date of the Japanese Obon Festival varies from region to region, although it is always celebrated in either July or August. According to Japanese Buddhist belief, the dead revisit the earth during this time; thus Buddhist families participate in special religious services and hold family reunions to honor the dead.

The festival begins with the lighting of small bonfires outside of homes to welcome the spirits of ancestors. A traditional meal of vegetables, rice cakes, and fruit is provided for the spirits who are included in family activities as if they were physically present. On the final day of the festival, another bonfire is lit outside to guide the spirits back to the netherworld. The climax of the Obon Festival is the Bon-Odori. During this event, the town is lit with paper lanterns and people participate in folk dances which comfort the souls of the dead.

Obon is an important Japanese festival throughout the world as Japanese communities in many countries observe the traditions. In the United States, the most elaborate celebrations take place in Chicago and various locations in California.

Marya
July or August; third day of waning half of the Hindu month of Sravana

According to Buddhist legend, when Gautama sat down under the Bo tree to await Enlightenment, Mara, the Buddhist Lord of the Senses and satanic tempter, tried a number of strategies to divert him from his goal. Disguised as a messenger, Mara brought the news that one of Gautama's rivals had usurped his family's throne. Then he scared away the other gods who had gathered to honor the future Buddha by causing a storm of rain, rocks, and ashes to fall. Finally, he sent his three daughters, representing thirst, desire, and delight, to seduce Gautama—all to no avail.

In the city of Patan, Nepal, a procession on this day commemorates the Buddha's triumph over Mara's temptations. A procession of 3,000 to 4,000 people, carrying gifts—usually butter lamps—for Lord Buddha, moves through the city from shrine to shrine. Some wear masks and others play traditional Nepalese musical instruments. The devil dancers and mask-wearers in the parade often pretend to scare the children who line the streets by suddenly jumping out at them.

August

Floating Lantern Ceremony (Toro Nagashi)
August 15

The Floating Lantern Ceremony, a Buddhist ceremony held in Honolulu, Hawaii, commemorates the end of World War II. This festival is part of the annual Buddhist Obon season during which the spirits of dead ancestors are entreated and welcomed back to earth with prayers, dances, offerings, and the ceremony of setting afloat several thousand colorful paper lanterns bearing the names of the dead.

September

Shinbyu
September 2

Shinbyu is a Burmese Buddhist initiation ceremony. Parents provide a feast for their sons who wear headdress and robes. After the meal, the boys are taken to the temple, their heads are shaved, and they enter the monastery for a period of time typically ranging from three days to three months.

Vatsa (Ho Khao Slak)
Three months beginning around September 22

In Laos the observation of the Buddhist Rains Retreat is called Vatsa or Ho Khao Slak. It begins later in the year than the traditional season observed in many other Buddhist communities. Customs associated with the day are also slightly different. In Laos, people draw the name of a monk in the monastery and bring him a gift of food, flowers, or one of the eight essential items a monk is permitted to own. Also, some parents give toys and candy to their children. At the end of the festival, boat races are held on the rivers in Laos at Vientiane, Luang Phabang and Savannakhet.

Autumnal Higan
September 23 or 24

The Autumnal Higan is a week of Buddhist services observed in Japan at the autumnal equinox, when day and night are of equal length. A similar observance is held at the spring equinox.

October

Bodhidharma Day
October 5

Bodhidharma was a Buddhist teacher during the sixth century C.E. Although his teachings were not consolidated until the eighth century, he is still considered the founder and patriarch of Zen Buddhism. Many Zen monasteries observe this day in his honor with an all-day sitting.

November

Tazaungdaing
November 19

In Burma (now officially called Myanmar) Burmese Buddhists honor the robe that Buddah's mother wove for him. The commemoration is observed by girls who enter weaving competitions to make an entire robe. Another festival activity is the offering of new robes to the monks to replace the soiled robes they have worn throughout the rainy season.

Festival of Lights (Ganden Ngamcho)
November or December; twenty-fifth day of the tenth Tibetan lunar month

This Tibetan festival commemorates the birth and death of Tsongkhapa (1357–1419), a saintly scholar, teacher, and reformer of the monasteries, who enforced strict monastic rules. In 1408 he instituted the Great Prayer, a New Year rededication of Tibet to Buddhism; it was celebrated without interruption until 1959 when the Chinese invaded Tibet. He formulated a doctrine that became the basis of the Gelug (meaning "virtuous") sect of Buddhism. It became the predominant sect of Tibet, and Tsongkhapa's successors became the Dalai Lamas, the rulers of Tibet.

During the festival, thousands of butter lamps (dishes of liquid clarified butter called ghee, with wicks floating in them) are lit on the roofs and window sills of homes and on temple altars. At this time people seek spiritual merit by visiting the temples.

December

Rohatsu (Buddha's Enlightenment)
December 8

Zen monasteries honor Buddha's enlightenment with an arduous retreat typically lasting a week.

CHAPTER 14

Taoism, Confucianism, and Chinese Folk Religions

Overview of Chinese Religious Thought

The Development of Chinese Religious Principles

The religions of ancient China, though diverse, often shared similar concepts and components. One of these was a view that the things in the natural world—the earth, the sky, the stars, the waters—were interrelated. Correspondences and dissonances among them had effects that could be recognized and used for benefit. The human role in the cosmos was one of responsibility. Ritual actions, whether performed by the shaman, the sage, or the emperor, ensured that seasons would change, that crops would grow, that epidemics would abate, and that human fertility would be protected.

The ebb and flow of human life and the cyclical patterns observed in nature gave rise to a concept of intertwined opposites. These are defined in Chinese culture as "yin" and "yang." Yin represents cold and darkness; yang represents heat and light. They are viewed as opposites but still part of the same thing, both emerging from and existing within the other.

From nature, the ancient Chinese also developed the concept chi (also spelled qi), the most basic substance from which all else derived. Chi, interacting with the five elements—wood, fire, earth, metal, and water—was responsible for the entire creation, animate and inanimate.

The Role of Ancestors and Gods

Another widespread component of Chinese religious thought focused on the role of ancestors. Ancestors were members of the family who had died. They were often consulted through divination, honored as if still present, and appeased through rituals to avoid trouble. Practices surrounding ancestor worship involved funeral rites in which a deceased family member was officially numbered among the ancestors. Wood inscribed with the name of the deceased was kept on a family altar. An offering of incense was kept burning. Spirits of the dead who were from outside the family were feared as ghosts and placated in annual rituals.

Nature gods also played a role in the development of Chinese religion. These included gods such as the earth, sky, sun, moon, water, and wind. At different periods during history, a supreme god was recognized. During the Shang Dynasty (1766–1122 B.C.E.) a reigning deity, called Shang-ti, ruled over the lesser gods of nature but was not intimately involved in the lives of men. During the Chou Dynasty (1122–249 B.C.E.), the supreme god was called T`ien. His role in human affairs was closer to that of an ancestor.

The Imperial Cult

An official state cult of the emperor arose in which the ruler, called the Son of Heaven, was seen as possessing divine ancestors. He was responsible for performing specific rituals, and his actions affected the fortunes of his empire. During the Han Dynasty (206 B.C.E.–220 C.E.) the cult of the emperor reached its full expression. Beneficial events, such as good harvests, were attributed to the virtue of the emperor; catastrophic events, such as droughts and floods, were blamed on the emperor.

The Ming (1368–1644) and Ching Dynasties (1644–1912) were especially well known for their assertion of the

177

imperial cult. In Beijing, the Imperial Palace (also known as the Forbidden City), was oriented so that its major buildings faced south signifying the sun's goodness and holiness. Ching emperors performed a ritual sacrifice to the earth at the summer solstice on a special square altar in the northern portion of the Palace grounds. Other sacrifices were made at the beginning of each of the four seasons and at the end of the year. A spring plowing ceremony conducted in the Temple of Agriculture and overseen by the emperor, marked the start of the farming season.

Local Cults

In addition to organized religious traditions, a myriad of folk religions also existed. Many local cults focused on specific gods who were sometimes honored at rural temples. By the tenth century local deities, called city gods (chenghuang), were often publicly worshipped. Typically they were understood to possess powers over nature, and their worshippers often included people who also adhered to other traditions such as Taoism or Buddhism. Some cults were forced into hiding by government sanctioned persecution; others became more widely accepted.

Secularism and Atheism

In the middle of the 19th century, the religious face of China changed. A reformer, Hong Xiuquan (1814–1864), influenced by Christian literature, asserted that he was a younger brother of Jesus. He began a civil war, called the T`ai-ping Rebellion, which crusaded against idolatry and promoted the causes of land reform and egalitarianism (a belief that all people should have the same political and social rights). After more than 15 years and the loss of an estimated 20 million lives, the T`ai-ping Rebellion was defeated. Its legacy helped usher in an age of secularism.

TABLE 14.1.
MAJOR CHINESE DYNASTIES

Approximate Dates	Name
1500–1040 B.C.E.	Shang
1040–256 B.C.E.	Chou
202 B.C.E.–220 C.E.	Han
266–316 C.E.	Ch`in
581–618 C.E.	Sui
618–907 C.E.	T`ang
960–1279 C.E.	Song
1264–1368 C.E.	Mongolian
1368–1644 C.E.	Ming
1644–1912 C.E.	Ching (Manchu)
1949 C.E.	Beginning of Communism

The Chinese Communist Party, under the leadership of Mao Tse-tung) (Mao Zedong), came to power in 1949, and China became an atheistic state. Temples, images of ancestors, and sacred books were burned. The Cultural Revolution (1966–1976) sought to silence the nation's religious voice. Beginning in the 1980s (following Mao's death in 1976), however, religious expression was once again more accepted. Seminaries were reopened, religious periodicals published, and temples rebuilt.

Overview of Confucianism

Confucian beliefs and practices are based on the teachings of Confucius, a Chinese sage from approximately the fifth century B.C.E. The primary Confucian focus is on human relationships rather than on worship and ritual. The five relationships defined by Confucius were: (1) between a ruler and a subject; (2) between a father and a son; (3) between a husband and wife; (4) between the eldest son and his siblings; and (5) between older and younger friends.

Whether Confucianism is properly classified as a philosophy or a religion is a source of debate. Although Confucius expressed a belief in heaven, he did not consider himself a divine messenger, and he did not promote the worship of any specific god or gods.

One of the central principles of Confucianism is noble conduct. Education, based on morals and cultural standards, also plays an important role. Confucius taught that political problems and improper moral and social behavior resulted from unsatisfactory human performance. Confucius felt that the ethics of his era had declined from the ideals of the previous dynasty (Chou 1040–256 B.C.E.) which he elevated as an example and a standard. His precepts were based on perpetuating the established traditions of the past.

Several key elements in Confucian teaching were the concepts of *li, hsiao, i,* and *jen*:

- *Li* (proper social ritual) focused on ceremonial formality. Confucius believed that li demonstrated respect for other people. The concept also involved using the correct forms of address for one's superiors.

- *Hsiao* (filial piety; also spelled xiao) refers to the respect children feel toward their parents and ancestors. Confucius felt that a child's relationship with his or her parents set the stage for relationships with others. Hsiao also implied loyalty, courage, and trustworthiness.

- *I* (propriety) was demonstrated in friendships through mutual obligations and accountability.

- *Jen* (human virtue) was viewed as the natural result of right living and the primary source of all virtue. It was the sum of li, hsiao, and i, and it encompassed the love of people one to another.

These elements combined to perfect a "junzi" (a virtuous gentleman) who exhibited five honorable traits: charity, justice, propriety, wisdom, and loyalty. Confucius's political ideals emphasized that men should rule based on their virtues, not on their social position. He also believed that all human beings had within themselves the ability to perfect their behavior.

The Relationship between Confucius and the People

Confucius made no divine claims and there is no central god in Confucianism. Confucius advocated pleasing T`ien (heaven) by perfecting one's moral attitudes and culture.

Authorities and Sacred Writings

Confucius did not write his teachings down. The books that are held in esteem by Confucians include classics of his day and books written by his followers. Confucian scriptures include:

- A collection called the *"Four Books"* compiled primarily during the T`ang Dynasty (seventh through tenth centuries C.E.).

- *Lun-yu* (*The Analects*), a collection of the sayings of Confucius, attributed to Mencius, a disciple of Confucius's grandson, Tzu-ssu (also spelled Zi Si).

- *Ta-hsueh* (*The Great Learning*), an ancient ritual collection that explained the relationship between individual spiritual development and society.

- *Chung Yung* (*The Doctrine of the Mean*) ascribed to Confucius's grandson, a treatise on human nature and the moral order of the universe.

- *Meng-tzu* (*The Book of Mencius*), a collection of the sayings of Mencius.

Other important books in Confucianism include texts that were existent in Confucius's era and from which he is reputed to have taught. Called the Five Classics, these are:

Shu Ching (*The Book of History*)
Shih Ching (*The Book of Odes*)
I Ching (*The Book of Changes*)
Ch`un Ch`ui (*Spring and Autumn Annals*)
Li Chi (*The Book of Rites*)

History

Confucius (a Latinized form of the Chinese name K'ung-fu-tzu) lived from 551 to 479 B.C.E. during a turbulent age in Chinese history marked by warring feudal states. He lived in the state of Lu, which is now located in the Shandong Province. During his lifetime, Confucius taught approximately 3,000 students and had fewer than 100 disciples. Two later followers of Confucius expanded his teachings, influence, and fame: Mencius (371–289 B.C.E.; also spelled Meng-tzu) and Hsun-tzu (300–230 B.C.E.; also spelled Xunzi).

Mencius was a follower of Confucius's grandson. His teachings focused on ending the warring among the feudal states of his era. Mencius believed that a virtuous leader would be acknowledged by heavenly mandate and, as a result, would be acknowledged by the people. To Confucius's original teachings, Mencius added the concept that every human possesses innate goodness. Mencius also supported the rights of the people to rebel against governments that did not conform to Confucian ideals.

Hsun-tzu, the third great Confucian philosopher, did not agree with Mencius about the natural condition of the human being. He believed that goodness was not innate, but that it had to be taught. He also had a different concept of heaven. He believed that it existed as a separate entity from the human world. He taught that people interested in pursuing goodness needed to do so without divine guidance.

During the Han Dynasty (202 B.C.E.–220 C.E.), the emperor Han Wu-ti adopted Confucianism as the official doctrine of the state. He commanded that it be taught in universities. He established the tradition of using Confucian sacred writings as the basis for civil service examinations.

After the collapse of the Han dynasty, however, other traditions in China emerged to challenge the authority of Confucianism. These included Taoism and Buddhism. Eventually Buddhism, perceived as a foreign religion, fell into disfavor and Chinese leaders of the Song Dynasty once again embraced Confucian ideals.

Song leaders reestablished the study of the Confucian classics. At the same time, some metaphysical elements of Taoism and Buddhism were incorporated. The Confucianism that emerged came to be called Neo-Confucianism by Western analysts. Neo-Confucianism held that an underlying universal principle bound people together with the cosmos and provided guidance in everyday life. During the Song Dynasty, the practice of using Confucian texts as a basis for civil service examinations was re-instituted, and it continued until the close of China's imperial age in the early twentieth century.

Confucianism Today

In China, the importance of Confucianism diminished in the wake of Communism. Communist leaders condemned Confucianism on the grounds that its rites and practices were elitist and an impediment to needed social change. Since the death of Mao Tse-tung in the 1970s, however, there has been a revived interest in Confucianism and renewed attention to ceremonies honoring Confucius's birth.

Worship

Confucius did not promote himself as divine. He did, however, advocate a limited number of things which were worthy of veneration. These included heaven, men of greatness, and the teaching of sages. In the past, some Confucians worshipped him in temples. During the twelfth century it was common practice to make offerings to T`ien (heaven), to local gods, and to the spirits of Confucius and his disciples. In more modern times, temples continue to exist, but Confucius is no longer worshipped. Some people continue to make pilgrimages to his tomb, but the main body of Confucianism is centered on correct mores and virtues. Worship involves the choices of everyday life rather than rites.

Sects

During the course of its development, three primary schools of Confucianism developed.

School of Principle

The School of Principle, founded by Chu Hsi (1130–1200 C.E., also spelled Zhu Xi) focused on intellectual study. It included the belief in a concept called the Great Ultimate (T`ai-chi) and a principle of physical matter called chi. According to the school's doctrines, a person who understood the nature of things reduced the chi in the mind. This permitted insight into universal truths which enabled the enlightened person to acquire virtue.

School of the Mind

The School of the Mind focused on intuition. Its concepts can be dated to the eleventh and twelfth centuries, but its practices did not become popular until the late fifteenth century under the leadership of Wang Yang-ming (1472–1529). In contrast with the School of Principle that taught that the mind contained chi (matter), the school of the Mind taught that the mind did not contain matter, which meant that the mind was basically good. As the school developed following Wang's death, it focused on more subjective principles and incorporated a Zen-like style of meditation.

School of Practical Learning

The School of Practical Learning developed during the late seventeenth century in response to the collapse of the Ming Dynasty. Confucian scholars felt that the dynasty's downfall was the result of misapplied Confucian principles. It rejected the mysticism related to the School of Principle and the subjectivity of the School of the Mind and instead focused on objective analysis.

Overview of Taoism

In contrast with the Confucian ideal that an individual should strive to conform to the expectations of society, Taoism promoted the idea that an individual should harmonize with the inherent patterns of the universe. Three important components of Taoism are the concepts of Tao, wu-wei, and yin and yang.

The Tao (the Way) refers to the reality that gives order to the physical world. The Tao expresses the undefinable manner of the cosmos.

To conform to the Tao, a person must practice "wu-wei," a principle that means "do nothing" in the sense of making no unnatural struggle against the natural order. The passivity of wu-wei imitates the effortlessness of nature.

Yin and yang represent opposite energies that work together to form harmony. Yin and yang are traditionally symbolized by a stylized circle divided equally into two colors (traditionally dark and light) by a curved line. Each portion of the circle contains a smaller circle of the opposite color.

Some Taoists are primarily philosophical Taoists. They seek to achieve humility and a mystical quiet for the purpose of gaining inner understanding. Philosophical Taoists seek harmony with the ultimate reality that permeates the universe.

Philosophical Taoism, blended with Chinese folk practices, yielded a spiritual Taoism with complex rituals and gods. Religious Taoists worship traditional gods and seek immortality. Some Taoists use magic and ritual to control nature. The ancient five elements (earth, wood, fire, metal, and water) are each associated with correspondences to colors and directions. Five sacred mountains are honored: Heng Shan (in the north) T`ai Shan (in the east—the most popularly visited of the five); Heng Shan (in the south); Hua Shan (in the west) and Sung Shan in the center.

Divination also plays an important role. The classical text *I Ching* (*Book of Changes*) serves as a tool for interpreting the meaning of Hexigrams. Hexigrams are formed by combining two Trigrams. A Trigram is formed by a series of three lines, broken and unbroken, representing yin (broken) and yang (unbroken).

Different patterns of lines yield one of eight different Trigrams. By combining sets of Trigrams, a total of 64 different Hexigrams can be drawn.

The Relationship between the Gods and the Taoist People

Taoism developed a pantheon of gods typically representative of qualities and attributes but also incorporating mythological and historical figures. These were often described in groups of threes such as the "Heavenly One," "Earthly One," and "Great One," who were honored by Taoists of the early Han Dynasty.

Later Taoists recognized a supreme ruler called The First Principle, an eternal deity, who is the source of all truth but who does not interact directly in human affairs. The highest god who interacts with people is called the Jade Emperor (Yu-huang). He rules over subordinate gods in the hierarchy of heaven. The Jade Emperor's jurisdiction includes lesser gods, buddhas, people, ghosts, and demons.

Authorities and Sacred Writings

The collection of Taoist scriptures is called the *Tao-tsang*; it comprises more than 1,400 separate texts which were compiled over a period of 1500 years.

One of the most important is the *Tao-te Ching* (*The Way and Its Power*), which is attributed to Lao Tzu. The word "Tao" in the title refers to the Tao, a way or a path, or alternately a way of behaving or teaching. The word "te" refers to virtue or power.

Other books important to Taoists include:

The Three Caverns, a collection of texts dating from the fifth century including esoteric knowledge, talismans, and rituals.

Chuang Tzu, a collection of parables and allegories attributed to Chuang-tzu, considered to be a formal presentation of Taoist philosophy.

T`ai-p`ing (*Classic of the Great Peace*), a work that dates from the seventh century C.E. and looks forward to an era of peace and the coming of a messiah-like figure.

History

Traditionally, the development of Taoism is traced to Lao Tzu (c. 551–479 B.C.E.), a Chinese philosopher and mystic. According to Taoist belief, Lao Tzu decided to leave civilization because of its declining condition. On his way to the frontier (between China and Tibet) he was asked by the guard of the border to write down his teaching. The resulting book was called the *Tao-te Ching*.

Chuang-tzu (c. 369–286 B.C.E.) was an early follower of the philosophies described by Lao Tzu. The book bearing his name is one of the classics in the Tao collection of revered writings. Chuang-tzu, who criticized the political leaders of his era, promoted the cause of intuition over reason and the use of figurative language over logic.

When the Han Dynasty rose to power in the second century B.C.E., China entered an era of relative political calm. A religious reformer of the time, Chang Tao-ling, was instrumental in refocusing Taoism as a religion. Claiming he had seen Lao Tzu in a vision, he organized a sect called the Heavenly Masters. Practices of the Heavenly Masters included making offerings of cooked vegetables instead of blood sacrifices, confession of sins, and healing.

In the second century C.E. following a civil war in western China a Taoist group called the Way of the Celestial Masters combined with an alchemist movement seeking to find an illusive elixir able to provide immortality. They were followed by other groups who received revelations from gods and divine messages associated with magical practices.

In the middle of the fifth century C.E. *The Canon of the Yellow Court*, a text used for meditation, helped to unify the many diverse and separate Taoist groups. This led to the development of a Taoist movement in which adherents recognized many shared beliefs, rituals, and festivals. Taoists priests served as mediators between people and spirits and other supernatural forces.

Taoism Today

In modern China, religious Taoism is less common than philosophical Taoism, but its presence continues to play an important role.

Worship

Taoist worship combines elements from nature and ancestor worship. Ceremonies and rituals vary according to the god or gods being honored. Priests are viewed as experts in the performance of rituals. Common ritual elements include the burning of paper charms and exorcisms for the healing of sickness. The use of incense represents spirits rising up to be with the gods. Mountains are viewed as sacred places where people can come in contact with the gods, and temples are often stylized to represent mountains.

Sects

Of the many Taoists sects to emerge during the religion's development, two continue to enjoy popularity. The Heavenly Masters school of Taoism predominates in southern China. Its priesthood is perpetuated through heredity and its emphasis is on the use of talismans. The Perfect Truth sect is more popular in the north. It incorporates concepts such as fasting and meditation.

TABLE 14.2.
CHINESE HOLIDAY CYCLE

First Lunar Month (January–February)

1 . . . . .Lunar New Year (Throughout East Asia)
9 . . . . .Making Happiness Festival (Folk)
15 . . . .Lantern Festival (Folk)
18 . . . .Star Festival (Folk)

Second Lunar Month (February–March)

~ . . . . .Monkey God Festival (Taoist)

Third Lunar Month (March–April)

4 or 5 . .Qing Ming Festival (Folk)
23 . . . . .Matsu Festival (Taoist; Buddhist; Folk)

Fourth Lunar Month (April–May)

~ . . . . .Chongmyo Taeje (Confucian)
8 . . . . .Tam Kung Festival (Taoist)
8-9 . . . .Birthday of the Third Prince (Taoist)

Sixth Lunar Month

13 . . . . .Birthday of Lu Pan (Taoist)

Seventh Lunar Month (July–August)

15 . . . .Festival of Hungry Ghosts (Taoist; Buddhist; Folk)

Eighth Lunar Month (August–September)

~ . . . .Monkey God Festival (Taoist)
15 . . . .Mid-Autumn Festival (Folk)

Ninth Lunar Month (September–October)

1-9 . . . .Festival of the Nine Imperial Gods (Taoist; Buddhist)
~ . . . . .Confucius's Birthday (Confucian)

Tenth Lunar Month

1 . . . . .Sending the Winter Dress (Folk)

Twelfth Lunar Month (December–January)

~ . . . . .Winter Solstice (Folk)
~ . . . . .Ta Chiu (Taoist)
23 . . . . .Kitchen God Festival (Taoist; Folk)

The symbol ~ indicates a date that is movable on the Chinese lunar calendar.

Chinese Lunar Calendar

A Lunisolar Calendar

As in many other Eastern religious calendars, the Chinese calendar emphasizes the ebb and flow of nature's patterns. In addition to charting the course of the year, the Chinese Lunar Calendar serves as a tool for divination.

Oracle bones, estimated to be from the 14th century B.C.E. Shang dynasty, provide details about one of the oldest and most accurate timekeeping systems known. The ancient Chinese followed a calendar that predicted a lunar cycle of 29½ days and intercalated a month of 29 or 30 days seven times during a 19-year period, yielding a solar year of 365¼ days. The ancient calendar fell into disfavor, however, and was replaced by another that used the sun's position to determine the timing of intercalated months.

Yin and Yang

The concepts of yin and yang also play an important role in the Chinese understanding of the calendar. Yin and yang, conceptual opposites, provide the harmony and necessary balance to keep the cosmos ordered. They are born at opposite points in the year and establish the basis of the ever-cycling sequence of years and also parallel the rhythms of life.

Yang is born at the winter solstice and strengthens and grows during the spring. The yang half of the year represents the human experiences of adolescence and entering maturity. Yin is born at the summer solstice and strengthens and grows during the summer. The yin half of the year represents old age and renewal or rebirth.

Religious Calendar

Although the solar calendar is currently used as the official calendar in China, many people still follow the lunar calendar for religious purposes. Most dates for major festivals are calculated on the basis of the lunar calendar. The first day of the month corresponds with the new moon and the fifteenth of the month marks the full moon. Similar to the ancient methods of intercalation, the Chinese lunar calendar is synchronized to the solar calendar by the addition of an extra month whenever the sun fails to progress to the next zodiac sign during the course of a month. This occurs in seven of every nineteen years.

Taoist Divinatory Eras

In addition, Taoists use the calendar in divination. Although the twelve animals representing the constellations of the Chinese zodiac are well-known in the west, their use is considered too simple to be accurate by religious Taoists. (The twelve are: rat, ox, tiger, hare, dragon, snake, horse, sheep, monkey, rooster, dog, and pig.) Instead, a complex system based on ten celestial signs called "stems" and twelve earth signs called "branches" is used. Stems and branches are combined to form sixty different pairs. These are associated with differing levels of power and energy.

Three sixty-year cycles, each with its own energy pattern, combine to form a larger unit of time equal to one hundred and eighty years. Within this larger period, a separate sequence also operates. Called the Nine Cycles, it comprises nine repetitions of a twenty-year pattern.

Ancestor Worship in a Chinese Home: Ancestor worship played an important role in the development of Chinese religious thought. Ancestors were members of the family who had died. They were often consulted through divination, honored as if still present, and appeased through rituals to avoid trouble.

Practices surrounding ancestor worship involved funeral rites in which a deceased family member was officially numbered among the ancestors. Wood inscribed with the name of the deceased was kept on a family altar. An offering of incense was kept burning. Spirits of the dead who were from outside the family were feared as ghosts and placated in annual rituals.

◈ ◈ ◈

Taoism, Confucianism, and Chinese Folk Religions Holidays

First Lunar Month (January-February)

Lunar New Year (Spring Festival; Yuan Tan; Tet; Sang-Sin; Je-sok)
First day of the first lunar month

Celebrations marking the beginning of the new year are the most important and the longest of all Chinese festivals. They are observed by Chinese communities throughout the world. The festival, believed to date back to prehistory, marks the beginning of the new lunar cycle. It is also called the Spring Festival, since it falls between the Winter Solstice and Vernal Equinox.

In China the first day of the new lunar year was formerly called Yuan Tan ("the first morning"), but the name was changed when the Gregorian calendar was officially adopted by the Republic of China in 1912. To differentiate the Chinese new year from the Western new year, January 1 was designated Yuan Tan. Today in China and in other Eastern nations, January 1 is a public holiday, but the Lunar New Year (Spring Festival) is the much grander celebration.

The Lunar New Year has certain variations from country to country, but they all include offerings to the household god(s), house-cleaning and new clothes, a large banquet, ancestor worship, and firecrackers. Preparations begin during the preceding month and include making traditional food, cleaning houses, settling debts, and buying new clothes. It is also customary to paste red papers with auspicious writings on the doors and windows of homes.

The high point of the festival occurs on the eve of the new year. Family members return home to honor their ancestors and enjoy a feast. The food served has symbolic meaning. Abalone, for example, promises abundance; bean sprouts, prosperity; and oysters, good business. It is also a night of colossal noise. Firecrackers explode and rockets whistle to frighten away devils. An old legend says that the lunar festival dates from the times when a wild beast (a nihn; also the Cantonese word for "year") appeared at the end of winter to devour many villagers. After the people discovered that the beast feared bright lights, red, and noise, they protected themselves on the last day of the year by lighting up their houses, painting objects red, banging drums and gongs, and exploding bamboo "crackers."

The explosions go on until dawn, and continue sporadically for the next two weeks.

On the first day of the new year, household doors are thrown open to let good luck enter. Families go out to visit friends and worship at temples. Words are carefully watched to avoid saying anything that might signify death, sickness, or poverty. Scissors and knives are avoided for fear of "cutting" the good fortune. Brooms are also not used lest they sweep away good luck. Dragon and lion dances are performed, with 50 or more people supporting long paper dragons. There are acrobatic demonstrations and much beating of gongs and clashing of cymbals.

An ancient custom is giving little red packets of money (called hung-pao or lai see) to children and employees or service-people. The red signifies good fortune, and red is everywhere at this time.

Families stay home on the third day of the holiday because the day is regarded as one of bad luck. On the fourth day, local deities return to earth after a stay in heaven and are welcomed back with firecrackers and the burning of spirit money. According to legend, the seventh day is the anniversary of the creation of mankind. The ninth day is the birthday of the Jade Emperor, the supreme Taoist deity. He is honored with firecrackers. In most Asian countries, people return to work after the fourth or fifth day of celebration.

In Taiwan, New Year's Eve, New Year's Day, and the two days following are public holidays, and all government offices, most businesses, restaurants, and stores are closed. The closings may continue for eight days.

Celebrations vary from country to country and region to region. In Vietnam, where the holiday is called Tet, the ancestors are believed to return to heaven on the fourth day, and everyone has to return to work. On the seventh day, the Cay Nev is removed from the front of the home. This is a high bamboo pole that was set up on the last day of the old year. On its top are red paper with inscriptions, wind chimes, a square of woven bamboo to stop evil spirits from entering, and a small basket with betel and areca nuts for the good spirits.

In Taiwan the festival is called Sang-Sin. Small horses and palanquins are cut from yellow paper and burned to serve as conveyances for the kitchen god. The New Year's feast is first laid before the ancestor shrine. About seven o'clock, after the ancestors have eaten, the food is gathered up, reheated, and eaten by the family. The greater the amount of food placed before the shrine, the greater will be the reward for the new year. After the banquet, oranges are stacked in fives before the ancestor tablets and household gods. A dragon-bedecked red cloth is hung before the altar. The dragon is the spirit of rain and abundance, and the oranges are an invitation to the gods to share the family's feasting.

In Korea, Je-sok (or Je-ya) is the name for New Year's Eve. Torches are lit in every part of the home, and everyone sits up all night to "defend the New Year" from evil spirits. In modern Seoul, the capital, the church bells are rung 33 times at midnight. A traditional food is duggook soup, made from rice and containing pheasant, chicken, meat, pinenuts, and chestnuts.

Making Happiness Festival (Tso-Fu Festival)
Ninth day of the first lunar month

The Making Happiness Festival is celebrated in Taiwan soon after the beginning of the Lunar New Year. The Happiness Master, headman, chief medium, and other villagers "invite the gods" by collecting a number of gods who normally dwell in various shrines and private homes and bringing them to the temple, accompanied by a hired band, children, gongs, and banners. Mothers of newborn sons pay their respects to the Heaven God by presenting hsin-ting ping ("new male cakes"). The following day they distribute these cakes to every household except those occupied by other new mothers. Elaborate sacrificial rites are performed in the temple and a special feast is held for villagers over 60 years of age, other important guests, and women who have given birth to sons during the year. At the end of the festival, the gods that have been brought to the temple are returned to their shrines.

Lantern Festival (Yuan Hsiao Chieh; Yuen Siu)
Fifteenth day of the first lunar month

Beginning on the thirteenth and fourteenth days of the new year, shops hang out lanterns in preparation for the Lantern Festival which falls the day of the first full moon of the new year. It marks the conclusion of the new year celebration.

According to one legend, the Lantern Festival originated with the emperors of China's Han dynasty (206 B.C.E.–221 C.E.) who paid tribute to the universe on that night. Because the ceremony was held in the evening, lanterns were used to illuminate the palace. The Han rulers imposed a year-round curfew on their subjects, but on this night the curfew was lifted, and the people, carrying their own simple lanterns, went forth to view the fancy lanterns of the palace.

Another legend holds that the festival originated because a maid of honor (named Yuan Hsiao, also the name of the sweet dumpling associated with the day) in the emperor's household longed to see her parents during the days of the Spring Festival. The resourceful

Dongfang Shuo decided to help her. He spread the rumor that the god of fire was going to burn down the city of Chang-an. The city was thrown into a panic. Dongfang Shuo, summoned by the emperor, advised him to have everyone leave the palace and also to order that lanterns be hung in every street and every building. In this way, the god of fire would think the city was already burning. The emperor followed the advice, and Yuan Hsiao took the opportunity to see her family. There have been lanterns ever since.

Star Festival
Eighteenth day of the first lunar month

When the Lunar New Year celebration is over, a day is set aside for men to worship the Star Gods. To the Chinese, the stars and planets are the homes of sainted heroes who have the power to influence the course of human destiny. Women are traditionally forbidden to participate in the ceremony, which consists of setting up a small table or altar in the courtyard of the house with a simple food offering (usually rice balls cooked in sugar and flour). Two pictures are placed on the altar, one of the Star Gods and another of the cyclical signs associated with them. In a sealed envelope is a chart of lucky and unlucky stars. The master of the house makes a special prayer to the star that presided over his birth and lights the special lamps, made of red and yellow paper and filled with perfumed oil, that have been arranged around the altar. They burn out quickly, after which each son of the house comes forward to honor his own star by relighting three of the lamps. If their flames burn brightly, it means he will have good luck in the coming year.

Second Lunar Month
(February-March)

Monkey God Festival
Celebrated on February 17 and September 12

Tai Seng Yeh, the popular Monkey God, is honored on both February 17 and September 12. According to Taoist belief, Tai Seng Yeh sneaked into heaven and acquired miraculous powers. He is thought to cure the sick and absolve the hopeless. He is the godfather of many Chinese children.

In Singapore, Taoist mediums go into a trance to let the god's spirit enter their bodies. Then, possessed, they howl and slash themselves with knives, and scrawl symbols on scraps of paper that are grabbed by devotees. There are also puppet shows and Chinese street opera performances at Chinese temples. The festival also may include demonstrations of fire walking.

Third Lunar Month
(March-April)

Qing Ming Festival (Ch'ing Ming; Festival of Pure Brightness; Cold Food Day; Han Sik-il; Han Shih)
Fourth or fifth day of the third lunar month

The Qing Ming Festival is a Confucian celebration that dates back to the Han Dynasty (206 B.C.E. to 221 C.E.). It is computed as 105 days after the Winter Solstice, Tong-ji. Its purpose is to honor the dead, and it is now a Chinese national holiday.

Qing Ming is observed by the maintenance of ancestral graves; the presentation of food, wine, and flowers as offerings; and the burning of paper money at the graveside to provide the ancestors with funds in the afterworld. Traditional Chinese belief holds that the afterlife is quite similar to this life, and that the dead live below ground in the Yellow Springs region. In ancient China, other festivities of the day included playing Chinese football and flying kites. Today, people picnic and gather for family meals.

The day is also called Cold Food Day because, according to an ancient legend, it was taboo to cook the day before. In Korea, the holiday's name is Han Sik-il; in Taiwan it is Han Shih. The Taiwanese observance includes a symbolic ritual of maintaining the home of one's ancestors. This is accomplished using strips of yellow paper about three inches long by two inches wide which are stuck in the ground by the grave. After this is completed, prayers and food offerings are made.

Matsu Festival (T'ien-hou Festival)
Twenty-third day of the third lunar month

Matsu (or Ma-cho or Mazu; also known as T'ien-hou), the Chinese Goddess of the Sea, is venerated on the day set aside to honor her birth. Fishermen honor her for protecting them from storms and disasters at sea. People pay homage to her at the Meizhou Mazu Temple on Meishou Island, in other Chinese communities, and on Taiwan.

On Taiwan, the most famous Matsu celebration site is the Chaotien Temple in Peikang, Taiwan's oldest, biggest, and richest Matsu temple, built in 1694. During the festival, a carnival-like atmosphere prevails, with watermelon stalls, cotton candy stalls, sling-shot ranges, parades of the goddess and other gods, altars for sacrifices of food and incense, and firecrackers. It has been estimated that 75 percent of all firecrackers manufactured on Taiwan are exploded in Peikang during the Matsu Festival. The festival is attended by hundreds of thousands of people, many of whom make pilgrimages from the town of Tachia about 60 miles north and spend a week visiting about 16 Matsu temples along the route.

The origins of the festival are uncertain. According to one Chinese legend, the goddess was born in about 960 C.E. and, because she never cried in the first month of her life, was named Lin Moniang (*moniang* means "quiet girl"). She began to read when she was eight, studied Buddhist and Taoist scriptures, became a believer in Buddhism at 10, studied magic arts when she was 12, and at 28 achieved nirvana and became a goddess. She is worshiped because she is believed to have performed many miracles during her life. Courts in successive dynasties issued decrees to honor her with such titles as "Holy Princess" and "Holy Mother."

In Taiwan, the story is that Matsu, a girl from the Hokkien Province in China, took up the fishing trade to support her mother after her fisherman father died. One day she died at sea, and because of her filial devotion, she came to be worshiped as a deity. During World War II, when American planes started to bomb Taiwan, many women prayed to Matsu, and it is said that some women saw a girl dressed in red holding out a red cloth to catch the falling bombs.

Fourth Lunar Month (April-May)

Chongmyo Taeje (Royal Shrine Rite)
First Sunday in May

This rite is a Confucian memorial ceremony held at Chongmyo Shrine in Seoul, Korea, to honor the Yi kings and queens of the Choson Dynasty (1392–1910). The shrine, in a secluded garden in the center of Seoul, houses the ancestral tablets of the monarchs. Each year elaborate rites are performed to pay homage to them, and a number of royal descendants, robed in the traditional garments of their ancestors, take part. The rites are accompanied by court music and dance. The ceremony is a grand expression of the widespread Confucian practice of honoring ancestors, either at home or at their graves.

Tam Kung Festival
Eighth day of the fourth lunar month

Tam Kung is a popular god among fisherfolk. Taoists believe his powers were apparent when he was only 12 years old. Although his greatest gift was controlling the weather, he could also heal the sick and predict the future. Residents of the Shau Kei Wan area believe he saved many lives during an outbreak of cholera in 1967. His birthday is marked with a grand procession, Cantonese opera, and lion and dragon dances.

Birthday of the Third Prince
Eighth and ninth days of the fourth lunar month

The Third Prince is a Taoist child-god. Taoists believe he rides on the wheels of the wind and fire and can work miracles. A festival in his honor is held in Singapore. Chinese mediums in trances dance, slash themselves with spiked maces and swords, and write charms on yellow paper with blood from their tongues. There is also a street procession of stilt-walkers, dragon dancers, and Chinese musicians.

Sixth Lunar Month June-July

Birthday of Lu Pan
Thirteenth day of the sixth lunar month

Lu Pan, the Taoist patron saint of carpenters and builders is honored on the day set aside to commemorate his birth. According to tradition, Lu Pan was born in 507 B.C.E. An architect, engineer, and inventor, Lu Pan is credited with inventing the drill, plane, shovel, saw, lock, and ladder. His wife is said to have invented the umbrella. Because his inventions are indispensable to building, it is common practice at the start of major construction projects for employees to have feasts, burn incense, and offer prayers to Lu Pan so that he may protect them and the construction work from disaster.

In Hong Kong, people in the construction industry observe Lu Pan's birthday with celebratory banquets to give thanks for their good fortune in the past year and to pray for better fortune in the year to come. They also pay their respects at noon at the Lu Pan Temple in Kennedy Town.

Seventh Lunar Month (July-August)

Festival of Hungry Ghosts
Full moon or 15th day of seventh lunar month

The Festival of the Hungry Ghosts is celebrated by both Taoists and Buddhists. Its origins probably date back to the sixth century and Confucius. It is observed in China and throughout the rest of eastern Asia.

According to Chinese legend, the souls of the dead are released from purgatory during this time to roam the earth. This makes it a dangerous time to travel, get married, or move to a new house. Unhappy and hungry spirits, those who died without descendants to look after them or who had no proper funeral, may cause trouble and therefore must be placated with offerings. Offerings are made by people who burn paper replicas of material possessions like automobiles, furniture, clothing, and paper money ("ghost money") believing that this frees these things for the spirits to use. Offerings of food are placed on tables outside people's homes. Prayers are said at Chinese temples and in Chinese shops and homes. The festival also includes open-air performances of street opera, called wayang, and puppet shows.

Eighth Lunar Month
(August-September)

Mid-Autumn Festival (Moon Cake Festival; Chung Ch'iu; Hangawi; Ch'usok; Trung Thursday; Tiong-chhiu Choeh)
Fifteenth day of the eighth lunar month

The Mid-Autumn Festival celebrates the birth of the moon goddess. The festival is a national holiday in China and observances occur throughout the Far East and in Asian communities all over the world. In Korea, it is called Hangawi or Ch'usok; in Vietnam Trung Thursday; in Hong Kong Chung Ch'iu; and in Taiwan Tiong-chhiu Choeh.

Several traditional activities are associated with the festival including family reunions, exchanging presents, feasting, and eating moon cakes. Some people also pray to the moon for protection, family unity, and good fortune.

There are varying legends associated with the origin of the festival, which is thought to date back to the ninth century. One story tells of a rabbit who can be seen on the dark side of the full moon. The rabbit, who makes a potion for immortality, is honored on this day which is believed to be his birthday, and moon cakes were made to feed the rabbits. Another version says that the day marks the overthrow of the Mongol overlords in ancient China; the moon cakes supposedly hid secret messages planning the overthrow. Another version of the day's origin is that the day is a harvest festival, and it occurs at a time when the moon is brightest.

Ninth Lunar Month
(September-October)

Festival of the Nine Imperial Gods
First nine days of the ninth lunar month

As celebrated today in Singapore, the Festival of the Nine Imperial Gods derives from an ancient Chinese cleansing ritual. The festival begins with a procession to a river or the sea to invite the Nine Imperial Gods to descend from the heavens into an urn filled with burning benzoin. The urn is then carried to the temple and put in a place where only Taoist priests and Buddhist monks are allowed to enter. Nine oil lamps representing the gods are hung from a bamboo pole in front of the temple. They are lowered and then raised again to signify that the gods have arrived. The ground below the lamps is purified every morning and afternoon with holy water. Worshippers enter the temple by crossing a specially constructed bridge, symbolizing the belief that they are leaving the evils of the past year behind.

Chinese operas known as wayang shows—some of which take two or more days to complete—are often performed during the nine days of the festival. On the ninth day, the sacred urn with the burning ashes is brought out of the temple and taken in procession back to the water's edge, where it is placed in a boat. The observers wait for the boat to move, indicating that the gods have departed—but what often happens is that other boats turn on their engines to churn up the water and send the gods on their way.

Confucius's Birthday (Teacher's Day)
September 28

Confucius, perhaps the most influential man in China's history, is honored on a day set aside to commemorate his birth. In Taiwan, the day is a national holiday. In Qufu, Shandong Province, China, the birthplace of Confucius, there is a two-week-long Confucian Culture Festival. In Hong Kong observances are held by the Confucian Society at the Confucius Temple at Causeway Bay near this date.

Commemorations in Taiwan take the form of dawn services at the Confucian temples. The Confucius Temple in Tainan was built in 1665 by Gen. Chen Yunghua of the Ming Dynasty and is the oldest Confucian temple in Taiwan.

Tenth Lunar Month
(October-November)

Sending the Winter Dress
First day of the tenth lunar month

By tradition, on this day the Chinese send winter garments to the dead. They are not real items of clothing but paper replicas packed in parcels bearing the names of the recipients. The gift packages are first exhibited in the home; the actual sending of the garments takes place in a courtyard or near the tomb, where they are burned.

TABLE 14.3. ALPHABETICAL LIST OF CHINESE HOLIDAYS

Holidays	Dates
Birthday of Lu Pan (Taoist)	Thirteenth day of the sixth lunar month
Birthday of the Third Prince (Taoist)	Eighth and ninth days of the fourth lunar month
Ch'ing Ming *see* Qing Ming Festival	
Ch'usok *see* Mid-Autumn Festival	
Chongmyo Taeje (Confucian)	First Sunday in May
Chung Ch'iu *see* Mid-Autumn Festival	
Cold Food Day *see* Qing Ming Festival	
Confucius's Birthday (Confucian)	September 28
Festival of Hungry Ghosts (Taoist; Folk)	Full moon day of the seventh lunar month
Festival of Nine Imperial Gods (Taoist)	First nine days of the ninth lunar month
Festival of Pure Brightness *see* Qing Ming Festival	
Han Shih *see* Qing Ming Festival	
Han Sik-il *see* Qing Ming Festival	
Hangawi *see* Mid-Autumn Festival	
Je-sok *see* Lunar New Year	
Kitchen God Festival (Taoist; Folk)	23rd night of the twelfth lunar month
Lantern Festival (Folk)	Fifteenth day of the first lunar month
Lunar New Year (East Asia)	First day of the first lunar month
Making Happiness Festival (Folk)	Ninth day of the first lunar month
Matsu Festival (Taoist; Folk)	Twenty-third day of the third lunar month

Holidays	Dates
Mid-Autumn Festival (Folk)	Fifteenth day of the eighth lunar month
Monkey God Festival (Taoist)	February 17 and September 12
Moon Cake Festival *see* Mid-Autumn Festival	
Qing Ming Festival (Folk)	Fourth or fifth day of the third lunar month
Royal Shrine Rite *see* Chongmyo Taeje	
Sang-Sin *see* Lunar New Year	
Sending the Winter Dress (Folk)	First day of the tenth lunar month
Spring Festival *see* Lunar New Year	
Star Festival (Folk)	Eighteenth day of the first lunar month
Ta Chiu (Taoist)	About December 27
Tam Kung Festival (Taoist)	Eighth day of the fourth lunar month
Teacher's Day *see* Confucius's Birthday	
Tet *see* Lunar New Year	
T'ien-hou Festival *see* Matsu Festival	
Tiong-chhiu Choeh *see* Mid-Autumn Festival	
Tong-ji *see* Winter Solstice	
Trung Thursday *see* Mid-Autumn Festival	
Tso-Fu Festival *see* Making Happiness Festival	
Tung Chih *see* Winter Solstice	
Winter Solstice (Folk)	About December 21
Yuan Hsiao Chieh *see* Lantern Festival	
Yuan Tan *see* Lunar New Year	
Yuen Siu *see* Lantern Festival	

Twelfth Lunar Month (December-January)

Winter Solstice (Tung Chih; Tong-ji)
During the twelfth lunar month; about December 21

The Chinese god T`ien is honored at the Winter Solstice. According to tradition, the ancient emperors of China would present themselves before the god at the Forbidden City in the capital of Beijing to offer sacrifices on behalf of the people. Modernly, the festival is commemorated on the longest night of the year. People visit temples and serve feasts in their homes to honor deceased family members.

Ta Chiu
During the twelfth lunar month; about December 27

Ta Chiu is a Taoist celebration of renewal. During the observance, gods and ghosts are summoned. Images of all patron saints are gathered in one place and people make offerings. A priest then reads the names of living persons. These are fastened to a paper horse and burned so that the smoke can rise to heaven.

Kitchen God Festival
Twenty-third night of the 12th lunar month

The Kitchen God Festival occurs during preparations for the new year. According to legend, at this time Zao Wang (which means "the Lord Who Watches over the Hearth") prepares for his journey to report to the Jade Emperor, who is supreme over all the gods. Zao Wang's mission is to tell the Jade Emperor about everyone's behavior. To send their Kitchen God on his way, households burn paper money and give him offerings of wine. To make sure that his words to the Jade Emperor are sweet, they also offer tang kwa, a dumpling that finds its way to the mouths of eager children.

CHAPTER 15

Shinto

Overview of Shinto

What Is Shinto?

The name Shinto was first employed during the sixth century C.E. to differentiate indigenous religions in Japan from faith systems that originated in mainland Asia (primarily Buddhism and Confucianism). The word is derived from two Chinese characters, *shen* (gods) and *tao* (way). Loosely translated, Shinto means "way of the gods." Its roots lie in an ancient nature-based religion. Some important concepts in Shinto include the value of tradition, the reverence of nature, cleanliness (ritual purity), and the veneration of spirits called kami.

Kami (which is both the singular and plural term) are honored but they are not all powerful. People descended from the kami, and the kami have influence over human life and the forces of nature. The kami can bestow blessings, but they are not all benign. Kami live in natural things such as trees, mountains, and rivers, and they are embodied in religious relics, especially mirrors and jewels. They also include spirits of ancestors, local deities, and holy people (both historic and legendary).

The human role is to worship the kami and make offerings. The ultimate goal of Shinto is to uphold the harmony between people and nature. One of the most important human tasks is to maintain ritual purity. Washing before coming into the presence of the kami is essential, and purity helps a person ascend towards the level of the gods.

The Relationship between the Gods and the Shinto People

The kami exist in all of nature, but in some places and at some times their presence is more manifest. Places marked for their geographic beauty, such as rock formations and waterfalls, are especially noted for the presence of local kami. As a result, some of the most picturesque areas in Japan boast Shinto shrines. The kami are also present when the weather changes, such as when storms brew.

In addition to the myriad of kami that inhabit the land of Japan, the Japanese people also recognize some kami of greater importance who serve as the gods and goddesses responsible for establishing and directing the course of the nation's development. According to Shinto legend, the first gods were born of the union between the first male and the first female who emerged from creation. Three of the most important deities were generated spontaneously by the male while he was washing in the sea. Amaterasu, the sun goddess, came from his left eye. Tsukiyomi, the moon god, came from his right eye; Susano-o, the god of the summer wind, came from his nostrils.

According to an ancient story, Susano-o, a temperamental god, frequently angered and insulted his sister. In one instance, she locked herself in the Rock Cave of Heaven and refused to come out. An assembly of 800 spirits gathered to extricate the goddess. They hung a mirror in a tree and performed loud, raucous dances. When Amaterasu emerged to investigate, the spirits roped off the Cave preventing her from returning to it. In remembrance of this event, the mirror continues to play a central role in Shinto and is often the focal point of a shrine.

Authorities

Priests

The central authorities in Shinto are the priests. Traditionally the duties of the priest were passed through lines of heredity, but in modern times, priests are trained on the basis of recommendation. The priests' duties include communicating with the kami and ensuring that ceremonies are properly carried out. Each individual priest is responsible for becoming ritually pure before performing required rites. Preparations include special bathing (ablutions), dietary rules, and sexual abstinence.

Books

Shinto has no one collection of sacred texts analogous to the Christian *Bible* or Islamic *Qur'an*, but several important books provide information and guidance.

Kojiki (*Records of Ancient Events*), compiled during the early eighth century C.E. under imperial command, is based on oral traditions. The text consists of three sections. The first section describes the mythic founding of Japan; the second and third sections include histories of the first emperors including time up to the reign of Empress Suiko in the early seventh century.

Nihongi (*Chronicles of Japan*), comprising thirty books, covers ancient Japanese history through the end of the seventh century C.E.

Engishiki (*Chronicles of the Engi*) contains ritual and ceremonial instructions along with prayers for sacred services.

History

Shinto grew out of the ancient worship of spirits in nature such as heaven, earth, mountains, rivers, seas, islands and forests. It began with the age of the kami. Kami were formed when the cosmos materialized out of chaos. The most important kami was the Sun Goddess Amaterasu. The relationship between Amaterasu and her brother, the god Susano-o, shaped the early history of Japan.

Amaterasu sent her grandson to the Japanese islands to establish rule because she was dismayed with the disorder that existed under the rule of Susano-o's son. When her grandchild, Ninigi, descended to the earth, the age of human history began. His great-grandson, Jimmu Tenno, was the first Japanese emperor of Japan. The traditional date for Jimmu's ascent to the throne is 660 B.C.E. (although many Western scholars place the date between the first century B.C.E. and the first century C.E.).

Because of this legendary history, emperors in Japan were viewed as having divine descent. Upon their ascension to power, they were given three symbols of the goddess Amaterasu: a mirror, jewels, and a sword. Early emperors were also believed to possess shamanistic powers and they served as a spokesperson for the gods. One early Japanese leader, Queen Himiko, who reigned during the late second and early third century, was reputed to serve the spirits and hold special powers over people.

By the time of the fourth and fifth centuries, the Japanese political system and the worship of the kami were closely interrelated. Rulers believed that the kami held power, influence, and protection. As the political system developed, the priesthood also became more organized.

Influences from China

Beginning in the sixth century C.E., the Japanese people began to come into greater contact with the people of mainland Asia. Religions from China, in particular Buddhism, Confucianism, and Taoism, were introduced and foreign concepts blended with ancient veneration of the kami. By the early ninth century, Buddhist and Shinto doctrines had merged to form Ryobu Shinto (Shinto of Two Kinds). The sect also incorporated some Confucian elements.

Buddhist temples often included shrines to local kami, and shrines contained Buddha figures. By the tenth century, two Shinto kami were identified as Buddhist bodhisattvas (incarnations). In the following years, more of the kami became identified with bodhisattvas. Shinto also had a profound effect on Japanese Buddhism. Several Buddhist schools developed out of syncretism with Shinto thought, but eventually Shinto practices faded as Buddhist customs rose in popularity.

Beginning in the eleventh century, Japan's cultural stability became threatened and fighting among feudal lords intensified. The emperor retained official status as the head of the Japanese government due to his divinity, but real power shifted to military rulers called shoguns.

During the thirteenth century, when stormy seas prevented a Mongol invasion of Japan, the preeminence of Shinto gods was asserted. By the fifteenth century, a doctrine with a nationalistic emphasis emerged. The kami were seen as fundamental and other Buddhist and Confucian manifestations were viewed as merely offshoots of the kami.

The seventeenth century saw the establishment of the Tokugawa Shogunate (1603–1867). Under its leadership the superiority of Japanese culture over Chinese culture was proclaimed. In a revival of Shinto, an effort was made to purify the ancient faith by purging Buddhist and Confucian elements. The National Learning Movement (Kokugaku) was formed to focus the attention of the Japanese people on developing an unadulterated Japanese ideology.

The rule of the shoguns came to an end following a civil war in the middle nineteenth century. In 1868 Emperor Meiji, asserting his divine right to rule, reorganized Japan's government according to its historic form and instituted changes that led to the establishment of State Shinto as the official religion of Japan.

With the rise in power of State Shinto, unauthorized sects were banned and persecuted. Eventually, the national government, under economic pressure from foreign governments, permitted some freedom of religion and officially recognized thirteen sects. According to many analysts, State Shinto became a tool used by the government for political purposes rather than a religion in the traditional sense.

Following Japan's defeat in World War II, State Shinto fell into disarray. The terms of Japan's surrender included a requirement that the emperor renounce his claims to divinity and that religious movements be severed from government control. The imperial family, however, continues to honor personal rituals as part of the country's traditional heritage.

Shinto Today

People

Despite the fall of the nationalistic State Shinto, other forms of Shinto continued to be practiced. By the early 1990s, there were more than 80,000 Shinto shrines in Japan. Estimates of the number of adherents varied widely, however, from 3 to 110 million. The lower figures reflected the number of people who identified Shinto as their primary or exclusive religion; the larger figures included people who participated in Shinto ceremonies, the vast majority of them also professing other religions (predominantly Buddhism). Most Shinto adherents live in Japan, but small communities also exist in Europe, Latin America, North America, and in the Pacific island nations.

Worship

Shinto shrines provide a place were people can go and worship or petition the kami. A typical shrine is located in a grove or other place of natural beauty. A pathway leading to it is often lined with lanterns. Most Shinto shrines have a gateway, called a torri, which usually consists of two pillars or columns with two cross beams at the top. The torri serves as a symbol of separation; it differentiates the holy place from the common world. Other elements found in many shrines include a place for ritual washing, a place to hang tablets with prayers and petitions, a platform where offerings can be made, and a place to house the sacred object in which the kami lives. The dwelling of the kami is typically located in an inner shrine, which only a priest may enter. The sacred object is frequently a mirror which represents Amaterasu.

In the modern era, many Shinto shrines are kept by priests who also have full time secular jobs. People who visit the shrines come to make offerings and venerate the kami with ritual bows and claps. During festival times, people may also make offerings of votive candles and buy special charms for good luck. Folded paper talismans (origami) or pieces of paper tied to trees help summon opportunity, dispel misfortune, and empower prayers.

Shinto rituals also often involve offerings of food and drink and performances of music and dance. Practitioners believe that the kami receive the gifts and in return bestow blessing on the givers. The priest may use a branch from a sakaki tree (a type of evergreen) to sprinkle water over worshippers to indicate the kami's blessing.

Major festivals are often marked by processions in which portable shrines carry the kami through the streets. The practice is believed to distribute the kami's blessings throughout an entire community.

In addition to shrine worship, many practicing Shintoists have small shrines in their homes. These family shrines, called kamidanas, consist of a sacred space where holy objects, candles and offerings are kept. They also typically include an amulet or some other representation of the kami being honored.

In some areas of rural Japan, mediums who communicate with the kami are common. The mediums, called miko, are typically female. Other holy people recognized by Shintoists include male and female ascetics who perform healing rituals and provide other spiritual services.

Sects

There are several Shinto sects currently recognized in Japan. They are classified into two major categories: Shrine Shinto and Sect Shinto. Another group, Confucian Shinto, also exists. It combines aspects of traditional Shinto with Confucian ethical principles and the metaphysical doctrines of the Neo-Confucians.

Shrine Shinto

The largest group of Shintoists are classified as belonging to the Shrine Shinto tradition. Followers venerate the kami historically recognized in Japan. During the era prior to World War II, many of the shrines were controlled by the government, but since that time the shrines have been restored to the priests. One of the best known shrines is located in Ise, and it is devoted to the sun goddess, Amaterasu.

Sect Shinto

Sect Shinto incorporates numerous small individual groups that operate independently. Many of the groups so classified trace their origins to the nineteenth century as people with perceived shamanic powers and supernatural experiences gathered followers. The types of groups include mountain sects (who venerate the kami of mountains), faith healing sects, and purification sects. The purification sects believe that individuals must maintain ritual purity in order to preserve physical and mental health.

The largest group within Sect Shinto is Tenrikyo (Heavenly Reason). It was established during the nineteenth century by two women who claimed divine encounters. The sect's teachings focus on mental and spiritual healing and the omnipresence of a divine spirit.

TABLE 15.1.
SHINTO HOLIDAY CYCLE

Dates	Holiday
January	
1-3	Ganjitsu
February	
3 or 4	Setsubun
8	Hari-Kuyo
May	
5	Children's Day
15	Aoi Matsuri
~18	Sanja Matsuri
June	
14 or 15	Rice Planting Festivals
17	Lily Festival
July	
17	Gion Matsuri
October	
20	Ebisu Festival
November	
15	Shichi-Go-San
December	
31	Omisoka

The symbol ~ indicates an approximate date.

Japanese Lunar Calendar and Modern Reforms

The Japanese Lunar Calendar

There are many similarities between the ancient Japanese and Chinese lunar calendars. One of the primary differences was in dating methods. Chinese calendars counted years based on the Chinese emperor's reign, and Japanese calendars reckoned their years based on the reign of the Japanese emperor.

There were also minor differences in recognizing the precise stage of the moon. These may have been attributable to differences in longitudes rather than differences in the underlying theories. The Japanese lunar calendar began each month with the new moon. The full moon occurred on the fifteenth day. The first full moon to occur after the winter solstice marked the beginning of a new year. In order to keep the lunar and solar cycles in harmony, intercalary months were added in seven years of every 19-year cycle. The twelve normal months of the year were named according to agricultural cycles.

Used for Divination

The ancient Japanese also used the calendar for divination. A complex system of ten celestial signs called "stems" and twelve earth signs called "branches" were used in combination to form a cycle consisting of sixty units. These units applied to cycles of sixty days

---

TABLE 15.2. ANCIENT JAPANESE MONTH NAMES

Name	Meaning
MuTsuki	Harmony
KisaRagi	Change of Dress
YaYohi	Grass Grows Dense
UTzuki	Plant Rice
SaTsuki	Rice Sprouts
MiNaTzuki	Put Water in the Field
FuTzuki	Letters
HaTzuki	Leaves
NagaTsuki	Autumn
KaNaTzuki	Gods
ShimoTsuki	Falling Frost
ShiHasu	Winter

and were used to divine "lucky" and "unlucky" days. Interest in divination and the perceived need to accurately predict auspicious times from inauspicious ones initially led to resistance against efforts to reform the Japanese calendar.

Calendar Reform

By the late seventeenth century, the Japanese calendar was approximately two days out of step with astronomical observations. Although some minor adjustments were made, it was not until the Gregorian calendar was adopted in 1868 that Japan's calendar achieved modern precision.

In modern times, three different calendars work in conjunction to order the timing of Shinto festivals: the solar calendar, which begins with the new year on January 1; the lunar calendar which begins with the first full moon after the winter solstice; and the Chinese almanac which charts lucky and unlucky days for the year.

White Lily: Lilies are gathered in preparation for the Lily Festival, and the Shinto temple priest offers a bouquet of lilies on the altar. The lily dance marks the end of the rainy season, and paraded lilies signify the purifying of the air.

Shinto Holidays

January

Ganjitsu (Japanese New Year)
January 1–3

The Shinto observance of the Japanese new year is focused on activities at shrines. Shrines and homes are typically decorated with symbolic emblems such as bamboo (representing sincerity), pine (constancy), and early-blooming flowers (renewed life). Other decorations include paper talismans to avert evil and bring good luck. Many people travel to visit a shrine and attend a morning ceremony or watch the sun rise.

February

Setsubun (Bean-Throwing Festival)
February 3 or 4

Setsubun occurs on the last day of winter according to Japan's lunar calendar. Observed in all major temples and shrines, it marks the beginning of spring. The day is celebrated by attending public ceremonies at temples and shrines in which beans are thrown to people who have gathered. The beans are thrown to drive away evil spirits, and catching one is considered good luck. Sardine heads are also used to ward off evil. People hang them in doorways because evil spirits dislike their smell.

Hari-Kuyo (Festival of Broken Needles)
February 8

This requiem service for needles is held throughout Japan. The ceremony of laying needles to rest dates back to at least the fourth century C.E. Today the services are attended not only by tailors and dressmakers but also by people who sew at home. Traditionally, a shrine is set up in the Shinto style, with a sacred rope and strips of white paper suspended over a three-tiered altar. On the top tier are offerings of cake and fruit, on the second tier there is a pan of tofu, and the bottom tier is for placing scissors and thimbles. The tofu is the important ingredient; people insert their broken or bent needles in it while offering prayers of thanks to the needles for their years of service. Afterwards, the needles are wrapped in paper and laid to rest in the sea.

May

Children's Day (Kodomo No Hi)
May 5

On children's day, children are blessed in Shinto shrines by having a priest wave paper streamers (white) over their heads. Originally only boys were blessed but more modernly boys and girls are both blessed. Another tradition associated with the day is the flying of a carp-shaped kite for each boy in the family. The carp symbolizes strength, courage, and determination.

Aoi Matsuri (Hollyhock Festival)
May 15

One of the three major festivals of Kyoto, Japan, Aoi Matsuri is believed to date from the sixth century. The festival's name derives from the hollyhock leaves adorning the headdresses of the participants; legend says hollyhocks help prevent storms and earthquakes. The festival owes its present form to the time in the Heian period (792–1099 C.E.) when imperial messengers were sent to the Kyoto shrines of Shimogamo and Kamigamo after a plague (or a flood) that came about because the shrines were neglected.

Today the festival, which was revived in 1884, consists of a re-creation of the original imperial procession. Some 500 people in ancient costume parade with horses and large lacquered oxcarts carrying the "imperial messengers" from the Kyoto Imperial Palace to the shrines to honor the god who protects the city.

Sanja Matsuri (Three Shrines Festival)
Weekend near May 18

The Sanja Matsuri is one of the most spectacular festivals in Tokyo, Japan. It is held to honor Kannon, the goddess of mercy (who is known as Kuan-yin in China), and the three fishermen brothers who founded the Asakusa Kannon Temple in the 14th century. The word Sanja means "three shrines," and matsuri is the Japanese term for festival.

According to legend, after the three brothers discovered a statue of Kannon in the Sumida River, their spirits were enshrined in three places. The annual festival has been held since the late 1800s on a weekend near May 18. Activities are focused on the Asakusa Temple and Tokyo's "Shitamachi" (downtown area).

More than 100 portable shrines (called *mikoshi*), which weigh up to two tons and are surmounted by gold phoenixes, are paraded through the streets to the gates of the temple. Carrying them are men in happi coats (traditional short laborers' jackets) worn to advertise their districts. There are also priests on horseback, musicians playing "sanja-bayashi" festival music, and dancers in traditional costume. On Sunday, various dances are performed.

June

Rice Planting Festivals
June 14 or 15

There are many rituals associated with the growing of rice in Japanese farming communities. Shinto priests are often asked to offer prayers for a good harvest season. The local Kami are also honored. In many rural celebrations, young women in costume perform rituals including planting seedlings while singing rice-planting songs to the accompaniment of pipes and drums. Sometimes women light fires of rice straw and pray to the rice god.

One of the better-known rice planting festivals occurs on June 14 in Osaka where thousands congregate to observe a group of young kimono-clad women plant rice and sing in the sacred fields near the Sumiyoshi Shrine. Working rhythmically to the music, the young women appear to be participating in a dance rather than the hard work of planting.

Lily Festival
June 17

The Lily Festival is a shrine celebration. Lilies are gathered in preparation for the festival and the temple priest offers a bouquet of lilies on the altar. The lilies are then blessed by seven women who wear white robes and perform a special dance. Afterwards, the lilies are mounted on a float and taken out in a procession. The lily dance marks the end of the rainy season, and the paraded lilies signify the purifying of the air.

July

Gion Matsuri
July 17

Gion Matsuri is the best-known festival in Japan and the biggest in Kyoto. It honors Susano-O, the brother of Amatersau (the sun goddess). Many smaller Gion festivals are held in other places throughout Japan in honor of the local kami.

The Gion Matsuri festival began in the year 869 C.E. when hundreds of people died in an epidemic that swept through Kyoto. The head priest of the Gion Shrine, now called the Yasaka Shrine, mounted 66 spears on a portable shrine, took it to the Emperor's garden, and the pestilence ended. In gratitude to the gods, the priest led a procession in the streets. Except for the period of the Onin War (1467–77), which destroyed the city, the procession has been held annually ever since.

There are events related to the festival throughout July but the main event is the parade of elaborate, carefully preserved floats on July 17. These gigantic floats include 29 hoko ("spears") floats and 22 smaller yama ("mountains") floats. The immense hoko weigh as much as 10 tons and can be 30 feet tall; they look like wonderfully ornate towers on wheels. They are decorated with Chinese and Japanese paintings and even with French Gobelin tapestries imported during the 17th and 18th centuries. Just under their lacquered roofs musicians play flutes and drums. From the rooftops of the floats two men toss straw good-luck favors to the crowds. The hoko roll slowly on their big wooden wheels, pulled with ropes by parade participants. Yama floats weigh only about a ton, and are carried on long poles by teams of men. Life-size dolls on platforms atop each float represent characters in the story the float depicts.

October

Ebisu Festival
October 20

The Ebisu Festival honors Ebisu, one of seven Shinto gods of good luck and the patron deity of tradesmen. Although he has a limited following in Tokyo where the shrine is located, a popular fair is held on the preceding day to provide people with items needed to participate in the commemoration. People buy wooden images of Ebisu, good-luck tokens, and large, white, pickled radishs (known as bettara).

November

Shichi-Go-San (Seven-Five-Three Festival)
November 15

This festival, possibly with roots in antiquity when children frequently died at a young age, honors children who have attained the ages of seven, five, and three. The children are attired in special dress (wearing kimonos) and presented at the shrine. There they are purified, and the priest prays to the tutelary deity for their healthy growth. At the end of the ceremony the priest gives each child two little packages: one containing cakes in the form of Shinto emblems (mirror, sword, and jewel), and the other with sacred rice to be mixed with the evening meal. Parents also give other gifts. Afterwards, there are often parties for the children. One custom is the giving of a special pink hard candy, called "thousand-year candy," which symbolizes hopes for a long life. Because Shichi-Go-San is

not a legal holiday in Japan, families observe the ceremony on the Sunday nearest November fifteenth.

December

Omisoka (Year's End)
December 31

The last day of the year serves as a day to prepare for the new year. Home and shrine altars are purified and rededicated. Some people also visit and tend to the graves of their ancestors. By making things clean, the spirits of the kami are honored.

TABLE 15.3. ALPHABETICAL LIST OF SHINTO HOLIDAYS	
Holidays	**Dates**
Aoi Matsuri	May 15
Bean-Throwing Festival *see* Setsubun	
Children's Day	May 5
Ebisu Festival	October 20
Festival of Broken Needles *see* Hari-Kuyo	
Ganjitsu	January 1–3
Gion Matsuri	July 17
Hari-Kuyo	February 8
Hollyhock Festival *see* Aoi Matsuri	
Japanese New Year *see* Ganjitsu	
Kodomo No Hi *see* Children's Day	
Lily Festival	June 17
Omisoka	December 31
Rice Planting Festivals	June 14 or 15
Sanja Matsuri	Weekend near May 18
Setsubun	February 3 or 4
Seven-Five-Three Festival *see* Shichi-Go-San	
Shichi-Go-San	November 15
Three Shrines Festival *see* Sanja Matsuri	
Year's End *see* Omisoka	

CHAPTER 16

Native American Tribal Religions

Overview of Native American Tribal Religions

What Are Tribal Religions?

Native Americans lived in thousands of tribes throughout North and South America. Each had its own religious traditions. Although many elements were shared in common, every tribe employed a unique blend of features that distinguished its faith from that of other tribes. In some instances the dissimilarities were slight; in others, the distinctions were more profound. Variations existed in basic beliefs, mythic content, customs, and ritual ceremonies.

Despite the diversity that existed, some general statements can be made. Most Native American religious systems sought to create or uphold the harmony between people and nature. In addition, many of the religions incorporated similar beliefs about the existence of spirits (especially guardian spirits) and practices related to taboos (prohibitions based on something's sacred status or perceived danger), animal ceremonialism, and shamanism. Many tribes also recognized an Ultimate or Supreme Being who presided over the universe. The Supreme Being was often viewed as distant and not directly involved with the day-to-day affairs of the people and animals who inhabited the earth.

The precise understanding of the Supreme Being varied, however. In some cases, the Supreme Being was viewed as a single deity, in others, as a force comprising more than one expression. One common motif coupled the Supreme Being with a cultural hero, often a legendary benefactor who provided societal knowledge (such as farming techniques) or who functioned as the progenitor of the tribe. Other popular beliefs linked the Supreme Being with a trickster god, typically one with grandiose intentions and a penchant for blunders. For many tribes, the sun was viewed as an expression of the Supreme Being's power. Rituals honoring the sun for this role were frequently mistaken by Europeans as ceremonies in which the sun itself was being worshipped.

In addition to the Supreme Being, other spirits were recognized. The Pueblo Indians of the southwest acknowledged the existence of hundreds of nature spirits called "katchinas." These were spirits of things such as clouds, trees, and rocks. Among the Hopi Indians, katchinas included ancestral and guardian spirits. Other types of spirits included those that presided over weather and those that inhabited animals.

Supernatural experiences, typically manifested as dreams or visions, were another important component of many Native American tribal religions. Such events, thought to originate with the spirits, were interpreted to give guidance to the individual or to the entire tribe. New instructions and innovative practices received through such supernatural channels led to increased diversity in religious expressions. As a result, different practices were sometimes observed even among clans of the same tribe.

Sacred Traditions and Authorities

Sacred Traditions

Native American tribal religions possess no written canonical texts. Native American languages had no writing until the Cherokee language was given a system of written notation by Sequoyah in the 19th century. Histories, myths, and legends were all passed on by oral tradition. Although the accounts of the past carried some authority, they were subject to change and reinterpretation as new visions were received.

Authorities

Depending on the tribe, authority was often shared by a tribal chief and a religious leader. Various types of religious leaders included medicine men, shamans, and specialists in seeing visions.

A medicine man (or sometimes woman) was believed to possess supernatural powers including the ability to heal. In some tribes, medicine men learned their trade from older practitioners and were skilled in using the curative powers found in natural substances. In other tribes the concept of medicine extended to an entire realm of mystic ability beyond the curing of physical disease. Sometimes this involved using trances to identify spirits responsible for diseases or calamities.

Medicine men, and sometimes other people within a tribe or clan, often possessed medicine bundles. The bundles included varying collections of objects believed to wield supernatural power. Items in the bundle varied significantly between tribes and even among individuals within the same tribe but often included ordinary objects such as feathers, bones, teeth, herbs, rocks, and hair. The power of the objects rested in their symbolism, and precise rituals usually governed the opening of a bundle. In some tribes, bundles were passed from one generation to the next; in others, individuals were responsible for collecting and assembling their own bundles.

A shaman operated in a similar fashion to a medicine man, but typically employed more power and focused more attention on supernatural experiences. Spiritual contacts included those made with spirits in other worlds (either subterranean or heavenly) and rituals conducted by or around the shaman were sometimes elaborate. Another feature of shamanism was the experience of spirit journeys in which it was believed that the shaman's spirit left his body and traveled to other places.

Specialists in seeing visions included those who practiced self-deprivation to induce visionary experiences and those who used psychotropic plants. Perhaps the most well-known psychotropic plant is peyote, a type of spineless cactus containing mescaline.

History

The history of Native American cultures dates back thousands of years into prehistoric time. According to many scholars, the people who became the Native Americans migrated from Asia across a land bridge that once connected the territories presently occupied by Alaska and Russia. The migrations, believed to have begun between 60,000 and 30,000 B.C.E. continued until approximately 4,000 B.C.E.

The religions among the early tribal settlers contained some elements similar to those found in other circumpolar groups. For example, many tribes shared creation stories that have parallel elements and a comparable

view of the cosmos. The cosmos was often seen as being layered with the heavens above and the underworld beneath. Although the number of heavens and the number of underworlds varied, the earth was in the middle. The different levels of the cosmos were typically connected by a tree, called the World Tree, which was represented in ceremonies with a pole. In a similar Norse legend, the earth was one of nine worlds, and the nine were connected by a World Tree. Modern followers of Asatru (Northern European Paganism) view the traditional May Pole as a representation of the World Tree (see CHAPTER 17—PAGANISM for a more complete description of Asatru beliefs and practices).

The historical development of religious belief systems among Native Americans is unknown. Most of the information available was gathered by Europeans who arrived on the continent beginning in the sixteenth century C.E. The data they recorded was fragmentary and oftentimes of questionable accuracy. The attempt to collect data was problematic due to two compounding difficulties: the Europeans did not understand the native cultures they were trying to describe, and the Native Americans were reluctant to divulge details about themselves.

Developmental Patterns

Many modern researchers note that religious ideas of individual tribes seem to have been closely related to the means employed to secure food. These included planting crops and hunting animals. Based on this premise, Native American religions can be grouped into two fundamental patterns: religions among agricultural tribes and religions among hunting tribes. Agricultural tribes often focused their attention on rain and crop cycles and ceremonies evolved that were suited for permanent settlements. Among hunting tribes, the religious focus centered on animals and spirits. Ceremonial practices were suited to a nomadic existence. The simple differentiation between hunters and growers helps explain patterns, but in practice many tribes participated in some aspects of both.

Many different tribes participated in Sun Dance ceremonies. Although the specifics varied, the rituals often occurred during the mid-summer months and the events emphasized individual bravery and courage. Among the Plains Indians, the Sun Dance served to reharmonize people with the natural environment (both plant and animal). This was accomplished through ritual participation in a re-telling of the creation myth.

Another common form of religious expression was found in animal ceremonialism, the ritual honoring of an animal that had been killed. The purpose of the ceremony was to appease the animal's spirit. It was most often performed with types of animals that were hunted, especially bears. The people believed that other animals would anticipate similar honors and, therefore, make themselves available.

Various tribes across the American continents believed that masters presided over the spirits of some types of animals. Typically animals with masters included those that served as a food source or that provided other significant benefits. The masters were responsible for controlling hunts and ensuring that hunters were worthy of their quarry. Spirit names and their allied animals varied in different areas. For example, one master of the spirits found among the Inuit Indians (commonly called Eskimos), was a goddess known as Sedna. Sedna, who was part animal and part fish, watched over the sea mammals.

Perhaps one of the religious artifacts most familiar to Europeans was the ceremonial pipe (also called a calumet pipe or peace pipe). Many Native Americans believed the smoke produced by the tobacco in the pipe carried prayers to the spirits. The decoration of the pipe itself also served to convey meaning. White feathers signified peace; red feathers meant war.

Contact with Europeans

The coming of Europeans to the American continents made a pivotal impact on the Native populations. In many cases early European settlers were viewed by Native Americans as a curiosity: European technology was interesting but cultural traditions were confusing. Europeans established themselves in permanent settlements from which movement would be difficult if local resources were depleted. In addition, the newcomers were often unprepared to cooperate with nature and its cycles.

Despite their peculiarities, however, the Europeans proved to be persisting and oppressive neighbors. Sickness (particularly smallpox) and war contributed to the deaths of thousands of Native Americans. Changes in land use caused disruptions in traditional cultural patterns. European notions of religion discounted the value of Native beliefs. Intensive missionary efforts succeeded in converting thousands of Native Americans to Christianity and impacted the faith systems of many thousands more.

In 1799 C.E., a prophet of the Seneca (part of the Iroquois nation), called Handsome Lake (Ganio `Daí Io), called for cultural reform and intertribal cooperation. His message, which serves as the basis for a tradition called Gaiwiio (Good Message), blended aspects of Christianity with traditional Native American concepts. Handsome Lake opposed the drinking of alcohol and sorcery; he advocated family and tribal life. His half-brother, Cornplanter (Kaiiontwa'ko), also advocated temperance and called for the restoration and preservation of Iroquois religious traditions.

Conflicts between Europeans and Native Americans continued. During the early nineteenth century, the newly established United States began implementing the practice of removing Natives from their ancestral lands. The Removal Act of 1830 displaced Native Americans from the Southeast to Oklahoma. The Cherokees, who were removed from their homeland in Georgia, endured a forced march that is remembered as "The Trail of Tears." An estimated 4,000 died as a result of insufficient food supplies, lack of blankets and warm clothing, and illness. Other tribes who were similarly moved from their traditional lands included the Creek, Chickasaw, Chocktaw, and Seminoles.

Persisting Tension

A shift in government policy took place during the late nineteenth century. Instead of segregating Native populations, efforts were made to convince Native Americans to assimilate into White society. Following the passage of the Dawes Act of 1887, Native American children were sent to boarding schools to be re-educated away from tribal influences.

As tensions between Native Americans and Whites escalated, interest among Native Americans in religious traditions increased. Prophecy, revelations, and promises of restored power attracted attention. Several movements, such as the Ghost Dance and peyote cults, became established during the turbulent years of the late nineteenth century.

In 1924, by an act of Congress, Native Americans were granted rights of citizenship in the United States. In 1934, the Indian Reorganization Act encouraged tribes to organize their own governments. By the end of the century, however, many controversial issues between Whites and Native Americans remained unresolved.

Native American Tribal Religions Today

People

Native Americans in the United States at the end of the twentieth century found themselves living in conditions far removed from the traditions of their ancestors. The loss of hunting lands and agricultural grounds resulted in economic collapse. The government policy of confining Native Americans to reservations produced living conditions in which status could not be attained by customary means and where ancient cultural practices were divorced from their relevance.

According to statistics gathered in 1990, an estimated two million Native Americans lived in the United States. Approximately one-third lived on reservations, and about one-half lived in urban centers, often in close proximity to reservations. The U.S. government held more than 55 million acres in trust for use by recognized tribes and other Native American groups. The Trust lands included reservations in 35 states, pueblos, and rancherias. The largest tribal group of Native Americans (in terms of both population and size of reservation) was the Navajo, with more than 100,000 members and over 15 million acres.

Worship

Although many Native Americans turned away from traditional belief systems and converted to Christianity, others preserved the practices of their forefathers. In several places increased pride in native languages and religions emerged to give new vitality to ancient rites. Some Native Americans began to look to their common heritage as indigenous people rather than to the practices of individual tribes.

The form of religious expression most closely associated with the Western concept of worship often took place within the context of a dance ritual. In some dances, participants wore costumes to represent animals or birds. The use of the costumes helped the spirit of the animal being invoked to be made manifest in the person performing the rituals. Things that were acted out represented a type of prayer for specific events.

Another type of ceremonial practice found among many different tribes was the powwow. Powwows featured gatherings during which ceremonies and other community activities were conducted. The purpose often included paying homage to spirits with ritual music and dance. Some powwows were observed at specified times and others were assembled on the basis of need, such as in response to a famine or epidemic.

Although some religious ceremonies took place out-of-doors in consecrated spaces, others occurred in special structures. A variety of temples, shrines, and sacred buildings existed among several tribes. Some Powhatan tribes had temples where dead bodies were kept until the bones were cleansed. In the southeastern region of the United States, some tribes maintained temples for sacred fires that were kept constantly burning.

Among the Delaware, the Big House was a structure used for ceremonies as well as a name for the ceremonies themselves. The four-sided building contained a partial roof that was open in the middle. A large pole, reminiscent of the World Tree and carved with an image depicting the supreme god, extended from the floor through the roof. The walls represented the four compass points, the floor signified the earth, and the opening in the roof was associated with the heavens. Ceremonies included proper circumambulations of the structure's interior.

Another type of sacred structure, called a kiva, was found in the American Southwest among the Pueblo Indians. The kiva was an underground room, cylindrical or rectangular in shape. It served to represent the womb of the earth, out of which men emerged. The walls of a kiva were typically decorated with sacred representations and depictions of everyday village life. The ceremonies that took place within the kiva were performed in secret by selected participants on behalf of the entire tribe.

Revival Movements

Ghost Dance

The Ghost Dance movement began during the late 1800s among the Paiute Indians in California and Nevada. From there it spread to Plains tribes. It was founded by Wovoka, a member of the Paiute tribe, who claimed to have seen God in a vision.

The Ghost Dance movement combined elements from Christianity (specifically, the resurrection of the dead) with traditional elements. It was named for a ceremonial round dance in which dances of the dead were imitated. The ecstatic dancing lasted for four or five days during which participants experienced visions of dead relatives. The purpose of the ceremony was to call the dead back to earth and restore the good times of the past.

The Ghost Dance movement culminated in anti-White sentiments that lead to U.S. military action against the Dakota Sioux Indians and their chief, Sitting Bull, in 1890. Many Indians who believed that wearing special clothing would make them invulnerable to bullets died at Wounded Knee on December 29, 1890. Although the popularity of the Ghost Dance waned when its prophecies remained unfulfilled, the movement led to greater cooperation among Native American tribes of diverse backgrounds.

Pan-Indianism

Pan-Indianism, a movement of the twentieth century, sought to recreate ancient tribal religions into a unified expression. With roots in the Ghost Dance movement, it grew out of an era of domination in an effort to define a shared identity and common expressions from history.

Native American Church

The Native American Church was organized in 1918. It grew out of a movement based on reviving ancient traditions surrounding the use of peyote, a psychotropic cactus that grew in the southwest. The cactus contained mescaline, which produced hallucinations. Rites governing the consumption of peyote were typically conducted at night and lasted for the entire night. The use of peyote among Indians was sometimes viewed as a counter-Christian movement in which peyote replaced Christ as the savior given by God.

The use of peyote became a source of conflict in some areas where local traditions had not previously included it. In many places visions were achieved through extreme personal effort, such as strict fasting, self-injury, and prolonged isolation. The use of peyote produced visions simply and instantaneously.

The Native American Church reported almost one quarter of a million members during the 1970s.

American Indian Movement (AIM)

Organized in 1968 in Minnesota, the American Indian Movement (AIM) began as a militant civil rights group. Its initial motivation was to protest the arrest of Native Americans in Minneapolis and St. Paul under conditions seen as discriminatory. Since its inception, the group's perspective broadened to include a religious aspect. By the 1980s, participation in a Sun Dance ritual was required of members, and membership totaled 5,000.

Bald Eagle: Many North American Indians associate the eagle with supernatural powers, particularly the power to control thunder and rain.

Seasonal Cycles

Among Native American tribes, time was viewed as a cyclical rather than a linear phenomenon. Instead of beginning at a point in the distant past and progressing toward culmination, time was understood as an extension of the repetitive patterns in nature.

In Mesoamerica, the Mayan and Aztec societies developed a sophisticated calendar for tracking time periods analogous to weeks and months as well as ceremonial cycles, solar years, and longer 52-year units. The Mayan Long Count Calendar extended to more than 5,000 years.

In North America, however, the use of calendars did not develop (or at least it was not known; native populations often kept sacred information secret from Europeans). Although time periods such as days, months, seasons, and years were recognized, they were not interrelated. They were merely counted and tracked independently.

The period of a day, a single cycle of daylight and night, was observed as a basic unit, but there is no historical evidence that days were named. Months were recognized as a cycle of the moon's phases. These often began at the new moon, but among some tribes, moons were reckoned based on the moon's position relative to the sun. The days of the month were sometimes counted in a progression leading to the full moon and then to the next new moon. One device for counting the days of the month was to relate each day to a specific body part (joint or bone) from the small finger of the right hand, up to the head (at the full moon), and then in reverse order down the left side until the next new moon.

The counting of seasons was typically related to changes in weather patterns rather than the passing of moons. The number of seasons varied between four and five.

Years were marked by the cycling of seasons, not by a fixed number of days. Some tribes counted the passing of twelve moons in a year, and a few tribes practiced intercalating a moon at different times. The Zuni Indians (New Mexico) used names for the moons. The first six were colors; the second six were directions.

Despite the consistency in recognizing the basic cycle of a year, its beginning was observed at different times in different areas. The equinoxes (vernal or autumnal) were used in some places. Among the Hopi, the new year began in November. The Creek Indians began their new year in the summer, but the precise date varied among individual settlements.

Time-Keeping Artifacts

One of the most basic devices for keeping track of time consisted of bundles of sticks. Each bundle contained a specified number of sticks, one of which could be removed on a daily basis. These types of bundles served to count down days until an event.

Notched sticks were sometimes employed to mark years after an important incident. These were most often used as mnemonic devices for recalling events in a series for story-telling, however, instead of counting.

Pictographs used by some tribes also marked the passing of years. One of the best known objects of this kind is a buffalo robe that begins in the year 1800 C.E. and is marked for 71 years.

Some tribes used devices called medicine wheels to trace the path of the sunrises and sunsets along the horizon. The wheels, made of stone and placed in a circle, were used as a type of calendar to determine certain significant dates with an astronomical basis, such as the summer solstice.

The Ceremonial Cycles

Although traditional calendars were not used, ceremonial cycles were often related to the patterns observed during the solar year. The Tewa (a Southwestern Pueblo people) ceremonial calendar consisted of two parts identified as winter and summer. Each part governed half of the year. The Tewa society was similarly divided into two units, called moieties. One moiety was identified with the winter cycle and the other with the summer cycle. The chief of each moiety ruled for half of the year. Within each half-year cycle, a progressive series of rituals served to bring supernatural assistance to the seasonal work being performed.

The Kwakiutl (inhabitants of the Pacific Northwest) also divided the year into two halves. During the summer half of the year (called basux) time was spent hunting and fishing. The people lived in isolated spots dispersed across broad territories and had little opportunity for contact. The winter, viewed as the opposite of summer, was called tsetseqa. It was marked by the return of the people to their village homes and the performance of many ceremonies. Often rituals focused on creation myths and the honoring of animal spirits (from whom people were believed to have descended).

The Hopi Indians also observed a ceremonial calendar in which the year was divided into two parts. During one half of the year the katchinas (nature, ancestral, and guardian spirits) lived in the village and revealed themselves to the people through ceremonial dances. During the other half of the year, the katchinas separated themselves from the village and returned to live in their homes in the mountains.

TABLE 16.2. NATIVE AMERICAN HOLIDAY CYCLE	
January	
10	Iroquois White Dog Feast
Winter	Kwakiutl Winter Ceremonial
24	Alacita (Aymara)
February	
16 days	Powamu Festival (Hopi)
March	
Early Spring . .	Eagle Dance (many tribes)
May	
Memorial Day Weekend . . .	Ute Bear Dance
June	
~	Strawberry Festival (Iroquois)
Late June	Sun Dance (Sioux and many others)
July	
3–7	Seminole Green Corn Dance
26	Niman Dance (Hopi)
August	
Middle to late August	Flute Ceremony (Hopi)
Middle to late August	Snake-Antelope Dance (Hopi)
Late Summer . .	Creek Green Corn Ceremony
September	
Late September .	Lakon (Hopi)
October	
First weekend .	Shiprock Navajo Nation Fair
November	
Eve of the new moon . .	Wuwuchim (Hopi)
Late Nov. or early Dec. . .	Shalako Ceremonial (Pueblo)
December	
Winter Solstice .	Soyal (Hopi)
December 21 . .	Guatemalan Winter Solstice (Mayan)

The symbol ~ indicates a variable date.

Native American Holidays

January

Iroquois White Dog Feast (Iroquois Midwinter Ceremony; Great Feather Dance)
January 10

The White Dog Feast was the traditional midwinter ceremony of the Iroquois Indians in Canada and the United States. It signified renewal for the tribe during the midwinter months and marked the Iroquois New Year. The festival was dedicated to Teharonhiawagon, the Master of Life. It was based on the belief that the sacrifice of a dog and an offering of tobacco were necessary to ensure the return of spring and the rebirth of life. A white dog was strangled so that no blood was shed or bones broken. It was decorated with ribbons, feathers, and red paint and hung from a cross-pole for four days. On the fifth day, it was taken down and carried to the longhouse or assembly hall, where it was placed on the altar and burned. A basket containing tobacco was also thrown on the fire, its smoke rising as incense.

The Great Feather Dance was performed on the sixth day as a way of giving thanks to the Creator for the crops. The False Face Dance, during which a pair of masked "uncles" would visit Iroquois homes and scatter ashes, was also performed during the White Dog Feast. Ashes were also blown directly on sick people in a curing ritual.

Kwakiutl Winter Ceremonial
Winter

The Kwakiutl people live along the western coast of the North American continent between Vancouver (Canada) and Alaska (United States). The winter season includes many rituals based on legendary events that occurred during the creation of the universe. Dances, masks and costumes evoke images of life, wealth, and death.

Alacitas
January 24

In South America (Bolivia) the Aymara people honor their god of prosperity, Ekeko, with a fair. Ekeko is depicted as a little man with a big belly, an open mouth, outstretched arms, and wearing a backpack. Miniature replicas of Ekeko are sold, as well as miniature items of food, clothing, and other goods that the Aymaras would like to have. They believe that if they fill one of Ekeko's packs with these miniature objects, he will bring them the real things they represent. The name from the fair is derived from the word meaning "buy me."

February

Powamu Festival
Sixteen days beginning after the new moon in February

The Powamu festival is celebrated annually by the Hopi Indians who live at the Walpi Pueblo in northeastern Arizona. It commemorates the final step in creation and serves to purify the year to come. The entire observance lasts sixteen days; eight days are dedicated to preparation and eight days are dedicated to rituals.

The Hopi Indians believe that for six months of the year ancestral spirits called the katchinas leave their mountain homes and visit the tribe, bringing health to the people and rain for their crops. During the Powamu Festival, the Hopi people celebrate the entry of the Sky Father (also known as the Sun God) into the pueblo by dramatizing the event. The Sky Father, represented by a man wearing a circular mask surrounded by feathers and horsehair with a curved beak in the middle, is led into the pueblo from the east at sunrise. There he visits the house and kiva (underground chamber used for religious and other ceremonies) of the chief, performing certain ceremonial rites and exchanging symbolic gifts.

March

Eagle Dance
Early spring

Many North American Indians associate the eagle with supernatural powers, particularly the power to control thunder and rain. In the Jemez and Tesuque pueblos in New Mexico, the eagle dance takes place in the early spring. Two dancers, representing male and female, wear feathered caps with yellow beaks and hold wings made out of eagle feathers. They circle each other with hopping and swaying motions. The Comanches hold an eagle dance where a single dancer imitates the eagle, who according to legend is the young son of a chieftain who was turned into an eagle when he died. Dancers in the Iowa tribe's eagle dance carry an eagle feather fan in their left hands, while the Iroquois eagle dance features feathered rattles and wands. Among some tribes, eagle feathers are believed to exert special powers. The Sioux wear them in their war bonnets for victory, while the Pawnee, Yuchi,

Delaware, and Iroquois Indians use them in ceremonial fans or brushes or as ornaments.

May

Ute Bear Dance
May, Memorial Day weekend

The Ute Bear Dance has its roots in an ancient ceremony of the Southern Ute Indians. Originally the ritual was held in late February or early March, at the time of the bears' awakening from their hibernation. It stemmed from the belief that the Utes were descended from bears, and the dance was given both to help the bears coming out of hibernation and to gain power from them, since bears were believed to cure sickness and to communicate with people in the Spirit World. Today the dance is largely a social occasion and it is held on the Sunday and Monday of Memorial Day weekend in Ignacio, Colorado.

June

Strawberry Festival
Strawberry time (typically June)

The Strawberry Festival is one of several annual festivals held by Iroquois Indians. The people congregate at Tonawanda, N.Y., in their longhouse to hear a lengthy recitation of the words of the Seneca prophet Handsome Lake (Ganio `Daí Io; 1735–1815) calling for cooperative farming, abstention from hard drink, abandonment of witchcraft and magic, the prohibition of abortion, and other instructions. This prophecy forms the basis of today's Longhouse religion.

Following the recitations and speeches are ceremonial dances accompanied by chants and the pounding of turtle-shell rattles. Lunch follows, with a strawberry drink and strawberry shortcake. The Iroquois say "you will eat strawberries when you die," because strawberries line the road to heaven.

Other traditional Iroquois celebrations are a New Year festival, a Maple Dance held at the time of making maple syrup and sugar, a Planting Festival, and the Green Corn Dance, at which the principal dish is succotash, made not just with corn and lima beans but also with squash and venison or beef.

Sun Dance
Late June

The Sun Dance is primarily a festival of thanksgiving during which the participants offer thanks for animals and the harvest. In many areas it is observed in conjunction with the summer solstice but in other places it is timed to coincide with the harvest.

Although many North American Indian tribes hold ritual dances in honor of the sun and its life-giving powers, the Sioux were known to hold one of the most spectacular. Usually performed during the Summer Solstice, preparations for the dance included the cutting and raising of a tree that would be considered a visible connection between the heavens and earth, and the setting up of tepees in a circle to represent the cosmos. Participants abstained from food and drink during the dance itself, which lasted from one to four days, and decorated their bodies in the symbolic colors of red (sunset), blue (sky), yellow (lightning), white (light), and black (night). They wore deerskin loincloths, wristlets and anklets made out of rabbit fur, and carried an eagle wing bone whistle in their mouths. The dance often involved self-laceration or hanging themselves from the tree-pole with their feet barely touching the ground. Sometimes the dancers fell unconscious or tore themselves loose, which was considered evidence that they had experienced a vision. After the dance, they were allowed to have a steam bath, food, and water.

Another group with a Sun Dance tradition is the Southern Ute tribe (in Ignacio, Colorado) whose annual two-day ritual is held beginning on the Sunday following July 4. The dancers who perform the ceremony are chosen from those who dream dreams and see visions. They fast for four days before the dance. One aspect of the ceremony involves chopping down a tree, stripping its bark and then dancing around it. Although the Sun Dance as performed by most Plains tribes usually incorporated self-torture, the Utes do not have such a practice.

July

Seminole Green Corn Dance
July 3–7

This four-day festival is observed by the Seminole Indians in the Florida Everglades region. It serves as a ritual to welcome the new year. The celebration includes feasting and traditional games. Dances include the catfish dance and the alligator dance. On the evening of the third day the Green Corn Dance is performed to give thanks for the harvest.

Niman Dance
July 26

The Niman dance is a summer-time ritual marking the home-going of the "katchinas" (mountain-dwelling, supernatural beings who are believed to live among the Hopi people from mid-winter to mid-summer). The ceremony honoring their departure serves to bring health and rain. Up to 75 dancers representing the katchinas spend an entire day singing and dancing. Children receive traditional gifts: Kachina dolls given to girls, and boys receive bows and arrows and rattles.

August

Flute Ceremony
Middle to late August

The Flute Ceremony is held once every two years by the Hopi people. Its observance alternates with the Snake-Antelope ceremony. It begins with a procession and concludes with flute music and song. The timing of the ceremony serves to commemorate the sun's journey to its summer home. Its purpose is to help the crops reach maturity and to bring rain.

Snake-Antelope Dance
Middle to late August

Among the Hopi Indians, the Snake-Antelope Dance is held in alternate years during the last dry week in August. It occurs over a period of several days during which snakes are gathered, bathed in a solution made from the yucca plant, and blessed. The purpose of the dance is to help bring rain.

The dance begins when the Snake and Antelope priests come out of the kiva (a special ceremonial room) where secret rituals are held, and perform a dance around the enclosure where the snakes are confined. Then they divide into groups of three, each consisting of a carrier, a hugger, and a gatherer. The carrier takes a snake in his mouth, the hugger puts his left hand on the carrier's shoulder, and the gatherer does the same thing to the hugger. Together they circle the area four times. Then the carrier releases the snake and the gatherer retrieves it. Eventually the snakes are set free so that they can carry out their mission and summon the rain.

Snake dances are common among Indian tribes, and vestiges of this ceremony can still be seen at the Zuni, Acoma, and Cochiti pueblos.

Creek Green Corn Ceremony
Late summer

The Muskogee-Creek Indians observe a religious harvest festival, not open to the public, in late summer on the ceremonial grounds in Okmulgee, Oklahoma. Each tribal group conducts its own Green Corn Ceremony on one of 12 such Creek ceremonial grounds in the state.

The dances for the ceremony are performed to the rhythm of turtle and gourd rattles. Women are designated "shell-shakers," and they dance in groups of four with shells (or sometimes today with juice cans filled with pebbles) around their ankles. Children are included in ceremonies from infancy as women dancers with babies carry them into the ceremonial circle. One dance, known as the ribbon dance, honors women and is performed only by women and girls.

Other elements of the festival are stickball games and cleansing ceremonies, but the affair is essentially religious. To worship the Great Spirit, Creeks perform rituals relating to wind, fire, water, and earth.

September

Lakon
Late September

Lakon is the most important of three harvest ceremonials performed among the Hopi people. (The other two are called Marawu and Owaqlt.) Ritual activities are done primarily by women and the rites serve to remind the people that life is temporary and that they must comply with the Creator's plans.

Preparations for Lakon begin during the planting time of year when designated women and one man (chosen to perform ceremonial tasks that only men are permitted to do) enter the kiva (special ceremonial room). There they fast, pray, and sing for eight days. The observance of Lakon concludes with another eight-day ritual held at harvest time, the precise dates are determined by the position of the sun.

October

Shiprock Navajo Nation Fair
Usually the first weekend of October

Also known as the Northern Navajo Fair, this harvest fair began in 1924 and is considered the oldest and most traditional of Navajo fairs.

The fair coincides with the end of an ancient nine-day Navajo healing ceremony called the Night Chant. The rituals involved in the Night Chant are complex and only portions are open to public attendance.

Other events of the fair include an all-Indian rodeo and inter-tribal powwow, a livestock show, a carnival, the Miss Northern Navajo Pageant, exhibits by Indian artisans, and a parade on Saturday morning.

November

Wuwuchim
Eve of the new moon in November

Wuwuchim is the new year for Hopi Indians. Observed by the Hopi people in northeastern Arizona, it is the most significant of the Hopi rituals because it serves to establish the rhythms for the year to come.

Over a four-day period, priests offer prayers, songs, and dances for a prosperous and safe new year. Other traditions include dances performed by men of the tribe costumed in embroidered kilts. Their dance is accompanied by the creation-myth chants of priests from the Bear Clan.

Shalako Ceremonial
Late November or early December

The Pueblo Indians at the Zuni Pueblo in southwestern New Mexico celebrate this impressive ceremonial dance in the fall of each year. Intended to commemorate the dead and entreat the gods for good health and weather in the coming year, the ceremony involves all-night ritual dances and chants, and the blessing of houses. The dance features towering masked figures with beaks who represent the rainmaker's messengers. Moving from house to house through the Pueblo, the dancers make clacking noises to indicate the houses receiving blessings. They stop at the designated houses, remove their masks, perform chants, and share food with the inhabitants. Others taking part in the ceremony represent rain gods, whip-carrying warriors, and the fire god.

December

Soyal
On or about the Winter Solstice; determined by solar observation

Among the Hopi Indians, the Soyal period was observed for the purpose of helping the sun turn from its departure and begin its return. The rituals associated with Soyal were held in the kiva (ceremonial rooms) and marked by fasting and silence.

Guatemalan Winter Solstice (Palo Voladore)
December 21

In Guatemala, Mayan Indians honor the sun god they worshipped long before they became Christians with a dangerous ritual known as the *palo voladore*, or "flying pole dance." Three men climb to the top of a 50-foot pole. As one of them beats a drum and plays a flute, the other two each wind a long rope attached to the pole around one foot and jump. If they land on their feet, it is believed that the sun god will be pleased and that the days will start getting longer.

TABLE 16.2. ALPHABETICAL LIST OF NATIVE AMERICAN HOLIDAYS	
Holidays	**Dates**
Alacitas (Aymara)	January 24
Creek Green Corn Ceremony	Late summer
Eagle Dance (many tribes)	Early spring
Flute Ceremony (Hopi)	Mid to late August
Great Feather Dance *see* Iroquois White Dog Feast	
Guatemalan Winter Solstice	December 21
Iroquois Midwinter Ceremony *see* Iroquois White Dog Feast	
Iroquois White Dog Feast	January 10
Kwakiutl Winter Ceremonial	Winter
Lakon (Hopi)	Late September
Niman Dance (Hopi)	July 26
Palo Voladore *see* Guatemalan Winter Solstice	
Powamu Festival (Hopi)	Sixteen days beginning after the new moon in February
Seminole Green Corn Dance	July 3–7
Shalako Ceremonial (Pueblo)	Late November or early December
Shiprock Navajo Nation Fair	Usually the first weekend of October
Snake-Antelope Dance (Hopi)	Mid to late August
Soyal (Hopi)	On or about the Winter Solstice
Strawberry Festival (Iroquois)	Strawberry time
Sun Dance (Sioux and others)	Late June
Ute Bear Dance	Memorial Day weekend
Wuwuchim (Hopi)	Eve of the new moon in November

CHAPTER 17

Paganism

Overview

What Is Paganism?

The term Paganism covers a variety of religions that share some common elements. These include nature worship, magic and divination, a belief in some kind of reincarnation, and a reverence for Goddesses and Gods (who may be viewed as abstract qualities or as literally existing). Most commonly these deities are drawn from the Celtic, Germanic, Norse, Greco-Roman, and Egyptian pantheons. For example, the Greek nature god Pan serves as a prototype for the Pagan Horned God; and Gaia, the Greek female spirit of the earth, becomes Mother Earth.

Modern pagan practices revive and reconstruct rituals based on interpretations of ancient mythologies. Although the rituals vary and individual groups may use different names, most pagans share a common set of eight holidays: the winter solstice; the spring equinox; the summer solstice; the fall equinox; and four days marking the midpoints between the solstices and equinoxes (traditionally February 1; May 1, August 1, and November 1).

Magic is one of the most basic elements of Paganism. Pagans believe that the visible world is only part of the world and that events in the unseen realm can impact the visible world. This type of interaction takes the form of receiving messages from the other world and employing its power.

The best known types of Pagans are Wiccans, Druids, the Asatru (consisting of Odinists and followers of other Northern European traditions), and Goddess Worshipers. Of these, the Wiccans probably have the greatest numbers. The groups, however, are not all mutually exclusive and practitioners in one may also be practitioners in another.

Authorities and Sacred Writings

The basic tenets of Paganism are typically taught by experience rather than authority. Different groups of pagans relate to authority in different ways. Among Wiccans it is common for the High Priestess to be considered as one among equals rather than as one with superior status. Typically, each coven operates independently in a democratic fashion. Other groups have a more clearly delineated line of prominence, but there is no one ultimate authority for all Pagans.

The types and kinds of writings held in esteem by Pagan groups and the level of that esteem vary. These may include official collections of ancient myths and a *Grimoire* (book of ceremonial magic). A group's *Grimoire* may be codified in a precise form or exist as an informal guideline. Two groups, each called The Odinic Rite, exemplify the difference. One group possesses *The Book of Blots* containing the final, authoritative version of all ceremonies; the other possess *The Book of Blotar of the Odinic Rite* which contains guidelines for rituals and other ceremonies. In Wicca, the *Book of Shadows*, includes rites, spells, chants, dances, and other elements of the religion, but there is no one definitive version of the *Book of Shadows*. In some Wiccan covens, each member compiles her or his own personal book.

Other subjects addressed in contemporary Pagan books include theology, ancient artifacts, Runes, and myths. These books, although not canonical, help individual pagans understand the complex interactions between themselves and the religious path they follow.

The History of Paganism

The history of modern paganism has been debated both within the Pagan community and outside it. Some claim that its traditions have been preserved by clandestine pagan groups and handed down secretly through generations of Christian dominion; they see folk customs and tales as being vestiges of a long religious heritage. Others suggest that the "ancient traditions" are twentieth century constructions for which folk customs and tales have provided inspiration for the imagination.

Whether Paganism is a continuation of an ancient religion or a modern innovation, events in European history helped produce a culture able to accept it as an alternate to mainstream religion in the middle and late twentieth century.

Historical Evidence

Researchers believe that ancient British society included people who were perceived as being exceptionally wise or who possessed healing powers. These people may have served their community in a capacity similar to that of a priest or priestess by overseeing spiritual events, like births, weddings, and funerals. Or, they may have served their communities in a more secular role, similar to that of a doctor. The historical record does not provide evidence that they worshiped the deities worshiped by modern Pagans. Nevertheless, modern Pagans (sometimes referred to as neopagans) view these ancient wise ones as their forbearers.

In the early centuries of the Common Era (C.E.), old religious practices were lost as Christianity gained political power and spread through northern Europe. In some instances, the old blended with the new. In other instances, the new persecuted the old and drove it either underground or to extinction.

One of the most perplexing issues in Pagan history relates to the European witch trials (1450–1700 C.E.). The witch trials, historically well-documented, are events that certainly occurred. But the question, "Who was burned?" lacks a definitive answer. Some historians have argued that the unfortunates were practitioners of an ancient pagan religion. Others believe that the "witches" who were burned were innocents selected for political or hysterical reasons.

Irrespective of which view most accurately described the historical event, several popular books on witchcraft written during the late nineteenth and early twentieth century asserted that actual witches had been burned. These witches were said to have been followers of an ancient religion that worshipped a female deity.

Magical Societies

In addition to popular belief in a goddess-based type of witchcraft, growing interest in magic and the occult also played a part in paving the way for modern Paganism.

The desire to control nature by magic and to manipulate events to one's own benefit has long been part of human history. In many cultures, legends of individual magicians can be found. In addition, several religions have magical offshoots, such as the Qabbalah. (Qabbalah is a form of mystical Judaism with roots in the early Christian era that became popular during the thirteenth century in Spain. Its followers use magic to achieve knowledge of God.)

Beginning with the seventeenth century, however, magical groups began to form. These magical societies included Rosicrucians, an occult group formed to impart secret wisdom, and Freemasons, a secret fraternal order established during the early 1700s from a consolidation of old stonecutters guilds. By the dawn of the twentieth century, many of these groups were operating with multiple levels of initiation into ritual practices and secrets, similar to modern Wiccan covens.

Poets and Other Authors

At the same time interest in magic increased, literary figures turned their attention to Pagan images. These included Robert Burns (Scottish poet, 1759–96), John Keats (English poet 1795–1821), and William Butler Yeats (Irish poet and dramatist 1865–1939). Drawing on ancient legend and cultural symbols, such writers found fertile ground with fairies and giants and other supernatural beings. They glorified pagan images, sometimes in opposition to Christian conventions or governmental authorities. The popularity of their ideas helped usher in a cultural atmosphere ready for magic and sexual freedom, two of the major components of modern Paganism.

The Beginnings of Modern Druidry and Wicca

The two most commonly known modern Pagan groups, Wicca and Druidry, can trace their beginnings to specific people and events. Revivals of Druidry began during the 18th century among Christians who saw Druids as monotheistic decedents from one of the Lost Tribes of Israel. The Ancient Order of Druids was founded in London in 1781. As societal interest turned to the occult and the patriarchal tendencies of the first Druid revivalists were softened, Druidry emerged as a Pagan religion.

Gerald Gardner is recognized as a founder or a cofounder of Wicca. Gardner, a Freemason, Rosicrucian, spiritualist, and a leader in the Druid order, published the first Wiccan publication in 1949. In 1951, when the remaining laws against witchcraft in Britain were repealed, the way for the current Wiccan revival was opened.

Paganism Today

In the 1960s, the movement became more organized and open to the public, which led to a surge in popularity during the 1980s when regional and national festivals were held that attracted hundreds and sometimes thousands of participants. Charlotte Hardman, one of the co-authors of *Paganism Today* (Thorson, 1995) estimates that the number of pagans in the United States is between 50,000 and 100,000 and the number in the United Kingdom is somewhere between 30,000 and 50,000.

According to some observers, the increasing popularity of Pagan religions may be tied to the effects of increased urbanization. As people become more and more inhabitants of cities, they long for the simpler times and have a deep desire to become re-connected with the things of nature.

Nature plays a central role in Pagan rites. Modern Pagan ritual ceremonies often take place within the context of a circle. This is typically done outside when circumstances permit. Among some groups being out of doors and in direct contact with the ground is essential, for others it is optional. The circle itself may be physically drawn or symbolically represented. The sacred items and symbols present will vary depending on the goddess(es) or god(s) being honored, the season, and the needs of the group.

Wiccans

Wiccans, known as witches, honor the Goddess (frequently identified with the earth). They celebrate according to the phases of the moon and typically conduct their rituals under the moon (ie., at night). Many Wiccan rites are private and open only to the attendance of the initiated. Initiation is done by degrees: first degree, second degree and third degree. Most often initiates must undergo specific training and wait a year and a day between the levels of initiation into the deeper mysteries of the craft.

The annual Wiccan holiday cycle is patterned after the human life cycle. The Great Mother Goddess and her consort, called the Horned God, give birth to the Divine Child of the new year at the winter solstice. At Beltane (or May Day) the Sacred Marriage and sexual union of the Goddess and God is celebrated. The deity dies at Mabon (the autumnal equinox) to be reborn at the winter solstice.

The Wiccan year is divided into two segments. During one, the Goddess presides; during the other the God rules. The Goddess is referred to as the triple goddess and she manifests herself in three attributes: as the beautiful young woman; the mother; and the old hag or crone. The Horned God manifests himself in different aspects depending on the season of the year. As the Holly King, he represents the death aspect; as the Oak King he represents the aspect of rebirth.

Druids

Although Druids hold many things in common with Wiccans their celebrations are more closely tied to the sun. Their festivals are conducted during the day where the sun serves as a symbol of spiritual light. Some Druids conduct their rites in private but many are public.

Like the Wiccan holiday cycle, the annual cycle within Druidry typically follows a human life pattern. For example, the British Druid Order follows the mythical story of Lleu Llaw Gyffes who was born at the Winter Solstice, named at Candlemas, and armed at the Spring Equinox. His bride-to-be, Blodeuedd, was created on the Eve of May. The Summer solstice marked the zenith of his power. Lleu Llaw Gyffes married Blodeuedd on Lammas and died at the hands of the Lord of Winter on Samhain, his spirit to be reborn again at the Winter Solstice.

The Asatru

The Asatru include groups that honor Northern European deities (Germanic and Scandinavian). Groups that specifically honor the God Odin are referred to as Odinists. They tend to be ecologically concerned and some distinguish themselves from other Pagan groups because they do not use an altar to separate themselves from the ground during their worship rituals.

Within the Asatru, some groups follow the traditional primary eight Pagan holidays. Others, however, do not. Instead they observe the solstices and equinoxes (four in total) along with other specified monthly festivals.

Goddess Worshippers

Goddess worship involves the veneration of a Goddess who is manifest in many forms. It differs from other Pagan groups who esteem both goddesses and gods.

Goddess worshippers follow the annual cycle of death and rebirth as depicted in the mythological story of Persephone (also called Kore) and her mother, Demeter. In the story Persephone is taken to be the wife of the God of the underworld—symbolic of her death—and her mother, grief-stricken, withholds fruitfulness from the world. A bargain is struck and Persephone walks on the world for six months during which the earth blooms. She returns to the underworld for six months and the earth suffers autumn and winter, awaiting rebirth in the spring.

⬧ ⬧ ⬧

The Pagan Calendar

Lunar and Solar Cycles

Pagan groups observe both lunar and solar cycles. For convenience, these are typically reconciled to the western civil calendar either by re-naming the twelve months (January through December) or by observing 13 lunar months and overlapping the beginning and ending moon where necessary.

The first month or moon of the year varies among the different groups. One of the most commonly used starting points of the year is the winter solstice—a time when the waning sun yields to the waxing sun. Other dates used as starting points include the spring equinox (when the growing season begins) and Samhain (a time when the death that leads to new life is celebrated).

Pagans claim one of the oldest calendar systems. The assertion is based on an artifact estimated to be 30,000 years old—a piece of bone with holes arranged in a manner suggesting counting in a series of sevens. The sequence may represent three cycles of the moon's phases from new to full, the approximate equivalent of a season.

Days

The measure of a day varies among modern pagan groups. Some prefer the common practice of beginning and ending a day at midnight. Others follow the example from ancient Greece and begin the day at dawn. For others, the day begins at sunset.

The way a day is determined affects the celebration of some festivals. In groups that celebrate a day beginning at sundown a holiday (day) and its eve (night before) will be seen as a single festival that was conceived on the eve, underwent gestation during the night and was fully birthed at dawn. For those who see the day beginning at midnight or dawn, the eve (or day before a festival) may be thought of as separate festival or as part of a two-day event.

Because of the relationship between some rituals, their magic, and events in nature, local time can be an important element. For example, the exact moment of sunrise or noon will vary depending on a locality's longitude. In some Pagan groups, awareness of the precise local time is important. In others, festivals and rituals are held when convenient at a time close to an astronomical event, such as delaying the celebration of a solstice until the weekend.

The Wheel of the Year

For most Pagans, the concept of the Wheel of the Year describes the turning of day to day, moon to moon, and season to season in a cycle that is continually repeated. Within the cycle some days are set aside as notable days. Similar to the notable days of many other religions, some of these days are "fixed" (that is they occur on the same calendar date every year) and some are "moveable" (their date of observance changes).

A common set of eight major notable days, called Sabbats, are shared by many Pagan groups. These Sabbats consist of four movable days, called Quarter Days, and four fixed days, called Cross-Quarter Days. The Quarter Days occur in conjunction with the sun's movements. (They are celebrated on the winter solstice, spring equinox, summer solstice, and autumn equinox.) The Cross-Quarter Days occur at the midpoints between the Quarter Days. (They are celebrated on February 1, May 1, August 1 and November 1.) The Sabbats of prime importance differ from group to group. In general, the quarter days tend to be more important to solar-dominated (ie., male) groups, such as Druids and Odinists. The cross-quarter days are more important to lunar-oriented (ie., female) groups, such as Wiccans and Goddess Worshipers.

Although most modern Pagan groups observe the Sabbats, they are known by different names. Table 17.1 presents some of the most familiar names for the celebrations.

The Lunar Cycles

In addition to observing the Sabbats, many groups within modern paganism also observe celebrations in conjunction with the moon. In Wiccan circles, lunar observances are called Esbats.

Within the solar year there are approximately 13 lunar cycles. Some Pagan groups observe the full moon;

TABLE 17.1. COMMON NAMES FOR THE EIGHT PAGAN SABBATS

Sabbat	Occurs
Yule	Winter solstice
Imbolg (or Brigid)	February 1
Ostara	Spring equinox
Beltane (or May Day)	May 1
Litha (or Midsummer)	Summer solstice
Lammas (or Lughnasadh)	August 1
Mabon	Autumnal equinox
Samhain	November 1

others observe the new moon (when no moon is visible). Because the lunar and solar cycles do not precisely coincide, a specific solar calendar may contain 12 full moons and 13 new moons, or 13 full moons and 12 full moons.

There are three commonly employed methods of reconciling the discrepancy between the lunar and solar cycles. For some the choice of celebrating a moon when it is new or full changes from year to year depending on which will yield 13 celebrations. For others, the last new or full moon may also be celebrated as the first. The third method moves the celebration of the 13th moon (when necessary) to a designated date prior to the winter solstice irrespective of the actual phase of the moon.

Various Calendar Systems

The Celtic Tree Calendar

One of the most popular calendar systems employed by modern Pagan groups is the Celtic Tree Calendar, developed by Robert Graves in the 1950s. Graves, in his *White Goddess*, presents a Tree Calendar (Table 17.2.), based on the eighteen-letter Gaelic alphabet. These are known as the Ogham runes and they are made with a pattern of slash marks either vertically or horizontally across or beside a base line. They represent thirteen consonants and five vowels. The thirteen consonants (B, L, N, F, S, H, D, T, C, M, Ng, G, and R) each correspond with a lunar month and its associated tree. The five vowel runes (A, O, E, U, and I) represent five seasons termed Rebirth, Spring, Summer, Autumn, and Death.

Graves's calendar uses the thirteen consonants of the tree alphabet as names of months and the five vowels as markers of quarter days. This configuration creates a calendar of thir teen 28-day months, plus an extra day (two in leap years) to make up the 365 days of a year. Although there is no plausible evidence that any such calendar was ever in general use in ancient Britain, it has been adopted by the Pagan movement and Pagan playwrights have composed special dramas based on the symbolism of the tree calendar for use in the celebration of their eight Sabbats.

The Asatru Calendar

Members of pagan groups worshipping the Northern European deities grouped together under the label Asatru. Asatru years are counted from the time Odin received the Runes; 1997 C.E. (Common Era) is equivalent to 2247 R.E. (Runic Era). Month names of the Asatru are shown in Table 17.3.

The Goddess Calendar

The Goddess Worshippers observe an annual progression of 13 months named in honor of various goddesses. The year begins after the Winter Solstice. The sequence of months is shown in Table 17.4.

TABLE 17.2.
THE CELTIC TREE CALENDAR

Date	Tree Calendar Month
December 23	Day of the Yew and Silver Fir (vowels: Idha, Yew; Alim, Silver Fir)
December 24	First day of the Birch (Rune: Beth)
January 21	First day of the Rowan (Luis)
February 18	First day of the Ash (Nion)
March 18	First day of the Alder (Fearn)
March 21	Day of the Furze (also known as Gorse) (vowel: Onn)
April 15	First day of the Willow (Saille)
May 13	First day of the Hawthorn (Huath)
June 10	First day of the Oak (Duir)
June 22	Day of the Heather (vowel: Ura)
July 8	First day of the Holly (Tinne)
August 5	First day of the Hazel (Coll)
September 2	First day of the Vine (Quert)
September 22	Day of the Aspen (vowel Eadha)
September 30	First day of the Ivy (Gort)
October 28	First day of the Reed (Ngetal)
November 25	First day of the Elder (Ruis)

TABLE 17.3.
THE ASATRU CALENDAR

Gregorian Month Name	Asatru Month Name
January	Snowmoon
February	Horning
March	Lenting
April	Ostara
May	Merrymoon
June	Fallow
July	Haymoon
August	Harvest
September	Shedding
October	Hunting
November	Fogmoon
December	Wolfmoon

TABLE 17.4.
THE GODDESS CALENDAR

Month Names	Approximate Gregorian Equivalents
Hestia	December/January
Birdhe	January/February
Moura	February/March
Columbina	March/April
Maia	April/May
Hera	May/June
Rosea	May/June/July
Kerea	June/July
Hseperis	July/August
Mala	August/September
Hathor	September/October
Cailleach	October/November
Astrea	November/December

Maypole: Dancing around the Maypole has heralded the beginning of spring for centuries. It remains a popular tradition associated with Beltane.

Pagan Holidays
Monthly

Esbats

Full moon of each month; sometimes at the new moon and sometimes at both the full and new moons, depending on the custom of a particular coven

Many modern Wiccan covens hold regular meetings, referred to as Esbats, on the most convenient evening nearest the full and/or new moon. Esbat rituals typically use color, nature symbolism, candles, and symbolic acts to enhance the significance of the attributes of a particular moon. Rituals serve as a form of worship, a means of teaching, an aide to meditation, and a form of communication between the practitioner and the Goddesses and Gods. Esbat meetings are usually open only to initiates because they are specifically intended to develop members who are in training for the priesthood of the religion.

Beginning with the full moon closest to the winter solstice, the names of the 13 moons of the year are:

- First moon: Oak Moon (Tree month name: Birch Moon)
- Second moon: Wolf Moon (Tree month name: Rowan Moon)
- Third moon: Storm Moon (Tree month name: Ash Moon)
- Fourth moon: Chaste Moon (Tree month name: Alder Moon)
- Fifth moon: Seed Moon (Tree month name: Willow Moon)
- Sixth moon: Hare Moon (Tree month name: Hawthorne Moon)
- Seventh moon: Dyad Moon (Tree month name: Door Oak Moon
- Eighth moon: Mead Moon (Tree month name: Holly Moon)
- Ninth moon: Wort Moon (Tree month name: Nut-Hazel Moon)
- Tenth moon: Barley Moon (Tree month name: Vine Moon)
- Eleventh moon: Wine Moon (Tree month name: Ivy Moon)
- Twelfth moon: Blood Moon (Tree month name: Reed Moon)
- Thirteenth moon: Snow Moon (Tree month name: Elder Moon)

Some groups may prefer to celebrate the full moons according to their traditional rural American names:

January: Wolf Moon

February: Snow Moon

March: Worm Moon or Sap Moon

April: Pink Moon

May: Flower Moon

June: Hot Moon or Strawberry Moon

July: Buck Moon

August: Sturgeon Moon or Corn Moon

September: Harvest Moon

October: Hunter's Moon

November: Beaver Moon

December: Cold Moon or Hunting Moon

Because there are 13 lunar cycles in one solar year, one month will have two full moons. The second full moon in a month is called the Blue Moon.

Maniblot

Full moons

Similar to esbats which are observed primarily by Wiccans, Maniblot rituals are observed by the Odinshof, a group devoted to the teachings of Odin.

Eight times per year

Sabbats

Quarter Days (Spring equinox, Summer solstice, Fall equinox, and Winter solstice) and Cross Quarter Days (February 1, May 1, August 1, and November 1);

The eight Sabbats are the major holidays celebrated by members of the various Pagan religions that have flourished in the United States since the mid-1960s. The Sabbats may sometimes be displaced from their traditional date in order to fall closer to that of a specific pagan festival. For example, the Eleusinian Mysteries in Greece were celebrated just after the full moon that fell closest to the fall equinox. Thus, if September 22 falls midweek, a coven observing the Greek traditions will often move its Sabbat to a weekend nearer the full moon.

Among covens meeting regularly for an Esbat at each moon during the year, a Sabbat is observed by means of a special ritual that is inserted into the middle of the coven's ordinary ritual. Hence, there is a set of eight such special rituals in a coven's liturgical manual or *Book of Shadows*.

Since 1970, the outdoor celebration of Sabbats in the United States has increased in popularity on both the

TABLE 17.5. THE PAGAN HOLIDAY CYCLE

December (beginning with the winter solstice)

~22	.Yule
~23	.New Year for Trees
~	.The Day that Is Not a Day
~	.Saturnalia
31	.Hogmany

January

~6	.The Twelfth Night
~7	.St. Distaff's Day
~	.Up-Helly-Aa

February

1	.Imbolg
1 or 2	.Gaelic Fire Festival
~	.Homstrom
14-15	.Lupercalia

March

~22	.Ostara
~22	.Iduna and Summer Finding

April

1	.All Fool's Day
21 or 22 . . .	.Earth Day
30	.Walpurgis Night

May

1	.Beltane

June

~21	.Midsummer Eve
~22	.Litha

July

~3	.Dog Days (until August 11 or 15)
31	.Lammas Eve

August

1	.Lammas
17-25	.Odin's Ordeal and the Discovery of the Runes
~	.Carnea

September

~22	.Mabon
~22	.Winter Finding

October

31	.Oidhche Shamhna

November

1	.Samhain
5	.Guy Fawkes' Night
11	.Old Halloween

December (before the winter solstice)

~21	.The Mother Night

The symbol ~ indicates a variable or approximate date.

local and national level. Although local gatherings may attract a few dozen to a few hundred people, there is now an annual cycle of festivals—approximately one for each Sabbat in each major region of the United States (e.g., New England, southern California, the upper Midwest, or the Southeast)—regularly attended by thousands of Pagan adherents. The Sabbat Ritual typically focuses on an aspect of the Goddess and her consort and combines drama, poetry, music, costume, and dance. The working of a newly written Sabbat Ritual is usually the climax of a festival.

Bonfire Nights
Dates usually falling near each of the eight Sabbats

In Britain there were many traditional nights during the year when a bonfire would be lit and danced around. Most of them fall on or near the dates for the eight Sabbats of the "Wheel of the Year." The specific list of bonfire nights is: Twelfth Night; Imbolg (or the Gaelic Fire Festival); Ostara; Walpurgis Night (May Eve); Midsummer Eve; Lammas Eve; and Oidhche Shamhna ("Vigil of Samhain" or Halloween).

Quarterly

Quarter Days
Spring equinox, Summer solstice, Fall equinox, and Winter solstice

During the middle ages, British landowners collected quarterly rents on or near the equinoxes and solstices. Eventually these days became known as quarter days, and they continued to be used into the early modern age.

Because of their association with the solstices and equinoxes, the quarter days have also gained religious connotations. In England, the quarter days are called: Lady Day (March 15), Midsummer Day (June 24), Michaelmas (September 29), and Christmas Day (December 25). In Scotland, the names and dates were slightly different. Candlemas fell on February 2; Whitsunday was observed on the seventh Sunday after Easter; Lammas was on August 1; and November 11 marked the celebration of Martinmas.

The observation of these days waned through the nineteenth century but has seen a resurgence in the twentieth century because of the increased popularity of the modern Pagan movement. The Quarter Days recognized by Pagans are Ostara (spring equinox, about March 22), Lithe or Midsummer (summer solstice, about June 22), Mabon (fall equinox, about September 22), and Yule (winter solstice, about December 22).

Cross-Quarter Days
February 1, May 1, August 1 and November 1

The cross-quarter days are the four traditional Celtic festivals celebrated by Pagans along with the quarter days. Together they make up the "Wheel of the Year." These holidays "cross" the quarter days (the solstices and equinoxes) about halfway in between. The most common names are Imbolg (February 1), Beltane (May 1), Lammas (August 1), and Samhain (November 1).

Annually

December (beginning with the winter solstice)

Yule (Alban Arthuan)
Winter solstice; around December 22

Yule, or the Winter Solstice, is a Quarter Day. It marks the beginning of many Pagan calendars. In the Celtic Tree Calendar, the Silver Fir, symbolic of birth, and the Yew, symbolic of death, are honored together on this day.

Yule is the longest night of the year and the day when the waning (lessening) sun yields to the waxing (growing) sun signifying rebirth or resurrection and the beginning of a new cycle. The Ancient Romans celebrated the winter solstice as Sol Invictus (The Undefeated Sun).

In many Pagan traditions, the concept of rebirth is expressed through the birth of a Divine Child. The celebration may include a vigil on the eve of Yule in anticipation of the birth. The child born at Yule is given different names in different legends. In Egyptian mythology the child is Horus; in Greco-Roman it is Apollo; in Norse it is Balder; in Phoenician it is Baal; and in Celtic it is Bel.

The Yule Sabbat ritual usually focuses on the themes of the returning light, the birth of the new king, and the giving of presents, which was a pagan custom long before Christianity. Mistletoe, a plant sacred to the Druids, is also traditionally gathered at Yule (and again at Midsummer).

One of the better known customs associated with Yule is the burning of the Yule log. The Yule log, a large piece from the trunk of an oak tree, may be burned according to the practice employed by a particular Pagan group. In one method, the piece is marked into four sections, one for each season of the year. At the beginning of each season, a fire is kindled to burn a portion of the log and people prayed to their gods for blessings on the season. In other practices, the log is burned only at Yule but a portion is left unburned and kept throughout the year. The unburned portion serves as an amulet of protection and is used to kindle the next year's Yule log, symbolic of the continuity of the cycle from one year to the next.

Another ritual associated with Yule among Wiccans is replacing and lighting altar candles which were extinguished at the preceding Samhain. The new candles serve to symbolize the sun's return.

New Year for Trees
Day after the winter solstice; around December 23

This day is observed by some Pagans who use Robert Graves' tree calendar. The New Year for Trees begins the day after the winter solstice. (See also the Jewish celebration of BI-SHEVAT occurring on the fifteenth day of Shevat).

The Day that Is Not a Day (The Extra Day of the Year; The Time that Is Not a Time)
Day after the winter solstice; around December 23

In the Celtic Tree Calendar, the day following the winter solstice is the extra day of the year. The concept of magical time between times, when it is not one time or another is celebrated. It is a day of liberation.

Saturnalia
Late December

The ancient Roman festival of Saturn (the father of the gods) was celebrated in late December, just about the same period now observed as the "Christmas season" in the United States. It was marked by "reversals": cross-dressing, Lords of Misrule, the rich serving the poor, and so on, as is still practiced to some extent in the German Fasching traditions. Many Pagans celebrate a revived Saturnalia as part of their Yule festival.

Hogmany
December 31

Hogmany originated in Northern England and Scotland. It was observed primarily by children who dressed in sheets, visited neighboring houses, recited rhymes, and received special cakes.

Some modern Pagans observe Hogmany as a day sacred to the solar deity, Hogmagog (or Magog). Participants, sometimes dressed up as animals, burn special sticks for protection against evil spirits. The spirits driven away represent any remaining ill from old year, thus making certain that only good welcomes in the new year.

January

The Twelfth Night
Early January

The Twelfth Night, counted from Yule, marks the ending of the Yuletide cycle of celebrations. By tradition, all Yule decorations around the house must be removed.

Mystical drama associated with the Twelfth Night depicts Persephone (Kore) preparing to rise from the underworld back into the world of the living.

St. Distaff's Day
Early January

Traditionally, St. Distaff's Day was the day after the "Twelfth Day." In the Christian calendar, the Twelfth Day (Epiphany) falls on January 6. As a result, St. Distaff's day is sometimes observed on January 7th; however, some prefer to observe St. Distaff's Day on January 12 (the Twelfth Day of January).

The "St. Distaff" honored is not a person. A distaff is a tool used to hold the wool or flax when spinning yarn. St. Distaff's Day marked the day when regular work resumed after the Yuletide break. It is observed by some modern pagans as a day to honor household gods.

Up-Helly-Aa
Last Tuesday in January

Up-Helly-Aa is an old Norse fire festival revived in 1889, during the first modern wave of Paganism. It is observed with reconstructed pagan rituals, including the burning of a Viking ship, at Lerwick in the Shetland Islands. The festival is also known as Antinmas, a name which may be derived from the Old Norse for "ending of the holy days."

February

Imbolg (Imbolc; Oimelc; Oimelg; Brigid; Brigantia; Gwyl Fair)
February 1

Imbolg, is the first Cross-Quarter Day of the year (the other three are Beltane—May 1, Lammas—August 1, and Samhain—November 1). The day is sometimes called Brigid, named for both the Irish goddess Brigid (also known as Bride, Bridget, Bridhe; patron of poets and daughter of the Dagda) and the Irish Saint Bridget, a historical figure who shares many of the goddesses' qualities and attributes. The Imbolg Sabbat is usually devoted to celebrations of light, poetry, and the overflowing bowl. It marks the time when the

Goddess sheds her guise as the old hag (or crone) and becomes the bride.

A ritual often associated with Imbolg is the placing of the "Brides Bed." By tradition, the last sheaf of grain harvested in the fall was believed to contain the spirit of the grain. This sheaf was saved, made into a human figure, and symbolically dressed with cloth. On Imbolg this figure is placed in a small basket and kept by the front door where it remains until Samhain. The "Brides Bed" by the door serves as a protective amulet and marks the home as a Pagan home. After Samhain, the grain is returned to nature either by scattering it as seed or by giving to the birds.

Gaelic Fire Festival (Candlemas)
February 1 or 2

The Gaelic Fire Festival (or Candlemas) is one of the traditional bonfire nights. It is sometimes observed as part of the Imbolg celebration rather than as a separate festival. (Firecraft is one of threefold attributes the associated with the Goddess Brigid; the others are healing and poetry.) Fires may be kindled as bonfires or through the ritualistic lighting of candles. The symbolic intent is that the old fire is extinguished and a new fire for the new year is kindled and blessed. This new fire symbolizes purity. Dried greens that were used to decorate for Yule are sometimes burned in the fire.

Homstrom
Usually the first Sunday of February

Homstrom is a Swiss festival celebrating the end of winter. One tradition associated with the day is the burning of a straw man symbolizing Old Man Winter. Homstrom is occasionally observed by Swiss-American communities on the first Sunday in February. It is reminiscent of the February 1 Celtic mid-winter festival of Imbolg (Brigid).

Lupercalia
February 14–15

With roots in ancient Roman Paganism, Lupercalia was a festival sacred to Faunus, the fertility god overseeing agriculture and flocks. On the first day of the festival, preparations for Lupercalia were made when men drew lots to select a female partner for the following day. Priests of Faunus, dressed in goatskin loincloths, struck women on their palms with thongs in a ceremony related to fertility. Some researchers believe that Lupercalia is the basis for modern-day Valentines traditions.

March

Ostara (Eostre; Alban Eilir)
The vernal (spring) equinox, about March 22

Ostara, the spring-equinox holiday, is one of the four Pagan Quarter Days. The other three are Litha (the summer solstice which is also known as Midsummer), Mabon (the fall equinox), and Yule (the winter solstice).

At Ostara the waxing daylight and waning night are again equal. The light, which is growing stronger than the darkness, is honored. Fires are set to commemorate the return of spring and honor the God and Goddess.

Ostara is also celebrated as a time of fertility and conception. In some Wiccan traditions, it is marked as the time when the Goddess conceives the God's child which will be born at the Winter solstice.

In Goddess mystical drama, Persephone (Kore) returns from the underworld to be reunited with her mother (Demeter). Celebrations commemorate the relationship between mothers and daughters and the bond between all women.

Many of the familiar secular symbols surrounding spring and the Christian observance of Easter have pagan roots. For example, eggs and rabbits both signify fertility.

Iduna and Summer Finding
Near the spring equinox

Among observers of Northern European Paganism, two festivals surround the spring equinox. Iduna is sacred to the Norse Goddess Iduna, who represents the half of the year in which the light overcomes the darkness. Summer Finding is observed as a day sacred to the God Thor. It marks the beginning of the farming season.

April

All Fool's Day (Festival of Fools)
April 1

All Fool's Day customs are popular in many communities and are so wide-spread they have become secularized. Some researchers theorize that the practice of setting one day aside to play tricks and practical jokes is a way to cope with the authority that rules the rest of the year. Although many festival celebrations begin on their eve and continue through the next day, All Fool's Day, begins in the morning and continues only until noon.

On All Fool's Day, Northern European Pagans honor the god Loki, who was known as a trickster.

Earth Day
April 21 or 22

Earth Day is a day on which the Mother Earth Goddess, Gaia (her Roman name), is honored. Modern environmental groups have chosen this day on which to encourage environmental responsibility.

Walpurgis Night (May Eve)
April 30

Walpurgis Night, one of the eight fire festivals, is dedicated to the German Goddess Walpurga. The night is considered a time of magic. Festivals are marked by revelry in anticipation of the coming summer. One ritual custom, that of leaping through or over the fire, is symbolic of purifying oneself. Some groups with Portuguese and Spanish roots, observe Walpurgis Night as a festival of the dead.

May

Beltane (Beltaine; May Day; Calan Mai)
May 1

Beltane is one of the four Cross-Quarter Days (the others are Lammas—August 1, Samhain—November 1, and Imbolg—February 1). The name Beltane is made of two parts: Bel is the name of the Celtic god; and tane (or tain) is a Celtic word meaning fire. Beltane is also the Irish Gaelic name for the month of May.

Beltane, or May Day, appears to have been a festival celebrating the beginning of the good weather season in northern Europe: when herdsmen could safely take the herds to the high summer pastures, and when wild fruits and berries began to grow and ripen. It celebrates the full blossoming of spring, the fertility of the Earth, and the rebirth of the flowers.

European folklore is full of May Day customs, many of them being folk-magic rituals for young women to use to reveal their future husbands. The wedding theme is also found in some Wiccan circles where Beltane marks the marriage of the Goddess and the Horned God. In some areas, the election of a May Queen is reminiscent of this sacred these Nuptials. Out of respect for the deities, however, May is considered an unlucky time for mortal marriages. As a result, June is a popular month for traditional weddings.

In Roman Catholic assemblies, the month of May was dedicated to Mary, and May Day was the traditional day for crowning the Blessed Virgin statues. It is often claimed that in the Middle Ages Mary was substituted for the pagan goddess to whom May was originally sacred.

One of the best known traditions associated with Beltane is the Maypole. Dancers circle the Maypole holding ribbons attached to the top. The dancers spiral inward as they dance, symbolizing the dual themes of death and resurrection. Odinists may see the Maypole as a representation of the World Tree that connects the nine worlds.

Other traditions associated with May include all-night outings to look for flowering branches and other prizes, picking flowers, making and exchanging wreaths, and kindling the Beltane fire.

Depending on the preferences of the people conducting the ceremony, the Beltane fire may be kindled on Walpurgis Night (May Eve) or on Beltane (May 1). By tradition, the Beltane fire contains bundles of nine different types of wood chosen for their symbolism and associated attributes. For example, hazel nuts are considered symbolic of wisdom, so adding hazel to the Beltane fire will bestow wisdom during the coming year.

June

Midsummer Eve
The evening before the summer solstice, about June 21

Midsummer Eve, celebrated in Shakespeare's *A Midsummer Night's Dream*, is noted for revivals of supposedly ancient rituals and the burning of bonfires. By tradition, the midsummer fire must lit by friction between fir and oak (fir representing rebirth and oak signifying magical power). Some groups, however, prefer to use modern utensils to light the fire but maintain the symbolism by using fir and oak in the kindling.

In the British Isles, Midsummer Eve is observed by the Ancient Order of Druids (founded in 1781) and various other British Druid orders, some of whom stay up all night to observe the Midsummer sunrise at Stonehenge. (The National Heritage will allow Druids into Stonehenge but limits the access of other Pagans and tourists.)

Litha (Midsummer; Alban Hefin)
Summer solstice, on or about June 22

Litha is one of the four Quarter Days. The other three are Ostara (spring equinox, about March 22), Mabon (fall equinox, about September 22), and Yule (winter solstice, about December 22).

The summer solstice occurs on the longest day of the year when the sun reaches its full power. The day is one of special significance among some Druid groups who gathered at Stonehenge to celebrate the Light which reaches its highest point at noon on the day of the solstice.

For many other Pagan groups, the day symbolizes maturity and fullness. One tradition holds that a fire kindled on Litha carries smoke that blesses. Some customs include burning sunwheels, carrying torches, or swinging burning brands. Midsummer is also a customary day for harvesting mistletoe which may be used as an amulet of protection.

July

Dog Days
July 3–August 11 or 15

This time period represents the hottest part of the year. According to ancient Roman tradition it is ruled over by the star Sirius, called the Dog Star. The determination was made because the star rose about the same time as the sun. Because the star was one of the brightest in the sky, people assumed that it added its heat to the heat of the sun. Among the Asatru, Sirius is known as Loki's Brand.

Lammas Eve
July 31

Lammas Eve, the night before Lammas is one of the eight traditional bonfire nights when special fires are kindled. The Lammas Eve fire may be burned as part of the Lammas Sabbat.

August

Lammas (Lughnasadh; Gwyl Awst)
August 1 (in some traditions July 31–August 1)

Lammas is one of the four Cross-Quarter Days (the other three are Samhain—November 1, Imbolg—February 1, and Beltane—May 1) and the first of three harvest festivals (the other two are Mabon and Samhain). The day is thought to have been a precursor of Thanksgiving in America and Canada's Harvest Festival.

Lammas celebrates the first harvest which is typically the grain harvest. In many Pagan traditions, grain symbolizes the concepts of death and resurrection, and although the festival focuses on the joy of harvest, it is also a day for mourning the loss of loved ones. One custom associated with the day is the baking of bread. The festival, originally celebrated as the Gule of August, became somewhat Christianized because of the practice of blessing the loaves. The name Lammas is a shortened form of "loaf mass."

Lughnasadh is an alternate name for the festival with a more Pagan origin. Lugh is the Celtic god of wisdom, and at Lughnasadh the Goddess is seen in her aspect as a pregnant mother. The Sabbat is usually celebrated outdoors during a weekend camp-out if possible. The ancient "games of Tara" are reenacted or an appropriate drama is performed.

Odin's Ordeal and the Discovery of the Runes
August 17–25

This holiday season of nine days commemorates Odin's crucifixion on the World Tree, called the Yggdrasill, and his resulting discovery of the Runes. According to the legend, Odin (the chief Norse deity) sacrificed himself and hung on the Yggdrasil, the tree that links the nine worlds together. (The manifest world inhabited by human beings is but one of the nine worlds.) After nine days and nine nights he received the Runes. The Runes are ancient alphabetic characters that can be used in divination.

Carnea
August

Carnea is an ancient Greek festival that was one of the three principle religious celebrations observed in Peloponnesus, Cyrene, and Magna Graecia of antiquity. Dating as far back as 676 B.C.E., the festival honored Apollo Karneios, the god of fertility and herding. Carnea derived its name from the month of Carneus (August) and primarily celebrated a bountiful harvest. The ritual celebration featured young men called *staphylodromoi* ("grape-cluster-runners") who pursued other celebrants draped in garlands presumably made of grape vines. Successful capture of the garland-bearing participants indicated a good omen.

In addition to entreating the god Apollo to ensure a good harvest, the Carnea was intended to secure the god's aid in battle. Ironically, military engagement was prohibited during the Carnea. Some historians have suggested that the smashing defeat of the Spartan forces by the Persians at Thermopylae may have been prevented if the main Spartan army had not been immobilized in honor of the Carnea.

September

Mabon (Alban Elfed)
Autumnal (fall) equinox, about September 22

Mabon is one of the four Quarter Days (the other three are Yule—winter solstice, Ostara—spring equinox, and Litha—summer solstice). It marks the second point in the year when the days and nights are equally long. At spring (Ostara), however, the waxing sun rises to preeminence; at Mabon, the waning sun rules.

Mabon marks a time when harvests are gathered and seeds stored for the next year. It is the second of three harvest festivals (the others are Lammas and Samhain) and it focuses on the fruit harvest.

When the autumnal equinox does not exactly coincide with a date that is convenient for the Pagan festival, Mabon may be displaced from its traditional date and observed at another time. For example, the Eleusinian Mysteries in Greece were celebrated just after the full moon that fell closest to the fall equinox; hence, if September 22 falls midweek, many covens that favor the Greeks will move their Mabon Sabbat to a weekend nearer the full moon.

In some Wiccan traditions, a coven's leadership will be transferred from the High Priestess to the High Priest, symbolic of the seasonal change from the time of year when the Goddess rules to the time of year ruled by the God, represented as the Horned Lord. As the earth rests, the Goddess rests and is not visibly manifest in nature during the coming season.

Winter Finding
Autumnal equinox

Among observers of Northern European Paganism, the autumnal equinox is observed as a day sacred to the God Frey, the Norse god of fertility.

October

Oidhche Shamhna (Vigil of Samhain; The Eve of Samhain; All Hallows' Eve; Halloween)
October 31

Some Pagans following the tradition of beginning a holiday celebration on the eve before the day (similar to the Jewish tradition of observing a day from sunset to sunset) begin their Samhain observances on the night more popularly known as Halloween (a shortened form of All Hallows' Eve, or the evening before All Saints' Day).

To the ancient Celts, and among some modern Pagan groups, Samhain Eve marked the end of the old year and Samhain the beginning of the new. As a result, the night is remembered as a time between the years, a time when the separation between the world of the living and the world of the dead is very thin. It is a favored night for divination and one of the eight traditional bonfire nights when special fires were kindled.

According to ancient Celtic belief the boundary between this world and the netherworld of fairies, gods, spirits, and magic was at its thinnest on the Vigil of Samhain. As a result, passage between the two dimensions was easier than at any other time. Visitations from the spirits of one's own departed ancestors, divine beings, or demons were believed to be possible, but not desirable.

Many of the customs that developed surrounding this night were directed toward understanding and appeasing these spirits, thus protecting one's family from their influences.

Halloween is a popular holiday in the United States because of the custom of "trick-or-treating," in which children dressed as ghosts, witches, and monsters go from house to house begging for treats. According to some, the costumed children represent the spirits of dead ancestors, fairies, and other supernatural beings who demand to be bribed with a treat to keep from working a trick on the inhabitants of the house. Other traditions associated with the Vigil of Samhain include setting places at the table for the dead, leaving food by the fireside, and wearing masks representing the goddesses and gods, spirits of the dead, or animal spirits.

Some pagan groups may choose to distance themselves from the commercial popularity of the secular observance of Halloween by displacing their Samhain celebrations to another day, such as the closest weekend, the closest new or last quarter moon, or a sign in nature, such as the first frost.

November

Samhain (Halomas; Festival of the Dead; Nos Galan Gaeof)
November 1

Samhain (pronounced "Sa-oo-en") is one of the four Cross-Quarter Days (the other three are Imbolg—February 1, Beltane—May 1, and Lammas—August 1) and the third harvest festival (the other two are Lammas and Mabon). The Samhain harvest is one of animals, when animals were traditionally slaughtered in preparation for the coming winter.

Samhain marks a turning point in the pagan year when death rules and the darker side of life is honored. A transition from light to dark, from physical to spiritual, takes place. In some Wiccan covens the Horned God rises to predominance; and to signify this, the Priestess may step aside yielding her position to a Priest.

The Sabbat Rituals of Samhain are focused on honoring the dead: celebrating life in death, calling out the names of those who have passed on, remembering what they did in life, and asking the gods to grant them a worthy rebirth. Some Wiccan covens observe a tradition of extinguishing altar candles at the end of the Samhain Sabbat; they are not re-lit until Yule, when the new year is reborn. The Goddess is seen in her aspect of the crone (hag), or destroyer.

Among Druids, Samhain is an important time for divination. Traditionally Druids were asked by kings to look into the future to discover events of the year to come.

TABLE 17.6. ALPHABETICAL LIST OF PAGAN HOLIDAYS

Holidays	Dates
Alban Arthuan	
see Yule	
Alban Eilir	
see Ostara	
Alban Elfed	
see Mabon	
Alban Hefin	
see Litha	
All Fool's Day	April 1
All Hallows' Eve	
see Oidhche Shamhna	
Beltaine *see* Beltane	
Beltane	May 1
Brigantia *see* Imbolg	
Brigid *see* Imbolg	
Calan Mai *see* Beltane	
Candlemas	
see Gaelic Fire Festival	
Carnea	During August
Day that Is Not a Day	The day after the winter solstice; around December 23
Dog Days	July 3–August 11 or 15
Earth Day	April 21 or 22
Eostre *see* Ostara	
Eve of Samhain	
see Oidhche Shamhna	
Extra Day of the Year	
see Day that Is Not a Day	
Festival of Fools	
see All Fool's Day	
Festival of the Dead	
see Samhain	
Gaelic Fire Festival	February 1 or 2
Guy Fawkes' Night	November 5
Gwyl Awst	
see Lammas	
Gwyl Fair *see* Imbolg	
Halloween	
see Oidhche Shamhna	
Halomas *see* Samhain	
Hogmany	December 31
Homstrom	Usually the first Sunday of February
Iduna and Summer Finding	Near the spring equinox
Imbolc *see* Imbolg	
Imbolg	February 1

Holidays	Dates
Lammas	August 1 (in some traditions July 31–August 1)
Lammas Eve	July 31
Litha	Summer solstice, on or about June 22
Lughnasadh	
see Lammas	
Lupercalia	February 14–15
Mabon	Autumnal (fall) equinox, about September 22
Martinmas	
see Old Halloween	
May Day *see* Beltane	
May Eve	
see Walpurgis Night	
Midsummer Eve	The evening before the summer solstice, about June 21
Midsummer *see* Litha	
New Year for Trees	The day after the winter solstice; around December 23
Nos Galan Gaeof	
see Samhain	
Odin's Ordeal	August 17–25
Oidhche Shamhna	October 31
Oimelc *see* Imbolg	
Oimelg *see* Imbolg	
Old Halloween	November 11
Old November Day	
see Old Halloween	
Ostara	The vernal (spring) equinox, about March 22
Samhain	November 1
Saturnalia	Late December
St. Distaff's Day	Early January (about January 7)
The Mother Night	Eve of the winter solstice
The Twelfth Night	Early January (about January 6)
Time that Is Not a Time	
see Day that Is Not a Day	
Up-Helly-Aa	The last Tuesday in January
Vigil of Samhain	
see Oidhche Shamhna	
Walpurgis Night	April 30
Winter Finding	Autumnal equinox
Yule	Winter solstice; around December 22

Guy Fawkes' Night
November 5

Guy Fawkes' Night is observed primarily in England as a day of deliverance from Roman Catholic domination but it is thought to be related to more ancient tradition of burning the effigies of evil spirits. Some modern Pagans celebrate Guy Fawkes' Night by lighting bonfires and burning effigies representing the sadness and ills from the year gone by.

Old Halloween (Old November Day; Martinmas)
November 11

In 1752 Britain adopted the Gregorian calendar which dropped ten days from the calendar and caused a discrepancy in dating. As a result the date for the Eve of Samhain (or Halloween) was moved. Some groups prefer to observe the date according to the old calendar. In the Christian church calendar, November 11 is called Martinmas Day.

December
(before the winter solstice)

The Mother Night
Eve of the winter solstice

Among observers of Northern European Paganism, the winter solstice is one of the most sacred days of the year. It is devoted to Odin, Ing, and Erda. Asatru followers believe that dreams on The Mother Night foretell events of the coming year.

CHAPTER 18

Western African Religions and Their New World Expressions

Overview of Yoruba Religious Traditions

The Yoruba people are indigenous inhabitants of Yoruba-land, a cultural area in Western Africa currently occupied by parts of Nigeria and Benin. The city of Ife, in Western Nigeria, serves as the religious center and seat of divine authority.

According to traditional Yoruba belief, all power in the universe emanates from a supreme being, Olorun. Although Olorun holds all power and is the giver of all life, he is not directly involved in the affairs of the earth. Other lesser deities, called orisa, serve as intermediaries between the people of earth and Olorun. The orisa, and not Olorun, are the objects of veneration and ritual obligation. The names and number of orisa varies according to local custom, and some are more widely known than others.

One of the most commonly honored orisa is Orisa-nla, also called Obatala. Orisa-nla was responsible for creating the earth and forming the first human beings. Differing accounts of the creation story exist, and some versions include a second orisa, called Ododuwa, who assisted Orisa-nla when the original plans went awry. Other important orisa include Orunmila (a deity associated with divination) and Esu (a trickster orisa with both good and bad aspects). Esu plays an important role in communicating between people and spirits. Because he serves as a mediator, he is summoned first in all ceremonies.

In addition to the orisa, the Yoruba people also honor two types of ancestor spirits. Communities revere spirits who played important historical roles; individual families pay homage to their worthy ancestors. Ogun, the first king, is worshipped as a dual being, as an orisa and as an ancestor.

Authorities

The Yoruba religion is based on oral traditions. Beliefs and practices are preserved by passing stories and customs from one generation to the next. Authority for interpreting events and establishing proper conduct rests with rulers who function in both religious and political realms.

The Oba is a chief who presides over the people within a geographic area. Under him are those with authority over smaller regions. Ultimately each family is presided over by a family head, called the olori ebi, who directs both religious activity and the day-to-day affairs of family members.

In addition to the hierarchy of rulers, other important people serve within specific spheres of influence. These include: mediums and mediators who communicate with the spirits of the orisa and the ancestors; diviners who use special objects, consult traditional oracles, and employ magical powers to reveal human destiny and recommend action; medicine men who work with diviners to help bring healing power; and priests who tend to various shrines and oversee the performance of specific rituals.

History

The origins of Yoruba religious practices extend back into pre-history and little is known with certainty. The city of Ife, currently located in Nigeria, is believed to be the place at which the world was created. The first Yoruba king, Ogun, ruled in Ife. In stories of the past, the kings of all surrounding territories received their authority from the reigning king in Ife.

Islam was introduced to western, sub-Saharan Africa during the seventeenth century. It was followed by Christianity in the nineteenth century. Both foreign religions produced intensive missionary efforts, and their precise impact on indigenous traditions is unknown. Some researchers believe that the concept of Olorun as a supreme god originated as a result of contact with the monotheistic traditions; others believe that the Yoruba understanding of Olorun pre-dates foreign contact and represents the native cosmology.

Yoruba Today

Estimates regarding the number of Yoruba people vary from five to 16 million. The largest number live in Nigeria, but smaller communities exist in Ghana, Togo, and Benin.

People

Although many of the Yoruba people live in cities, the primary occupation is farming. Cities are often surrounded by farmland and workers travel between their homes and the fields. Many religious practices focus on agricultural themes.

Worship

Yoruba worship involves the proper performance of rituals. Several different types of priests fill various spiritual roles. An elegun is a person who experiences spiritual possession that results in ecstatic states during which communication takes place. An egungun is a dancer who wears a special costume and concealing mask that is believed to be endowed with spiritual power from the ancestors. A babalawo is a priest skilled in divination. An oloogun works with the babalawo to cure sickness.

Overview of Voodoo

Voodoo (also called Voudoun) is a faith that combines Western African elements with French Roman Catholic characteristics. The word comes from the Fon language (indigenous to Nigeria) and means "spirit." The religion began in Haiti when African slaves from various tribes with diverse backgrounds were brought together under harsh conditions. Over time, the slaves developed a consolidated belief system with blended rituals to form the new religion.

The supreme being recognized by Voodoo practitioners is known as Bon Dieu. Other spiritual beings include ancestors (or the dead in general), twins, and a diverse pantheon of gods called loa that are typically associated with Roman Catholic saints.

The History of Voodoo

Western African religious thoughts and practices were introduced to the New World as a result of slave trading during the eighteenth and nineteenth centuries. Slaves, often forcibly baptized into Christian traditions, combined elements from their past culture with symbols from new religions to form syncretistic faith systems. Of these innovative faiths, Voodoo is one of the best known.

French rulers in Haiti outlawed Voodoo practices but the religion continued as an underground faith. From Haiti, it spread to other areas of the Caribbean, to Brazil, and to the United States, particularly in Louisiana.

During the nineteenth century in New Orleans, Voodoo enjoyed a period of popularity. Although most voodoo ceremonies were held in secret, the New Orleans authorities allowed slaves to dance in Congo Square on Sunday afternoons under the watchful eye of government authorities. One ritual, called the Calinda Dance, was performed on the eve of St. John's Day (June 23; St. John's Day is June 24) by a voodoo priestess. The dance imitated the undulations of a snake in a sensual way. In 1843 its performance was banned on the grounds that it was obscene.

Voodoo Today

Voodoo Practitioners

The largest Voodoo population center is in Haiti but other communities, called société centers, exist in places such as New Orleans, Miami, and New York City.

Worship

Voodoo ceremonies take place within a group of initiated practitioners called a hounfort. Worship often entails the performance of dance rituals that may be conducted by a priest (called a houngan) or a priestess (called a mambo). During the ceremony drums help summon the spirits who enter dancers and cause ecstatic trance states during which prophecies may be delivered. Although many people commonly associate Voodoo with menacing sorcery, only a small minority of Voodoo practitioners participate in black magic rituals.

Overview of Santeria

Santeria is a faith that combines Western African elements with Spanish Roman Catholic characteristics. The word Santeria means Way of the Saints; some practitioners prefer to de-emphasize the role of European saints and call the faith La Regla Lucumi (Regla means way or path; Lucumi refers to the people and culture that developed in Cuba from Yoruba traditions).

Santeros believe in one God, called Olorun who is viewed as the source of everything. Olorun is served by spiritual beings called orisas who are identified with Roman Catholic saints. Some of these correspondences are shown in Table 18.1.

History of Santeria

The origins of Santeria can be traced to Cuban slaves. Spanish rulers required that all slaves be baptized into the Roman Catholic church. Within the Cuban Catholic church, African ethnic societies called cabildos were formed. The cabildos functioned as social and religious organizations in which members aided each other. Church holidays were celebrated by the cabildos with African traditions, especially drumming and dancing.

The orisas that had been honored in Africa were paired with saints of the church. According to some researchers, the initial impetus for the matching of orisas with saints may have been to promote secret worship of the African spirits. Over time, however, the distinctions between the orisa and the saints became less clear.

When Cuba gained its independence from Spain the cabildos also gained independence from the Catholic church. They formed individual groups called reglas (which means path or way) based on the African ethnicity of the group's members. From the reglas the religion called Santeria emerged as an autonomous faith.

After the revolution in 1959, many Cubans left the island and migrated to North and South America. Included in their number were Santeros who carried their faith with them into exile.

TABLE 18.1. SELECTED ORISAS AND CORRESPONDING ROMAN CATHOLIC SAINTS

Orisa	Saint
Ogun	Peter
Shango	Barbara
Obatala	Mercedes
Esu	Anthony
Ibeji	Cosums and Damien
Babaluaye	Lazarus
Oxossi	George

Santeria Today

People

Since its beginnings, Santeria has been a secret faith. As a result the number of followers is unknown. The largest Santerian population center is believed to be in the Caribbean islands, particularly in Cuba. In the United States the largest Santerian populations are located among Hispanic groups in New York City and Florida. According to some estimates in the early 1990s, there were approximately one million Santeros in the United States.

Worship

Worship in Santeria involves interaction and communication with the orisas. Some of the ways this takes place is through ceremonial ritual, prayer, divination, and sacrificial offerings. The purpose of the ritual is to achieve spiritual possession in which the orisa being summoned enters the participants who then speak for the orisa.

One of the most controversial aspects of Santeria involves the use of animal sacrifice. According to Santerian belief, animal sacrifice is needed to feed the orisas. The most common animals used in sacrificial offerings are chickens and goats. In 1993, the United States Supreme Court upheld the right of Santeros to practice animal sacrifice.

Overview of Candomblé

Candomblé is a generalized name given to a diverse expression of African-based religious traditions in Brazil. Through the use of ethnic drum music, practitioners seek to manifest ancestral spirits within the community.

Like many other African-based sects in the New World, however, Candomblé also incorporated images of saints from Roman Catholicism. The orixa (the Brazilian form of orisa is traditionally spelled orixa) are often symbolized with small statues of the saints which are adorned in distinctive dress, and Olorun (the supreme being) is frequently equated with the Christian God.

History of Candomblé

The largest number of African slaves were transported to Brazil during the nineteenth century. The principal port of entry was located in Salvador da Bahia (often called Bahia). Communication and travel between Bahia and Africa were maintained by free blacks seeking to ensure that African religious traditions were preserved.

During the years of slavery, ceremonies were typically conducted in secret. Following the emancipation of

Brazilian slaves in 1888, some gatherings were held in the open and others chose to remain concealed. The gatherings, organized into communities, centered around a local leader, most often a priestess. Although individual Candomblé centers shared a common heritage, they were also differentiated in practice. Some focused on maintaining the purity of African traditions; others freely incorporated Roman Catholic elements and even added some gods from the Native American culture to their pantheon.

TABLE 18.2. CYCLE OF WESTERN AFRICAN-BASED HOLIDAYS

Dates	Holidays
March	
~20	Ibu Afo Festival
~	Bobo Masquerade
Holy Week	Rara Festival
May	
Mid-May	Ibeji Ceremony
June	
~	Egungun Festival
24	St. John's Day
Late June	Eje
July	
early to mid	Pilgrimage of Saut D'Eau
August	
Late August	Gelede
September	
27	Cosmas and Damian Day
December	
26–January 1	Kwanzaa

The symbol ~ indicates a movable date.

Seasonal Timekeeping and Roman Catholic Influences

Uncertain Origins

The origins of timekeeping systems in Western Africa are unknown. The cycling of days, as a natural phenomenon, was a progression observed by people all over the world. In different areas, however, the significance attributed to specific days and the number of days that comprised longer periods of time varied.

In tribal Africa, individual days and parts of days were often described according to the activity that was customary. For example, among one tribe in Central Africa the late afternoon/early evening hours were called by a name that meant "the cows come home." Among the Yoruba people, the days were numbered around agricultural cycles. A market day, observed every sixteen days, served as the focal point in a 16-day cycle somewhat analogous to a week.

Months and Years

Archeological evidence from central Africa suggests that some tribes may also have observed months. Markings on bones have been interpreted by some researchers as representations of the waxing and waning periods of the moon. Notches seem to count 14 and 15 day periods from the first appearance of a waxing crescent moon to the full moon and from the full moon to the last crescent of the waning moon.

Although the passing of the solar year was noted, there is no evidence that ancient African societies used the zodiac constellations or planetary cycles in their timekeeping systems. There is also no evidence that written calendars were developed. It is possible, however, that calendars and information about celestial signs were transmitted orally and that the stories have been lost.

The year was probably marked as the passing of a cycle of seasons. The recognition of seasonal variations in rainfall and other patterns of relevance to agricultural communities served to relate human activities to environmental phenomenon. Festivals related to agriculture occurred at specified times in conjunction with activities related to the seasons. Many other festivals were held at times determined by divination according to need.

The Igbo people of Nigeria celebrated the coming of the new year around the time of the vernal equinox with a solemn ceremony marking the end of the old year and heralding the arrival of the new. The council of elders, who were responsible for setting the annual calendar, determined the exact hour at which the year ended.

Roman Catholic Influences

In the New World, many people of Western African descent were baptized into the Roman Catholic church. As a result, traditional festivals were celebrated in secret often in conjunction with festival days in the Roman Catholic calendar. In addition, the identification of African spirits (orisas) with Roman Catholic saints gave rise to the practice of honoring the spirits on their associated saint days.

TABLE 18.3. ALPHABETICAL LIST OF WESTERN AFRICAN-BASED HOLIDAYS

Holidays	Dates
Bobo Masquerade	Late March
Cosmas and Damian Day	September 27
Egungun Festival	During June
Eje	Late June
Gelede	Late August
Ibeji Ceremony	Mid-May
Ibu Afo Festival	On or near March 20
New Yam Festival see Eje	
Pilgrimage of Saut D'Eau	Early to mid July
Rara Festival	Holy Week in the Christian calendar; March or April
St. John's Day	June 24
Kwanzaa	December 26–January 1

Holidays Related to Western African Religions

Ibu Afo Festival
On or near March 20

The Igbo people of Nigeria celebrate their New Year's Eve around March 20 with a solemn ceremony marking the end of the old year and heralding the arrival of the new. The council of elders who fix the annual calendar determine the exact hour at which the year will end. When it arrives, a wailing noise signals the departing year, and children rush into their houses, lock the doors to avoid being carried away by the old year as it leaves, and bang on the doors to add to the din. As soon as the wailing dies down, the doors are thrown open and everyone greets the new year with spontaneous applause.

Bobo Masquerade
Late March

The Bobo people of Burkina Faso celebrate the balance between the sun, the rain, and the earth. The god Dwo is honored in this festival that features painted masks and costumes. The event repels evil and maintains natural balance necessary for crops to thrive.

Rara Festival
Holy Week in the Christian calendar; March or April

This Haitian celebration of spring with deep ties to voodoo incorporates some elements of Christianity and bears a superficial resemblance to Carnival celebrations. The highpoint of the festival occurs between Palm Sunday and Easter and features a procession and exhibition by a Rara band (also spelled Ra-Ra). Each Rara band consists of a musical group, a band chief, a queen with attendants, a women's choir, and vendors selling food. The observance begins by calling on Legba (an old man, trickster spirit) who is the guardian of thresholds and crossroads. The group's leader often dresses like a jester and twirls a long baton known as a jonc.

Preparations for the Rara Festival begin on Shrove Tuesday night as the Christian lenten season gets underway. The Rara bands perform a Bruler Carnival in which they carry out the ritual burning of various carnival objects and then make a cross on their forehead with the ashes. Weekend dance processions take place during lent and culimnate in conjunction with Easter.

Ibeji Ceremony
Mid-May

Among Yoruba people twins are called ibeji and people believe that twins have special powers. The Ibeji ceremony is conducted at a supper to which the mother of twins invites friends. If one of the twins is dead, a doll is substituted.

Ibeji is also the name of the twin-child orisa (divine being or saint) honored by people who practice Santeria. Ibeji is associated with the Roman Catholic saints Cosmas and Damian, Christian medical practitioners who were martyred under Diocletian in the early fourth century C.E.

Egungun Festival
June

The Egungun is a secret society among the Yoruba people of Ede, Nigeria. The major Egungun festival takes place in June, when members of the society come to the market place and perform masked dances. The masks they wear represent ancestral spirits and may cover the whole body or just the face. It is considered dangerous to see any part of the man who is wearing the mask—an offense that was at one time punishable by death.

The masqueraders all dance simultaneously, although each has his own drum accompaniment and entourage of chanting women and girls. The festival climaxes with the appearance of Andu, the most powerful mask. It is believed that the spirits of the deceased possess the masqueraders while they are dancing, and although it promotes a feeling of oneness between the living and the dead, the festival also inspires a certain amount of fear.

St. John's Day
June 24

A family of yellow-flowered plants, commonly called St.-John's-wort, is used by voodoo conjurors and folk medicine practitioners to ward off evil spirits and ensure good luck. In the southern United States, all species of the plant are called John the Conqueror root, or "John de Conker," and all parts of it are used: the root, leaves, petals, and stems. The plant's imagery is often mentioned in African-American folklore and blues music.

The leaves, and often the petals, contain oil and pigment-filled glands that appear as reddish spots when held to the light. According to legend, these spots are John the Baptist's blood, and the plant is most potent if rituals are performed on his birthday.

Eje (New Yam Festival)
Late June

The Eje celebration among the Yoruba people is an elaborate harvest festival that takes place over a two-day period and consists of purification rites, presentation rites, divining rites, and thanksgiving rites.

The first day of the festival serves to prepare for the rites that will follow on the second day. A shrine to the sea god, Malokun, is erected and a scared space is purified. Yams are gathered and presented to Malokun as the people welcome the harvest. Rituals of thanksgiving occur during the night.

On the second day, the festival's focus shifts to ascertaining the future prospects of the community. In one divination rite, a recently harvested yam is divided into two parts. They are thrown on the ground, and if one lands face up and the other face down, this is considered a positive sign for the life of the community and the success of crops in the coming year. If both fall face down or face up, problems lie ahead.

Pilgrimage of Saut D'Eau
Early to mid July

This Haitian observance combines elements of Roman Catholic tradition and voodoo. It honors both Our Lady of Mount Carmel and Ezili Freda, the voodoo spirit of love. The pilgrimage begins with prayers of celebration and lasts six days. It concludes at the Church of Our Lady of Mount Carmel in Haiti.

Gelede
Late August

This Yoruba festival honors witches in an effort to appease them so that they will do good and not evil. Two types of masked dancers perform. The Efe dance at night in jest of people who may have foolishly irritated a witch. The Gelede dancers dance during the day; they wear masks resembling witches and try to please them.

Cosmas and Damian Day
September 27

In Brazil, Cosmas and Damian (Christian medical practitioners who were martyred under Diocletian in the early fourth century C.E.) are regarded as the patron saints of children. They are honored by giving children candy. Brazilians of African descent link Cosmas and Damian with the sacred orixa Ibeji. Sometimes children receive a special dinner of okra, a vegetable that is associated with Ibeji.

Kwanzaa
December 26–January 1

Kwanzaa, an African-American celebration of family and black culture, combines many diverse elements to form an ethnic expression. The holiday was created in 1966 by Maulana Karenga, chairman of the Black Studies Department at California State University in Long Beach. Although it is not directly linked to any specific religion, it incorporates some features representative of pan-African spiritualism.

In Swahili, Kwanzaa means "first fruits of the harvest," and first-fruit practices commonly found throughout Africa were adapted for the celebration. Each day of the seven-day festival is dedicated to one of seven principles: umoja (unity), kujichagulia (self-determination), ujima (collective work and responsibility), ujamaa (cooperative economics), nia (purpose), kuumba (creativity), and imani (faith). Families gather in the evenings to discuss the principle of the day, and then light a black, red, or green candle and place it in a seven-branched candleholder called a kinara to symbolize giving light and life to the principle. On the evening of December 31, families join with other members of the community for a feast called the karamu. Decorations are in the red, black, and green that symbolize Africa, and both adults and children wear African garments. Increasingly, colleges and museums are holding Kwanzaa events during some of the days.

Kwanzaa is observed by an estimated five million Americans and perhaps 10 million others in Africa, Canada, the Caribbean, and parts of Europe.

CHAPTER 19

Unclassified Holidays

Theosophical Society

Founded by Helena Petrovna Blavatsky (1831–91) and Henry Olcott (1832–1907), the Theosophical Society combined ancient European and Egyptian thought with Hindu and Buddhist elements. Blavatsky, a Russian-born aristocrat, developed a belief about the nature of the universe based on her participation in occult and psychic phenomenon coupled with secret revelations received from hidden spiritual guides in Tibet. She became acquainted with Olcott in 1873, and together they established the Theosophical Society in 1875.

The basic beliefs of the Society are that there is only one Universal Spirit behind all that exists and that the universe is cyclical in its development, reaching a zenith then diminishing into quiescence. All souls, or Monads, emanate from the Universal Spirit and are thus eternal and divine, but each must be enlightened once it becomes encased in matter—animal, vegetable, or mineral.

The cosmology presented by the Theosophical Society includes a hierarchically arranged pantheon of deities. The supreme deity, called God or Cosmic Logos, is expressed in a trinitarian formula of creator, preserver, and destroyer. Seven other rulers, called Planetary Logoi, hold dominion over all the stars. They are served by angelic beings called Devas.

Each human being is also viewed as possessing a hierarchically arranged multi-leveled self comprising seven types of bodies. These fall along a continuum from pure spirit to pure physical. Through a process of reincarnations, humans seek to eliminate the material aspects of themselves to become pure spirit. Supernatural guides assist in the process.

The popularity of the Theosophical Society in Europe and India increased under its second leader, Annie Besant (1847–1933). In the United States, William Judge ascended to the highest position. Ultimately followers of Besant and Judge formed two organizations: the Theosophical Society (loyal to Judge) and the Theosophical Society in America (loyal to Besant, with international headquarters in India).

Thesophical Holiday

Death of Helena Petrovna Blavatsky
May 8

Helena Petrovna Blavatsky, founder of the Theosophical Society, died on May 8, 1891. Theosophists around the world remember her on this day each year.

Arcane School

The Arcane School was founded in 1923 by Alice Baily (1880–1949), a former member of the Theosophical Society. Baily wrote nineteen books which were ascribed to clairvoyant transmission from a spiritual master. Although her first writings were accepted within the Theosophical Society, she was later expelled for maintaining contact with an unsanctioned master.

Arcane School Holiday

World Invocation Day (Festival of Goodwill)
Spring of each year at the full moon in Sagittarius

World Invocation Day, also called the Festival of Goodwill, is a holiday observed by the Arcane School and the churches and organizations descended from it. The focus of its observance is a prayer written by Bailey, known as the Great Invocation, which is recited by people at meetings around the world. This festival is the forerunner of recent examples of "world-wide prayer meetings," such as the Harmonic Convergence in 1988.

The Church of Scientology

Scientology is based on the writings of L. Ron Hubbard (1911–1986). During the 1940s and 1950s, Hubbard formed a theory of human mental development which he described in *Dianetics: The Modern Science of Mental Health.* According to Hubbard's teachings, the mind consists of two parts, an analytical part and a reactive part. The Reactive Mind was responsible for formulating abnormal behavior patterns on the basis of recorded perceptions of trauma called engrams. The focus of Scientology is a process known as auditing, through which participants discover and remove engrams. The American Psychological Association and the American Medical Association rejected Hubbard's beliefs, but Scientologists attributed their positions to persecution motivated by self-interest.

The first Church of Scientology was established in Los Angeles, California in 1954; a second was established in Washington, D.C., the following year.

Since its creation, the Church of Scientology has experienced controversy and legal difficulty. During the 1960s the U.S. Food and Drug Administration confiscated devices called E-Meters (used to identify engrams) on the basis that they were not medically valid. The Church of Scientology ultimately won a court decision on religious grounds and the E-Meters were returned. In other instances, the church has faced suits from former members and from the U.S. Internal Revenue Service.

Despite the controversies, the Church of Scientology experienced rapid growth. By the end of the 1970s, the organization reported an estimated world-wide membership of five million.

Scientology Holidays

Birthday of L. Ron Hubbard (Founder's Birthday)
March 13

L. Ron Hubbard, founder of Dianetics and Scientology, was born March 13, 1911, at Tilden, Nebraska. This date is celebrated internationally by the Church of Scientology as the Founder's Birthday.

May 9 Day
May 9

The ninth of May is celebrated internationally by the Church of Scientology as its Founding Day. The date May 9, 1950, marked the date of publication of L. Ron Hubbard's *Dianetics: The Modern Science of Mental Health,* the foundation document of Scientology.

Parent's Day
First weekend in June

During the first weekend in June, Scientologists observe a holiday on which family members get together to celebrate the family unity made possible through Scientology.

World Peace Day
August 24

The Church of Scientology celebrates this day to commemorate their first International Conference for World Peace and Social Reform, held at Anaheim, California, in 1976.

Auditors' Day
Second Sunday in September

Auditors' Day is observed by the Church of Scientology. The day allows auditors (a rank/profession within the church) to get together for a social and professional conference.

Freedom Day
December 30

Freedom Day is celebrated by Churches of Scientology in the United States (and some other countries) on December 30. It commemorates the Federal Court decision in 1974 that gave official recognition to the Church of Scientology as a religion.

PART THREE

Appendix, Bibliography, and Indexes

APPENDIX

Internet Sources
for More Information

This listing of calendar and holiday-related web sites includes site names, addresses (URLs), and descriptions of the sites. The sites were chosen to represent a broad sampling of material available on the World Wide Web and the sites are thought to be relatively stable. Inclusion in this list does not constitute an endorsement; omission does not imply criticism.

Calendars in General

CalendarLand
http://website.juneau.com/home/janice/calendarland/

Major sections at the CalendarLand site include Celestial Calendars, Cultural and Religious Calendars, Calendar Indexes, Information and Resources, Holidays, and Millenium Information. Additional sections include links to downloading calendar software, interactive calendars, and information on calendar reform. If you want to know what happened in history today, the answer is here.

Ari's Today Page
http://www.uta.fi/~blarku/today.html

At this site, the current day is presented with its placing in the year, by the week and the month. Users can find information about historical events, sports records, space projects, or famous birthdays occurring on the date the site is visited. Times are also given for the sun rises and sets around the world along with information on current astronomical events and a listing of upcoming holidays in the Christian, Judaic, and Islamic calendars.

Calendar Conversions
http://genealogy.org/~scottlee/calconvert.cgi

This page allows visitors to convert dates among the Gregorian, Julian, Jewish and French Republican calendars. Search results provide the day of the week as well as the date (month, day, and year). Also

included are descriptive overviews of the historical development of the featured calendars.

Festival and Holiday Chart
http://www.hooked.net/users/twerp23/festchartch art.html

Located at this address is a seasonally based chart listing dates with the corresponding holiday, origin, and description. Also included are links to further information on the major holidays listed. Visitors are invited to comment, correct, or contribute additional data.

One-World Global Calendar
http://www.zapcom.net/phoenix.arabeth/1world.html

One-World Global Calendar lists thousands of multicultural holidays and celebrations, modern, tribal, and ancient. It turns an eye to the sky with listings for meteors, moons, and eclipses. The site is updated weekly.

Baha'i

General

Baha'i Faith Page
http://www.colostate.edu/Orgs/MSA/docs/holidays.html

Baha'i Faith is a thorough and fast loading page. Well maintained, it offers a daily reading and prayer. Topics covered are an overview of the faith, sacred writings, and history. There are also links to Baha'i sites by organizations and individuals.

Calendar

Small Utilities for the Baha'i Calendar
http://www.annan.demon.co.uk/bahai/index.htm

This site allows visitors to download a Baha'i calendar conversion program for Microsoft Word versions 2, 6, and 7. This program enables users to add Baha'i dates to documents, convert dates, and print conversion calendars.

Holidays

Baha'i Holy Days
http://www.wwnet.com/~rreini/bahai/holyday.html

This site lists eleven religious days of the Baha'i faith and provides a short explanation of each. The page is sponsored by the Spiritual Assembly of the Baha'is of Canton Township and the Baha'is of Westland, Michigan.

Buddhism

General

Buddhism On the Web
http://www.inet.co.th/cyberclub/bow/main_conten ts.html

Dedicated to promoting Buddhism worldwide, this page has extensive links, all within the Theravada school. Visitors to this site can see the life of the Buddha documented and illustrated in loop animation. Contemporary issues are addressed and there is an open forum for discussion.

BuddhaNet
http://www2.hawkesbury.uws.edu.au/BuddhaNet/

A uniquely structured site, the Buddhist Information Network opens up multiple browser windows allowing visitors to switch between the main page, Buddhazine, and the Dhammapada with a mouse click. BuddhaNet also includes a chat area and a self-contained search engine.

Calendar

Buddhist Meditation Retreats and Events Calendar
http://www.dharmanet.org/calendar.html

At this location, one can find a compiled listing of Buddhist teachings, retreats, and other events. The list is arranged by months, is international in scope, and inclusive of all Buddhist traditions.

Christianity

General

Crosssearch
http://www.crosssearch.com/

Set up like many of the general Internet search engines, Crosssearch also provides a list of numerous subcategories. Subcategories include apologetics, art, ministry resources, bibles, history, literature, youth, music, news, mailing lists, and churches. This page is a service of Gospel Communications Network.

Christianity.Net
http://www.christianity.net/

Christianity.Net, a comprehensive Christian web index with pointers to over 1500 sites, is produced by Christianity Today, Inc. The net search feature, an extensive reference tool for laypeople and academicians, includes more than 4000 resources. The site also offers news briefs, message boards, and a church locator.

Calendar and Holidays

Ecclesiastical Calendar
http://cssa.stanford.edu/%7Emarcos/ec-cal.html

Entering a year of choice, this page calculates Easter Sunday and moveable feasts, in both the Western and Eastern Christian traditions. Feasts specific to the Catholic calendar are also calculated. A short history of the calendar is available, as well as resources and related links.

Hinduism

General

The Hindu Universe
http://www.hindunet.org/

This colorful site, sponsored by the Hindu Students Council, is very informative. There is an introduction to Hinduism, full text versions of the Ramayana, Mahabharata, and the Bhagavad Gita, and a detailed description of the saints. The page also touches on some of the fringes of the religion such as the Return to Sanskrit movement, Yoga, and vegetarianism. Also included are links to newsgroups, publications, organizations, temples, festivals and events.

Calendar

The Hindu Calendar
http://hindunet.org/hindu_calendar/

This page has a full and detailed explanation of the Hindu calendar that includes the days, months, years and ages of Hindu history. Delving into the esoteric, the page also includes a daily ephemeris for use in a branch of Vedic astrology. Also included is a link to an essay on the Hindu concept of time.

Holidays

Major Hindu Festivals
http://www.uic.edu/~rrajbh1/festivals.html

Major Hindu Festivals is a simple page that explains the Hindu festivals of Holi, Janamastami, Diwali, and Navaratri. The legends behind each holiday are told. A link back to the home page of the Hindu Students Council at the University of Illinois, leads to more Hindu resources.

Islam

General

Islam: The Divine Path of Peace
http://www.best.com/~informe/mateen/Islam/islam
   .html

Visitors to this site can read about the Divine Law, study the *Qur'an*, and investigate Sufism. The Divine Path to Peace provides access to mailing lists, newsgroups, and university based Muslim organizations.

Calendar

Gregorian-Hijra Dates Converter
http://www.cs.pitt.edu/~tawfig/convert/

This page is a simple, straight-forward program that converts Gregorian dates to Hijri dates and vice-versa. An introduction covers the history and motivation behind the lunar based Islamic calendar.

Establishing Ramadhan and Other Islamic Dates
http://www.qss.org/cgi-bin/showfile.cgi?article
   s/moon/text

This section of the Al-Qur'an was-Sunnah Society page cites scripture for the correct establishment of the month by natural astronomic observation to explain how new moons determine Islamic dates. This site also features an introduction to Islam, over 100 links to additional information, and a search engine for visitors to find exactly what they are looking for in this massive site.

Holidays

Islamic Holidays and Observances
http://www.colostate.edu/Orgs/MSA/docs/holidays
   .html

Here one can find a listing of the upcoming dates for the Islamic Holy Days. The meaning of Ramadan

is explained in detail. 'Id-al-Fitr, Hajj, and 'Id-al-Adha are each briefly described.

Jainism

General

Jain Studies
http://www.dmu.ac.uk/~pka/guides/jain.html

This site is a compendium of basic general resources on this ancient Indian religion. Reading lists are available, as well as links to online libraries with Jainist materials, references to discussion lists and various articles. This page is sponsored by the DeMontfort University Jain Studies Programme.

Jainism: Principles, Sources, Images, History
http://www.cs.colostate.edu/~malaiya/jainhlinks.html

This extensive and thorough page, covers a wide range of topics relating to Jainism. Visitors will find hundreds of links to texts, and information subjects such as vegetarianism, pilgrimages, and yoga. "Jainism Through the Eyes of Others" is a unique sub-category that links to various sites with controversial or confused views on Jainism.

Calendar and Holidays

Jain Festivals
http://www.cs.colostate.edu/~malaiya/calendar.html

This page is a simple chart, listing the names of the Indian months, the corresponding Gregorian months, and any Jain festivals occurring in each month. There is also a good list of links for various calendars and astronomical time-keeping methods.

Judaism

General

Judaism and Jewish Resources
http://shamash.org/trb/judaism.html

Perhaps the most extensive resource to all things Judaic on the Internet, this site includes lists of FTP sites, Gopher sites, mailing lists, newsgroups and Frequently Asked Questions. The many topics covered include education, communities, art, languages, Israel, news, services, and religious texts.

Calendar

Judaism 101
http://members.aol.com/jewfaq/index.htm

Judaism 101 has a Jewish Calendar section which explains the background and history of the Jewish calendar, the numbering of years, and provides a list of the Jewish months, their length in days, and their Gregorian equivalents. This site also has links to brief descriptions of Jewish holidays, and additional links to definitions of words in the Judaism 101 glossary.

Holidays

Jewish Holidays
http://bnaibrith.org/caln.html

This chart, offered by B'nai B'rith, gives the dates on which important Jewish holidays will fall through the year 2006. The site links back to the B'nai B'rith Interactive page which explains the international charitable organization and its services and programs. The group's magazine, *Jewish Monthly*, is available here in an online version.

Native American Tribal Religions
General

NativeTech's Religion and Cosmology Links
http://www.lib.uconn.edu/ArchNet/Topical/Ethno/NativeTech/links/religion.html#TOP

Over thirty diverse links and articles are featured including "Animal Symbolism in the Plains Indian Sun Dance" and "Native American Religious Freedom." Central America is represented with an Aztec calendar and links for Mayan cosmology and astronomy.

Calendar

The Aztec Calendar
http://napa.diva.nl/~voorburg/aztec.html

This site explains the method for configuring the Aztec calendar. It also includes shareware programs of the Aztec calendar for all platforms. Also included at this site is an artist's rendering of the Sunstone, and a list of related links.

Pow Wow's
http://www.ellabird.com/powwows.html

This frequently updated page is an annual national list of Native American Pow Wow's, maintained by craftswoman, Ella Little Bird.

Paganism
General

Rain Puddles
http://teleport.com/~rain/

Rain Puddles provides many links to a wide variety of Pagan web sites including Wiccan, Druidry, Goddess Worship, and Asatru. Links are organized by category. Some of the categories offered are: "Favorite Puddles" (sites), "Organizations," "Student Groups," "Usenet and FAQS" (Frequently Asked Questions), and "FTP files for Wiccan, Pagan, and Druidic Files."

Calendar and Holidays

WHUUPS Rituals Page
http://world.std.com/~notelrac/cuups.dir/rituals.dir/index.html

This page is sponsored by Wiccan identified peoples within the Unitarian Universalist church. There are numerous worship ideas for each of the eight Pagan sabbats that comprise "The Wheel of the Year". Standard and non-standard rituals are included for many other occasions from the blessing of a new house to the vows of marriage.

Sikhism
General

Introduction to Sikhism
http://photon.bu.edu/~rajwi/sikhism/mansukh1.html

Introduction to Sikhism is a site with almost everything one could want to know about Sikhism, put into a simple question and answer format. Topics covered include God, principles, history, literature, and worship. The topic "Sikhism and Modern Problems" discusses the Sikh attitudes regarding dancing, divorce, family planning, and mercy killing.

Calendar and Holidays

The Sikh Gurupurab Calendar
http://www.comland.com/~amar.p.s/

This site, offered by Gurmat Prakash Publications, briefly explains the term Gurupurab. It provides Gregorian calendar equivalents for significant dates associated with each of the ten Sikh Gurus and the Sikh holy scriptures, the Guru Granth Sahib. Gregorian months may also be selected to display the Sikh holidays by the date for the current year.

Shintoism
General

Shintoism
http://www.interinc.com/Allfaiths/Shintoism/

Shintoism is not well represented on the World Wide Web. At this site, however, one will find a synopsis and history as well as small sections featuring information on education, literature, martial arts, and shrines. This site also has links to libraries that have extensive Shinto-based holdings.

Holidays

Annual Events and Festivals
http://www.jnto.go.jp/07annualevents/annualeven
ts.html

Japan has many festivals which this page lists. Some have religious significance while others honor historic personages or occasions. For each festival a brief explanation is offered.

Taoism, Confucianism, and Other Chinese Folk Religions

General

Chinese Philosophy Page
http://www-personal.monash.edu.au/~sab/index.html

Covering Chinese schools of thought such as Confucianism and Taoism among others, this scholarly page is available in both Chinese and English. Links are provided in the areas of philosophy, Chinese culture, and Chinese language.

Calendar

Chinese Calendar Home Page
http://www.cnd.org:8018/Other/calendar.html

This home page has a simple calendar conversion program available in Chinese and English. The creators of the program explain its functions and proper use in detail.

Holidays

Chinese Festivals
http://science.gmu.edu/~jwang/china/holiday.html

Chinese Festivals lists the Chinese holidays, covering official, traditional, and minority celebration days. Each holiday in the Official and Traditional sections includes a brief description of its origin, and in some cases, its traditional celebration.

Western African Religions

General

Vodoun Information Pages
http://www.vmedia.com/shannon/voodoo/voodoo.html

A simple page with a wealth of information on the complex world of Voodoo. Study the Voodoo cre-

ation myth, learn basic rituals, and find out about black magic here. This site includes a glossary, bibliography, and links to other Voodoo related sites.

Calendar and Holidays

Calendar of Voudon Ceremonies
http://www.vmedia.com/shannon/voodoo/calendar.h
tml

At this location one finds a simple monthly calendar of Voudon ceremonies with highlighted links leading to a glossary of terms.

Zoroastrianism

General

Traditional Zoroastrianism: The Tenets
http://www.ozemail.com.au/~zarathus/tenets33.html

Featuring basic beliefs, religious articles and stories, an explanation of the unique treatment of their dead, and the matrimonial page, this site appears to be the most comprehensive covering this faith on the World Wide Web. The Saga of the Aryans, a semifictional historical novel, detailing Aryan migrations and the life of Zarathushtra, is available as well.

Calendar and Holidays

Zoroastrian Religious Calendar
http://www.avesta.org/zcal.html

This page explains the names of the spiritual beings that preside over each day and each month of the Zoroastrian religious calendar. The names of the prayers for different times of the day are given. This site also includes a list of the important festivals of the Zoroastrian faith.

The Zoroastrian Calendar
http://palette.ecn.purdue.edu/~bulsara/ZOROASTR
IAN/calendar.html

In Zoroastrian thought, the calendar holds great importance as it is a marker on the way to the time when heaven will be on earth. This site explores this notion in detail. An illustrated calendar of days, as well as an article on historical content, is presented as well.

Bibliography

This bibliography provides a starting point for further research into religions, calendars, and holidays. Materials are presented in a topical arrangement. General works are listed first followed by books about calendars and timekeeping systems. Individual religions are then listed in alphabetical order. The bibliography concludes with a list of books from which illustrations were taken for use in this volume

General

Appiah, Kwame Anthony and Henry Louis Gates, Jr. *The Dictionary of Global Culture*. New York: Knopf, 1997.

Bradley, David G. *A Guide to the World's Religions*. Englewood Cliffs, NJ: Prentice-Hall, 1963.

Campbell, Joseph. *The Masks of God, Vol. 3: Occidental Mythology*. New York: Viking, 1964.

Campbell, Joseph, ed. *The Mysteries: Papers from the Eranos Yearbooks.* Translated by Ralph Manheim & R. F. C. Hull. Princeton, NJ: Princeton University Press, 1955.

Clark, Peter B. Ed., *The World's Great Religions: Understanding the Living Faiths*. Pleasantville, NY: Readers Digest Association, Inc., 1993.

Earhart, H. Byron (ed.) *Religious Traditions of the World*. New York: Harper Collins, 1993.

Ellwood, Robert S., Jr. *Religious and Spiritual Groups in Modern America.* Engleweed Cliffs, N.J.: Prentice-Hall, Inc., 1973.

Enroth, Ronald, et al. *A Guide to Cults and New Religions*. Downers Grove, IL: Inter-Varsity Press, 1983.

Green, Marian. *A Calendar of Festivals*. Rockport, MA: Element, 1991.

Green, Marian. *A Harvest of Festivals.* London: Longman, 1980.

Gregory, Ruth W. *Anniversaries and Holidays.* 4th ed. Chicago: American Library Assn, 1983.

Hammond, N. G. L., and H. H. Scullard. *The Oxford Classical Dictionary.* 2d ed. Oxford, Eng.: The Clarendon Press, 1970.

Harper, Howard V. *Days and Customs of All Faiths.* New York: Fleet Publishing, 1957.

Hutchison, Ruth, and Ruth Adams. *Every Day's a Holiday.* New York: Harper & Row, 1951.

Ickis, Marguerite. *The Book of Festivals and Holidays the World Over*. New York: Dodd, Mead, 1970.

Ickis, Margureite. *The Book of Religious Holidays and Celebrations*. New York: Dodd, Mead, 1966.

Kightly, Charles. *The Customs and Ceremonies of Britain: An Encyclopaedia of Living Traditions.* London: Thames & Hudson, 1986.

Langley, Myrtle. *Religions*. Elgin, IL: David C. Cook, 1981.

Mathers, S. L. MacGregor, ed. and trans. *The Greater Key of Solomon.* Chicago: De Laurence, Scott, 1914.

Melton, Gordon J. *The Encyclopedia of American Religions.* 3d ed. Detroit, MI: Gale Research Inc., 1989.

Mossman, Jennifer, ed. *Holidays and Anniversaries of the World.* Detroit, MI: Gale Research, 1985.

National Geographic Society. *Great Religions of the World*. Washington, DC: National Geographic Society, 1971.

Oxtoby, Willard G. ed. *World Religions: Eastern Traditions*. New York: Oxford University Press, 1996.

Parrinder, Geoffrey ed. *World Religions: From Ancient History to the Present.* New York, NY: Facts on File, 1983.

Pike, Royston. *Round the Year with the World's Religions.* New York: Henry Schuman, Inc., 1950. Republished by Omnigraphics, Detroit, 1993.

Religions of the World Interactive CD-ROM. Distributed by Mentorom Multimedia, Ontario, Canada. Copyright 1994 Interactive Learning Productions, a division of International Thomson Publishing.

Shemanski, Frances. *A Guide to World Fairs and Festivals.* Westport, Conn.: Greenwood Press, 1985.

Smart, Ninian. *The Religious Experience of Mankind.* New York: Charles Scribner's Sons, 1969.

Spangler, David. *Festivals in the New Age.* Moray, Scotland: Findhorn Foundation, 1975.

Spicer, Dorothy Gladys. *The Book of Festivals.* Detroit, MI: Gale Research, 1969.

Three Festivals of Spring (The). Ojai, CA: MGNA Publications, 1971.

Van Straalin, Alice. *The Book of Holidays Around the World.* New York: E.P. Dutton, 1986.

Wasserman, Paul, Esther Herman, and Elizabeth Root, eds. *Festivals Sourcebook.* Detroit, MI: Gale Research, 1977.

Calendars

Arcana Workshops. *The Full Moon Story.* Beverly Hills, CA: Arcana Workshops, 1967.

Asimov, Isaac. *The Clock We Live On.* Revised ed. New York: Abelard-Schumann, 1965.

Aveni, Anthony F. *Empires of Time: Calendars, Clocks, and Cultures.* New York: Kodansha International, 1989,

Colson, F.H. *The Week.* Cambridge, Eng.: Cambridge University Press, 1926.

Nilsson, Martin P. *Primitive Time-Reckoning: A Study in the Origins and First Development of the Art of Counting Time Among the Primitive and Early Culture Peoples.* Lund, Norway: Gleerup, 1920.

Old Farmer's Almanac (The). 1997 ed. Dublin, NH: Yankee Publishing, 1996.

O'Neil, W. M. *Time and the Calendars.* Sydney, Australia: Sydney University Press, 1975.

Parise, Frank, ed. *The Book of Calendars.* New York: Facts on File, 1982.

Renfrew, Colin. "Carbon-14 and the Prehistory of Europe." *Scientific American,* Oct. 1971:63-72.

Renfrew, Colin. "The Origins of Indo-European Languages." *Scientific American,* Oct. 1989:106-114.

Wilson, P. W. *The Romance of the Calendar.* New York: Norton, 1937.

Wright, Lawrence. *Clockwork Man: The Story of Time, Its Origins, Its Uses, Its Tyranny.* New York: Horizon, 1968.

Zerubavel, Eviatar. *The Seven-Day Circle: The History and Meaning of the Week.* New York: Macmillan Free Press, 1985.

Individual Religions

Baha'i

Baha'i Meetings: The Nineteen Day Feast; Extracts from the Writings of Baha'u'llah, `Abdu'l-Baha, and Shoghi Effendi. Wilmette, IL: Baha'i Publishing Trust, 1976.

Esslemont, John E. *Baha'u'llah and the New Era.* Wilmette, IL: Baha'i Publishing Trust, 1950, 1970, 1980.

Gaver, Jessyca Russell. *The Baha'i Faith.* New York: Award Books, 1967.

National Spiritual Assembly of the Baha'is of the United States. *The Baha'i World: A Biennial International Record* XII (1950-1954) Wilmette, IL: Baha'i Publishing Trust, 1956.

Perkins, Mary, and Philip Hainsworth. *The Baha'i Faith.* London: Ward Lock Educational, 1980.

Buddhism

Ch'en, Kenneth Kuan Sheng. *Buddhism: The Light of Asia.* Woodbury, NY: Barron's Educational Series, 1968.

Domoulin, Heinrich, ed. *Buddhism in the Modern World.* New York: Macmillain, 1976.

Donath, Dorothy C. *Buddhism for the West: Theravada, Mahayana, Vajrayana.* New York, NY: Julian Press, 1971.

Humphreys, Christmas. *Zen Buddhism.* New York: Macmillan, 1948?.

Jumsai, M. L. Manich. *Understanding Thai Buddhism.* 2d ed. Bangkok, Thailand: Chalermnit Press, 1973.

Waddell, L. A. *The Buddhism of Tibet or Lamaism.* 2d ed. Cambridge, Eng.: Heffer, 1939.

Zen Lotus Society. *Handbook of the Zen Lotus Society.* Toronto: Zen Lotus Society, 1986.

Christianity

Allen, Richard. *The Life Experience and Gospel Labors of the Rt. Rev. Richard Allen.* Nashville: Abingdon Press, 1960.

Attwater, Donald. *The Penguin Dictionary of Saints.* New York: Penguin, 1965.

Barrett, Michael. *Footprints of the Ancient Scottish Church.* N.p., 1914.

Bede. *A History of the English Church and People.* Translated by Leo Sherley-Price. Baltimore, MD: Penguin, 1955.

Butler, Alban. *The Lives of the Fathers, Martyrs, and Other Principal Saints.* 12 vols. 1846. Reprint (12 vols. in 4). New York: Sadlier, 1857.

Cowie, L. W., and John S. Gummer. *The Christian Calendar: A Complete Guide to the Seasons of the Christian Year.* Springfield, MA: Merriam-Webster, 1974.

De Bles, Arthur. *How to Distinguish the Saints in Art by Their Costumes, Symbols, and Attributes.* New York: Art Culture Publications, 1925.

Deems, Edward Mark. *Holy-days and Holidays.* 1902. Reprint. Detroit, MI: Gale Research Co. , 1968.

Delehaye, Hippolyte. *The Legends of the Saints.* Translated by D. Attwater. New York: Fordham University Press, 1962.

Delaney, John J. *Dictionary of Saints.* New York: Doubleday, 1980.

Drake, Maurice, and Wilfred Drake. *Saints and Their Emblems.* 1916. Reprint. Detroit: Gale Research, 1971.

Engelbert, Omer. *The Lives of the Saints.* Translated by Christopher Fremantle and Anne Fremantle. David McKay, 1951.

Kenneth, Br., C.G.A. *A Pocket Calendar of Saints and People to Remember.* Oxford, Eng.: A. R. Mowbray, 1981.

National Conference of Catholic Bishops. *Holy Days in the United States: History, Theology, Celebration.* Washington, D.C.: United States Catholic Conference, 1984.

Roeder, Helen. *Saints and Their Attributes, with a Guide to Localities and Patronage.* London: Longmans, Green, 1955.

Weiser, Francis X. *Handbook of Christian Feasts and Customs: The Year of the Lord in Liturgy and Folklore.* New York: Harcourt, Brace, 1952.

Weiser, Francis X. *The Holyday Book.* New York: Harcourt, Brace, 1956.

Hinduism

Berry, Thomas. *Religions of India.* New York: Bruce, 1971.

Fasts and Festivals of India. New Delhi: Diamond, n.d.

Hopikins, J. T. *The Hindu Religious Tradition.* Encino, CA: Dickenson, 1971.

O'Flaherty, Wendy Doniger. *Hindu Myths.* Middlesex, England: Penguin Books, 1975.

Pitt, Malcolm. *Introducing Hinduism.* New York: Friendship, 1965.

Stutley, M. and J. Stutley. *Harper's Dictionary of Hinduism.* New York: Harper, 1977.

Stutley, Margaret. *Hinduism.* Wellingborough, Northamptonshire: The Aquarian Press, 1985.

Zaehner, R.C. *Hinduism.* New York: Oxford University Press, 1962.

Islam

Farah, C.E. *Islam: Beliefs and Observances,* Woodbury, NY: Barrons, 1968.

Gibb, H.A.R, and Kramers, J.H. *Shorter Encyclopedia of Islam.* Ithaca, NY: Cornell University Press, 1953.

Hughes, Thomas Patrick. *A Dictionary of Islam.* London, Allen, 1885.

Rahman, Fazlur. *Islam.* Chicago: University of Chicago Press, 1979.

Wilson, J.C. *Introducing Islam.* New York: Friendship, 1958.

Jainism

Jaini, Jagmanderlal, M.A. *Outlines of Jainism.* Cambridge: At the University Press, 1940. Republished by Hyperion Press, Inc., Westport, CT, 1982.

Judaism

Bamberger, Bernard J. *The Bible: A Modern Jewish Approach.* New York: B'nai B'rith Hillel Foundations, 1955.

Bloch, Abraham P. *The Biblical and Historical Background of the Jewish Holy Days.* New York: Ktav, 1978.

Diamant, Anita and Howard Cooper. *Living a Jewish Life.* New York: Harper Collins, 1991.

Eisenberg, Azriel Louis. *The Story of the Jewish Calendar.* London and New York: Abelard-Schuman, 1958.

Gaster, Theodore H. *Festivals of the Jewish Year: A Modern Interpretation and Guide.* New York: William Sloane, 1953.

Gaster, Theodore H. *Thespis: Ritual, Myth, and Drama in the Ancient Near East.* 2d ed. New York: Doubleday, 1961.

Goodman, Philip. *The Rosh Hashanah Anthology.* Philadelphia: The Jewish Publication Society of America, 1973.

Pfeiffer, Robert H. *Introduction to the Old Testament.* 2d ed. New York: Harper, 1948.

Rosenau, William. *Jewish Ceremonial Institutions and Customs.* 4th ed. New York: Bloch, 1929.

Strassfield, Michael. *The Jewish Holidays: A Guide and Commentary.* New York: Harper and Row, 1985.

Tillem, Ivan L. *The Jewish Directory and Almanac.* Vol. I. New York: Pacific Press, 1984.

Trepp, Leo. *The Complete Book of Jewish Observance.* New York: Behrman House and Summit Books, 1980.

Mythology (Greek and Roman)

Brand, John, and Henry Ellis. *Observations on the Popular Antiquities of Great Britain.* 3 vols. London: Bohn, 1853.

Burkert, Walter. *Homo Necans: The Anthropology of Ancient Greek Sacrifician Ritual and Myth.* Berkeley: University of California Press, 1983.

Clinton, Kevin. "The Sacred Officials of the Eleusinian Mysteries." *Transactions,* n.s. Vol. 63, pt. 3. Philadelphia, 1974.

Cook, Arthur Bernard. *Zeus: A Study of Ancient Religion.* 3 vols. Cambridge, Eng.: Cambridge University Press, 1914-1940.

Farnell, Lewis R. *The Cults of the Greek States.* 5 vols. London: Oxford University Press, 1896-1909.

Ferguson, John. *The Religions of the Roman Empire.* Ithaca, N.Y.: Cornell University Press, 1970.

Fontenrose, Joseph. *Python: A Study of Delphic Myth and Its Origin.* Berkeley: University of California Press, 1959.

Fowler, W. Warde. *The Roman Festivals of the Period of the Republic: An Introduction to the Study of the Religion of the Romans.* London: Macmillan, 1899.

Graves, Robert. *The Greek Myths.* 2 vols. New York: Penguin, 1955.

Harrison, Jane Ellen. *Prolegomena to the Study of Greek Religion.* 1903. Reprint. Princeton: Princeton Univer. Press, 1991.

Jung, Carl G., and C. Ker,nyi. *Essays on a Science of Mythology: The Myth of the Divine Child and the Mysteries of Eleusis.* Translated by R. F. C. Hull, 1949. 2d ed. Reprint. Princeton, NJ: Princeton University Press, 1963.

Kerényi, C. *Eleusis: Archetypal Image of Mother and Daughter.* Trans. by Ralph Manheim. 1960. Reprint. New York: Pantheon, Bollingen Series 65:4, 1967.

Mylonas, George E. *Eleusis and the Eleusinian Mysteries.* Princeton, NJ: Princeton University Press, 1961.

Neugebauer, Otto, and H. B. van Hoesen. *Greek Horoscopes.* Philadelphia: American Philosophical Society, 1959.

Nilsson, Martin P. *Greek Folk Religion.* New York: Columbia University Press, 1940.

Ogilvie, R. M. *The Romans and Their Gods in the Age of Augustus.* New York: W.W. Norton & Company, Inc., 1969.

Pollard, John. *Seers, Shrines, and Sirens: The Greek Religious Revolution in the Sixth Century B.C.* New York: A. S. Barnes, 1965.

Rose, H. J. *A Handbook of Greek Mythology.* 6th ed. London, England: Methuen & Co. Ltd., 1958.

Rose, H. J. *Religion in Greece.* New York: Harper, 1946.

Rose, H. J. *Religion in Greece and Rome.* New York: Harper, 1948.

Stapleton, Michael. *The Illustrated Dictionary of Greek and Roman Mythology.* London: The Hamlyn Publishing Group Ltd., 1978.

Thomson, George. *Studies in Ancient Greek Society.* Vol. I. 3d ed. London: Lawrence & Wishart, 1961. Vol. II, London: Lawrence & Wishart, 1955.

Wolverton, Robert E. *An Outline of Classical Mythology.* Totowa, N. J.: Littlefield, Adams & Co., 1975.

Zuntz, Günther. *Persephone: Three Essays on Religion and Thought in Magna Graecia.* London: Oxford University Press, 1971.

Native American

Caso, Alfonso. *The Aztecs: People of the Sun.* Lowell Dunham tr. Norman, OK: University of Oklahoma Press, 1958.

Danziger, Edumnd Jefferson, Jr. *The Chippewas of Lake Superior.* Norman, OK: University of Oklahoma Press, 1979. repr 1990.

Fergusson, Erna. *Dancing Gods: Indian Ceremonials of New Mexico and Arizona.* Albuquerque, NM: University of New Mexico, 1931; repr 1991.

Fewkes, Jesse Walter. *Hopi Snake Ceremonies.* Albuquerque, NM: 1986, 4th ed 1991.

Fewkes, Jesse Walter. *Tusayan Katchinas and Hopi Altars.* Albuquerque, NM: Avanyu Publishing, 1990.

Gill, Sam D. *Native American Religions.* Belmont, Ca: Wadsworth Publishing, 1982.

Hultkrantz, Ake. *The Religions of the American Indians.* Trans. Monica Setterwall. Los Angeles, CA: University of California Press, 1979.

Waters, Frank. *Masked Gods: Navaho and Pueblo Ceremonialism.* Athens, OH: Swallow Press, 1950.

Waters, Frank. *Book of the Hopi.* New York: Ballantine, 1963.

Paganism

Adler, Margot. *Drawing Down the Moon: Witches, Pagans, Druids, and Other Goddess-Worshippers in America Today.* 2d ed. NY: Viking Press, 1979. Boston: Beacon Press, 1987.

Buckland, Raymond. *The Tree: The Complete Book of Saxon Witchcraft.* York Beach, ME: Samuel Weiser, 1974.

Burland, C. A. *Echoes of Magic: A Study of Seasonal Festivals Through the Ages.* London: Peter Davies, 1972.

Campanelli, Pauline. *Wheel of the Year: Living the Magical Life.* St. Paul, MN: Llewellyn Publications, 1989.

Crowley, Aleister. *Magick in Theory and Practice.* NY: Dover Publications, 1976.

Farrar, Stewart, and Janet Farrar. *Eight Sabbats for Witches.* London: Robert Hale, 1981.

Farrar, Stewart, and Janet Farrar. *The Witches' Way: Principles, Rituals, amd Beliefs of Modern Witchcraft.* London: Robert Hale, 1984.

Ferguson, Diana. *The Magickal Year: A Pagan Perspective on the Natural Year.* New York: Quality Paperback Book Club, 1996.

Fitch, Ed, and Janine Renee. *Magical Rites from the Crystal Well.* St. Paul, MN: Llewellyn, 1984.

Frazer, Sir James G. *The Golden Bough.* 3d ed. 13 vols. London: Macmillan, 1912.

Gardner, Gerald B. *Witchcraft Today.* London: Jarrolds, 1954.

Graves, Robert. *The White Goddess: A Historical Grammar of Poetic Myth.* 3d ed. London: Faber & Faber, 1948.

Glass-Koentop, Pattalee. *Year of Moons, Season of Trees.* St. Paul, MN: Llewellyn Publications, 1991.

Harvey, Graham and Charlotte Hardman. *Paganism Today.* San Fransicso: Thorsons (an imprint of Harper-Collins), 1995.

Hawkins, Gerald S. *Stonehenge Decoded.* NY: Doubleday, 1965.

Hoyle, Sir Fred. *Stonehenge.* San Francisco: W. H. Freeman, 1976.

Matthews, Caitlín. *The Celtic Book of Days: A Guide to Celtic Spirituality and Wisdom.* Rochester, VT: Destiny Books, 1995.

Murray, Margaret A. *The God of the Witches.* London: Oxford University Press, 1931.

Murray, Margaret A. *The Witch-Cult in Western Europe.* London: Oxford University Press, 1962.

Pennick, Nigel. *The Pagan Book of Days.* Rochester, VT: Destiny Books, 1992.

Price, Nancy. *Pagan's Progress: High Days and Holy Days.* London: Museum Press, 1954.

Rees, Aylwin, and Brinsley Rees. *Celtic Heritage: Ancient Tradition in Ireland and Wales.* London: Thames & Hudson, 1961.

Regardie, Israel. *The Golden Dawn: An Account of the Teachings, Rites, and Ceremonies of the Order of the Golden Dawn.* 2d ed. Minneapolis, MN: Hazel Hills, 1969.

Ross, Anne. *Pagan Celtic Britain: Studies in Iconography and Tradition.* New York: Columbia University Press, 1967.

Starhawk. *The Spiral Dance: A Rebirth of the Ancient Religion of the Great Goddess.* 2d ed. San Francisco, CA: Harper & Row, 1989.

Valiente, Doreen. *The Rebirth of Witchcraft.* London: Robert Hale, 1989.

Scientology

Hubbard, L. Ron. *What Is Scientology?* Los Angeles, CA: Church of Scientology of California, 1978.

Sikhism

Arora, Ranjit. *Sikhism.* New York: Bookwright Press, 1987.

Cole, W. Owen, and Piara Singh Sambhi. *The Sikhs: Their Religious Beliefs and Practices.* London: Routledge & Kegan Paul, 1978.

Shintoism

Bauer, Helen and Sherwin Carlquist. *Japanese Festivals.* Garden City, NY: Doubleday, 1965.

Hori, Ichiro. *Folk Religion in Japan: Continuity and Change.* Chicago: University of Chicago Press, 1968.

Ono, S. *Shinto: The Kami Way.* Rutland, VT: Bridgeway, 1962.

Ross, F. H. *Shinto: The Way of Japan.* Boston: Beacon, 1965.

Taoism, Confucianism, and Chinese Folk Religions

Creel, Henlee Glessner. *Confucious and the Chinese Way.* New York: Harper, 1960.

Gerth, Hans H., ed. *The Religions of China: Confucianism and Taoism.* Glencoe, IL: Free Press, 1951.

Liu, Wu-chi. *Confucious: His Life and Time.* Westport, CT: Greenwood, 1972.

Wong, Eva. *The Shambhala Guide to Taoism.* Boston, MA: Shambhala, 1997.

Theosophical Society

Ryan, Charles J. *H. P. Blavatsky and the Theosophical Movement.* Pasadena, CA: Theosophical University Press, 1974.

West African Religions and New World Expressions

Anderson, David A. *The Origin of Life on Earth: An African Creation Myth.* Mt. Airy, MD: Sights Productions, 1991.

Barashango, Ishakamusa. *Afrikan People and European Holidays: A Mental Genocide, Book I.* Washington, D.C.: IV Dynasty Publishing, 1980.

Huxley, F. *The Invisibles, Voodoo Gods in Haiti.* New York: McGraw Hill, 1969.

Murphy, Joseph M. *Santeria: African Spirits in America.* Boston, MA: Beacon Press, 1988; repr 1993.

Murphy, Joseph M. *Working the Spirit: Ceremonies of the African Diaspora.* Boston, MA: Beacon Press, 1994.

Zoroastrianism

Boyce, Mary. *Zoroastrians: Their Religious Beliefs and Practices.* London: Routledge and Kegan Paul, 1979.

Mehr, Farhang. *The Zoroastrian Tradition,* Rockport, MA: Element Books, 1991.

Pangborn, Cyrus R. *Zoroastrianism: A Beleaguered Faith.* New York: Advent Books, 1983.

Illustrations

Brewster, H. Pomeroy. *Saints and Festivals of the Christian Church.* New York: F.A. Stokes, 1904. Republished by Omnigraphics, Detroit, MI, 1990.

Chambers, Robert. *The Book of Days, Vol 1.* London: W. & R. Chambers, 1862-1864. Republished by Omnigraphics, Detroit, MI, 1990.

Cole, Herbert. *Heraldry and Floral Forms as Used in Decoration.* Drawings by the author. New York: Dutton, 1922. Republished by Omnigraphics, Detroit, MI, 1992.

Edidin, Ben M. *Jewish Holidays and Festivals.* Illustrations by Kyra Markham. New York: Hebrew Pub. Co., 1940. Republished by Omnigraphics, Detroit, MI, 1992.

Pike, Royston. *Round the Year with the World's Religions.* Drawings by E. C. Mansell. New York: Henry Schuman, 1950. Republished by Omnigraphics, Detroit, MI, 1993.

Alphabetical List of Holidays

Holidays shown in **bold** are primary entries in the text. Holidays shown in roman type are alternate names and variant spellings.

Holidays shown in **bold** are primary entries; roman type indicates alternate names and variant spellings.

Holidays shown in **bold** are primary entries; roman type indicates alternate names and variant spellings.

Holidays shown in **bold** are primary entries; roman type indicates alternate names and variant spellings.

Holidays shown in **bold** are primary entries; roman type indicates alternate names and variant spellings.

Holidays shown in **bold** are primary entries; roman type indicates alternate names and variant spellings.

Holidays shown in **bold** are primary entries; roman type indicates alternate names and variant spellings.

Holidays shown in **bold** are primary entries; roman type indicates alternate names and variant spellings.

Holidays shown in **bold** are primary entries; roman type indicates alternate names and variant spellings.

Holidays shown in **bold** are primary entries; roman type indicates alternate names and variant spellings.

Holidays shown in **bold** are primary entries; roman type indicates alternate names and variant spellings.

Chronological List of Holidays

The dates contained in this list have been compiled from many different, and sometimes contradictory, sources. The dates presented, especially for movable holidays, are approximate.

Fixed holidays are denoted by roman type; movable holidays appear in italicized type. Movable dates are placed according to their position in 1997 with these exceptions: Asarah be-Tevet (Judaism) is listed on the Gregorian date for 1998 because the holiday will not occur on any date in 1997. The Annunciation of the Blessed Virgin Mary (Christian) is listed on its typical date of March 25; however, the observance will be displaced to April 1 in 1997 because March 25 falls during Holy Week.

The symbol ~~ denotes a variable date. These holidays are listed in the month during which they typically fall but the exact date is variable, determined by divination, or otherwise unknown.

Holiday seasons are listed according to the the date on which they begin.

Zoroastrian dates are placed according to the Fasli calendar; for Shahanshahi and Qadimi equivalents, see the individual entries.

Islamic dates move back approximately 11 days every calendar year and move through all the months every 33 years.

January

01 Feast of the Circumcision (Christian) 78
01 Ganjitsu (Shinto). 195
01 Oshogatsu (Buddhism). 170
01 *God's Day* (Unification) 78
05 *Epiphany Eve* (Christian) 78–79
05 *Universal Week of Prayer* (Christian) 78
06 Epiphany (Christian) 79
06 Old Christmas Day (Christian). 79
06 *True Parents' Birthday* (Unification) 79
07 *Carnival* (Christian) 81
09 *Asarah be-Tevet* (Judaism). 47
10 Iroquois White Dog Feast (Native American) 205
10 *Ramadan* (Islam) 109
12 *Feast of the Baptism of the Lord* (Christian). 79–80
12 *Feast of the Holy Family* (Christian) 79
13 Death of George Fox (Christian). 80
13 *Maghi* (Sikh) 161–62
13 *Plough Monday* (Christian) 80
14 *Makar Sankranti* (Hindu). 140
14 *Vasant Pañcami* (Hindu) 141

15 *Guru Gobind Singh's Birthday* (Sikh). 161
16 Feast of Vohuman (Zoroastrian) 59
16 *Bhishma Ashtami* (Hindu) 141
19 *Blessing of Animals* (Christian) 80
19 *World Religion Day* (Baha'i) 118
20 *Birthday of Martin Luther King, Jr.* (Christian) . 80
23 *Magha Purnima* (Hindu) 141–42
23 *Minakshi Float Festival* (Hindu) 142
23 *Tu Bishvat* (Judaism) 47
24 Alacitas (Native American, Aymara) 205
25 Conversion of St. Paul (Christian). 80
27 *Sakata Chauth* (Hindu). 142
27 *Up-Helly-Aa* (Pagan) 217
30 *Kitchen God Festival* (Chinese) 189
~~ *Kwakiutl Winter Ceremonial* (Native American) 205
~~ *Lohri* (Sikh) 161
~~ *Pongal* (Hindu). 140
~~ *St. Distaff's Day* (Pagan) 217
~~ *Thaipusam* (Hindu) 140–41
~~ *Twelfth Night* (Pagan) 217

Roman type denotes fixed dates; *italic* type denotes movable dates; ~~ indicates a variable date.

February

March

April

Roman type denotes fixed dates; *italic* type denotes movable dates; ~~ indicates a variable date.

May

June

Roman type denotes fixed dates; *italic* type denotes movable dates; ~~ indicates a variable date.

Roman type denotes fixed dates; *italic* type denotes movable dates; ~~ indicates a variable date.

~~ *Gelede* (Yoruba) 230
~~ *Indra Jatra* (Hindu) 134
~~ *Onam* (Hindu) 132
~~ *Partyshana Parva* (Jain) 153–54
~~ *Snake-Antelope Dance* (Native American, Hopi) . 207
~~ *Tirupati Festival* (Hindu) 132

September

02 Feast of San Estevan (Christian) 92
02 Shinbyu (Buddhism) 175
03 *New Year for the Herds* (Judaism) 44
06 *Sante Fe Fiesta* (Christian) 92–93
08 Nativity of the Blessed Virgin Mary
   (Christian) 93
10 *Dussehra* (Hindu) 135
11 Coptic New Year (Christian) 93
12 Monkey God Festival (Taoist) 185
12 Paitishahem (Zoroastrian) 57
12 St. Matthew's Day (Christian) 93
14 Triumph of the Holy Cross (Christian) 93
14 *Auditors' Day* (Scientology) 232
15 Mary as Our Lady of Sorrows (Christian) . . 93
16 *Kojagara* (Hindu) 135
16 *Mid-Autumn Festival* (Chinese) 187
16 *Sharad Purnima* (Hindu) 135
16 *Valmiki Jayanti* (Hindu) 135–36
17 Feast of Mithra (Zoroastrian) 57
21 World Peace Day (Baha'i) 118
22 *Mabon* (Pagan) 220–21
22 *Vatsa* (Buddhism) 175
22 *Winter Finding* (Pagan, Odinist) 221
23 *Autumnal Higan* (Buddhism) 176
27 Cosmas and Damian Day (Candomblé) . . . 230
28 Confucius's Birthday (Confucian) 187
29 Michaelmas (Christian) 93
~~ *Dasain* (Hindu) 135
~~ *Durga Puja* (Hindu) 134–35
~~ *Lakon* (Native American, Hopi) 207
~~ *Laksmi Puja* (Hindu) 134
~~ *Pitra Visarjana Amavasya* (Hindu) 136

October

01 *Childrens Day* (Unification) 93
01 *Festival of the Nine Imperial Gods* (Taoist) . . . 187
02 Guardian Angels Day (Christian) 94
02 Mihragan (Zoroastrian) 58
02 *Govardhan Puja* (Hindu) 136–37

02 *Teshuva* (Judaism) 45
02 *Rosh Hashanah* (Judaism) 44–45
03 *Bhaiya Duj* (Hindu) 137
03 *Fast of Gedaliah* (Judaism) 45
04 *Shiprock Navajo Nation Fair* (Native American) 207
05 Bodhidharma Day (Buddhism) 176
05 *Rally Day* (Christian) 94
07 Mary as Our Lady of the Rosary (Christian) . 94
07 *Surya Shashti* (Hindu) 137
11 *Yom Kippur* (Judaism) 45
12 Ayathrem (Zoroastrian) 58
12 *Devathani Ekadashi* (Hindu) 137
15 *Kartika Purnima* (Hindu) 137
15 *Puskar Mela* (Hindu) 137
16 *Sukkot* (Judaism) 45–46
18 St. Luke's Day (Christian) 94
19 *Karwachauth* (Hindu) 137–38
20 Ebisu Festival (Shinto) 197
22 *Hoshana Rabbah* (Judaism) 46
23 *Shemini Atzeret* (Judaism) 46
24 *Simhat Torah* (Judaism) 46
26 Aban Parab (Zoroastrian) 58
26 Feast of Christ the King (Christian, Roman
   Catholic) 94
28 St. Simon and St. Jude's Day (Christian) . . . 94
28 *Dhan Teras* (Hindu) 138
29 Birth of the Bab (Baha'i) 118
29 *Narak Chaturdashi* (Hindu) 138
30 *Dewali* (Hindu) 138
30 *Dewali* (Jain) 153
31 Oidhche Shamhna (Pagan) 221
31 Reformation Day (Christian, Protestant) 94
31 *Sending the Winter Dress* (Chinese) 187
~~ *Birthday of Guru Ram Das* (Sikh) 161
~~ *Kartika Snan* (Hindu) 136
~~ *Skanda Shashti* (Hindu) 136
~~ *Tihar* (Hindu) 138

November

01 All Saints' Day (Christian) 94–95
01 Samhain (Pagan) 221
02 All Souls' Day (Christian) 95
05 Guy Fawkes' Night (Pagan) 223
08 Dedication of St. John Lateran (Christian) . . . 95
08 Saints, Doctors, Missionaries, and Martyrs
   Day (Christian) 95
10 Birthday of Martin Luther (Christian) 95
11 Old Halloween (Pagan) 223

Roman type denotes fixed dates; *italic* type denotes movable dates; ~~ indicates a variable date.

December

Roman type denotes fixed dates; *italic* type denotes movable dates; ~~ indicates a variable date.

Calendar Index

This index is divided into two parts. The first section contains references to all the calendars discussed in the text. The second section contains an alphabetical listing of all the month names from the various calendars and provides page ranges for the holidays that fall within each month.

Master Index

Arabic names beginning with abd, abu, ibn, or umm are indexed under the first letters of these compounds. Al- means the; names beginning with al- are alphabetized under the first letter following al-. Japanese, Indian, and Vietnamese names are inverted as in English, but Chinese names are not inverted: the last (or family) name appears first, and the first name follows.

Tables are denoted by the letter t following the page number.

Tables are denoted by the letter t following the page number.

Tables are denoted by the letter t following the page number.

Tables are denoted by the letter t following the page number.

B

Tables are denoted by the letter t following the page number.

Tables are denoted by the letter t following the page number.

Tables are denoted by the letter t following the page number.

Tables are denoted by the letter t following the page number.

Tables are denoted by the letter t following the page number.

Tables are denoted by the letter t following the page number.

Tables are denoted by the letter t following the page number.

Tables are denoted by the letter t following the page number.

E

Tables are denoted by the letter t following the page number.

Tables are denoted by the letter t following the page number.

F

Tables are denoted by the letter t following the page number.

Tables are denoted by the letter t following the page number.

G

Tables are denoted by the letter t following the page number.

Tables are denoted by the letter t following the page number.

Tables are denoted by the letter t following the page number.

Tables are denoted by the letter t following the page number.

I

Tables are denoted by the letter t following the page number.

Tables are denoted by the letter t following the page number.

Tables are denoted by the letter t following the page number.

Tables are denoted by the letter t following the page number.

Tables are denoted by the letter t following the page number.

Tables are denoted by the letter t following the page number.

Tables are denoted by the letter t following the page number.

294

Tables are denoted by the letter t following the page number.

Tables are denoted by the letter t following the page number.

Tables are denoted by the letter t following the page number.

Tables are denoted by the letter t following the page number.

Tables are denoted by the letter t following the page number.

Tables are denoted by the letter t following the page number.

Tables are denoted by the letter t following the page number.

Tables are denoted by the letter t following the page number.

Tables are denoted by the letter t following the page number.

Tables are denoted by the letter t following the page number.

Tables are denoted by the letter t following the page number.

Tables are denoted by the letter t following the page number.

Tables are denoted by the letter t following the page number.

Tables are denoted by the letter t following the page number.

Tables are denoted by the letter t following the page number.

T

Tables are denoted by the letter t following the page number.

Tables are denoted by the letter t following the page number.

U

Tables are denoted by the letter t following the page number.

Tables are denoted by the letter t following the page number.

Tables are denoted by the letter t following the page number.

Tables are denoted by the letter t following the page number.